ETHNIC AND RACIAL IMAGES
IN AMERICAN FILM AND TELEVISION

Garland Reference Library
of Social Science
(Vol. 308)

ETHNIC AND RACIAL IMAGES
IN AMERICAN
FILM AND TELEVISION
Historical Essays and Bibliography

Allen L. Woll
Randall M. Miller

GARLAND PUBLISHING, INC. • NEW YORK & LONDON
1987

Library of Congress Cataloging-in-Publication Data

Woll, Allen L.
Ethnic and Racial Images in American Film and
Television.

  (Garland Reference Library of Social Science;
vol. 308)
Includes index.
1. Minorities in motion pictures—United States—
Bibliography. 2. Minorities in television—
United States—Bibliography. 3. Minorities in
motion pictures—United States. 4. Minorities in
television—United States. I. Miller, Randall M.
II. Title. III. Series: Garland Reference Library
of Social Science; v.308.
Z5784.M9W65 1987   016.79143'09'093520693   84-48883

[PN1995.9.M56]
ISBN 0-8240-8733-X (alk. paper)

Printed on acid-free, 250-year-life paper
Manufactured in the United States of America

To my brother Richard--for all those Saturdays
together at the Century and Pantheon theaters in
Chicago and for once saving me when I believed the
creature from 20,000 leagues under the sea was
real.---R.M.M.

To Myra---A.L.W.

CONTENTS

Acknowledgments   ix
Abbreviations   xi
Introduction   xiii
I.   General   3
II.   Afro-Americans   39
III.   Arabs   179
IV.   Asians   189
V.   East Europeans & Russians   203
VI.   Germans   221
VII.   Hispanic Americans   243
VIII.   Irish   261
IX.   Italians   275
X.   Jews   309
XI.   Native Americans   327
XII.   Others   343
Author Index   353
Film and Television Show Index   371
Subject Index   385

ACKNOWLEDGMENTS

Film and television are forms of collective or group artistry, with so many hands engaged in production that it is almost impossible to assign responsibility to any particular individual. The names in the credits or on the marquees identify only some of the producers and players. So it is with our book. The credits surely include all the writers listed in this bibliography, but they represent only part of the collective effort that transformed an idea into a book. The credits should also note those who provided encouragement and suggestions. They are: John Appel, Gretchen Bataille, George Beichl, Edward D. C. Campbell, Christine Choy, Carlos Cortes, Patricia Erens, Lester Friedman, Joseph Giordano, Larry Gross, Phyllis Klotman, Daniel Leab, J. Fred MacDonald, Michael T. Marsden, Lary May, James Monaco, Jack Shaheen, Charles L. P. Silet, William Van Deburg, Paul J. Vanderwood, and Stephen Whitfield. The librarians at the Annenberg School of Communications at the University of Pennsylvania and the Free Library of Philadelphia, especially Geraldine Duclow of the Theater Collection, were unfailingly helpful. We also benefited from the resources at the Balch Institute, the Chicago Public Library, Haverford College, the Library of Congress, the Museum of Modern Art, the New York Public Library and especially its Billy Rose Theater Collection, the Philadelphia College of Art, Swarthmore College, and Temple University. Special thanks go to Barbara Lang and Norma DiStefano of the inter-library loan service at Saint Joseph's University and Rutgers University, Camden, respectively, for acquiring many rare and unusual sources. Gail Farr at the University of Pennsylvania, Margaret A. Fitzpatrick at Saint Joseph's University, and Matthew Podlas at Rutgers University provided a wide variety of tasks from word-processing to checking references which speeded the completion of this book.

ABBREVIATIONS

J	Journal
Q	Quarterly
R	Review

INTRODUCTION

Although such recent films as Fort Apache--The
Bronx, Year of the Dragon, and The Color Purple
consider diverse subjects, all were greeted with
varying degrees of criticism (from boycotts to
newspaper editorials) for their presentation of
minority groups on film. Critics were concerned
about the possible effects these popular movies
might have on an individual's perception of Hispanics, Asian Americans, or Afro-Americans. The
nature and importance of mass media stereotypes and
their effects on society have been debated in
recent years by scholars from a wide variety of
disciplines. Some have analyzed the history of
popular stereotypes; others have argued about the
effects of these images on the viewing audience;
while others have considered the reasons for the
evolution of these stereotypes in American popular
culture.
     One difficulty of much of this research has
been that it has tended to be fairly insular. Most
scholars have studied only one ethnic group in the
their analysis and have considered it primarily
from an individual discipline. As a result, there
have been few valid generalizations emerging from
recent literature on this subject. While the number
of studies of this field has been voluminous (as
this bibliography will certainly attest), few individuals have ventured out of the realm of their
particluar field of study to consider new ap-
proaches or methodologies. Therefore, Ethnic and
Racial Images in American Film and Television:
Historical Essays and Bibliography is an attempt to
unite the work from a wide variety of disciplines,
languages, and fields of study in order to expand
the vistas of scholarly research in this area.
     This bibliography provides both a listing as
well as an analysis of books, dissertations, master's theses, articles in scholarly journals, popular periodicals, and newspapers, as well as reports
by government agencies, private communications
companies, and public service organizations. Material was gathered by the use of indexes, citations,
abstracts, reviews, computer searches, as well as
yearly surveys of the journals most likely to consider this issue. In a similar fashion, question-

naires were sent to the foremost individuals who have analyzed this topic in their writings. Their gracious and helpful responses often revealed obscure citations which we might not otherwise have noted. The bibliography is comprehensive for American sources, and material from elsewhere is included when appropriate. For example, the chapter on Hispanics includes literature from Mexican journals, while the section on Germans naturally includes relevant German-language materials. The listing comprises studies from many disciplines, especially history, sociology, psychology, mass communications, and literature. Certain materials have been excluded such as book reviews (unless of an "essay" form), biographical and promotional articles, studies concerning educational films, documentaries, animated cartoons, or television commercials, and ethnographic or anthropological works. Any material received by the authors after March, 1985, could not be included in the final text.

This work is divided into twelve chapters, with each considering specific ethnic or racial groups. The first chapter offers general considerations on the subject, while each succeeding section provides an analysis of (in alphabetical order): Afro-Americans, Arabs, Asians, Eastern Europeans and Russians, Germans, Hispanics, Irish, Italians, Jews, and Native Americans. A final chapter, "Others," discusses the wide variety of groups, from Africans to Turks, which have received only scant scholarly attention.

The introductory essay for each chapter provides a general overview of the history of each group's film and television images from the turn of the century to the present. This is followed by an analysis of the literature included in the bibliography, as well as suggestions for future areas of research. The inclusion of this section supercedes the necessity of individual annotations for each entry in this bibliography. Instead, the entries are discussed in an analytical essay, thus avoiding the one or two sentence summaries found in annotated bibliographies which tend to highlight each work in isolation instead of in the context of current research on the subject. Concluding each essay is a listing of the major motion pictures and television shows discussed in the bibliographical citations. These items tend to offer either lengthy analyses or novel interpretations of these cinematic or television offerings. The mere mention of a film in a book or article is not sufficient to warrant inclusion in either this section or the index. After all, virtually every article on Afro-American images in film refers to The Birth of a Nation, but only a small proportion offer significant comments on this D. W. Griffith classic. Only these latter studies are included in the essay and in subject index references for this film.

References to the appropriate bibliographical citations throughout this essay are included in parentheses following either a discussion of the item or a mention of a particlular film or television show. The arabic numeral indicates the reference in the bibliography at the end of each chapter. If the arabic numeral is preceded by a roman numeral, this cross-reference directs the reader to another chapter for additional discussion of the work.

Each chapter bibliography consists of listings in alphabetical order by author of works considering questions of film and television images of ethnic and racial groups. Complete bibliographical citations as defined by the Chicago Manual of Style are included for each item with the exception of articles cited from collections of readings, which appear in complete citation form only in the first listing. A parenthetical designation will guide the reader to the initial reference.

Three indexes will assist the reader in determining the content of each bibliographical entry. These include an author index, a film and television show index, and a subject index. In these sections the index numbers refer to the chapter number and the item number. Thus, 6-2 refers to chapter VI, item 2.

While both co-authors are jointly responsible for the compilation, writing, and editing of Ethnic and Racial Images in American Film and Television: Historical Essays and Bibliography, Professor Miller provided chapters 1, 2, 3, 5, 6, 9, and 12, while Professor Woll supplied the introduction and chapters 4, 7, 8, 10, and 11. Yet, it is difficult to draw a distinct line dividing our efforts. Genuine cooperation was the prime rule throughout the three years of our collaboration. All future projects should be as congenial and rewarding.

Ethnic and Racial Images
In American Film and Television

I. GENERAL

The role film and television play in shaping images of various ethnic and racial groups has occasioned a large, if somewhat contradictory, literature. While virtually all observers agree that mass media convey social messages, behavioral scientists have been unable to identify precisely how audiences receive, distill, and believe such messages. Much of the work on film and television images has focused on specific movies or television programs, rather than tracking patterns within each medium, or across media, over time. The biases of a filmmaker, television producer, or whomever might be known, but once the images are projected on the screen, they can assume meanings for different audiences that the filmmaker or television producer might never have anticipated or even condoned.

Scholarship on imagery in film and television has been inextricably bound up with mass media's effects on the audience. This connection largely stems from society's recognition that mass media can and do influence behavior, especially that of children. Almost from the inception of film, movies were regarded as educational instruments. Throughout the 1920s and 1930s social scientists attempted to measure film's effects and concluded that the movies shaped young viewers' attitudes, influenced their play, provided them with information, and formed stereotypes in their minds. One only had to observe the public's adulation of film stars and its emulation of movie fashions and manners to appreciate the cultural power of commercial movies. The universality and popularity of the film medium (like television later on) concerned scholars and public policymakers who worried about the social and political implications of leaving so formidable a power unregulated. Some "reformers" threatened hostile legislation and court action aimed at controlling film content. The industry's efforts at self-regulation were a response to such threats.

3

Studies of the relationship between film and
audience do suggest that films can affect the attitudes, beliefs, images, and opinions of the
viewers. As part of the Payne Fund project conducted in the early 1930s on the effects of movies
upon children, for example, Ruth Peterson and L. L.
Thurstone discovered that high school students who
had little exposure to blacks, Chinese, and Germans
had their perceptions of these groups significantly
shaped by films depicting the groups.(116)   The
U.S. government's use of film for propaganda purposes during World War II, which led to such films
as the "Why We Fight" series and The Negro Soldier
(1944), was based on studies showing that a balanced presentation of a subject might persuade an
intelligent viewer to accept the film's message.
Irwin Rosen, among others, reported in 1948 that
the film Gentleman's Agreement (1947), which
treated anti-Semitism in a discreet manner, influenced viewers to be more conscious of anti-Semitism
in their midst,(See X-72) a finding reconfirmed by
Russell Middleton in 1960.(102) How films shaped
viewers' attitudes remained unclear. These and
other studies lacked sufficient theoretical depth
and evidentiary breadth to make them applicable to
film generally.

If scholars cannot determine with precision how
mass media affect audience attitudes, beliefs, and
behavior, they do agree that the recurrent images
in film and television reflect the mass culture
that produced and sustained them by its patronage.
Engaged in the mass production of goods for a
national market, neither the film nor the television industry has dared to move too far away from
(or to offend) the common culture. As early as 1933
Irving Thalberg of Metro-Goldwyn-Mayer articulated
what was already, and would remain, production
policy in the entertainment business--namely, that
to create demand it was necessary to play to the
audience's predominant interests and values. In a
seminal study of national types in Hollywood films,
published in 1949, Siegfried Kracauer made a similar point. He noted how many groups appeared only
briefly in film, which he attributed to audience
interest and attitudes. While political attitudes
toward foreigners influenced production decisions
in Hollywood, market considerations outweighed all
other factors in determining how, even if, a group

would appear in a Hollywood film. Subjective images thus conformed to public attitudes, although, Kracauer conceded, Hollywood films might sometimes volunteer additional information about foreign peoples.(83) Commercially successful movies and television shows sense the public mood, and especially perceptive or timely ones capitalize on shifts in that mood--a fact amply illustrated by the recent box-office punch of <u>Rambo</u> and other film salutes to the muscular "patriotism" of the 1980s.

Where it once was believed, as recorded by Hortense Powdermaker and others in the late 1940s, that the audience was passive and so readily manipulated by a "totalitarian" filmmaker, the conventional wisdom now assumes that viewers respond to those messages that converge with their own values and prejudices; consequently, movies (or television) reinforce rather than form images and ideas. (e.g., 71) As such, movies (or television) serve as barometers of popular belief about groups or other subjects. Film and television do not necessarily create and fix images of groups or subjects, though they might focus attention on them. Pressure groups trying to remove offensive images from the screen instinctively draw upon both older and more current theories of audience involvement (for even the reinforcement of negative images by their repetition in powerful media poses social dangers to the group so maligned), and many writers concerned about ethnic and racial images in American film and television continue to operate from the older assumption of a passive audience. Still, scholarship generally appreciates some connection between screen images and mass culture, recognizing that both the creator and the audience influence film (or television) content. Stereotypes of groups, then, are not invented by filmmakers (or television producers), for they must derive from popular beliefs and prejudices to have meaning for audiences.(e.g., 96, 154) And, as Maurice Yacowar argues, stereotypes are necessary to artistry because they are "realistic" metaphors in that they reflect popular perceptions.(174)

Commercial considerations have governed both film and television and strongly influenced the images and messages conveyed in those two media. The marriage of art and commerce which has characterized American film and television has directed

scholars to consider how the structural aspects of
the entertainment industry have intersected with
the artistic and cultural sensibilities of the
artists (filmmakers, writers, directors, actors).
Much of that literature, however, mentions ethnic
and racial imagery only incidentally, if at all.
Understanding how the partners in that marriage
have interacted to produce images of groups is no
easy task, for, as Arthur Schlesinger, Jr., has
observed regarding film, in such an arrangement
compromises between art and commerce foster images
of countries and people that are simultaneously
true and false.(132)

Ethnic and racial images frequently receive
mentions in general studies of film, but most often
without any discussion of the origins and meaning
of such images. A typical approach in general histories of the industry is the 1957 survey by
Richard Griffith and Arthur Mayer, which traces the
development of the industry and the movies' effects
on American culture, from the early days of film to
the early 1950s. Griffith and Mayer make passing
references to images of Germans in war movies,
Latin lovers and Arab sheiks in Hollywood potboilers, and blacks in epics about the Civil War
and the American South. The authors include references to particular ethnic groups in specific film
genres and historical circumstances, but they are
not concerned with group images themselves.(62)
More recently, the Polish scholar Jerzy Toeplitz
incorporates discussions of specific ethnic images
(Asians, blacks, American Indians, Italians) in
trying to show the changing social consciousness of
the American film industry, but even though he is
sensitive to ethnic portrayals, he uses them to
illustrate Hollywood's changing face, not to locate
the historical roots and meaning of the images
themselves.(149)

Garth Jowett's detailed analysis of the American film industry and the social science literature on and about the movies well appreciates the
importance of Afro-American, Asian, and German
images as indices of Hollywood's sociological development and their connection to American political and social currents, particularly wartime
propaganda, and it notes group portrayals in assaying film content and themes. But Jowett, too,
does not explore the cultural or social antecedents

of group images in film, "the democratic art."(74)
Likewise, in his cultural history of the movies,
which examines the responses of American filmmakers
to political and social pressures on the industry
and identifies film's own culturally and socially
liberating messages and influences on Americans,
Robert Sklar includes observations on racial and
ethnic images in film, but, again, such material is
important only so much as it illustrates American
film's development.(138)

In an effort to link film content to social
currents, Charles Champlin offers a decade-by-
decade review of film fare, which includes discussions of Hollywood's uses of the past and the
emergence of ethnic and racial subjects and stars
in films of the 1970s.(28) Eugene McCreary looks at
films of the 1940s from a comparative perspective
(American, German, French, and Russian) and concludes that film images are dependent on mass
support.(93) Reflecting contemporary ethnic consciousness perhaps, James Monaco devotes considerable attention to Afro-American, Italian, and
Jewish ethnicity in the artistry and direction of
recent movies--all in the context of noting the
fundamental shifts underway in the organization and
control of the film industry.(107)

Richard Maltby argues that the business of
Hollywood has fostered an ideology of consensus--a
set of cultural values and assumptions with which
the broadest possible audience will feel comfort-
able.(95) Such a consensus limits the range of
ethnic and racial images available to Hollywood
filmmakers. Indeed, as Michael Wood comments, the
tendency in film has been to blur distinctions.
Ethnic images serve only as metaphors for those
film characters who are outsiders. Ethnic images
are interchangeable then, and no group achieves a
full and true identity.(171)

More to the point of the film industry's structure and film content is the observation by Jeremy
Tunstall and David Walker that the concentration of
commercial film and television production in Hollywood distorts the vision of image makers, who live
in a socially insulated community and mistake California culture for American culture.(152) Randall
Miller's two introductory essays to collections on
ethnic/racial images and popular mass media,(105,
106) and Edward Jurewicz's brief argument that the

increase in ethnic portrayals in film and television during the 1970s reflected a heightened social consciousness within the entertainment industry and audience demands for such fare,(75) also attempt to make explicit the connections between the structure and business of the film industry and the development of ethnic and racial images generally. On the whole, however, the development and complexity of those linkages remain largely unexplored.

By examining the leitmotifs of films in specific eras it is possible to delineate the social, cultural, and political contexts that foster the development and use (or absence) of particular images. In his discussion of film during the silent era, for example, William Everson notes D. W. Griffith's and others' use of racial/ethnic portraiture in the context of the cultural and political moods of the early twentieth century, when caricature of blacks and immigrants was common on the stage and when World War I made Germans targets for film propaganda.(45) Lewis Jacobs argues that during the Progressive era filmmakers attempted to portray ethnic groups fairly, but Griffith's powerful and influential Birth of a Nation and World War I encouraged negative racial and ethnic images in films.(70) In a rare study of audience interaction with early film, Elizabeth Ewen describes the interplay between immigrant moviegoers and silent films about immigrant/ethnic subjects and how American film socialized the immigrant viewers.(47)

D. W. Griffith was so influential in defining American film artistry and audience that students of early film necessarily begin by looking at his images in their efforts to understand the culture and content of movies. Griffith used and reinforced racial themes and many group stereotypes in his movies. As Jack Temple Kirby observes, Griffith showed sympathy for some groups, especially American Indians, and prejudices toward others, especially blacks, but his racial portraiture in many ways mirrored the values of his era.(80) Other students of Griffith and his age make a similar case, although most are primarily concerned with explicating Griffith's work rather than discussing ethnic and racial imagery.(e.g., 114, 138)

According to Andrew Bergman, the Depression bred self-doubts about American institutions and revived American social conscience--all of which

led to films addressing such ills as slum life,
poverty, and racial injustice.(14) Nick Roddick
notes that during the Depression era race and ethnicity became more explicit in Hollywood fare
partly because movie stars had grown more ideolog-
ically conscious.(124) Roger Dooley remarks on
Hollywood's willingness to treat such previously
taboo subjects as miscegenation in films of the
1930s, changes which he attributes to liberal
values in Hollywood.(41)

World War II was a watershed in racial/ethnic
images in films. On the one hand, Hollywood marched
in step with governmental pronouncements that America was in the war for democracy. Thus, war movies
teemed with multi-ethnic fighting units demon-
strating the unity of Americans.(70, 76, 77, 82,
91, 167) But war also made government and filmmakers more conscious of film's potential as a
socializing agency. Liberals gained control over
filmmaking policy in government, and in Hollywood
to a lesser extent, and used film to effect social
change in America by portraying blacks and other
minorities more favorably.(73, 74, 82, 91) Indicative of the new-found sensitivity to film's propagandistic power was the Writers' Congress held at
the University of California in 1943, during which
several prominent writers and artists reviewed
film's patterns of racial/ethnic discrimination and
negative imagery and called on the industry to mend
its ways.(173)

During the Cold War the "social problem" films,
or "message movies," of the 1930s-1940s gave way to
themes of consensus. Peter Biskind comments on the
absence of ethnicity during the 1950s, when consensus politics demanded everyone plunge into the
melting pot. In that regard, the filmmakers' use of
ethnically identifiable characters, such as Irish
or Italian mobsters, established the characters
immediately as enemies of the American way.(19)
International politics during the Cold War also
shaped the images of several groups. The Russian
image, for example, metamorphosed from being America's trustworthy ally in World War II films into
being the nefarious, brutal enemy of freedom in
Cold War-era fare.(131)

Films of the 1960s and 1970s had a darker
face--both in their criticism of American social
institutions and behavior and in their more diverse

ethnic and racial castes and themes. James Monaco
recognizes ethnic and racial consciousness as a
significant force driving several prominent directors in recent American film.(107) John Powers
points out that during the 1970s numerous films
presented the Western culture (embodied in America)
as evil. In the process of criticizing the West for
imperialism and inhumanity, such films moved beyond
obvious stereotypes of particular races to forge a
monolithic, one-dimensional Third World image with
no distinction between different peoples.(117) Kiku
Adatto, however, maintains that a conservative
cultural ethos continued to pervade Hollywood
products in the 1970s. The rugged individual remained as hero, or anti-hero, and ethnic or racial
identities were subsumed in the ethic of indivi-
dualism.(4)

The study of particular genres has provided
occasions to examine ethnic and racial imagery in
American film. The serials, for example, teemed
with cultural and group stereotypes.(141) Studies
of the crime and detective genres have yielded much
information about popular associations between
particular ethnic groups and anti-social behavior,
views which have been transferred from popular
literature to film and, from the 1930s on, also
have been developed independently by filmmakers.
(e.g., 46, 128) The social problem film, which
emerged as a Hollywood genre during the 1930s,
gained currency in the war years and immediately
after. As Peter Roffman and Jim Purdy demonstrate,
issues of class more than ethnicity informed such
films, but films of social conscience inevitably
moved to attacks on prejudice and persecution and
raised social consciousness on issues relating to
race.(125)

Movies with working-class subjects and themes
became popular again in the 1970s, when, amidst an
"ethnic revival" in the United States, the working-
class "ethnic" assumed heroic stature for some
critics of the impersonal, modern age.(119) Hollywood has remained ambivalent about class issues,
but independent filmmakers have risked tackling
controversial subjects on ethnic and working-class
culture. As Lynn Garafola (50) and others (e.g., 8)
have argued, recent films on the ethnic working
class tend to counterpose a supposedly family-
centered past with a culturally barren and socially

corrupting present and evoke a nostalgia with their
own stereotypes of class and culture. Many of the
films depicting ethnic working-class culture or
subjects were set in the 1930s. The association of
particular groups with particular social classes,
however, has reinforced old steretypes and generated new ones.(97)

More than any other genre, war films invariably
involved some representation of ethnic or racial
images. Films about World War II purveyed messages
of American social unity, as evinced in the American combat units composed of diverse ethnic groups
but committed to common ideological goals. Indeed,
the melting pot metaphor was a central theme of
American propaganda during the war. Blacks, too,
benefited from the government's efforts to enlist
all Americans in the cause; in the service of total
war, American films included blacks in American
service units, even though, in reality, black
soldiers remained segregated in the services.(76,
77, 91, 130, 134, 167) Not surprisingly, as many
authors have observed, the demands of war led to
negative portrayals of America's enemies.(e.g.,
135) Allen Woll adds a new dimension to the analysis of war and film by detailing how a particular
genre (in his case, Hollywood musicals), with its
own tradition of ethnic and racial representation,
was affected by wartime exigencies.(170)

Few scholars have explored the carryovers in
imagery and representation from film to television.
In a seminal collection of essays, sponsored by the
Anti-Defamation League of B'nai B'rith in 1959,
several scholars discussed the characteristics of
stereotypes and their manifestations in film and
television.(12) Robert Toll takes the long view,
describing and connecting the motifs and uses of
entertainment from the nineteenth-century popular
stage and minstrel shows to modern television.(150)
Arthur Asa Berger finds conscious symbolic meaning
attached to television's borrowing of ethnic images
from film and other sources. He views television as
a socializing process engaged in a dialectic between East and West, the former represented by
Asians and Indians and the the latter by WASPs and
cowboys.(13) In the form of reruns of serials and
old movies, television perpetuated Hollywood's
images, even after the film industry had altered or
discarded them.

Regarding television, most surveys of the industry's evolution have identified commercial factors as the key elements shaping program content and the representation of groups. During the 1950s, an age of consensus in politics and society, television, like film, became increasingly bland in content and homogeneous in ethnic ascription. In television, observes Erik Barnouw, sponsors sought to avoid controversies that might become associated with their products, and they sought to promote a uniform national personality type and lifestyle as a means of encouraging consumption of their products by building on a middle-class, white, Anglo-Saxon Protestant image that viewers would want to emulate.(10)

Confrontation and ethnic pluralism replaced consensus as the dominant themes of American culture in the 1960s and 1970s, and television accommodated to the new order--to a degree. More black faces appeared in television commercials and on programs because of the civil rights movement and the growth of the black market, but market forces still dictated television's messages. Television producers "de-ethnicized" subjects and characters so as not to offend consumers.(10) Indeed, David Karp, writing in 1968, observed a decline in ethnic images; ethnicity on television existed only in humor. Karp maintained that advertisers, who had developed sophisticated techniques for targeting specific television markets, were more willing to present racial and national diversity than were network executives who lacked clear messages on ethnic preferences from national audiences.(78) The introduction of "ethnic programming" in the 1970s was a response to market forces, but the shows often degenerated into caricature or abandoned explicitly ethnic or racial themes in order to appeal to larger audiences. More than anything else, argues Rose Goldsen, ratings pressures killed cultural pluralism in television; ethnic characters survived by becoming ambiguous in their ethnicity.(60)

In his work on prime-time programming, Todd Gitlin stresses that the preeminent concern among television executives has been, and remains, reaching the largest possible target audiences, which has meant providing simple, familiar characters and stories. A banality and uniformity con-

tinue to characterize television fare because the
industry complex has been, and is, demographically
narrow and socially insulated. Political, social,
and cultural currents influence television, but
appear on the screen in forms so diluted that they
pose no danger of alienating any important audience. Such processes, Gitlin argues, exclude serious treatment of Afro-American or any minority
subjects, except in the most superficial ways.(59)

Benjamin Stein echoes Gitlin's (and Tunstall
and Walker's [152]) point on the social insulation
of Hollywood producers, who, writes Stein, repli-
cate a super-clean world of Los Angeles where the
slums are spotless, poverty is a social malfunc-
tion, poor people are honest or quaint, and busi-
nessmen are evil.(142) Such distortion is dangerous
because it creates its own false reality, which, by
the ubiquity and seductiveness of television, per-
vades American culture. Media images, insists Jerry
Mander in an argument on the supreme power of
television, replace or displace real images of
foreign people and places.(98) Michael Novak warns
that television inflicts a class bias on viewers
that affects their way of perceiving and approaching reality. The television viewer has only a
limited range of human consciousness. Despite
"ethnic programming," television characters lack
true, definable ethnic identities. Even their accents are muted to conform to national tastes.(111)

Other scholars have documented the class bias
of recent television and remarked that lower-class
images remain linked to ignorance and bigotry.
(e.g., 16) Unwilling to risk depictions of real
social ills, television ignores those groups who
command no market or whose ideologies, culture, or
behavior offend national norms, except to ridicule
or caricature them in the most simplistic ways. Or,
contends Cedric Clark, it regulates them by making
them appear as protectors of the dominant American
culture--thus ethnic and racial minorities (those
who benefit least from the dominant society) become
policemen on television, thereby protecting the
social order.(29) Mark Miller and Karen Runyon
concur. They argue that the seeming diversity of
ethnic characters on television in fact promotes
the concept of the family of man; television in-
vokes diversity only to subvert it with subtle
endorsements of the power structure. Minority

figures are never in control.(103) Alexis Tan maintains that television and newspapers socialize
minorities to accept common values and to support
the established political and social system.(148)
    Concern over the impact of television on audi-
ences has stimulated much research, if little
agreement. Writing in 1966, Samuel Becker, for
example, insisted that television's reporting and
exploring of racial and ethnic themes and issues
had no discernible effect on viewers' beliefs on
those themes and issues.(11) In 1980 Joseph Boskin,
however, established a link between anti-urban
messages in television and negative perceptions of
dark-skinned minorities. Americans' long-standing
distrust of cities was heightened by fears of
"aliens" inhabiting them. Removing such minority
and lower-class associations, argued Boskin, would
contribute to healthy racial relations.(20) Regarding ethnic and racial images in television generally, the Columbia University project summarizes
the literature on the subject through the mid-1970s
and stakes off the boundaries of dispute regarding
television and human behavior.(31)
    Scholars do agree that children are especially
susceptible to television's messages. Numerous
studies affirm the socializing influence of the
medium on young viewers. In 1975 Grant Noble reported that young children were considerably more
prone to television's ability to shape their attitude toward foreigners than were teenagers.(110)
Gordon Berry, in 1980 and again in 1982, explained
that television teaches children about social class
roles and social issues. Even though the children
do not fully understand what they see, they learn
vicariously from the "unplanned educational curriculum" that is television. Such "learning" occurs
especially among minority viewers who have few
other sources of information.(17, 18) George Comstock and Robin Cobbey earlier had reported similar
findings and emphasized the reliance of minority
children on television for information about social
behavior and social types.(32) In 1978 they also
dismissed the roughly 2300 social and behavioral
studies on television and the socialization of
minority children as largely useless because all
but 7 percent of the studies lacked scientific
rigor.(33) Since 1978 (as revealed in the citations
throughout this book) significant new work on

ethnicity/race, television, and the socialization
of children has occurred, although scholars have
yet to achieve much consensus on the precise ways
television influences viewers.

All such arguments to some extent assume the
viewer is passive and uninformed--assumptions challenged by other students of television's effects.
In studying political correlates of television
viewing, for example, George Gerbner and others
discovered that heavy television viewers approached
the political world in homogeneous conventional
terms, as it is generally presented on television,
but they do not argue that television itself is the
force for moderation.(54) In summarizing the influential studies conducted at the University of
Pennsylvania on television's effects on viewers,
Gerbner stated that the persistent and pervasive
violence on television made heavy viewers of television feel more threatened by and estranged from
the real world, which they perceived as more crime-
ridden than it really was. But television, in that
regard, did not invent such fears so much as it
reinforced and exaggerated them among viewers who
interacted with television's messages.(52) Timothy
Rook recognizes that different personality types
may respond differently to the same visual images.
(127) Todd Gitlin assumes the growing sophistication of television audiences by arguing that when
television's images conflict with viewers' own
experience, the audience recognizes simplified,
stereotyped presentations for what they are; the
result is that such television images magnify the
audience's distrust of the medium.(58) In the most
comprehensive compendium of data and survey of the
literature on television and human behavior, the
Columbia University research team led by George
Comstock discovered many ways in which audience
perceptions and responses influenced television
production.(31)

Several general surveys of television make
observations on ethnic and/or racial images in
programming. They include Muriel Cantor's discussion of content and control in prime-time television,(26) Harry Castleman and Walter J. Podrazik's overview of television programming over four
decades,(27) Mary Coakley's attack on television
violence and sexuality,(30) Marc Eliot's synopses
of network prime-time shows from 1946 to 1980,(43)

Katie Kelly's warning that viewers must remain
vigilant lest television distort all reality,(79)
Richard Levinson and William Link's examination of
production processes in prime-time television (with
observations on the external and internal social
pressures on producers to show ethnic/racial groups
fairly),(89) David Marc's discussion of television
as a lens for American culture,(99) and Martin
Mayer's survey of programming and production
factors (with attention to the sources of racial
comedy and audience responses).(100) Among genre
studies of television, only Ralph and Donna Brauer,
who examine the changing images of the television
western, discuss ethnic or racial imagery. They
remark that television westerns continue to cast
blacks, Indians, and Mexicans as "outsiders" who
threaten the values of the white male hero.(22)
    Early studies of program content reported few
instances of ethnic, racial, or working-class
images in prime-time television. Sydney Head's
pioneering count in 1954, which discovered very low
representation of non-whites in network drama
programs, used content analysis of drama programs,
establishing the basic methodology of content analysis and the principal focus on prime-time drama
programming which would guide subsequent surveys.
(67) Researchers were not content just to count
appearances of groups or describe images; they also
made judgments about the quality of representation
and images and occasionally predicted future
trends. One 1961 study, for example, confirmed
earlier reports regarding working-class portrayals
but added that, over time, characters in prime-time
programs with an ethnic identity become less stereotypical and more "positive" in their appeal.(51)
In 1980 Mauricio Gerson published his "message
system analysis" of minority representation in
network television drama during the years 1970-
1976, which included a brief history of past practices. Gerson discovered that minority representation grew substantially from the late 1960s
through the mid-1970s and that blacks and Hispanics
especially had larger roles in drama.(55)
    The steady increase in roles for minorities was
hardly a surprise, given the growth of the minority
consumer market in the United States, the civil
rights movement, and the surge of "ethnic consciousness" during the 1970s. Such change was

almost too obvious to report.(65) In 1973 the Michigan State University project on "Communication
Among the Urban Poor" issued its report on employment, regulation, and legislation related to improving minority access to mass media; on television portrayals of minority groups; and on social
changes affecting program content. The report
linked the improvements in minority representation
and imagery in television to the growth of minority
media and growing public sensitivity to ethnic and
racial issues.(61) Optimism was not universal. In
the same year Edith Efron reported on minorities'
complaints about their underrepresentation in the
industry.(42)

The production, and popularity, of such shows
as All in the Family and Roots in the late 1970s
attested to television's maturity regarding once
prohibited or sanitized ethnic and racial subjects.
(143, 144) As Howard Suber observed in 1975, in the
span of a few years television had moved from a
position of virtually denying minority representation to an obsession with ethnic and racial themes
and characters, though, he added, minorities seldom
appeared in any sustained way in a manner that had
anything to do with their numerical significance,
historical importance, or real relation to society.
Minorities were attractive because of their nov-
elty, but television made them appealing by humanizing and homogenizing them.(147) In 1983 Arthur
Unger insisted that television offered a fairer,
more balanced set of ethnic images than did
American film--an argument that has found few
takers.(155)

By 1981, however, several critics noted a
change in the number and kind of ethnic and racial
depictions in television. The ethnic revival seemed
to invite self-deprecation and excesses, which
themselves became caricatures. Surveying Italian
and Jewish images in television series about gangsters or crime, Jean Grillo complained that ethnic
slurs were back.(63) Writing in TV Guide in 1984,
Michael Leahy and Wallis Annenberg maintained that,
based on an Equal Employment Opportunity Commission
survey of minority representation in television,
"tokenism" ruled the airwaves. Minority characters
failed to develop, minority actors were dispens-
able, and shows about minorities, written by minority writers, received no encouragement or support

from television producers who remained convinced
such material would alienate the national market.
(87) As is evident from the studies listed in the
several chapters of this book, each ethnic/racial
group has registered its own complaints about the
kind and degree of involvement in the industry. No
group has expressed satisfaction with its images or
influence.

Among the most sophisticated samplings of
ethnic and racial images and representation in
television is one conducted by the Annenberg School
of Communications (University of Pennsylvania). It
is a content analysis of women and minorities in
television drama, counted for the years 1969 to
1978, that looks at aggregate systems of messages
rather than individual programs, networks, or productions. The project reported, among other
findings, that blacks and Hispanics were underrepresented in day- and prime-time programming and
that "majority types" (white males) had proportionately more leading roles than minority persons.(53)
Especially important in conducting such research is
the development and application of clear models.
Nancy Signorielli, a member of the University of
Pennsylvania team, cautioned researchers that in
formulating their hypotheses and constructing their
models to count minority, or any kind, of representation in television,it is necessary to know what
already exists, what is important, what is right,
and what is related to what.(137) Too much survey
research has been subjective, even polemical, and
too little conducted systematically over long
periods of time; consequently, the actual size and
character of ethnic and racial participation in
television remains elusive.

Content analysis bears directly on the political manipulation of television. Using modern
sampling techniques and drawing upon recent research, with a historical narrative to set its
findings in context, the U.S. Commission on Civil
Rights linked the prevalence and persistence of
negative stereotypes in television to the underrepresentation of minorities and women in in the industry. The Commission reported its findings first
in its broad survey of television (images, representation, content analysis, production, news
programming, prime-time programming), which it released in 1977, and then in a 1979 update that

recorded little progress in all categories for
minorities or women in television.(157, 156) The
two reports provide histories of television's development and minorities' and women's involvement
in the industry, statistics, and proposals for
changing industry practices. Highly critical of
industry practices, such governmental reports
spurred calls for governmental intervention to
force greater integration of the industry and to
introduce more balanced programming. In 1969 and
1970 Congress conducted hearings on minority participation in the television medium, issuing reports on films and broadcasts demeaning to ethnic,
racial, or religious groups,(160, 161) and in 1983
Congress again held hearings on the subject, which
then largely focused on Afro-American testimony and
complaints.(See II-600)

As a licensed public medium, television, more
than film, is vulnerable to pressure groups who
want to control its constitution and content.
Throughout the 1970s various pressure groups challenged local television station licenses in those
instances where they believed the stations were
treating minorities unfairly. The success of black
challengers in getting the Federal Communications
Commission to revoke the license of a station in
Jackson, Mississippi, encouraged other such efforts
and convinced broadcasters that they could not
ignore completely minority groups' demands for
better representation in the industry.(7) With
mixed success, in the early 1970s minority group
organizations pressured local television stations
showing old movies to ban or edit severely the
films the groups considered offensive.(25) Others
encouraged support for ethnic television (designed
and programmed for specific audiences) on UHF channels, which, according to one study, prospered in
Los Angeles where sizeable ethnic communities
created cultural and commercial demand.(146)
Critics also worked to convince advertisers to
remove such obnoxious stereotypes as the "Frito
Bandito" from television commercials.(64) By 1975
Harry Waters was asking if minority pressure
groups, which he thought exercised considerable
influence on entertainment content, were ruling
television.(164)

Studies of the relationship between special-
interest groups and television's images record

ethnic and racial groups' responses to television's
symbols and content and reveal something about
strategies for political intervention in the production process.(e.g., 23, 42, 64, 164) The two
U.S. Commission on Civil Rights studies mentioned
above (and, for film, a special study on equal
employment opportunity in the movie industry, prepared in 1978 by the California Advisory Committee
to the U.S. Commission on Civil Rights [158])
provide the most complete summaries of the issues
and the prospects for such intervention, but
studies of particular group responses (as revealed
in studies listed especially in the following
chapters on Afro-Americans and Hispanics) add other
glimpses of particular moments of crisis and
subjects of concern. Both general and individual
group studies, however, often lack longitudinal
perspectives on images and/or representation in
popular culture. The politics of television imagery
remains a subject needful of detailed examination.

Some scholars have sought ways to bring mass
media images into the formal learning process.
Randall Miller briefly surveys treatments of the
immigrant/ethnic experience in American film, with
an eye to using such films to show popular cultural
beliefs on immigration.(104) Daniel Walden also
recommends ways teachers might use films with
ethnic themes or images.(162) Thomas Cripps looks
at urban, ethnic, and racial images in early films
and television in order to suggest how to introduce
such materials in discussions of modern society.(37) Acknowledging the role of film and television in teaching children social roles and introducing them to ethnic and racial issues, Carlos
Cortes urges Americans to incorporate television
into American education, which, he states, first
demands that viewers understand the processes and
images in mass media.(34,35) Joseph Giordano argues
that ethnic stereotypes in television can contribute
to children's prejudices against particular groups,
but rather than concede to television such influence, he asks viewers to dissect the images they
see and pressure television producers to remove
offensive ones.(56, 57)

The numerous studies relating to ethnic and
racial images in American film and television
attest to the importance of the subject. In suggesting how images influence inter-group relations

and shape self-concepts, how they both reflect and affect American culture, they remind us, too, that American film and television have never been mere entertainment.

1. Anon. ATTI DEL CONVENGO SU METODI DI RICERCA E
    RISULTATI SUL RAPPORTO TRA VIOLENZA LA
    TELEVISIONE E CRIMINALITA [Proceedings of
    the Meeting on Research Methods and Results
    Concerning   the   Relationship   between
    Violence in Television and Criminality].
    Torino, Italy: ERI--Edizione rai Radiotele-
    visione Italiana, 1975.

2. ————. IN   SEARCH   OF   DIVERSITY--SYMPOSIUM
    ON   MINORITY   AUDIENCES   AND   PROGRAMMING
    RESEARCH: APPROACHES   AND   APPLICATIONS.
    Washington, D.C.: Corporation for Public
    Broadcasting, 1981.

3. ————. FIGHTING TV STEREOTYPES. Newtonville,
    Mass.: Action for Children's Television,
    1982.

4. Adatto, Kiku. "American   Fantasy: Social
    Conflicts and Social Myths in Films of the
    1970s." Ph. D. diss., State University of
    New York at Stony Brook, 1982.

5. Adler, Richard P., ed., ALL IN THE FAMILY: A
    CRITICAL   APPRAISAL.   New   York: Praeger,
    1979.

6. Arlen, Michael J.   THE VIEW FROM HIGHWAY 1:
    ESSAYS ON TELEVISION. New York: Ballantine
    Books, 1977.

7. [Astor, Gerald]. MINORITIES AND THE MEDIA. New
    York: Ford Foundation, November, 1974.

8. Auster, Al, and Lynn Garafola, Dan Georgakas,
    Leonard Quart, and Fred Siegel. "Hollywood
    and the Working Class: A Discussion."
    SOCIALIST R 9 (July-August 1979): 109-21.

9. Axthelm, Kenneth W. "Minority   Groups: Our
    Majority Audience." FILM LIBRARY Q 1
    (Summer 1968): 25.

10. Barnouw, Erik. TUBE OF PLENTY: THE EVOLUTION
    OF AMERICAN TELEVISION. New York: Oxford
    University Press, 1975.

11. Becker, Samuel. "Research Findings in Broadcasting and Civil Rights." TELEVISION Q 5 (Fall 1966): 72-82.

12. Belth, Nathan C. and Morton Puner, eds. PREJUDICE AND THE LIVELY ARTS. New York: Anti-Defamation League of B'nai B'rith, [1959].

13. Berger, Arthur Asa. THE TV-GUIDED AMERICAN. New York: Walker & Company, 1976.

14. Bergman, Andrew. WE'RE IN THE MONEY. New York, New York University Press, 1971.

15. Bergsten, Bebe, ed. BIOGRAPH BULLETINS, 1896-1908. Los Angeles: Locare Research Group, 1971.

16. Berk, Lynn M. "The Great Middle American Dream Machine." J OF COMMUNICATION 27 (Summer 1977): 27-31.

17. Berry, Gordon L. "Children, Television, and Social Class Roles: The Medium as an Unplanned Educational Curriculum." CHILDREN AND THE FACE OF TELEVISION (item I-115), pp. 71-81.

18. ――――, and Claudia Mitchell-Kernan, eds. TELEVISION AND THE SOCIALIZATION OF THE MINORITY CHILD. New York: Academic Press, 1982.

19. Biskind, Peter. SEEING IS BELIEVING: HOW HOLLYWOOD TAUGHT US TO STOP WORRYING AND LOVE THE FIFTIES. New York, Pantheon Press, 1983.

20. Boskin, Joseph. "Denials: The Media View of Dark Skins and the City." SMALL VOICES AND GREAT TRUMPETS: MINORITIES AND THE MEDIA. Edited by Bernard Rubin. New York: Praeger, 1980, pp. 141-47.

21. Bowser, Pearl, ed. IN COLOR: SIXTY YEARS OF IMAGES OF MINORITY WOMEN IN THE MEDIA... 1921-1981. New York: Third World Newsreel,

[1983].

22. Brauer, Ralph, and Donna Brauer. THE HORSE,
     THE GUN, AND THE PIECE OF PROPERTY:
     CHANGING IMAGES OF THE TV WESTERN. Bowling
     Green, Ohio: The Popular Press, 1975.

23. Brazaitis, Thomas J. "Ethnics Fear Images
     Warped." [Cleveland] PLAIN DEALER, February
     13, 1977, I, 20ff.

24. Breitenfeld, Frederick, Jr. "Speeding Down the
     Wrong Track." TV GUIDE 23 (January 25-31,
     1975): 22-23.

25. Brown, Les. "Ethnic Pressures are Effective in
     Barring 'Offensive' TV Films." NEW YORK
     TIMES, November 28, 1973, pp. 1, 90.

26. Cantor, Muriel G. PRIME-TIME TELEVISION:
     CONTENT AND CONTROL. Beverly Hills, Ca.:
     Sage, 1980.

27. Castleman, Harry, and Walter J. Podrazik.
     WATCHING TV: FOUR DECADES OF AMERICAN
     TELEVISION. New York: McGraw-Hill, 1981.

28. Champlin, Charles. THE FLICKS, OR WHATEVER
     BECAME OF ANDY HARDY? Pasadena, CA.: Ward
     Ritchie Press, 1977.

29. Clark, Cedric C. "Television and Social
     Controls: Some Observations on the
     Portrayals of Ethnic Minorities." TELE-
     VISION Q 8 (Spring 1968): 18-22.

30. Coakley, Mary Lewis. RATED X: THE MORAL CASE
     AGAINST TV. New Rochelle, N. Y.: Arlington
     House, 1977.

31. Comstock, George, and Steven Chaffee, Natan
     Katzman, Maxwell McCombs, and Donald
     Roberts. TELEVISION AND HUMAN BEHAVIOR. New
     York: Columbia University Press, 1978.

32. ————, and Robin E. Cobbey. TELEVISION AND
     THE CHILDREN OF ETHNIC MINORITIES. [mime-
     ographed report] Syracuse, N. Y.: S. I.

Newhouse School of Public Communications, Syracuse University, 1978.

33. ———. "Research Directions for the Study of Television and Ethnicity: Methodological Considerations." [mimeographed report] Syracuse, N. Y.: Syracuse University, April, 1978.

34. Cortes, Carlos E. "The Role of the Media in Multicultural Education." VIEWPOINTS IN TEACHING AND LEARNING 56 (Winter 1980): 38-49.

35. ———. "The Societal Curriculum and the School Curriculum: Allies or Antagonists?" EDUCATIONAL LEADERSHIP 36 (April 1979): 475-79.

36. ———, and Leon G. Campbell, eds. RACE AND ETHNICITY IN THE HISTORY OF THE AMERICAS: A FILMIC APPROACH. Riverside, Cal.: University of California, Riverside, Latin American Studies Program Film Series, no. 4, 1979.

37. Cripps, Thomas. "Early Films and Television: With Special Reference to Urban, Ethnic and Black Studies." [mimeographed report] Baltimore: Morgan State University, April 1972.

38. Cross, Donna Woolfolk. MEDIASPEAK: HOW TELEVISION MAKES UP YOUR MIND. New York: Coward-McCann, 1983.

39. Davies, Philip, and Brian Neve, eds. CINEMA, POLITICS AND SOCIETY IN AMERICA. New York: St. Martin's Press, 1981.

40. de Grazia, Edward, and Roger K. Newman. BANNED FILMS: MOVIE CENSORSHIP IN THE UNITED STATES. New York: Bowker, 1982.

41. Dooley, Roger. FROM SCARFACE TO SCARLETT: AMERICAN FILMS IN THE 1930S. New York: Harcourt, Brace, Jovanovich, 1981.

42. Efron, Edith. "Report on Minorities: Minority
     Complaints about Television." TV GUIDE 21
     (October 27, 1973): 6-11.

43. Eliot, Marc. AMERICAN TELEVISION: THE OFFICIAL
     ART OF THE ARTIFICIAL. Garden City, N.Y.:
     Anchor Press/ Doubleday, 1981.

44. Epstein, Benjamin R. "'Art' vs. People: A
     Summing Up." PREJUDICE AND THE LIVELY ARTS
     (item I-12), pp. 21-23.

45. Everson, William K. AMERICAN SILENT FILM. New
     York: Oxford University Press, 1978.

46. ————. THE DETECTIVE IN FILM. Secaucus, N.
     J.: Citadel Press, 1972.

47. Ewen, Elizabeth. "City Lights: Immigrant Women
     and the Rise of the Movies." SIGNS: J OF
     WOMEN IN CULTURE AND SOCIETY 5 (Spring
     1980): 45-65.

48. Foner, Eric. "The Televised Past." TELEVISION
     Q 16 ([Spring] 1979): 59-60, 62-63.

49. Gans, Herbert J. POPULAR CULTURE AND HIGH
     CULTURE: AN ANALYSIS AND EVALUATION OF
     TASTE. New York: Basic Books, 1974.

50. Garafola, Lynn. "Hollywood and the Myth of the
     Working Class." RADICAL AMERICA 14 (no. 1
     1980): 7-15.

51. Gentile, Frank, and S. M. Miller. "Television
     and Social Class." SOCIOLOGY AND SOCIAL
     RESEARCH 45 (April 1961): 259-64.

52. Gerbner, George. "The Mainstreaming of
     America: Television Makes Strange Bed-
     fellows." TV GUIDE 32 (October 22, 1984):
     20-23.

53. ————, and Nancy Signorielli. WOMEN AND
     MINORITIES IN TELEVISION DRAMA, 1969-1978:
     A RESEARCH REPORT. Philadelphia: Annenberg
     School of Communications, University of
     Pennsylvania, 1979.

54. ———, and Larry Gross, and Michael Morgan. "Political Correlates of Television Viewing." PUBLIC OPINION Q 48 (Spring 1984): 283-300.

55. Gerson, Mauricio. "Minority Representation in Network Television Drama, 1970-76," MASS COMMUNICATIONS R 7 (Fall 1980): 10-12, 16.

56. Giordano, Joseph. "Families: What TV Teaches Children." ATTENZIONE 3 (December 1981): 76, 78, 80.

57. ———, and Philip Franchione. "Time to Change TV's Pictures of the 'Ethnics.'" NEW YORK DAILY NEWS, March 4, 1981, p. 17.

58. Gitlin, Todd. "Fourteen Notes on Television and the Movement." LEVIATHAN 1 (July/August 1969): 3-9.

59. ———. INSIDE PRIME TIME. New York: Pantheon, 1983.

60. Goldson, Rose K. THE SHOW AND TELL MACHINE: HOW TELEVISION WORKS AND WORKS YOU OVER. New York: Dial Press, 1977.

61. Greenberg, Bradley S., and Sherrie L. Mazingo. RACIAL ISSUES IN MASS MEDIA INSTITUTIONS [Project CUP: Communication Among the Urban Poor. Report 16]. East Lansing, Mich.: College of Communication Arts, Michigan State University, 1973.

62. Griffith, Richard and Arthur Mayer. THE MOVIES: THE SIXTY-YEAR STORY OF THE WORLD OF HOLLYWOOD AND ITS EFFECT ON AMERICA FROM PRE-NICKELODEON DAYS TO THE PRESENT. New York: Simon & Schuster, 1957.

63. Grillo, Jean Bergantini. "Ethnic Slurs Are Back." TV GUIDE 29 (June 13, 1981): 35-36, 38.

64. Gunther, Max. "Life in a Pressure Cooker." [Part 1 of series "How Special Interest

Groups Pressure TV"] TV GUIDE 22 (February
9, 1974): 4-8; "Men in the Middle" [Part
2] TV GUIDE 22 (February 16, 1974): 33-36,
39-40.

65. Hall, Jane. "After the Bad Guys Bite the Dust
... the Good Guys Take Over on 'Americans
All.'" TV GUIDE 22 (August 17, 1974):
28-29.

66. Handelman, Janet. "Report on the FLIC-EFLA
Minorities Film Workshop." FILM LIBRARY Q 4
(Winter 1970-71): 7.

67. Head, Sydney. "Content Analysis of Television
Drama Programs." Q OF FILM, RADIO AND
TELEVISION 9 (Winter 1954): 175-94.

68. Helffrich, Stockton. "Editing the Airwaves."
PREJUDICE AND THE LIVELY ARTS (item I-12):
14-16.

69. Higham, Charles and Joel Greenberg. HOLLYWOOD
IN THE FORTIES. New York: A. S. Barnes &
Co., 1968.

70. Jacobs, Lewis. THE RISE OF THE AMERICAN FILM.
New York: Harcourt, Brace & Company, 1939.

71. Jarvie, I. C. MOVIES AS SOCIAL CRITICISM:
ASPECTS OF THEIR SOCIAL PSYCHOLOGY.
Metuchen, N. J.: Scarecrow, 1978.

72. Jeffres, Leo W., and K. Kyoon Hur. "White
Ethnics and Their Media Images." J OF
COMMUNICATION 29 (Winter 1979): 116-22.

73. Jones, Dorothy B. "Tomorrow the Movies IV: Is
Hollywood Growing Up?" THE NATION 160
(February 3, 1945): 123-25.

74. Jowett, Garth. FILM: THE DEMOCRATIC ART.
Boston: Little, Brown, 1976.

75. Jurewicz, Edward J. "Films, Television and
Ethnic Identity." ETHNIC FORUM 1 (December
1980): 22-24.

76. Kane, Kathryn Rose. "A Critical Analysis of
    the World War II Combat Films, 1942-1945."
    Ph. D. diss., University of Iowa, 1976.

77. ————. VISIONS OF WAR. HOLLYWOOD COMBAT
    FILMS OF WORLD WAR II. Ann Arbor, Mich.:
    UMI Research Press, 1982.

78. Karp, David. "Who Stole the Melting Pot?"
    TELEVISION Q 7 (Summer 1968): 62-69.

79. Kelly, Katie. MY PRIME TIME: CONFESSIONS OF A
    TV WATCHER. New York: Seaview Books, 1980.

80. Kirby, Jack Temple. "D. W. Griffith's Racial
    Portraiture." PHYLON 39 (June 1978): 118-
    27.

81. Klapp, Orrin. HEROES, VILLAINS, AND FOOLS: THE
    CHANGING AMERICAN CHARACTER. Englewood
    Cliffs, N.J.: Prentice-Hall, 1962.

82. Koppes, Clayton R., and Gregory D. Black.
    "What to Show the World: The Office of War
    Information and Hollywood, 1942-1945." J OF
    AMERICAN HISTORY 64 (June 1977): 87-105.

83. Kracauer, Siegfried. "National Types as
    Hollywood Presents Them." PUBLIC OPINION Q
    13 (Spring 1949): 53-72.

84. Kurnitz, Harry. "Screen Humor." PROCEEDINGS
    (item I-173), pp. 230-35.

85. Landry, Robert J. "The Menace of the Naive
    Artist." PREJUDICE AND THE LIVELY ARTS
    (item I-12), pp. 8-9.

86. ————. "The Movies: Better Than Ever?"
    PREJUDICE AND THE LIVELY ARTS (item I-12),
    pp. 10-11.

87. Leahy, Michael, and Wallis Annenberg.
    "Discrimination in TV: How Bad Is It?" TV
    GUIDE 32 (October 13, 1984): 6-8, 10-14.

88. Leifer, Aimee Dorr, Neal J. Gordon, and
    Sherryl Browne Graves. "Children's

Television More Than Mere Entertainment."
HARVARD EDUCATIONAL R 44 (May 1974):
213-45.

89. Levinson, Richard, and William Link. STAY
    TUNED: AN INSIDE LOOK AT THE MAKING OF
    PRIME-TIME TELEVISION. New York: St.
    Martin's Press, 1981.

90. Linton, James M., and Garth S. Jowett. "A
    Content Analysis of Feature Films." REPORT
    OF THE ROYAL COMMISSION ON VIOLENCE IN THE
    COMMUNICATION INDUSTRY, Vol. III: VIOLENCE
    IN TELEVISION, FILMS AND NEWS. Toronto:
    Royal Commission on Violence in the
    Communications Industry, 1977, pp. 465-580.

91. McClure, Arthur F. "Hollywood at War: The
    American Motion Picture and World War II."
    J OF POPULAR FILM 1 (Spring 1979): 123-35.

92. ———, Alfred E. Twomey, and Ken D. Jones.
    MORE CHARACTER PEOPLE: SUPPORTING PLAYERS
    IN THE AMERICAN MOTION PICTURE. Secaucus,
    N. J.: Citadel Press, 1984.

93. McCreary, Eugene. "Film and History: Some
    Thoughts on Their Interrelationship."
    SOCIETAS 1 (no. 1 1971): 51-66.

94. MacDougall, David. "Prospects of the
    Ethnographic Film." FILM Q 23 (Winter
    1969-70): 16-30.

95. Maltby, Richard. HARMLESS ENTERTAINMENT:
    HOLLYWOOD AND THE IDEOLOGY OF CONSENSUS.
    Metuchen, N.J.: Scarecrow Press, 1983.

96. Manchel, Frank. FILM STUDY: A RESEARCH GUIDE.
    Rutherford, N.J.: Fairleigh Dickinson
    University Press, 1973.

97. Mandelbaum, Juan Pedro. "The Portrayal of
    Social Class in Hollywood Films." M.A.
    thesis, Annenberg School of Communications,
    University of Pennsylvania, 1980.

98. Mander, Jerry. FOUR ARGUMENTS FOR THE

ELIMINATION   OF   TELEVISION.   New   York:
Morrow, 1978.

99. Marc, David. "Democratic Vistas: Television in
American Culture." Ph. D. diss., University
of Iowa, 1982; Philadelphia: University of
Pennsylvania Press, 1984.

100. Mayer, Martin.   ABOUT   TELEVISION. New York:
Harper & Row, 1972.

101. Mendelsohn, Harold.   "Social   Need   or Sacred
Cow?--A Sociological   Perspective."   J   OF
COMMUNICATION 28 (Spring 1978): 30-35.

102. Middleton, Russell.   "Ethnic   Prejudice   and
Susceptibility   to   Persuasion."   AMERICAN
SOCIOLOGICAL R 25 (October 1960): 679-86.

103. Miller,   Mark   Crispin,   and   Karen   Runyon.
"Television."   THE   NATION   230 (April   26,
1980): 506-508.

104. Miller, Randall M.   "American   History Through
Film: The   Immigrant   Experience."   ORGAN-
IZATION   OF AMERICAN   HISTORIANS NEWSLETTER
12 (May 1984): 24-25.

105. ————,   ed.   ETHNIC IMAGES IN AMERICAN FILM
AND   TELEVISION.   Philadelphia: The   Balch
Institute, 1978.

106. ————,   ed.   THE   KALEIDOSCOPIC LENS: HOW
HOLLYWOOD VIEWS ETHNIC GROUPS.   Englewood,
N. J.: Jerome S. Ozer, 1980.

107. Monaco, James.   AMERICAN FILM NOW: THE PEOPLE,
THE POWER, THE MONEY, THE MOVIES. New York:
New American Library, 1979.

108. Neale, Steve. "The Same Old Story: Stereotypes
and   Difference."   SCREEN   EDUCATION   nos.
32/33 (Autumn/Winter 1979): 33-37.

109. Nobile, Philip, ed.   FAVORITE MOVIES: CRITICS'
CHOICE. New York: MacMillan, 1973.

110. Noble, Grant. CHILDREN IN FRONT OF THE SMALL
     SCREEN. Beverly Hills, Cal.: Sage Publica-
     tions, 1975.

111. Novak, Michael. "Television Shapes the Soul."
     TELEVISION AS A SOCIAL FORCE: NEW AP-
     PROACHES TO TV CRITICISM. Edited by
     Douglass Cater and Richard Adler. New
     York: Praeger, 1975, pp. 9-21.

112. O'Connor, John. AMERICAN HISTORY/AMERICAN
     TELEVISION: INTERPRETING THE VIDEO PAST.
     New York: Frederick Ungar, 1983.

113. ———, and Martin Jackson, eds. AMERICAN
     HISTORY/AMERICAN FILM: INTERPRETING THE
     HOLLYWOOD IMAGE. New York: Frederick
     Ungar, 1979.

114. O'Dell, Paul, with Anthony Slide. GRIFFITH
     AND THE RISE OF HOLLYWOOD. New York: A. S.
     Barnes, 1970.

115. Palmer, Edward L. and Aimee Dorr, eds.
     CHILDREN AND THE FACE OF TELEVISION:
     TEACHING, VIOLENCE, SELLING. New York:
     Academic Press, 1980.

116. Peterson, Ruth Camilla, and L. L. Thurstone.
     MOTION PICTURES AND THE SOCIAL ATTITUDES
     OF CHILDREN. New York: MacMillan, 1933.

117. Powers, John. "Saints and Savages." AMERICAN
     FILM 9 (January-February 1984): 38-43.

118. Pozner, Vladimir. "Adult or Adulterated."
     SCREEN WRITER 2 (April 1947): 14-17.

119. Quart, Leonard, and Albert Auster. "The
     Working Class Goes to Hollywood." CINEMA,
     POLITICS AND SOCIETY IN AMERICA (item
     I-39), pp. 163-75.

120. ———, and Barbara Quart. "Ragtime with-
     out a Melody." LITERATURE/FILM Q 10 (no. 2
     1982): 71-74.

121. Ramsaye, Terry. A MILLION AND ONE NIGHTS: A
      HISTORY OF THE MOTION PICTURE. 2 vols. New
      York: Simon & Schuster, 1926.

122. Ransom, Jo. "On Key with Tin Pan Alley."
      PREJUDICE AND THE LIVELY ARTS (item I-12),
      pp. 17-18.

123. Real, Michael. MASS-MEDIATED CULTURE. Engle-
      wood Cliffs, N.J.: Prentice-Hall, 1977.

124. Roddick, Nick. A NEW DEAL IN ENTERTAINMENT:
      WARNER BROTHERS IN THE 1930S. London:
      British Film Institute, 1983; Urbana,
      Ill.: University of Illinois Press, 1984.

125. Roffman, Peter, and Jim Purdy. THE HOLLYWOOD
      SOCIAL PROBLEM FILM: MADNESS, DESPAIR, AND
      POLITICS FROM THE DEPRESSION TO THE
      FIFTIES. Bloomington: Indiana University
      Press, 1981.

126. Rollins, Peter C., and Harry W. Menig.
      "Regional Literature and Will Rogers: Film
      Redeems a Literary Form." LITERATURE/FILM
      Q 3 (Winter 1975): 70-82.

127. Rook, Timothy E. "The Role of Divergent
      Personality Patterns as Pertaining to
      Individual Viewer Assessment of Minority
      Characters on Commercial American Tele-
      vision." Ph. D. diss., Bowling Green State
      University, 1982.

128. Rosow, Eugene. BORN TO LOSE: THE GANGSTER
      FILM IN AMERICA. New York: Oxford
      University Press, 1978.

129. Rubin, Bernard, ed. SMALL VOICES AND GREAT
      TRUMPETS: MINORITIES AND THE MEDIA. New
      York: Praeger, 1980.

130. Sauberli, Harry A. "Hollywood and World War
      II: A Survey of Themes of Hollywood Films
      About the War, 1940-1945." M. A. thesis,
      University of Southern California, 1967.

131. Sayre, Nora. RUNNING TIME: FILMS OF THE COLD

WAR. New York: Dial Press, 1982.

132. Schlesinger, Arthur, Jr. "Un hermafrodita: el
      cine." ["A Hermaphrodite: the Cinema"]
      PANORAMAS (Mexico) 3 (no. 15 1965): 117-
      26.

133. Seggar, John F., and Penny Wheeler.   "The
      World of Work on TV: Ethnic and Sex
      Representation in TV Drama." J OF
      BROADCASTING 17 (Spring 1973): 201-14.

134. Shain, Russell Earl. "An Analysis of Motion
      Pictures about War Released by the Amer-
      ican Film Industry, 1930-1970."   Ph. D.
      diss., University of Illinois, Champaign-
      Urbana, 1971; New York: Arno Press, 1976.

135. Shindler, Colin. HOLLYWOOD GOES TO WAR: FILMS
      AND AMERICAN SOCIETY, 1939-1952. London:
      Routledge & Kegan Paul, 1979.

136. Shulman, Arthur, and Roger Youman. HOW SWEET
      IT WAS, TELEVISION: A PICTORIAL COM-
      MENTARY. New York: Bonanza, 1966.

137. Signorielli, Nancy. "Content Analysis: More
      Than Just Counting Minorities." IN SEARCH
      OF DIVERSITY--SYMPOSIUM ON MINORITY AUDI-
      ENCES AND PROGRAMMING RESEARCH: APPROACHES
      AND APPLICATIONS. Washington, D.C.:
      Corporation for Public Broadcasting, 1981,
      pp. 97-108.

138. Sklar, Robert. MOVIE-MADE AMERICA: A CULTURAL
      HISTORY OF AMERICAN MOVIES. New York:
      Random House, 1975.

139. ————. PRIME-TIME AMERICA: LIFE ON AND
      BEHIND THE TELEVISION SCREEN. New York:
      Oxford University Press, 1980.

140. Small, Melvin. "Motion Pictures and the Study
      of Attitudes: Some Problems for Histor-
      ians." FILM & HISTORY 2 (1972): 1-5.

141. Stedman, Raymond W. THE SERIALS: SUSPENSE AND
      DRAMA BY INSTALLMENT. Norman: University

of Oklahoma Press, 1971.

142. Stein, Benjamin. THE VIEW FROM SUNSET
     BOULEVARD: AMERICA AS BROUGHT TO YOU BY
     THE PEOPLE WHO MAKE TELEVISION. New York:
     Basic Books, 1979.

143. Stein, Howard F. "All in the Family as a
     Mirror of Contemporary American Culture."
     FAMILY PROCESS 13 (1974): 279-315.

144. ————. "In Search of 'Roots': An Epic of
     Origins and Destiny." J OF POPULAR CULTURE
     11 (Summer 1977): 11-17.

145. Sterritt, David. "Minorities in the Media."
     CHRISTIAN SCIENCE MONITOR, May 9, 1983, p.
     13.

146. Stoloff, David L. "Ethnic Television in Los
     Angeles." Ph. D. diss., University of Cal-
     ifornia, Los Angeles, 1982.

147. Suber, Howard. "Television's Interchangeable
     Ethnics: 'Funny They Don't Look Jewish.'"
     TELEVISION Q 12 (Winter 1975): 49-56.

148. Tan, Alexis S. "Media Use and Political
     Orientations of Ethnic Groups." JOURNALISM
     Q 60 (Spring 1983): 126-32.

149. Toeplitz, Jerzy. HOLLYWOOD AND AFTER: THE
     CHANGING FACE OF MOVIES IN AMERICA.
     Chicago: Regnery, 1975.

150. Toll, Robert C. THE ENTERTAINMENT MACHINE:
     AMERICAN SHOW BUSINESS IN THE TWENTIETH
     CENTURY. New York: Oxford University
     Press, 1982.

151. Tunstall, Jeremy. THE MEDIA ARE AMERICAN. New
     York: Columbia University Press, 1977.

152. ————, and David Walker. MEDIA MADE IN
     CALIFORNIA: HOLLYWOOD, POLITICS AND THE
     NEWS. New York: Oxford University Press,
     1981.

153. Turow, Joseph. "Casting for TV Parts: The
      Anatomy of Social Typing." J OF COMMUNI-
      CATION 28 (Autumn 1978): 18-24.

154. Tyner, Howard A. "Stereotypes in Films Can Be
      Useful." CHICAGO TRIBUNE, March 4, 1981,
      pp. 1, 4.

155. Unger, Arthur. "Minorities in the Media."
      CHRISTIAN SCIENCE MONITOR, May 10, 1983,
      pp. 12-13.

156. U. S. Commission on Civil Rights. WINDOW
      DRESSING ON THE SET: AN UPDATE. Washing-
      ton, D. C.: U. S. Commission on Civil
      Rights, 1979.

157. ————. WINDOW DRESSING ON THE SET: WOMEN
      AND MINORITIES IN TELEVISION. Washington,
      D.C.: U. S. Commission on Civil Rights,
      1977.

158. ————, California Advisory Committee.
      BEHIND THE SCENES: EQUAL EMPLOYMENT
      OPPORTUNITIES IN THE MOTION PICTURE
      INDUSTRY--A REPORT PREPARED BY THE CALI-
      FORNIA ADVISORY COMMITTEE TO THE U. S.
      COMMISSION ON CIVIL RIGHTS. Washington,
      D.C., U. S. Commission on Civil Rights,
      1978.

159. ————, Montana Advisory Committee. THE
      MEDIA IN MONTANA: ITS EFFECTS ON
      MINORITIES AND WOMEN. Washington, D. C.:
      U. S. Commission on Civil Rights, 1976.

160. U. S. Congress, Committee on Interstate and
      Foreign Commerce, Subcommittee on Communi-
      cations and Power. FILMS AND BROADCASTS
      DEMEANING ETHNIC, RACIAL, OR RELIGIOUS
      GROUPS. Washington, D. C.: GPO, 1970.

161. ————. FILMS AND BROADCASTS DEMEANING
      ETHNIC, RACIAL, OR RELIGIOUS GROUPS.
      Washington, D. C.: GPO, 1971.

162. Walden, Daniel. "American Ethnic Studies and
      Film." SIGHTLINES 11 (Fall 1977): 18-19.

163.   Walker, Alexander. THE SHATTERED SILENTS: HOW
       TALKIES CAME TO STAY. New York: William
       Morrow & Company, 1979.

164.   Waters, Harry F. "TV: Do Minorities Rule?"
       NEWSWEEK 85 (June 2, 1975): 78-79.

165.   Westen, Tracy A. "Barriers to Creativity." J
       OF COMMUNICATION 28 (Spring 1978): 36-42.

166.   White, David Manning, and Richard Averson.
       THE CELLULOID WEAPON: SOCIAL COMMENT IN
       THE AMERICAN FILM. Boston: Beacon Press,
       1972.

167.   Willett, Ralph. "The Nation in Crisis:
       Hollywood's Response to the 1940s."
       CINEMA, POLITICS AND SOCIETY (item I-39),
       pp. 59-75.

168.   _____. "Nativism and Assimilation: The
       Hollywood Aspect." J OF AMERICAN STUDIES 7
       (no. 2 1973): 191-94.

169.   Williams, Carol Traynor. THE DREAM BESIDE ME:
       THE MOVIES AND THE CHILDREN OF THE
       FORTIES. Rutherford, N. J.: Fairleigh
       Dickinson University Press, 1980.

170.   Woll, Allen. THE HOLLYWOOD MUSICAL GOES TO
       WAR. Chicago: Nelson-Hall, 1983.

171.   Wood, Michael. AMERICA IN THE MOVIES, OR,
       "SANTA MARIA, IT HAD SLIPPED MY MIND!" New
       York: Basic Books, 1975.

172.   Wright, Charles R. MASS COMMUNICATION: A
       SOCIOLOGICAL PERSPECTIVE. New York: Random
       House, 1959.

173.   Writers' Congress. THE PROCEEDINGS OF THE
       CONFERENCE HELD IN OCTOBER 1943 UNDER THE
       SPONSORSHIP OF THE HOLLYWOOD WRITERS'
       MOBILIZATION AND THE UNIVERSITY OF
       CALIFORNIA. Berkeley: University of
       California Press, 1944.

174. Yacowar, Maurice. "Aspects of the Familiar: A
      Defense of Minority Group Stereotyping in
      the Popular Film."   LITERATURE/FILM Q 2
      (Spring 1974): 129-39.

II. AFRO-AMERICANS

Afro-Americans have probably been more profoundly affected by film and television than any
other racial group. Early depictions of blacks on
screen, however, were neither wholly prejudicial
nor much planned. Before the development of editorial cutting no sustained screen narrative was
possible. Filmmakers could not easily transfer the
prevailing popular stereotypes of blacks from stage
and literature (the tragic mulatto, the jiving
sharpster, the bestial brute, the shuffling Sambo,
the blackface clown) to the screen and generally
had to represent blacks, like all subjects, in the
various places and circumstances in which they
existed.(181, 226, 387)
    All that changed soon enough--and with drastic
consequences for the Afro-American image in film.
In the early twentieth century America was still
basking in the theme of sectional reconciliation.
Southern "local color" stories and appeals to the
unity of the Anglo-Saxon race enjoyed favor among
whites both North and South. When filmmakers
learned to select, cut, and edit their shots for
narrative effect, they grabbed the popular cultural
symbols and fare at hand. Blacks, or whites in
blackfaces, began to appear in movies as they did
in minstrel shows, in vaudeville, and in potboilers
--that is, often as "darkies" of the "Old Virginny"
type. Despite several important exceptions--espe-
cially Edwin S. Porter's Uncle Tom's Cabin (1909),
which restored some of the abolitionist energy of
the novel and inspired several remakes through
1927, and Jack Johnson's boxing pictures--black
images on the screen increasingly mirrored the
narrow opportunities and racist images in society
at large.
    In the age of Jim Crow and in the absence of a
powerful, consistent black voice, filmmakers borrowed their racial themes and characters from white
sources. Unwilling or unable to develop new mate-

rial while churning out countless shorts for a
growing movie audience, many filmmakers shamelessly
played on race humor, with blacks as the butts of
jokes and pranks. Even in Africa, where they might
have been expected to dispense with old stereotypes
and let reality sell itself, documentary filmmakers
arranged their pictures in terms of European or
American colonialist perspectives. The "natives" on
screen seemed dull, impotent, and almost unworthy
of "civilization." A few documentary filmmakers,
like Martin and Osa Johnson who did not frame their
shots to conform to racial or imperial priorities,
continued to enjoy commercial and artistic success
through the 1920s by focusing their lens on "primitive" black Africa, itself an image potentially
damaging to blacks. But in Africa, as in America,
the white man's fiction and fantasies ruled. Tarzan
subdued the blacks in popular novels and then in
media-made Africa, while the Ku Klux Klan and other
whites did the job in fact and on film in the
United States.(181, 182, 387, 390, 466, 652)
    By the 1910s American movies were expanding
outward from their early storefront and nickelodeon
environments and catering to a wider audience. The
change in audience, the increased costs in production, and the new filming techniques combined to
make American moviemakers more attentive to the
demands of those who could pay. White, middle-class
audiences wanted good stories and action, and they
had their own ideas about the proper social order.
They also had nostalgic feelings about a pastoral
idyll seemingly lost in modern, urban America. In a
mood of sectional reconciliation, which intensified
in anticipation of and during the fiftieth anniversary of the Civil War, popular tastes craved
stories about the supposed rural innocence of the
"Old South," a theme southern writers of the "Lost
Cause" school had been peddling in magazines,
books, and theater for over a generation. Blacks,
and especially black-related subjects with an urban
setting, began to fade from the silver screen,
except as faithful retainers or gullible, rowdy
town blacks easily duped by northern white Radicals
in stories about the Civil War and Reconstruction.
A series of Civil War movies fed the white audiences' appetite for action, narrative, and sentimentality, while also showing blacks in old stere-

otypes dusted off from white southern lore.(120,
181, 182, 387)

In 1915 blacks' place in film, and in the
popular imagination, became fixed for over a generation, with the showing and enormous artistic and
commercial success of David Wark Griffith's The
Birth of a Nation. The film was, and remains,
controversial and a classic. It signalled the birth
of a significant American film art and transformed
both the conception and content of film. It synthe-
sized a generation of new advances and techniques
in filmmaking and invented several new ones. Its
narrative and visual sweep and its scale awed audiences and critics alike. Indeed, it attracted huge
audiences, with probably more paid admissions than
any other film in history, and it earned the impri-
matur of President Woodrow Wilson who reportedly
likened Griffith's movie to "writing history with
lightning."(226, 559)

Griffith's history, however, recalled the "Lost
Cause" myth, and dressed it up with glory in
battle, and pathos and courage in defeat. A South-
erner by birth and inclination, Griffith sought to
tell the "southern" side of the great struggle. He
drew upon Thomas Dixon's novel and stageplay, The
Clansman, for plot and characters, and worked with
Dixon in developing the film, but The Birth of a
Nation owed much to Griffith's own views of the
plantation ideal, war, and race relations. Griffith
intended the movie to demonstrate the tragedy of
war. Coming at the high tide of the Civil War
anniversary celebrations, its effect, however, was
broader and, in some cases, contradicted Griffith's
own intentions.(71, 91, 130, 181, 308, 439, 540,
573, 604, 631)

The advertising campaign promoting the film,
which included billboards featuring nightriders,
and even hired robed horsemen riding through the
streets of New York City, generated excitement and
closed the historical distance between the film and
its audience. For many of those who had worked on
the film and who saw it, the Civil War had been a
personal, even a central, event in their own lives.
For them, the "Lost Cause" was real and palpable.
(90, 112, 120, 121, 130, 181, 226, 244, 374, 516,
573, 601)

Griffith's powerful images of blacks (many
played by whites in blackface because of the

shortage of blacks in southern California [226, 537]) included the trusting, loyal slave who shared the master's kindness and values in the big house, the malevolent mulatto who sowed discord, and the ignorant black field hands and town dwellers who succumbed to blandishments and promises of power by corrupt (and corrupting) northern agents. Griffith also conjured up sexual fantasies about black lasciviousness and designs against white women, which he tried to make viewers believe justified the harsh and "necessary" punishments the Klan meted out at the end of the film to protect white womanhood and to overthrow the "tyranny" of the black South.(120, 181, 246, 369, 387, 601, 604)

— Griffith offered little that was new regarding black images. His work derived from southern mythology and common racial stereotypes long circulating in the popular culture, and for several years prior to The Birth of a Nation Griffith and others had been trotting out such images in a string of Civil War films.(55, 120, 121, 130, 140, 181, 182, 230, 369, 370, 387, 392, 573, 601) Griffith's contribution was his scale and his cinematic force, conveyed by the dynamic quality of the film. Nobody had previously put together so long a film (twelve reels, three hours in length), with such a compelling narrative. The imagination and persuasive power of the film admitted no alternative vision, and, as William Everson observes, with audiences then unfamiliar with film technique, viewers did not understand how the movie "was manipulating them."(226) Many viewers accepted Griffith's message and imagery as a "true" account of the war and its aftermath, and, then, too, of black character. Leading contemporary historians, philanthropic and religious figures, and politicians praised the film's historical "authenticity" and validity. Combined with the film's power, artistry, and trappings of historical accuracy, such accolades further confirmed the "truth" of Griffith's images in the public mind.(120, 130, 140, 181, 226, 374, 387, 392, 440, 537, 604)

— Blacks understood immediately the implications of Griffith's images. The National Association for the Advancement of Colored People (NAACP) launched a campaign assailing the film's stereotypes, urging boycotts at showings, seeking to cut offensive scenes from the prints, and initiating legal action

to prevent the film's exhibition.(180, 181, 187,
202, 235, 355, 387, 461, 466) Griffith stepped
into the fray with a pamphlet attacking censorship
and defending his historical interpretations, and
other filmmakers and critics joined in what became
the first full-dress public debate on the relationship between film content and racial prejudices. Despite several victories, including major
excisions in the film before it opened in Boston,
the NAACP lost the first war over The Birth of a
Nation.(40, 50, 235, 258, 288, 300, 308, 540, 631)

      In a larger sense, however, the campaign
against Griffith's film gave new direction and
purpose to civil rights activities and stirred
Afro-American cultural consciousness. The film's
commercial and critical success, which isolated
black critics from many white liberal friends of
civil rights who fell under the film's visual and
narrative power, caused blacks to rethink their own
strategies in confronting racism. Both political
action, which brought local factions of black
leaders together in a national effort, and the
recognition of the mass media's importance in
shaping and reinforcing cultural images flowed from
the NAACP's efforts to censor and, then, counter
The Birth of a Nation. Black critics cultivated a
black aesthetic, which grew in the hothouse of the
Harlem Renaissance and "New Negro" movements in the
1920s and 1930s, and several black actors, filmmakers, and entrepreneurs established a black cinema.(181, 190, 387)

      The NAACP and Booker T. Washington both sought
to develop a black motion picture company, but
their efforts failed for want of white financial
backing and confusion among blacks about what
message they wanted to convey. An ambitious dream
of mounting a grand film epic on black progress,
entitled Lincoln's Dream, was scaled down to become
The Birth of a Race (1919), which floundered in
conception and got little reception. But several
black actors saw a market in the black urban film
audience. Brothers George P. and Noble Johnson
formed the Lincoln Motion Picture Company to
portray blacks with dignity and humanity in their
"every day life." With meagre funds, they relied on
friends and good organization to produce such films
as The Realization of a Negro's Ambition (1916) and
The Trooper of Company K (1916). The Johnsons'

modest success encouraged other black entrepreneurs
and players to form motion picture companies, which
quickly glutted the market.(91, 157, 158, 167, 180,
181, 206, 384, 387, 466, 654)

The Johnsons' approach illustrated the limits,
and possibilities, in making "race movies." They
used light-skinned "colored players" in their films
and preached a black bourgeois gospel of uplift.
Although they experimented with themes such as
miscegenation and passing, the content of most
films followed that of Hollywood. Underfinanced in
an industry demanding greater investments in tech-
nology and production, the black companies remained
poor stepchildren, even to black audiences who
preferred the more technically sophisticated,
better-made fare offered by the major white film
companies. Still, as Hollywood ignored black life,
or mocked and misrepresented it in the 1920s, black
film companies survived to supply urban black audiences with films that seemingly spoke to their own
concerns.(140, 159, 167, 169, 170, 181, 206, 289,
358, 359, 384, 387, 539)

Blacks, however, never developed a coherent
black film aesthetic capable of nurturing and sustaining a major black film art or industry. Most
"black" film companies were partly, and sometimes
wholly, owned and run by whites and simply made
low-budget films using Hollywood themes with black
casts. Although several race movies rose above
their underfinanced production companies because of
good stories and acting, most remained hardly dis-
tinguishable from low-budget Hollywood potboilers,
except, of course, by the color of their players
and by their more primitive sets and poor-quality
prints.(159, 181, 206, 319, 384)

The race movies of the 1920s reflected the
ambitions of the black bourgeoisie who produced
them. They urged black audiences to aspire to
middle-class values and status, retailing black
Horatio Alger success myths and condemning the
corruptions of ghetto existence--themes which
reached their apogee in The Scar of Shame (1927), a
production of Philadelphia's white-owned Colored
Players studio. Even independent black filmmaker
Oscar Micheaux, who produced the best-cut and most
original race movies in the 1920s, including Body
and Soul (1924) starring Paul Robeson, accepted the
uplift formula. Micheaux's films exemplified the

race movies of the period. His heroes struck it
rich in scores of various ways, but invariably in
fields requiring little rigorous training or education. Preaching a bonanza approach, Micheaux and
the others suggested that group progress would come
from individual success. Whatever its limits for
most blacks in the 1920s, that message had virtually no appeal when the Great Depression smashed
the illusions of a beneficent, expanding capitalism
upon which it had been built.(159, 165, 169, 170,
177, 178, 181, 206, 272, 358, 359, 384, 387, 492,
536)

The end of the silent era brought black voices
into the movie houses, ushered in by Hollywood's
all-black musicals Hallelujah! (1929) and Hearts in
Dixie (1929), which drew off black audiences from
race movies. Lacking funds to shoot sound film and
losing their small market to Hollywood, poor black
film companies folded. Those that survived became
even more imitative of Hollywood. During the 1930s
race movies fell in with the collectivist themes
prevailing in Hollywood films. Group organization
and cohesion emerged as an important feature in
race films, which by their all-black casts paradox-
ically promoted racial unity while, by implication,
accepting segregation. But the ghetto remained the
enemy, the evil environment to be cleansed in
1930s-style by group effort.(140, 181, 206, 393,
536)

Most race movies were black only in casting,
for a coterie of white entrepreneurs gained control
over the production of race movies, without significantly improving the technical or narrative quality of the genre. With blacks appearing more favorably and frequently in Hollywood's own productions
during the 1930s and 1940s and with black audiences
unwilling to tolerate the second-rate production
qualities of race movies in which black cowboys and
gangsters aped their Hollywood models, the market
for race movies evaporated. Consisting of remakes,
shorts, and shameless (and often improbable) dupli-
cations of Hollywood roles and plots, race movies
had lost whatever social vision and purpose they
once professed. By the late 1930s the race companies abandoned melodrama and social themes for
musicals, which at least had the virtue of showcasing genuine black talent.(169, 178, 181, 206,
299, 358, 359, 387, 393, 536)

A few independent producers in America and in Europe turned out films with powerful black characters--especially Paul Robeson in Borderline (1929) and The Emperor Jones (1933)--and pointed the way for black cinema in the future, but their products reached only the small, yet loyal and dependable, "art film" audience. Political censorship, distributor and exhibitor hostility (or at least indifference), and inadequate financing kept the independents out of the major markets. For a commercially viable, socially-conscious cinema, most filmgoers would have to look to Hollywood.(90, 91, 181, 206, 387)

From World War I through the 1920s blacks found little social conscience or opportunity in Hollywood. During World War I black fighting units got scant attention from the camera, and black motion picture companies received few contracts to provide war-related footage. Exclusion became more pronounced in the 1920s as the film industry catered to white, middle-class tastes. The industry's interest in stories drawn from literary classics, its self-regulation under the Hays Office which prohibited treating such issues as miscegenation, and its emphasis on upper-class settings and subjects left blacks out of the picture, except in stereotypical roles as servants or as elements of "scenery" to establish place and atmosphere. Black actors scraped by playing stooges in costume dramas or savages in jungle flicks. Only the post-war decline of the Civil War genre prevented further embarrassments. Noble Johnson and a few other actors broke the Sambo pattern, playing skulking, sinister parts or the "good-bad nigger," and by the end of the decade, several black males appeared in complex, if still supporting roles. Black women and children found work as trusted domestics or playmates of whites. Realistic black images and black characters who interacted meaningfully with white ones still waited on changes in Hollywood, where few blacks lived and worked anyway.(129, 169, 170, 174, 181, 210, 387)

The industry's shift away from rural and southern subjects in favor of urban milieus, and the growing awareness of the Harlem Renaissance in artistic circles, promised opportunities to represent blacks in contemporary circumstances. So, too, did the advent of sound film. In too many instances, however, such promise remained unrealized.

Sound allowed several black voices to be heard in Hollywood films. Although black critics resented the depiction of black life passing into white hands and being addressed to white audiences, black actors appreciated that sound film afforded them opportunities to participate in high-quality technical productions the black cinema could not match. The all-black musicals Hallelujah! and Hearts in Dixie presented blacks in sentimental rural repose, which they contrasted with images of a corrupted urban black milieu, but the music won over audiences and critics.(605) By earning favorable reviews and modest box-office receipts, the two films encouraged further experimentation with black subjects and players. The films were also important in that King Vidor's efforts to evoke a realistic setting caused him to seek technical advice from blacks in making Hallelujah!, and the central place of blacks in story and song allowed actors, such as Clarence Muse in Hearts in Dixie, to show they could do more than shuffle and dance. (77, 181, 314, 387, 472, 473, 605)

Attuned to Afro-American spirituals and jazz-related music, urban audiences were willing to pay to see and hear black entertainers. The musicals suggested one way to tap that interest, by attempting to present an "authentic" black sound. The danger of blacks' appeal as musical performers was that it reinforced both the rural vision of black life--an image in musicals that did not allow for black frustrations or discussions of contemporary social issues--and the studios' investment in a one-dimensional Negro.

Hollywood musicals at least gave black performers work.(56) In the sound era, musical talent and experience determined black actors' chances in Hollywood. Radio, records, and nightclub shows introduced Afro-American singers and musicians such as Louis Armstrong, Cab Calloway, Duke Ellington, and Ethel Waters, among others, to national audiences and encouraged Hollywood studios to incorporate contemporary "urban" black sounds into their productions. First in all-black musical shorts and later in "integrated" full-length movies, the industry expropriated and exploited black talent in a host of musicals throughout the 1930s and 1940s,

although, significantly, the studios continued to
shoot the black musical parts of their films in
segregated sections so that they could be cut out
of the film when necessary to accommodate the so-
called southern market.(79, 181) Several black
entertainers prospered as butlers/maids who danced,
sang, and loved their white patrons, while also
being a little flippant and familiar. Black
critics charged them with betrayal for playing in
traditional roles, but the working black actors
responded that their individual successes and
"star" status provided models of uplift and that
their roles in Hollywood films undermined white
fears about blacks mixing with whites. Black cinema
also fell in with the prevailing tune, cranking out
musicals in rhythm with the Hollywood beat.(181,
387)

Lincoln Perry, as Stepin Fetchit, symbolized
the dilemma of the "colored movie star" in 1930s
Hollywood. Often seen solely as the personification
of the obsequious, bumbling Uncle Tom, Fetchit, in
Peter Noble's words, seemingly perpetuated the
"popular myth that the American Negro was a happy,
laughing, dancing imbecile, with permanently
rolling eyes and widespread, empty grin" (473)--a
charge echoed by critics thereafter,(90-92, 181,
200, 387, 389, 466) and one Perry eventually con-
tested in a law suit.(1, 406, 490) But during the
1930s at least, Fetchit, particularly in his roles
with Will Rogers, as in Steamboat 'Round the Bend
(1935), came across as both sassy and servile,
incisive and dim-witted.(530)

Within the limited confines of Hollywood a
small troupe of black "stars" emerged as new roles
in urbane comedies or social-conscience films
became available for black actors. The 1930s Hollywood black actors ventured more rounded black characters than did their 1920s predecessors. Louise
Beavers, Hattie McDaniel, George Reed, Bill Robinson, and even Stepin Fetchit projected undertones
of disagreement and distance and overtones of dignity and discernment while playing roles as domestics, entertainers, and even criminals (e.g.,
Louise Beavers as the numbers queen in Bullets or
Ballots [1936]). Paul Robeson brought a sexuality
and intelligence to his roles, as in Showboat
(1936) with its subplot of interracial marriage,
that contrasted sharply with the 1920s Stepin

Fetchit style of many black performers, including
Fetchit himself in the 1929 version of Showboat.
Robeson's politics, his outspoken condemnation of
racism in the industry, and his screen presence,
however, were all too radical for the Hollywood
moguls' sensibilities. Black actors prospered by
not being overly "uppity" and taught themselves to
score artistic and social points by nuance rather
than proclamation.(91, 92, 177, 181, 190, 387, 620)
        The Great Depression, however, brought several
glimmers of contemporary race-related issues to
Hollywood productions. In the "social problem"
films which became increasingly prevalent in the
1930s, Hollywood studios, especially Warner
Brothers, addressed a number of social and political subjects previously shunned by the industry.
The protagonists and antagonists in films about
chain gangs (I Am a Fugitive from a Chain Gang
[1932]) or sharecropping (A Cabin in the Cotton
[1932]) were white, but audiences could not fail to
notice that the problems affected blacks as well.
The appearance of blacks in such films linked white
and black in a common cause, and especially in the
case of the reformist prison movies, blacks
achieved a crude equality with whites by eating at
the same mess and by laboring in the same chain
gang. In another context, Farina's membership in
"Our Gang" placed her in the same urban neighborhood as her white friends.(80, 181, 387, 466,
527) In films about city life blacks in supporting
roles sometimes served, in Thomas Cripps's words,
as "a plastic material through which moviemakers
shaped their vision of the city."(181)
        In a few instances, filmmakers bestowed dignity
on black characters, and risked box-office re-
jection, by depicting Afro-Americans in non-tradi-
tional roles (e.g., Clarence Brooks playing a
doctor in Arrowsmith [1931]). Several films touched
on controversial subjects involving blacks. A subplot in The Imitation of Life (1934), with Louise
Beavers and Fredi Washington, dealt sympathetically
with the subject of racial "passing" and won
applause from black audiences, although black
critics accused the film of rationalizing racial
prejudice.(109, 210, 466) In Golden Boy (1939) an
Italian-American boxer, angry over his own exploitation in the sport, literally kills his black
opponent (tagged "Kid Chocolate" lest anyone not

know his race) in the ring, while a Harlem crowd
looks on in distress. The victim's father (Clinton
Rosamond) fails to get justice in the subsequent
trial of his son's killer, thereby suggesting the
inequities of a social and legal system that
allowed the exploitation of blacks and lower-class
whites.

In the main, however, studios balked at presenting blacks as central characters, or even
victims, in social problem films. Asians, Mexican
Americans, and Native Americans were all treated as
sympathetic figures and victims of racism and prejudice in several Hollywood films during the 1930s,
while blacks were usually connected to such
subjects by implication only. In the Warner
Brothers film They Won't Forget (1937), for example, the plot turns on sectional antagonism as
the source of southern lynch law; it ignores racial
matters altogether, save for the appearance of a
quaking black janitor called as a witness.(80, 527)

The ambiguity of black images became apparent
in the revival of the Civil War genre, which
straddled the demands of the southern box-office
and the industry's experiments, however timid and
halting, with complex black characters. Old South
plantation settings, which included banjo-strum-
ming, dancing slaves, remained de rigueur; so, too,
did assumptions about the paternalism of masters.
In the big house, however, the mammies and faithful
retainers who continued to proliferate in Civil War
movies seemed to stoop less and sass more than
their counterparts in pre-1930s films. In So Red
the Rose (1935) King Vidor compromised the integrity of his black characters by having them capi-
tulate to the daughter of the dying plantation
owner and by surrounding them with many old stereotypes, but by having insolent, rebellious slave
characters appear at all, Vidor called into
question the plantation ideal of earlier films.
Jezebel (1938), set in New Orleans, extended the
Old South mythology and racial conservatism to the
city, but the movie's black maid confidante to
Bette Davis was no sycophant. Amply endowed black
women, as domestics, could sneak in wisecracks and
raised eyebrows while tightening their mistresses'
corsets and observing the white women's foolishness.(120, 121, 203, 210, 601)

The production history of David O. Selznick's
Gone With the Wind (1939) best illustrated the
ambiguities, and contradictions, in Hollywood's
portrayal of blacks. Helped along by the popularity
of Jezebel and the national passion for Margaret
Mitchell's bestseller, Selznick overcame the industry's timidity regarding "southern flicks,"
which had not done well at the box office in northern cities during the 1920s and 1930s. He committed
himself to a grand, historically accurate portrayal
of the South and the war, and he recruited the best
possible talent for the parts. Selznick managed a
delicate compromise whereby he remained faithful to
Mitchell's story and romantic vision of the Old
South, which captivated Selznick as well, while
introducing changes in the scale and casting of the
drama. In addition to Mitchell's book and consul-
tation, Selznick drew upon a generation of movie-
made images of southern and black life and added a
few of his own, as in the splendor of Tara and his
use of Technicolor to show off the land. Selznick's
debt to Griffith's Birth of a Nation became apparent in the film's rendition of an uncomplicated,
paternalistic antebellum southern society, which
became the counterpoint to the greed, mendacity,
and chaos of the post-war period, and in absolving
the South of any blame or responsibility for having
caused the war and the troubles following it. Gone
With the Wind had its share of slaves singing in
the fields and being overly attached to their be-
nevolent masters, and in the case of Prissy (the
slave girl who dissolves when called upon to assist
in the delivery of Scarlett O'Hara's baby), it
recalled the stereotype of the hysterical black
woman.(120, 181, 233, 634)

Where Selznick departed from the traditional
plantation model, however, was in his perception of
blacks and their place in the historical drama.
Selznick wanted blacks to "come out decidedly on
the right side of the ledger" in his story, and he
raised the importance of Mammy's role in the narrative by making her one of the principals. In
recruiting seasoned professional blacks for the key
parts and treating them with respect on the set,
including listening to their suggestions for improvements in the film, Selznick was acknowledging
the importance of black involvement in a major
movie production.(181, 183)

Black actors and actresses repaid the confidence with excellent performances. Butterfly McQueen later publicly regretted her role as Prissy, which she regarded as a slur on black character. Hattie McDaniel, as Mammy, however, undercut the traditional mammy stereotype by looking white folks directly in the eye, by passing on the wisdom of their actions (often with only a remark or an expression to make the point), and by exuding a personal inner strength superior to almost every white character (save the saintly Melanie).(210, 233, 532) When McDaniel received an Oscar for her supporting role and accepted it with grace, she inevitably diverted attention from the film's weaknesses in racial portraiture and came to symbolize new opportunities for blacks to play serious, integral roles in major Hollywood films. Black critics divided on the film for those reasons.(181, 210, 574)

Black actors looked to brighter days in the industry after Gone With the Wind. Thomas Cripps has concluded that the movie and McDaniel's Oscar signalled a watershed in the industry, "after which blacks were owed some due in roles and in public attention to their feelings."(181) Other observers have disagreed, noting that, at best, blacks remained relegated to supporting roles. By sharing secrets with Humphrey Bogart and Ingrid Bergman in Casablanca (1942) and being his own man in the film's subplot of racial tolerance, Dooley Wilson, as Sam the piano player, showed how a supporting character could become central to a movie's themes and principal characters. Until World War II, few other such opportunities arose for black players. Certainly, McDaniel did not benefit artistically by her performance in Gone With the Wind, for she remained type-cast thereafter in mammy-like roles.(181, 203)

Many old stereotypes lingered during the 1930s. The assembly-line "B" movies especially relied on well-worn roles, as did costume dramas and films geared to the southern market. The jungle movies were the worst of the lot in perpetuating cinematic racism, inspired by the box-office appeal of Tarzan, The Ape Man (1932) and its sequels, which used stock footage and stereotypes of jungle savagery. In more benign roles, blacks continued to appear as genial Uncle Toms who might share kind-

ness and folk wisdom with a white child star (e.g.,
Bill Robinson in the Shirley Temple films), or as
singers, musicians, or vaudevillians not integrated
into the movie plots.(181, 387, 466, 467)

The black press and liberal white filmmakers
and filmgoers grew increasingly intolerant and
weary of such images. Changing social and aesthetic
priorities relegated most overt racism to the back
lots, where it survived in cartoons, newsreels, and
pulp for the "B" houses. Meanwhile, World War II
made accommodations to black sensibilities necessary.(114, 140)

During World War II the nation had to confront
honestly the issue of discrimination. The United
States government condemned Hitler's racism and
viewed the struggle as a people's war for democracy
(and against fascism) that would, among other ac-
complishments, benefit minorities around the world.
The need for black manpower at home and in the
armed forces forced the government to respond to A.
Philip Randolph's, and other black civil rights
leaders', demand for "democracy in Alabama" as a
condition of black support for the war. Film as an
instrument of propaganda also assumed importance
during the war. The government urged Hollywood to
produce films explaining the war's meaning and
encouraging American involvement. When Hollywood
failed to come forth with interesting and effective
films promoting the principles for which Americans
fought, the government stepped in to commission
movies and to make its own films. Black images improved as a result. The Office of War Information
(OWI) specifically criticized negative racial portrayals, and through its manual on filmmaking and
policy of reviewing rough cuts, it stipulated film
content.(355) It also responded to black criticisms
of films. In the case of the movie Tennessee
Johnson (1942), for example, the OWI deferred to
NAACP protests and insisted that MGM revise its
portrayal of Andrew Johnson and Reconstruction.
(161, 171)

In Frank Capra's Why We Fight series, which was
mandatory viewing for American soldiers at training
camps, the War Department demonstrated its ability
to produce powerful, complex films defining war
aims and gave the film industry a standard for its
own war-related films. The government, too, used
the Capra series as a model for The Negro Soldier

(1944), its most explicit film statement fusing
racial tolerance with the unified national war
effort. An overworked Capra allowed Carlton Moss, a
young black writer, almost complete autonomy in
producing The Negro Soldier, which benefited from
technical assistance by Hollywood regulars in the
service and by Moss's access to black writers and
actors who had gravitated to southern California
during the 1930s and 1940s. Even though the film
did not violate Army policy toward racial segregation, it did preach a message of black achievement and involvement in the nation's development
and defense. The film combined clips of prominent
blacks and recreations of American history involving blacks with scenes of a well-dressed, ob-
viously intelligent black congregation listening
and responding to a handsome young preacher
(Carlton Moss) explain why World War II was the
blacks' fight too. Black audiences took pride in
the high technical quality of the film and its
message of black contributions to America. Black
critics and civil rights organizations heaped
praise on the film, which they claimed as their
own, and lobbied successfully for its distribution
to all service units and to commercial movie
houses. After the original 43-minute version failed
at the box office, the film was recut to a 20-
minute two-reeler, which made it more palatable to
commercial exhibitors.(59, 159, 161, 181, 185, 508,
616)

     The success of The Negro Soldier brought white
liberals and black critics together in calls for
integrationist movies.(238, 297, 418, 466)   As
early as 1943 in several Hollywood productions,
blacks were included in the integrated war units
that appeared in film (though not in fact). In
Bataan (1943) a black soldier (Kenneth Spencer)
died valiantly with the rest of the multi-ethnic
American platoon; in Crash Dive (1943) a black
messman (Ben Carter) on a submarine showed his
courage by saving the life of his commander; and in
Alfred Hitchcock's Lifeboat (1944) a black cook
(Canada Lee) shared rations and suffering with the
survivors of a torpedoed vessel. Still, Hollywood
waffled regarding blacks' true place in society.
Blacks continued to occupy subservient positions in
films and were rarely fully integrated into the
group. In Lifeboat, for example, the black alone

did not vote in group decisions and served in a
"janitorial position" on the boat.(387, 450) In
the wartime musicals black performances too often
continued to be segregated from the body of the
film, and so easily cut out, even though, as Allen
Woll points out, the songs the blacks sang "often
reinforced the image of racial democracy that the
musicals were trying to maintain."(639) Hollywood
resolved the contradiction in part by producing
all-black musicals (e.g.,the two Lena Horne vehicles, Cabin in the Sky [1943] and Stormy Weather
[1944]).(140, 181)

The war had matured the industry and the nation
about film's importance and methodology. The NAACP
appreciated anew the power of film's indirect
messages and established a committee on film propaganda to protect black interests. At the 1943
Writers' Congress, sponsored by the Hollywood
Writers' Mobilization, several sessions on film
addressed the issue of propaganda and minority
representation. At the meeting and afterward Dalton
Trumbo criticized Hollywood's past injustices
toward minorities and called for a new black image,
(593, 594), and William Grant Still, a black com-
poser employed by various studios, charged that
white producers routinely disregarded blacks' suggestions on film content and style, even in matters
of Afro-American music.(576, 577)

In the immediate post-war period Hollywood
experimented with a series of "message films" intended to draw attention to and stimulate discussion of controversial domestic subjects. The war
had made politically liberal writers, actors, and
filmmakers aware of the connections between human
psychology and the persuasive power of film, and
they sought to expand and perfect the social
problem genre. Discrimination and prejudice especially came under attack, with two films about
anti-Semitism (Crossfire [1947] and Gentleman's
Agreement [1948]) setting the tone. Several individuals who had worked on wartime documentaries
consciously carried themes of racial liberalism
into their own work after the war (e.g., Carl
Foreman, who wrote Home of the Brave [1949], Stuart
Heisler, who indicted the Ku Klux Klan in Storm
Warning [1950], and Stanley Kramer, who persisted
in the "message" films involving race through the
1950s and 1960s, as in The Defiant Ones [1958] and

Guess Who's Coming to Dinner? [1967]).(185) Long
conditioned by the southern box office, the industry was reluctant to take up the issue of
racism, but the appearance of sympathic black
characters in several European productions (e.g.,
Paisan and Men of Two Worlds) and the insistence of
such individuals as Elia Kazan and Stanley Kramer
forced the issue into Hollywood. In 1949 alone such
films as Home of the Brave, Intruder in the Dust,
Lost Boundaries, and Pinky tackled the post-war
adjustment problems of black army veterans, southern lynch-law mentality, and racial passing. To
contemporaries, Pinky seemed controversial enough
that it became entangled in a censorship lawsuit
involving the industry's code.(90, 153, 162, 163,
224, 375, 528, 559, 619)

    Hollywood's interest in social problem films
proved short-lived after the war. Fundamental
shifts in the film industry affected film content
and blacks' place and images in Hollywood during
the 1950s. Changing leisure-time habits cut into
movie attendance, while production costs skyrock-
eted. Anti-trust proceedings against the industry
dismantled the studio system, which, among other
effects, caused studios to trim payrolls and
thereby reduce dramatically the small stable of
black stars. The break-up of the studio system, the
demise of the Production Code, and the Supreme
Court's 1952 Miracle decision entitling motion
pictures to First Amendment protection seemingly
afforded independents a larger role in film production and promised a greater variety of subject
matter in film fare. The economics of the industry
and its inherent social conservatism dictated otherwise. Eager to regain audiences lost to television and other pastimes, the industry resorted to
gimmicks, such as 3-D films, and moved toward a
blockbuster mentality in production. The industry
turned out fewer films, eliminating the "B" film
almost completely, and increasingly lavished its
attention, resources, and promotion on epics. Opportunities for black actors and black-related
subjects dried up in the 1950s. Stories about black
athletes provided some work (e.g., The Harlem
Globetrotters [1951] and The Joe Louis Story
[1953]). More often, blacks were only faces in the
crowd, extras like the eunuchs in Bible epics who

were denied even the possibility of passion.(59, 86, 115, 140, 181, 355, 387)

The anti-Communist crusade of government witch-hunters directed at Hollywood in the House Un-American Activities Committee hearings from 1947 to 1952 further dampened a nervous industry's willingness to essay controversial subject matter that political conservatives might in any way construe as "anti-American." Liberal thought in the industry had been receding almost from the war's end anyway. "Message" films themselves conveyed a sense of doubt, for they offered no solutions to the problems they exposed. Besides, the message movies involving racial issues did poorly at the box office.(86, 355, 528)

According to Thomas Cripps, in the backlash against McCarthyism during the late 1950s, post-war liberalism reasserted itself. Black actors and subjects began to reappear in Hollywood movies so long as they remained non-threatening. Black actors hardly had a choice about their careers, for the humanity of black images in The Negro Soldier and the early post-war message movies ironically had ended the raison d'etre for race movies. The independent black film industry collapsed, leaving black performers to accommodate themselves to the white-controlled entertainment business.(17, 162, 163, 181)

Black actresses especially felt the pinch of limited dramatic roles. Only Dorothy Dandridge seemed likely to escape the mammy stereotype, but her career ended in professional disappointment and personal tragedy. In Carmen Jones (1954) she earned an Oscar nomination for best actress for her part as a temptress.(62) Dandridge commanded star treatment and pay and sought roles other than those as sluts or domestics. She did not find them. In Island in the Sun (1957), with its double plot of interracial romance, Dandridge participated in liberating Hollywood from its taboo on miscegenation themes and got to play a respectable West Indian shop girl. Otherwise, the industry pressed her into parts as a sexy native girl or a siren (e.g., the disastrous Porgy and Bess [1959], also starring Sidney Poitier and Sammy Davis, Jr., which reviewers scorned for its poor production qualities and black critics skewered for its perpetuation of old caricatures).(387, 589)

Meanwhile, in Thomas Cripps's judgment, Sammy
Davis, Jr., Harry Belafonte, and especially Sidney
Poitier "enjoyed lively careers" depicting "inoffensive and deserving black characters whose manner
promised an easy integration of American society."
Their work prolonged liberal consciousness in the
medium and transformed stereotyping into "a weapon
of liberals." Davis burlesqued racism in his films
and nightclub routines, and Belafonte taught by
homily, as in The World, the Flesh, and the Devil
and Odds Against Tomorrow (both 1959).(162)
More than anyone else, Poitier defined the new
images of blacks in Hollywood film who attacked
racism by indirection and compassion. Poitier established the pattern as early as 1950 in No Way
Out, a film also remarkable for its attempt to
depict black middle-class family life, when he
played a black doctor who tries to save the life of
a white bigot who had shot him.(638) In various
roles Poitier befriended whites and improved their
world by his presence. Thus, he comes to the aid of
a white teacher in an inner-city classroom (Blackboard Jungle [1955]), sacrifices his own freedom to
stay with a white fellow escapee from a southern
prison (The Defiant Ones [1958]), builds a chapel
for white nuns in the wilderness (Lilies of the
Field [1963]), staves off outlaws in the West (Duel
at Diablo [1966]), and solves a murder and erodes
the bigotry of a white police chief (In the Heat of
the Night [1967]). Although a screen hero, Poitier
succeeded by being an asexual, non-threatening one.
His manner disarmed whites and affirmed the liberal
belief in integration.(38, 91, 102, 189, 347, 366,
421, 427) In all these performances, as Martin
Dworkin has noted, Poitier interacted with whites
"in areas of conscience, not sex."(217) Even when
he finally matches up with a white woman (Guess
Who's Coming to Dinner [1967]), he is cast as an
articulate, well-educated professional, distinguished from his understanding prospective white
in-laws only by his color. Black critics recognized
how little Poitier's interracial dynamic spoke to
the real world of American blacks by dismissing the
movie as "Abie's Irish Rose in blackface."(61, 63,
91, 93, 102, 225, 310, 318, 387, 511)
By the late 1960s Poitier's cool demeanor had
become dated and irrelevant. Black rage demanded
more forthright assaults on racism than the too-

reasonable Poitier characters provided, and a new
generation of black actors supplied urban black
audiences with models born in the mean streets of
ghetto America. Poitier defended himself from
charges of cozying up to whites by asserting that
his roles served black interests, in that they suggested the possibility of meaningful black-white
interaction and racial integration. He added that
the absence of other blacks and of black roles in
film showed how little the industry would tolerate
anyway.(15, 274, 322, 471, 504) At least he was
working. He also marked progress by being selected
to star in a movie in which race was not a factor
at all (The Bedford Incident [1965]). Black critics
who once viewed Poitier's success as a milestone
were unconvinced. They tagged Poitier as a "show-
case nigger"(431). In 1970 film critic Vincent
Canby added that Poitier's milestone had become a
millstone because Poitier's blackness was "invisible."(123)

Poitier reacted to such criticisms with anger
and with fresh departures in his screen personae.
(15, 91, 93, 225, 322, 504, 505) In For Love of Ivy
(1968), which he helped to write, he had a romantic
relationship with a black woman, and in The Lost
Man (1969) he wore a leather jacket, sunglasses,
and a scowl in his role as a black "militant"
leader. He also directed himself in Buck and the
Preacher (1972) and other films during the 1970s,
and found commercial, if not critical, success in
Let's Do It Again (1975), a sequel to his Uptown
Saturday Night (1974), in which he again teamed
with Bill Cosby in an amiable caper film.(366)

Recent critical assessments of Poitier's career
now concede his important transitional role in
moving black actors onto center stage. In Donald
Bogle's estimation, Poitier made whites take a
black person seriously, "at least while they sat in
the movie theater."(90, 91, 151) His presence alone
set a precedent, even if his "ebony saint" image
was forced on him by an industry indifferent or
hostile to black concerns.(63, 387) Poitier be-
queathed to black actors a legacy of grace under
pressure. According to Thomas Cripps, "a broad
spectrum of black performers," ranging from Diahann
Carroll to ex-football players turned actors (e.g.,
Jim Brown, Bernard Casey, and O.J. Simpson) to
"every single character in Roots I and II," owed

Poitier "debts of style, manner, business, stifled
smiles, flashes of silent anger, rhetorical pauses,
and standing up to whites with more at his disposal
than mere empty rage."(162)

Within the southern, or plantation, genre,
blacks had nowhere to go in terms of character
development. With but few exceptions (e.g., Band of
Angels [1957] in which the relationship between the
white, played by Clark Gable, and the slave, played
by Sidney Poitier, was marked by tension and showed
both characters as tangles of good and evil), they
became new one-dimensional stereotypes, flippant
and savvy, but still loyal to a white master or
mistress. In the 1960s and 1970s several filmmakers, who wanted to make their own racial
statements and to appear avante-garde and shocking
by putting black over white, challenged the older
plantation ideal by depicting whites as stupid
sadists and blacks as victims and rebels in plantation movies (e.g., Mandingo [1975] and Drum
[1976]), but in doing so, they created their own
set of cardboard black figures. If anything, by
bedding the slaves down with the masters or mistresses, the 1970s films played to racial fantasies
about blacks as over-sexed creatures of passion.
(119-21)

In the late 1960s through the early 1970s black
anger burst forth in a wave of films. Where several
films of the 1960s departed from the Poitier-style
by using sexual titilation or rugged urban milieus
(e.g., My Baby is Black [1965] and The Cool World
[1964]), it was not until television had made visible to all America the black "militants" and
street fighters of the 1960s that film discovered
the box-office potential of black nationalism.(387,
423, 427, 459) The industry's need to fill empty
downtown movie theaters after white flight from the
cities and its recognition that urban black moviegoers preferred action films with black heroes and
heroines to any genre featuring whites led the
studios to hire black performers and sometimes even
black writers and directors to produce "black-
oriented" fare. More than two hundred such movies
followed and became known in the trade papers as
"blaxploitation" films. Most blaxploitation films
were simple rehashes of stories from white sources.
Cheaply made productions directed solely to the so-
called black market, the films lacked social vision

and cultural integrity. Their principal legacy was
stylized, choreographed violence and a new set of
stereotypical images of blacks who lived by their
fists and loins and whose vocal utterings were
intended to outrage rather than inform. When young
black audiences tired of the genre, they switched
readily to martial arts films to find their political metaphors.(59, 162, 206, 387)

A few products of the genre, however, introduced new black talent and seethed with an authentic black anger. As the black civil rights
struggle veered toward black nationalism and away
from integrationist impulses, Afro-American artists
sought to inject racial politics into a distinctly
black visual art. Ossie Davis, Gordon Parks, Melvin
Van Peebles, and several others combined stylistic
flair with racial consciousness to make movies
celebrating the ethos of black ghetto life and
making heroes of dope pushers, pimps, and gangsters
in biting attacks on white society's social conven-
tions.

Ossie Davis' Cotton Comes to Harlem (1970) set
the standard for quality productions by assembling
an excellent cast and by shooting it on location in
Harlem. The commercial success of Cotton Comes to
Harlem, which satirized ghetto inhabitants and
habits and eschewed the blood and guts of most
blaxploitation films, encouraged other studios to
engage black directors and allowed Davis to set up
his own film company, Third World Cinema Corporation, to nurture black artistic talent and to make
movies free of white manipulation.(4, 127, 446)
Gordon Parks, who was coming off the tepid reception to his slow-paced autobiographical film The
Learning Tree (1968), provided the macho tone for
the blaxploitation genre with his Shaft (1971), in
which Richard Roundtree, as private eye John Shaft,
seized the detective genre for blacks and gave
audiences a street-wise, brave, tough, and angry
superman (a black James Bond, according to MGM
publicists) who outsmarted and outmuscled
"whitey."(356, 387, 435, 446, 459)

Melvin Van Peebles traded on the box-office
receipts from his Watermelon Man (1970), an improbable and embarrassing story about a white bigot who
wakes up to find himself turned black, to finance
the most controversial of the blaxploitation films,
Sweet Sweetback's Baadasssss Song (1971). Van

Peebles exploited all the cliches in the genre to
assail racial fantasies.(124, 159, 206, 387, 397,
458, 489) Sweetback (Van Peebles) is the quintessential black buck, who runs, shoots (and kicks,
stomps, and slashes, too, for that matter), and
fornicates his way free from "the Man" (white
police specifically, white society generally).(435,
436, 459)

Van Peebles was unusual in his willingness to
gamble with unknown and untested talent and in his
refusal to infuse his film with didacticism (for,
as Van Peebles put it, whites would be involved in
distributing and exhibiting the film and audiences
were dulled to low attention levels). But he understood the film industry. He pandered to audience
cravings for sex and violence and capitalized on
the shock his outspoken, naked hostility generated
among whites to get free publicity. In James Monaco's assessment, Van Peebles' film brought to the
movie screen a genuine black militancy, but one in
which the only lesson taught was survival. Sweetback was for the 1970s what Bigger Thomas was for
the 1940s, except for the very real difference that
in the 1970s Sweetback actually possesses the white
woman and escapes his pursuers.(446)

Moviegoers paid to see black superheroes win.
Shaft alone grossed over $12 million in its first
year. Studios rushed to crank out sequels to and
imitations of the successful formulas. A horde of
new black superheroes (many of them ex-athletes)
rumbled through violent ghettoes. White characters
became synonymous with greed, sadism, unalloyed
racism, and evils of every sort, thus seemingly
providing justification for the black superheroes
to practice any manner of cruelty on them to right
past wrongs. In many such films black criminals
wage war against white police and criminals (who
are often indistinguishable from one another). The
most profitable of the Shaft spin-offs was Superfly
(1972), in which a dope pusher manages to fend off
black hoodlums and white police, while satisfying
the sexual needs of black and white women
alike.(459) The genre even begat the female "superspade" who proved as deadly as her male counterpart
(e.g., Pam Grier in Coffy [1973] and Foxy Brown
[1974]).(387)

After Sweet Sweetback, Shaft, and Superfly, the
genre had nowhere to go artistically or politi-

cally. It rapidly degenerated into pointless violence and predictable outcomes. As James Monaco
observes, scriptwriters copied white action genres
(police, private eye, caper, and a few westerns),
replacing black actors with white ones,"reversing
racial stereotypes, and occasionally (at their
best) even injecting a little Black sensibility."
(446) The genre's political purpose was lost in
excesses of gun blasts or kung fu acrobatics. Its
artistry and talent was coopted by film and television producers who sought to cash in on the box-
office appeal of black actors and actresses for
productions geared to black and white audiences.
And the films were increasingly under fire from
black critics.

The appeal of blaxploitation films among young
people caused black critics to decry the genre for
its distortions of Afro-American life and emphasis
on sex and violence. They blasted such films as
Super Fly for glorifying dope pushers and criminal
life.(111, 139, 199, 256, 324, 352, 442, 575, 607,
612, 613) Black psychiatrist Alvin Poussaint warned
that blaxploitation films had an "insidious effect
on young lives" by encouraging "misguided feelings
of machismo" and that they legitimated in subtle
ways age-old stereotypes of blacks as "violent,
criminal, sexy savages who imitate the white man's
ways as best they can from their disadvantaged
sanctuary in the ghetto."(509) The NAACP and other
civil rights groups, who differed among themselves
on other policy issues, concurred in their condemnation of blaxploitation films as "a rip-off" "potentially far more dangerous than 'step-n-fetch it'
and his -lot."(13, 14, 50, 154, 387) In several
instances Afro-American community leaders returned
to the NAACP's policy of 1915, in its response to
Birth of a Nation, by seeking legal censorship to
prevent theaters from showing the films.(202) Black
critics divided on the merits of the few truly
well-made blaxploitation films. Some few, for example, praised Sweet Sweetback for its honesty.
(206, 292, 469, 646, 648) Others, especially Lerone
Bennett, Jr., rejoined that the film revived stereotypes and, worse, was "neither revolutionary nor
black," being, on the contrary, reactionary by
suggesting that black people were "going to be able
to s*** their way across the Red Sea."(78, 522)

Such criticisms elicited mixed reactions from
black artists and performers. Blaxploitation films,
after all, provided work. The Coalition Against
Blaxploitation, a black protest group which pushed
for improved images of blacks in film and for
better jobs for blacks behind the cameras, discovered the force of industry inertia when its
efforts failed partly because the black actors and
actresses who played in the blaxploitation films
feared its activities threatened their jobs.(11)
Socially-conscious Afro-American artists and
players also pointed out that the genre gave blacks
valuable technical experience and that profits from
films and performances could underwrite the development of a truly black cinema.(18, 87, 194) Ossie
Davis was a case in point with his Third World
Cinema, which served as a job-training organization
and succeeded in producing such films as Claudine
(1974) and Greased Lightning (1977).(127) A score
of black actors and actresses and several filmmakers achieved recognition by way of the blaxploitation film and parlayed their audience appeal into
lucrative opportunities within the industry. Even
though the heyday of the genre was short (roughly
1968-1974), the commercial success of the movies
demonstrated to Hollywood that black could be box
office and awoke the industry to the economic potential of the black audience. If nothing else,
blaxploitation validated blacks' existence in the
movie business--to a degree.(43, 87, 206, 239, 240,
446)

The "success" of blaxploitation films in the
marketplace and in showcasing black talent, rather
than black criticism of their content, finally led
to the genre's demise.(624) White film producers
looked at the receipts and figured they could tap
the black market without having to make wholly
black films. Black audiences turned out for blockbusters like The Godfather (1972) as well as for
blaxploitation offerings, so the industry began to
graft black images and talents onto essentially
white productions in order to capture black and
white audiences. As early as the mid-1960s Hollywood experimented with its own new screen image of
the "hip," aggressive black male in action movies,
a role Jim Brown especially made his own in such
films as Rio Conchos (1964), The Dirty Dozen
(1967), Dark of the Sun (1968), 100 Rifles (1969),

and El Condor (1970), to name several.(387) In
westerns, war movies, and crime films, black men
embraced white women, sometimes violently, in explicit sexual scenes, and advertising campaigns
highlighted the interracial sexual nature of the
films by picturing black and white together. The
revival of the southern genre especially turned on
themes of interracial sexual union (see above).

Hollywood also entered the market with less
sensational fare. Paramount took over Lady Sings
the Blues (1972) from Ossie Davis and made a tidy
profit, thanks to the singing ability of Diana Ross
and the softening of the story line to appeal to a
national, interracial market. In Sounder (1972)
Twentieth Century-Fox introduced Cicely Tyson and
an evocative, sympathetic story about black share-
croppers in Depression-era Louisiana, in which both
black and white characters had an authenticity and
dignity about them rare for films set in the South,
and earned rave reviews from black and white
critics and good financial returns for its efforts.
(36, 370) Increasingly in the 1970s Hollywood studios made "crossover" films (movies in which blacks
appear as principal, integral characters) that
displaced blaxploitation films in the major
markets. Hollywood's strategy included recruiting
recognizable black talent from allied entertainment
fields outside the film industry (e.g., James Earl
Jones and Cicely Tyson from the New York stage,
Diana Ross from music, Jim Brown and O.J. Simpson
from football) and, in some cases, buying proven
products for the screen, even though movies from
black sources and with all-black casts did not
always do so well at the box office as they had
done in their original form (e.g., Broadway hits
such as The Wiz, which was made into a film
[1978]).(162, 446)

Black films also declined in the 1970s because
television expropriated black talent and themes.
Cicely Tyson moved from stage and one successful
film to national acclaim in made-for-TV movies,
especially The Autobiography of Miss Jane Pitman
(1974). Paul Winfield, who had starred with Tyson
in Sounder, also found work and recognition by
appearing in made-for-TV movies (e.g., It's Good to
Be Alive [1974], in which he portrayed baseball
great Roy Campanella) and in TV miniseries (e.g.,
King [1977], in which he portrayed Martin Luther

King, Jr.). Television simply absorbed the small
reservoir of nationally-known black actors and
actresses. The enormous success of the twelve-hour
Roots (1977) and the fourteen-hour Roots: The Next
Generations (1979), which derived in part from the
contributions and appeal of well-known black actors
and actresses who came over from film, seemingly
promised increased opportunities for blacks in
television and redirected attention away from black
films. Blacks were garnering regular employment in
supporting roles in several prime-time television
series, and young black players looked to television to gain exposure and credits. As the film
industry settled into its pattern of making fewer
pictures in the 1970s and 1980s and investing its
money and promotion on those films producers believed would be blockbusters, television became the
principal outlet for black talent.(416, 446)

A few black filmmakers continued to find financial backing in the 1970s and 1980s, but they
largely survived by working within the Hollywood
system. Among them, Michael Schultz was unique in
putting together a string of successful films and
retaining some measure of black cultural integrity
in an industry wary of all-black films for the
general market. His Cooley High (1975) and Carwash
(1976) both did well with viewers and critics.
Schultz succeeded, too, because he hitched up with
the rising star of Richard Pryor, who starred in
such Schultz films as Which Way Is Up? (1977) and
Greased Lightning (1977). Overall, however, black
filmmakers in the 1970s and 1980s remained in the
industry ghetto, making action films for the inner-
city trade, or they moved into television or left
Hollywood altogether to struggle in relative obscurity as independent filmmakers.(446)

More blacks were working in the film business
than before, but only a few comedians exercised any
say in their work, or even worked regularly during
the 1970s and early 1980s.(204) In music, perhaps
the one field blacks might have expected to claim
as their own, black songwriters and musicians
played supporting roles and watched "black sound"
homogenized to attune it to the national audience.
As the California Advisory Committee to the U.S.
Commission on Civil Rights reported in 1978, studios met affirmative action guidelines by hiring
blacks for their administrative and clerical staffs

rather than integrating them into all levels of production. Blacks did not control much behind the camera--or on it.(106, 446, 598)

In film, most roles for blacks remained confined to race-related subjects and the images they projected still carried some unflattering connotations. Critics reminded their readers that the negative film images were subtle rather than blatant, unintentional rather than malicious in intent, but they persisted all the same. In Rocky (1976) a white club fighter gets to realize the American Dream by knocking down the black heavyweight champion (who seemed a parody of Muhammad Ali),(386) and in the Rocky sequels Rocky takes the title from the black and then brings him over into his corner. In the Star Wars trilogy (1977-1983) the only black (Billy Dee Williams, as Lando Calrissian, the smuggler turned rebel general) does not appear until The Empire Strikes Back (1980), and in his contrived role hardly counterbalances the black force of the arch-villain Darth Vader, who wears basic black and speaks (in the voice of James Earl Jones) from behind a black mask.

In less subtle ways blacks also reappeared as villains and toughs in films or as cardboard victims for easy preachments on the wrongs of the modern America. Charles Bronson's Death Wish (1974-1985) series preyed on white fears of urban (read interracial) crime and offered white audiences vicarious relief by having Bronson as a one-man vigilante force blow away black and other urban night stalkers. In such recent action films as King Solomon's Mines (1985) and Sheena,, among many others, media-made African natives have returned as the quintessential loin-clothed cannibals and savages. Films cashing in on musical fads (e.g., Breakin' [1984] and Purple Rain [1984]) at least offered up black characters who were not menacing. Such films spawned sequels which fared less well, and their appeal, geared as it was to the youth market, hinged too much on movement and music to carry any black aesthetic or social vision very far. Blacks who jived, gave high-fives, or highstepped were always welcome in the entertainment game.(529)

The lucrative contracts of several very popular black comedians mask the still limited opportunities in Hollywood films. Richard Pryor and Eddie

Murphy alone of black actors have established
enough box-office clout to pick their own roles.
Pryor showed dramatic talent in Blue Collar (1978),
in which he played an autoworker, but his fame
rides on his comedy. In choosing roles Pryor has
not always been wise, as evidenced in his subju-
gation in the tasteless, supposedly anti-racist
satire, The Toy. Murphy has tried to escape the
"vaudeville Negro" image by parodying it in his
television routines and by his brash satires, as in
Beverly Hills Cop (1985), which earned Murphy new
respect for his acting skills and a larger national
following. Murphy concedes, however, that black
stars remain comics. He has no illusions about
blacks' place in film. As he stated in 1984, "I
don't think the country is ready for black leading
men."(151)

Or for black leading women. Black women have
wondered aloud if there is any future for them in
Hollywood films because they have had so few good
movie parts available recently.(291) The NAACP grew
so disgusted with the meagre, and demeaning, roles
for black actresses that it suspended its Image
award for best actress in 1981. In 1982 no Hollywood film featured a black woman in a starring
role. In 1984 the only black woman who shared top
billing in a "major" feature film was the amazonian
Grace Jones who flexed muscles with Arnold Schwarz-
enegger in Conan the Destroyer.

Black dramatic actors have not prospered much
better, except in supporting roles.(407, 628, 629)
In 1983, for example, less than one dozen of the
142 films released by major studios had blacks in
starring roles. Louis Gossett, Jr., won an Oscar
(for best supporting actor) in 1983 for his part as
a sergeant training a young white enlistee in officer's school (An Officer and a Gentleman), and he
gained additional credit for his title role in the
made-for-TV movie Sadat. Gossett stood almost alone
in parlaying dramatic roles into other good parts.
There were few such parts to go around. Howard E.
Rollins, Jr., for example, had an Oscar nomination
for his part in Ragtime (1981), but he did not make
another feature film until A Soldier's Story
(1984), a taut drama from black playwright Charles
Fuller that explores black and white racism in a
military setting. The commercial success of A
Soldier's Story at least augured better days ahead,

for it was written as well as performed by blacks.(151) A few white directors and producers have also hinted at more and better roles for blacks by risking capital and reputation in movies with blacks or black-related subjects figuring prominently. John Sayles put up his own money to finance the inventive satire, The Brother from Another Planet (1984), and Stephen Spielberg ventured his own reputation in making a film adaptation of Alice Walker's A Color Purple in 1985. As black actors attest, they need such help. Lacking it in a film industry enslaved to a blockbuster mentality, many blacks had long turned to television to find work and expression.(416)

The Afro-American performers' gravitation toward television was a logical consequence of the intimate relationship that had evolved between blacks and the medium. Commercial television emerged during the brief post-World War II liberal consensus when the nation and the entertainment industry were becoming attentive to black aspirations and talent, and, as J. Fred MacDonald has emphasized, the medium "matured in the midst of the civil rights movement" during the 1960s.(413) It became, in fact, the principal instrument black civil rights leaders used to carry their social crusade to the nation. As heavy consumers of video fare since the 1960s, blacks were also peculiarly sensitive to the imagery and social messages purveyed on the small screen. The public nature of the medium, licensed and regulated by the federal government, made television potentially responsive to political pressure from blacks, just as the cruder devices of the boycott might be applied to sponsors and programs unmindful of black concerns. From the advent of commercial television in the 1940s to the present, when 99 percent of the households in the United States have a television set, Afro-Americans have sought access to the medium and, over time, developed images and gained influence in television that both reflected and transcended their experience in film.

The early years of television seemed to promise many opportunities for black entertainers and even to suggest a willingness on the part of the major broadcasting networks to provide fair and sensitive portrayals of minorities on television. Needful of talent to fill its growing air time, the new in-

dustry recruited black singers, musicians, dancers,
and comedians. While several black performers
brought the stereotypical roles of sassy mammy,
rascally "coon," and Tomish servant from the movies
to television, many others simply played themselves
in variety shows. Influential variety show hosts
who featured black entertainers, especially Ed
Sullivan of Toast of the Town and Steve Allen of
the Tonight show, responded to criticism from prejudiced viewers and concerned advertisers by stating
unequivocally that television needed and benefited
from black performers. Allen and Sullivan, at
least, consciously sought to undermine racism by
bringing black personalities (and in Allen's case,
civil rights issues as well) to their national
audiences. Black performers appreciated those opportunities television afforded during the 1950s,
when film was retreating from its post-war liberalism and offering fewer parts even for musically
talented black stars. The television networks also
seemed determined to resist overt racism by
drafting guidelines to improve the black image in
productions. Blacks even hosted two network musical
series (The Billy Daniels Show [1952] and Sugar
Hill Times [1949]). Blacks appeared as contestants
on game and quiz shows, showed up on sports
programs (especially boxing), and had parts in
several dramas. Hopeful about television's possibilities and its early responsibility, Ebony magazine, which devoted considerable space to blacks in
film and television, proclaimed in 1950 that television had lifted racial barriers.(413)

     The early promise was, however, partial and
incomplete. Stereotypical and demeaning roles entered the medium and compromised the many positive
images of blacks in early television. The structure
of television simply could not prevent older images
from spilling over into the new medium. In its
efforts to build an audience, television looked to
radio, the medium from which it had evolved. Television adopted many of the story lines and stereotypes already successful in radio and film. The
popularity of such radio programs as "Amos 'n'
Andy" and the familiarity of black domestics in
radio series (e.g., Eddie Anderson as Rochester,
Jack Benny's valet and "conscience") invited emulation in television. (413)

The Columbia Broadcasting System (CBS) launched
The Amos 'n' Andy Show television series in 1951,
amid much publicity and furor over the use of black
actors (two whites having played the major characters in the radio broadcasts) and the minstrel
stereotypes the show perpetuated. The producers,
who worried about white audiences becoming discom-
fitted by black actors, eliminated all possible
black-white interaction by setting the show in an
all-black environment and coached the black actors
to assume stereotypical postures of conniving
"coons" and other vulgar caricatures borrowed from
the blackface minstrel tradition. Such policies may
have satisfied some white viewers, but they outraged black critics and many liberal white ones as
well.(156, 413, 519)

The reaction of the black press and civil
rights organizations to the show was immediate and
vocal. At its 1951 annual convention the NAACP
summed up the black critics' indictments against
the show, and implicity against those who produced
it, charging that every character "in this one and
only TV show with an all-Negro cast is either a
clown or a crook" and that the show, like the radio
series from which it came, reinforced "the conclusion among uninformed and prejudiced people that
Negroes are inferior, lazy, dumb and dishonest."
The NAACP demanded that CBS take the show off the
air, and brought suit to effect that result.(50,
156, 357)

CBS had tied up $2.5 million just to get rights
to the show and kept it alive until 1953, when it
released it for syndication. After years of litiga-
tion CBS finally withdrew the show from circulation
in 1966, but until that time, wherever it appeared
in local outlets, The Amos 'n' Andy Show continued
to evoke sharp criticism for its stereotypes and
patronizing view of black society. Like Birth of a
Nation in film, the controversy over Amos 'n' Andy
at least served to remind blacks at an early stage
in the development of a mass medium that they would
have to remain vigilant regarding the uses of their
images and that they could not assume that any mass
medium was culturally or socially neutral.(413)

The attention focused on Amos 'n' Andy deflected criticism from other shows or presentations
unflattering to blacks. Blacks in comedy shows
regularly appeared as variations of traditional

stereotypes of domestics or menial servants (e.g.,
the maids in Beulah [1950-1953], Rochester in The
Jack Benny Show [1950-1965], and especially the
ubiquitous, and seemingly mindless Willy Best as
the handyman in Trouble with Father [1950-1955],
the elevator operator on My Little Margie [1952-
1955], and the handyman on Waterfront [1954-
1956]).(305, 340) Local television stations' reliance on old movies, especially the cheaply rented
or purchased film libraries of B-movie fare, filled
non-prime-time programming hours with Hollywood's
old stereotypes. The old B movies also inspired
cheap imitations.   The various jungle shows (e.g.,
Ramar of the Jungle [1952-1954] and Jungle Jim
[1955]), for example, were cloned from filmdom's
Tarzan and other series and teemed with ignorant,
cowardly natives. In more subtle ways, too, the
very "progress" of blacks in television obscured
their limited gains, for the most successful blacks
on the small screen were those who could sing or
dance.(66)
     Dramatic parts for blacks simply did not exist
in the 1950s. The lily-white world of television
theatre rarely admitted blacks. Only one local
series, Harlem Detective, which aired on station
WOR-TV in New York City between October 1953 and
mid-January 1954, risked a principal black character, but the show died aborning due to a low
budget and a small audience. Blacks would have to
wait until 1965 when I Spy with Bill Cosby provided
a sympathetic, realistic black character in a lead
role. In the meantime, black dramatic actors had to
remain satisfied with minor supporting roles, or no
work at all.(340, 376, 413)
     The legacy of racial proscription and pre-
scription borrowed from other mass media strongly
influenced television's exclusion of blacks from
drama. As in film, blacks found work in television
dramas "only when a script specifically called for
black characters."(413) And, like film, television
imposed racial quotas so as not to make shows
appear too black. When such organizations as the
NAACP protested the color line in television and
demanded more and better portrayals of blacks, the
effect was often to remove black roles completely.
Producers did not want to be bothered with disputes
over racial representation and portraiture.(176)

Equally important in excluding blacks from dramatic parts was the structure of television itself. Like radio, early television earned revenue by selling air time to sponsors, who, in turn, interrupted television programs with commercials to sell their products. Throughout the 1950s sponsors exercised a preponderant control over program content because they actually produced most of the shows on network schedules. Program decisions in television, like those in radio, were thus subject to commercial considerations, and any social issues potentially threatening to the sponsors' interests had no chance of finding outlets on network television. Sponsors wanted to avoid controversial subject matter that might reflect badly on their products.(69)

Sponsors sought "happy shows" that would "create a bright sales atmosphere" for their products. Advertisers who were trying to "upgrade" American consumers and their buying habits studiously avoided subjects and settings related to poverty and social problems. Writers and directors for television dramatic anthology series (e.g., Studio One, the Philco Television Playhouse, Ford Theater, and Kraft Television Theater) suffered regular interference from sponsors and their agencies, who revised or scrapped scripts and monitored plot details closely. Sponsors were especially leery of plots depicting blacks, or any minorities, in a realistic light, for such stories raised too many troubling social and political issues which could not be readily resolved. The interference killed the anthology series. Leading anthology writers and directors took their talents elsewhere, television drama was left increasingly in the hands of formula writers and producers who could churn turn out inoffensive, upbeat stories. The formula show offered the security of predictability and simplicity wherein solutions to problems were as clearcut as the commercials sponsoring them.(69)

The most celebrated instance of preproduction censorship rooting out any connection with blacks was the adaptation of Reginald Rose's play, Thunder on Sycamore Street, for Studio One in 1954. The play was based on an actual event in which a Cicero, Illinois, white neighborhood tried to drive out a black family who had just moved into its midst, but the television version removed all references to blacks and made the central character an ex-convict instead. According to Rose, the producers feared a black character would "appall" southern viewers especially.(69, 413)

Throughout the decade producers capitulated to the southern market and refused to underwrite stories with racial themes or implications. The increasing visibility on television newscasts of the black struggle against Jim Crow pointed up the explosive issues involved with race and, ironically, frightened many sponsors away from any depictions of blacks. Local television stations outside the southern market did not compensate with their own programming, however, suggesting that black exclusion was an industry-wide policy. A few breakthroughs in drama did occur--most notably James Edwards in "D.P." on the General Electric Theater (1955) and Sidney Poitier in "A Man Is Ten Feet Tall" on the Philco Television Playhouse (1955)--but if blacks appeared at all, it was in predictable, safe, and stereotypical roles, as in remakes of The Green Pastures, which appeared three times on network television during the 1950s.(413)

The short life of the Nat King Cole Show (1956-1957) illustrated the difficult time blacks had gaining complete acceptance. NBC valiantly carried the program without a commercial sponsor, although it eventually attracted Rheingold Beer as a co-sponsor, but the show failed of support because advertisers did not want their products associated with blacks.(138, 412, 413, 519) If an assimilated and popular performer like Cole could not get complete sponsorship, it seemed almost futile to risk capital and time in proposing programs featuring less well-known blacks.

By the early 1960s the picture began to change rapidly. One important factor was the homogenizing influence of the medium, which through network programming and advertising purveyed a common culture. The increase in network news programming also served to create a national image of society and politics. Although Martin Luther King, Jr., and other black leaders did not get invited to shows such as Person to Person, they did command attention on news programs because they made news. Television became, in the words of William B. Monroe, Jr., "the chosen instrument" for the black

civil rights struggle. Recognizing its influence,
civil rights leaders pitched their messages and
marches to use television to good effect. Bringing
one-quarter million civil rights marchers to Washington in 1963, for example, was a major news event
no station could ignore. As the civil rights
struggle became a daily feature on television, the
social force of the medium became increasingly
apparent.(57, 413, 422, 491, 569)

The effects of showing the "good life" to
blacks in network programs and advertising and
exposing cruelties against blacks in network newscasts were powerful. The southern market lost its
grip on television content as advertisers studied
demographic facts about purchasing power and as
liberal consciousness arose during the civil rights
demonstrations.(69, 176, 413) As early as 1963 S.I.
Hayakawa predicted that a liberal, national message
regarding civil rights emanating from television
would bring blacks and whites "together in their
tastes and aspirations, in spite of the best
efforts of the White Citizens Councils and the
Black Muslims."(304)

The color line in television faded. Networks
hired black reporters to cover the civil rights
stories. Black civil rights groups pressured television to increase the coverage and to improve the
images of blacks in television. In Jackson, Mississippi, black citizens challenged the licenses of
the network affiliates, pointing out that, although
they constituted 45 percent of the viewing
audience, the stations ignored them in programming
and blacked out news about desegregation. The
federal courts upheld the black complaints and
forced the Federal Communications Commission to
vacate the license of Jackson station WLBT-TV in
1964.

The WLBT-TV case prompted other southern
stations to reassess their hiring and news policies. It also encouraged similar license chal-
lenges in northern markets. The New York Ethical
Culture Society, for example, monitored the three
network stations in New York City and concluded
that the stations needed to improve both the representation and portrayal of blacks in the medium.
The Society especially condemned the industry for
not integrating its national programming as rapidly
as local stations were doing. Only in appearances

in advertising and public service announcements did
the Society note a strong improvement in black
representation. In North and South television was
under pressure to integrate.(499-502)

Blacks began to benefit immediately from the
pressures and from changes in television's
structure. In the 1960s the networks assumed
control over program production and schedules, and
sponsors became advertisers who purchased minutes
of advertising time from networks, rather than
controlling longer time slots as they had done
previously. At the same time, the networks engaged
in "counter programming"--scheduling programs to
draw audiences away from rival networks. Sponsors
lost power but not influence in the process, and,
in some ways, the ability to purchase time slots
rather than having to associate their products with
particular programs freed sponsors to respond to
what D. Parke Gipson termed "the $30 Billion Negro"
consumer market of television viewers.(69, 257)
Counter-programming led to an increase in action
shows, which were very popular in the 1960s, and
sponsors watched the ratings and calculated the
demography of viewers to locate specific markets
for their wares. As voracious consumers of television and as a rising consumer force, blacks attracted increasing attention from both network
programmers and advertisers. Blacks began to appear
in programs and on advertisements in increasing
numbers.

Television turned to social issues for stories,
and problems relating to race crept into series
such as The Defenders and Ben Casey. Series with a
social mission were aired, most notably David Suss-
kind's realistic East Side/West Side (1963-1964),
with Cicely Tyson, about inner-city life. Police
shows seeking realism began to include blacks as
officers (e.g., Car 54, Where Are You? [1961-1963],
with Ossie Davis and Nipsey Russell). As entertainers, blacks continued to find regular television outlets; indeed, because such shows as American Bandstand regularly featured black music and
stars and because black music informed American
popular music so profoundly during the age of rock
and roll, black singers and black bands gained ever
larger numbers of video supporters, black and
white. Until the success of I Spy in 1965, however,
blacks remained supporting characters--"tokens"

according to critics--in the white-dominated world
of network prime-time programming.(376, 413, 420,
422, 519)
     In terms of prime-time programming, I Spy
signaled a watershed in the depiction and representation of blacks on television. The show capitalized on the then current rage of spy thrillers,
but it brought to the screen American humor and a
black presence in comedian-actor Bill Cosby, who
played agent Alexander Scott, a graduate of Temple
University (like Cosby in real life) and an Oxford
scholar whose language skills were vital to
missions conducted throughout the world. Cosby was
the first black to star in a network drama series,
and he proved equal to the role. His easy manner,
humor, and integrity made him popular and earned
him three Emmy awards. More than that, Cosby was no
"superspade" stereotype; rather, he emerged as a
believable black hero, one who felt and expressed
emotions, which even included interracial love
affairs in at least two episodes. The show did not
prosper so well in the ratings, but NBC stuck with
it for three seasons (1965-1968) before selling it
for syndication. During its three years I Spy also
provided acting opportunities for a host of other
black performers. Cosby's personal popularity gave
him a voice in promoting black talent, as he did as
a guest host on The Tonight Show, and as a critic
of racial injustice, as he did in hosting the
seven-part CBS television documentary, Of Black
America (1968), which included a discussion of
black stereotypes in the mass media (in the first
installment, entitled "Black History: Lost, Stolen
or Strayed").(376, 402, 413, 618)
     After 1965 blacks appeared frequently and reg-
ularly in prime-time television comedy and drama
series. They played high school teachers (e.g.,
Room 222 [1969-1974] and The Bill Cosby Show [1969-
1971]); police officers, both in uniform and in
mufti (e.g., Ironside [1967-1975], N.Y.P.D. [1967-
1969], and The Mod Squad [1968-1973]); lawyers
(e.g., The Young Lawyers [1970-1971] and The Storefront Lawyers [1970-1971]); an electronics expert
and secret missions agent (Mission: Impossible
[1966-1973]); a prisoner-of-war during World War II
(Hogan's Heroes [1965-1971]); a medical intern (The
Interns [1970-1971]); a bounty hunter (The Outcasts
[1968-1969]); a secretary (Mannix [1968-1975]); and

a twenty-second-century starship communications officer (Star Trek [1966-1969]); among other roles.
Blacks also entered daytime television in soap
operas, although only as minor characters. Many of
the prime-time programs were short-lived, and some
popular entertainers suffered early cancellations
of variety shows (e.g., The Sammy Davis, Jr. Show
[1966] and The Leslie Uggams Show [1969]), which in
the case of The Leslie Uggams Show relied too
heavily on black casts and settings. The future for
blacks in television, however, seemed promising. If
nothing else, the networks' shift in the mid-1960s
away from shows featuring rural life, which largely
appealed to older audiences, and toward "relevant"
melodrama in urban settings to reach the youth
market bode well for blacks.(413)

      In another sense, the late 1960s failed to
realize the diversity of black images and voices
available. Blacks found places in television series
almost wholly in so-called salt and pepper combi-
nations with blacks invariably in subordinate
roles. Most of the black characters were bland and
integrated into the white worlds in which they
worked; they rarely threatened the dominant white
culture.(422, 587) The "hip" counterculture
language and dress and the full "Afroed" hair of
Linc Hayes (Clarence Williams, III) in The Mod
Squad, for example, could not disguise the fact for
viewers that the black undercover policeman worked
"for the system."(94) Whether in the police station
or on a starship, blacks were team members; their
blackness hardly mattered at all. Strong, virile,
and angry black characters did not survive long, as
evinced in the short screen life of The Outcasts,
starring Otis Young as a bounty hunter who operated
as much against the white man's law as for it.(320)
Blacks were expected to play by the rules in television, and during the late 1960s the integrationist theme still ran strong among liberal whites
and many blacks, even in the face of urban race
riots and calls for black nationalism coming from
"militants." In such circumstances, no black performer could satisfy the cultural and psychological
needs of all black people.(99, 315, 413, 587)

      The critical reception to Julia (1968-1971),
starring Diahann Carroll, illustrates the point.
Carroll played Julia Baker, a young, attractive,
articulate, middle-class widowed nurse whose life

in a medical office and at home provided the focus
for the series. Julia was almost totally assimilated; she lived in an integrated neighborhood and
interacted easily with whites. She had black boy-
friends, but she seemed never to confront questions
of race in her work or life. The series strived to
avoid racial or socially topical issues. Carroll
herself described the character as "a white Negro"
and increasingly felt uncomfortable in the role.
Critics labeled the series a sellout to racism, for
it implied that the "good life" of middle-class
America was available to all blacks who did not
protest or criticize "the system." Despite very
good ratings, Carroll and others connected with the
show gave it up.(403, 413, 434, 543) The direction
in situation comedies was changing anyway. Where
Julia was originally offered as a counter to The
Doris Day Show, which aired in the same season, by
the early 1970s Norman Lear had redefined situation
comedies in such a way as to put "white Negroes"
out of work--or so it would seem for a while.
     Producers discovered that by the early 1970s
viewers had grown very tired of "relevant" social
dramas. Television abandoned many dramatic series
in which blacks had participated. In their place
came a rash of situation comedies, many of them
assailing controversial, contemporary social
problems, including racism, with humor and satire.
For blacks, the trend toward "realistic" situation
comedies was a mixed blessing. While the new comedies provided numerous new outlets for black
talent and promised critical, if somewhat light,
pokes at racism and other prejudices, they also
tended to recast blacks as clowns by having blacks
parody themselves.(67, 413, 448)
     The success of self-deprecating humor was dem-
onstrated by The Flip Wilson Show which enjoyed
widespread popularity in the early 1970s. Black
comedian Flip Wilson mocked black culture, joking
about skin color and hair texture. In his various
personae (especially, the sassy, street-wise black
momma Geraldine Jones who absolved herself of all
responsibility by screeching "The Devil made me do
it!" and the con-artist, revival preacher Reverend
Leroy of the Church of What's Happening Now) Wilson
paraded inner-city black stereotypes before millions of viewers. Critics charged that Wilson's
comedy fueled rather than dispelled racial bigotry,

but in the copy-cat, competitive world of counter-
programming television the Wilson style invited
emulation and duplication.(94, 413, 422)

The principal architects of the realistic situation comedies in the 1970s tapped the "new racial
humor" for their own productions. Led by Norman
Lear and Bud Yorkin, producers of situation comedies in the 1970s attempted to use comedy to
address such contemporary social problems as abor-
tion, aging, alcoholism, death, mental health,
racism, and rape. The pioneer program in this new
style was Lear's All in the Family, which focused
on the life of Archie Bunker (Carroll O'Connor), an
uneducated, outspoken, working-class white bigot
who believed every stereotype he had ever heard or
seen and who spewed forth racial and sectarian
bilge at anyone who was not of his color and faith.
Unhappily for Archie, he could not escape contact
with minorities, for they worked beside him, lived
next door, and finally moved into his house when
his daughter married a Pole. Archie's favorite
racial targets were his next-door neighbors, the
Jeffersons, a black family newly arrived in
Archie's neighborhood. Lear countered Archie's
bigotry with the liberal jabs of Archie's daughter
and son-in-law and the innocent, native goodness of
Archie's wife, and he had the victims of Archie's
prejudices outpoint Archie at every turn, often by
acting out or repeating in satirical ways the stereotypical behavior Archie attributed to them.
Confrontational humor became a weapon against
racism, or so Lear argued in justifying his series.
Lear developed Archie as a lovable bigot so that
viewers would identify with him and come to see
their own prejudices. Archie's bigotry, Lear explained, was born of fear, not hatred.(53, 413,
422)

The show almost immediately set off a spirited
argument among psychologists, sociologists, and
others about the effects of Archie's bigotry on
viewers. Indeed, ABC backed away from the series as
too controversial, and CBS broadcast it as adult
entertainment and, in the early episodes, with a
disclaimer stating that the show did not consciously intend to demean any group. Several
studies concluded that Archie's behavior actually
reinforced prejudice, for racist viewers could not
see that the show was intended to satirize prej-

udices.(103, 603) Critics added that hearing the words "coon," "jig," "jungle bunny," and "spade" (Archie only once used the word "nigger") regularly on network television gave such slurs a currency and legitimacy no amount of disclaimers and counter humor could match. Some black families saw in Archie Bunker the epitome of white racism and used the show to introduce their children to a kind of bigotry they should expect in a white-ruled world.(413) The congressional black caucus lodged an official complaint with the FCC concerning All in the Family, and the Anti-Defamation League criticized the show's producers for imbedding prejudices in the public mind. On the other side of the ledger, some critics applauded the show's topicality and suggested that its approach forced viewers to reassess their own values. And the Los Angeles chapter of the NAACP, among other black organizations, gave the show a "brotherhood" award for its anti-racism.(339, 413)

Whatever the sociological effects of All in the Family, the show was immensely popular. Its success spawned spinoffs and imitations, and in the words of one CBS network executive literally "changed the face of television."(39, 325) The spinoff habit of 1970s television programming led to several shows coming from All in the Family characters. Most notably for blacks were The Jeffersons (1975-1985), based on Archie's black neighbors who move uptown to success, and Maude (1972-1978), which introduced Maude's black maid Florida Evans, whose character in turn spun off to become a lead in Good Times (1974-1979), about Evans and her lower-middle-class family who lived in a high-rise housing project. Blacks in situation comedies became regular fare as television networks scrambled to find variations of the Lear/Yorkin formula. Lear and Yorkin alone created several popular shows on their own theme, including Sanford and Son (1972-1977), starring Redd Foxx as a 65-year-old junk dealer who tried to con his way to advantage; What's Happening!! (1976-1979), about three black, urban high school students; Carter Country (1977-1979), about a black big-city policeman who comes to a small Georgia town to work for a redneck police chief; and Diff'rent Strokes (1979-), about two black orphans from Harlem adopted by a wealthy white man. In each instance the

black characters were "hip" and often played on
racial humor. And as J. Fred MacDonald observes, in
the case of Diff'rent Strokes the jokes recalled
the stereotypes of the Our Gang and Little Rascal
comedy films, for the show's premise hinged on
exploiting the children as black curios in a white
world.(413)

The black characters and circumstances in these
and other "black-oriented" comedies have been subjected to sustained criticism.(83, 212, 213, 245,
321, 339, 413, 422, 434, 445, 477, 514, 582) According to one critic, the new comedies distort
"authentic issues in the black community" by suggesting that blacks can solve problems with wisecracks and luck, rather than by hard work and
intelligence. Young black male characters come
across as loud-mouthed, jiving sharpsters, and the
women as modern-day mammies. Especially disturbing
was the character J.J. Evans (Jimmie Walker) on
Good Times, the teenager who rolled his eyeballs
and grinned widely in good minstrel fashion and who
mugged for a laugh and connived for advantage to
such a degree he seemed a throwback to the "coon
comics" of early films. The show's star, Esther
Rolle, grew so disenchanted by the negative role
model J.J. provided black youth, with his constant
womanizing and scheming, that she left the
show.(213, 413, 449) The social issues in the show,
set in Chicago's Cabrini-Green housing project,
were lost in J.J.'s antics. Self-deprecating racial
humor became distressingly common fare during
prime-time and late-night viewing hours, and Gar-
rett Morris and later Eddie Murphy on Saturday
Night Live built careers by parodying the parodies
of blacks. The cool, discerning manner of Ron Glass
(as the articulate, natty detective in Barney
Miller) and the equally urbane Robert Guillaume (as
the savvy butler on Soap, a role which he spun off
into Benson) offered viewers more refined versions
of black comedians whose humor played on their skin
color.

The character of George Jefferson (Sherman
Hemsley) in The Jeffersons evoked considerable
comment because he seemed to embody all that was
wrong with the "realistic" situation comedies. In
his condemnation of black situation comedies as
demeaning to blacks, columnist Lance Morrow singled
out George Jefferson as the archetypal new black

stereotype on television--a "black bigot, a sple-
netic little whip of a man who bullies like a de-
mented overseer, seldom speaks below a shriek and
worships at the church of ostentation."(395, 449)
In the show the Jeffersons move to a luxury high-
rise apartment in Manhattan, but George cannot
escape his own rascality and racism. His wife
Louise is intelligent and well meaning, and his son
Lionel is likewise, and the Jefferson's have neighbors who include a racially mixed couple. But the
show centers on George's egomania and get-rich-
quick schemes, and Hemsley plays George as a blackface clown who regularly gets his come-uppance in
the end, often from the black maid who mocks
George's words and actions.

As the show grew more popular, however, the
central characters underwent a subtle transformation. In a perceptive commentary on the show critic
Mary Helen Washington observed that by the early
1980s the Jeffersons had whitened up in their dress
and manner. George did not use the word "nigger"
anymore, and he no longer spoke about his past in
reform school. The producers discovered that the
Jeffersons commanded a large white audience and
began to restyle George into a "Mr. Everyman," a
little guy who makes it big in the world and
battles adversity. According to the show's producers, they consciously downplayed skin color and
sought out themes that would allow the white
viewers to identify with the central characters. As
George became less "black," ratings went up,
although George never could escape his color altogether and race humor continued to provide easy
laughs. The significance of the show's changes was
not lost on critics who recognized how little
media-made black characters actually represented
real life experiences and needs of blacks.(617)

Eugenia Collier argued in 1974 that the basic
problem with black characterization in television
was that whites controlled the medium and created
black characters to suit their white view of Afro-
American culture(142, 143)--a charge echoed by
numerous other critics.(146, 348, 534) Indeed,
access to the production side of television
(writing, directing, producing) became the rallying
cry of blacks critical of television fare. The
meagre Afro-American representation in the industry's technical aspects was well documented in

the U.S. Civil Rights Commission's two reports on
minorities in the media (in 1977 and 1979),(596,
597) and it was the central theme of the hearings
on "Minority Participation in the Media," held in
Congress in 1983.(600) Redd Foxx gave that concern
dramatic attention in 1974 when he walked off the
Sanford and Son set in protest over the almost
complete absence of black scriptwriters or directors for the series. Foxx returned to production
when Lear/Yorkin gave him and costar Demond Wilson
unequivocal veto power over any material they
deemed offensive to black viewers--a policy, once
in force, that made Foxx and Wilson implicitly
responsible for the black images projected in the
show.(215) Several studies of the portrayal of
blacks in comedy series in the 1970s found that
black shows emphasized humor, that black characters
(especially the young and the elderly) often appeared as nonproductive, shiftless persons, and
that few blacks (indeed, very few women) were cast
as professionals and that those who were so cast
came across as less professional than their white
counterparts.(146, 245, 518, 582)

Black viewers, too, have been critical of the
situation comedies, but studies of black viewers
have documented a profound ambivalence regarding
blacks in television comedies. In a survey by the
Corporation for Public Broadcasting, for example,
only a small percentage of black respondents
thought such shows as Sanford and Son and The Flip
Wilson Show were offensive or harmful, although,
significantly, many black respondents chose to
register no opinion at all on the subject. According to other studies, many black viewers
strongly objected to the portrayals of black racism
and foolishness in such programs as The Jeffersons
and Sanford and Son, and few such viewers person-
ally identified with the programs. Yet, at the same
time, comedies with black stars were very popular
among black viewers, who seemed to prefer seeing
demeaning portrayals than to have no black roles at
all.(196, 197, 396)

The recent critical and ratings triumphs of
Bill Cosby in The Cosby Show, a series about a
sober, decent middle-class black family, suggests
that white audiences will accept black comedy
without minstrel-style racial humor, and, given
Cosby's conscious effort to direct the content and

flow of images in the program, it also provides a
case study of how to create "positive" images by
having considerable black artistic and technical
input into the production. But, as critics point
out, Cosby's show remains almost alone as a "serious" situation comedy in which blacks do not in
some ways mock themselves.

Studies on television and the socialization of
minority children, conducted by Bradley Greenberg
and researchers at Michigan State University in the
mid-1970s, discovered a "black ghetto" in television fiction. They reported that roughly one half
to three-fourths of all black characters appeared
on only a few shows on daytime and prime-time
programming, all of which were either cartoons or
situation comedies. The characters were disproportionately poor, jobless, or in low-status occupations.(279, 284, 557) The studies observed that,
compared to white children, minority children from
low-income families watched more television, more
readily accepted what they watched on television as
true, and relied more on television for information. Although white and minority children alike
indicated a marked inability to distinguish television fiction from "reality," and although white
and black children used television to learn how
different people behaved, dressed, talked, and
looked, low-income black children and adolescents
had a very high propensity to believe in what they
saw, even when their own life experiences contradicted the television messages.(278-281, 285, 411)
This was especially true in the black children's
acceptance of the occupational roles of minority
characters on television as being like those occupations minorities held in real life(306, 411)--a
conclusion supported by other researchers as
well.(51, 146, 196, 342, 588)

The Greenberg group's studies also reported
that the depiction of minorities in comic roles had
a deleterious effect on children's attitudes toward
minorities. In testing to find what personality
traits white children attached to television characters, the researchers discovered that the
children associated humor with lack of "smartness"
in black characters and that the children did not
wish to emulate those characters. The exact socializing effects of television on children remain in
dispute--with some studies suggesting that children

do not necessarily perceive the language or situations of black characters on television as true--but the consensus among researchers and community leaders alike is that repeated images of blacks in comedic roles and in low-status occupations on television must in some ways negatively affect black childrens' aspirations and attitudes.(23, 46, 84, 128, 136, 145-148, 196, 211, 276, 404, 483, 578, 585, 636)

Researchers on viewer attitudes toward television characters have observed that whites perceive blacks in negative terms in part because blacks appear almost entirely in situation comedies. White television characters, too, are often ridiculous and self-parodying, but whites are seen in a wide variety of other roles and situations. In those non-comedic roles blacks regularly occupy, they often have been part of a tough, crime-ridden urban world. In the areas of children's programming (especially Sesame Street with its positive interplay among different ethnic groups),(68, 621, 622) news programming, and sports programming blacks have achieved high positive visibility, but in prime-time programs blacks show up as comedians, singers, or characters on crime/police programs. Whites who know little about blacks and who regularly watch prime-time television might conclude that Afro-Americans are in reality as whites see them on the home screen--comical, musical, or somewhat dangerous.(136, 211, 278, 414)

In television drama during the 1970s and 1980s blacks have been largely associated with the urban crime/police genre. Blacks have appeared as pimps (e.g., "Rooster" on Baretta) and private detectives (Shaft [1973-1974] and Tenafly [1973-1974]), but most often they have been police officers. The black private detective series never caught on with viewers, partly because of scheduling problems but also because the television versions of blaxploitation characters Shaft and Tenafly were so tempered in language and tame in style and so accommodating to the white establishment that they lacked the energy and insouciance which had won over moviegoing audiences.(413, 587) Attempts to create a flip black private detective type in the mold of white heroes (e.g., Tenspeed and Brown Shoe [1980-1981], starring Ben Vereen) have also met cool audience responses.

More enduring were the black patrolmen and
undercover officers for metropolitan police de-
partments. Indeed, it was Georg Stanford Brown's
depiction of a steady, responsible policeman committed to humane methods of law enforcement in The
Rookies (1972-1976) that persuaded producers to
experiment with other black characters in police
dramas. The first weekly detective show with a
black in the starring role was Get Christie Love
(1974-1975), with Teresa Graves as a "supercop" in
undercover jobs. The stories, however, were often
improbable, and Graves's sexy persona could not
sustain audience interest alone. Likewise, Paris
(1979-1980), starring James Earl Jones as a well-
educated police captain, failed with viewers. The
successful formula for blacks in crime/police was
for them to belong to the team as supporting
players.(413) Michael Warren and Taureen Blacque as
policemen on Hill Street Blues have remained subordinate to white characters in rank and in air
time, although in recent years Warren has emerged
as a popular personality and has been the focus of
subplots.(316) In Miami Vice Philip Michael Thomas
shares equal billing with Don Johnson, but the
stories generally revolve around Johnson's character and actions. Whatever their prominence in
crime/police shows, the black characters inhabited
violent and crime-filled worlds. In the absence of
alternative depictions, blacks in drama series
could hardly escape being associated with the
underside of American life, even though blacks are
rarely portrayed as criminals themselves.(414, 566)

For a brief moment in television it appeared
that black actors and black perspectives might find
an audience in television drama. Beginning in the
early 1970s several historical black figures have
been the focus of biographical treatments on made-
for-TV movies. Many of the programs have been about
popular sports personalities (e.g., Brian's Song,
It's Good to Be Alive, and Wilma), capitalizing on
the prominence of blacks in sports programming no
doubt,(273) but other black personalities have
received attention too. Especially noteworthy was
The Autobiography of Miss Jane Pittman (1974),
which viewed the southern world of segregation from
a black woman's experience and made racism in the
South a subject for television drama.(623)

The theme of southern race relations surfaced
in other dramas--most memorably in Melvin Van
Peebles' Just an Old Sweet Song (1976), about differences for blacks living in the North and South,
and in the miniseries Roll Thunder, Hear My Cry
(1978), about a black family in Depression-era
Mississippi. The subject of interracial love also
captured viewer interest, from the controversial My
Sweet Charlie (1970), which profited in the ratings
from the national discussion regarding its propriety,(401) to the sensitive Wedding Band (1974), to
the passionate A Killing Affair (1977). The popularity of these dramas notwithstanding, serious
dramas focusing on black characters remained underrepresented in television offerings in the 1970s
and 1980s. The unrealized promise of black-oriented
dramas became all the more remarkable because it
followed the broadcast of Roots (1977), which had
garnered the highest ratings ever for a television
miniseries.

It is somewhat paradoxical, observes J. Fred
MacDonald, that, in the face of discrimination,
exclusion, and bias, the most popular series of
programs in television history focused on the Afro-
American experience.(413) In January, 1977, the
twelve-hour miniseries Roots, based on Alex Haley's
best-selling autobiographical novel/history about
his family, achieved the enormous ratings. According to the Nielsen ratings, about 85 percent of
the American households with television sets tuned
in at least part of the series, and estimates
suggest that the series pulled in audiences of 130
million viewers or more. The fourteen-hour sequel,
Roots: The Next Generations, which aired in February, 1979, did less well, but still claimed a 41
percent share of the audience for its time-slot and
ranked second only to Roots in weekly ratings for
television.

In Roots audiences saw a heroic black wrested
from a pastoral African setting and then struggling
to survive the degradations of bondage in America.
The series dealt graphically with slavery, depicting the savage cruelty of whippings and rapes
and efforts to strip the enslaved blacks of their
heritage, even their names. Roots celebrated the
blacks' resiliency, their human dignity, which was
reflected in Kunta Kinte's refusal to acknowledge
the name given to him by his master. From Kunta

Kinte (LeVar Burton) to Chicken George (Ben Vereen) to Tom Murray (Georg Stanford Brown), the great-grandson of "the Old African" Kunta Kinte, the black characters (men and women) evinced many skills and stratagems in holding on tenaciously to their familial and cultural roots. In the sequel--principally set in late nineteenth- to early twentieth-century Tennessee in which Jim Crowism, disfranchisement, lynching, sharecropping, and black capitalism provide the narrative context--the themes of family integrity and unity again res-onate. They culminate with Halcy (James Earl Jones) returning to his ancestral roots in Africa to mark the spot from which Kunta Kinte had been kidnapped over two centuries earlier.

The two miniseries featured numerous black stars, two of whom received Emmy nominations (Louis Gossett, Jr., and Olivia Cole). Among the Afro-American actors were former athletes and singers and dancers who acquitted themselves very well in dramatic roles. Save for Gossett and Ben Vereen, however, few black actors' careers immediately benefitted from the series. Roots did not generate spin-offs or even imitations, and serious roles for black actors were no more abundant after the Roots phenomenon than before it. If anything, Roots probably built false expectations about fundamental changes occurring in television programming and casting.(413, 558)

The Roots phenomenon was an aberration with surprisingly little impact on television. A few more autobiographical accounts of blacks reached production (e.g., Maya Angelou's I Know Why the Caged Bird Sings [1978]), but such accounts have been diluted by commercial considerations. In her 1978 criticism of white control of black images on television, Pamela Douglas predicted that the Roots phenomenon would accomplish nothing more than some Roots-type projects with historical and rural set-tings so that whites will not have to confront "real" contemporary life and with the blacks as victims who will find solutions to their problems within the American system.(213) Even such Roots-style projects have not been forthcoming. The pro-ducers of Roots themselves were reluctant to make further sequels for both commercial reasons (the belief that American audiences had seen quite enough of the Roots-style genre) and political ones

(the belief that any sequel might be perceived as
exploitive, a conviction reinforced by Ben Vereen's
refusal to return to the role of Chicken George ,
charging the producers with trying to "rip-off"
black sensibilities by manufacturing the first
sequel).(413, 640)

It is also perhaps significant that the black
perspective on slavery, central to Roots, has received no further treatment in prime-time network
programming, being relegated to public broadcasting
productions such as A House Divided: Denmark
Vesey's Rebellion.(241, 413, 592, 601) Indeed,
television seemed to regress in 1980 when NBC offered the Civil War romance Beulah Land, which
offended black actors and the NAACP because of its
background of happy, subservient slaves cut in the
mold of southern romantic potboilers once common in
movies.(462, 583, 601) It is even more significant
that the subject of black kinship has struggled to
find serious dramatic outlet, as evinced in the
failure of Kinfolks even to be aired after it was
produced and in the early cancellation of Harris
and Company in 1977. Black families are marketable
commodities in television only so much as they are
funny.(560)

Many thousands of viewers, and of students who
participated in college credit courses based on the
series, got their first lessons in slavery from
Roots, much as previous generations "learned" about
slavery and blacks from The Birth of a Nation and
Gone with the Wind. They were lessons, however,
which did not readily translate into greater interracial understanding or applications to contemporary social issues. The basic problems were ones
of interpretation and presentation. However much
Roots rebutted The Birth of a Nation, it did not
present a black perspective on blacks' own history.
Roots was adapted from Haley's book and relied on
black performers to interpret the scenes, but the
scripts had been developed by white writers, shot
under white directors, and shaped by white producers.(415, 591, 601, 630)

The series failed as history anyway. The publicity about the series, which caused Haley himself
to redirect his own interpretation of his book,
stressed the brutal and shocking events in the
first episodes and deflected discussion away from
the historical validity and significance of the

subject matter.(232, 560, 601) The frequent flog-
gings and tortures, including rapes, reminded audiences of slavery's horrors, but by pandering to
audience desires for titillation, the television
production vitiated its force as history. Frank
Mankiewicz and Joel Swerdlow have surmised that, as
much as anything else, the repeated brutality
whites inflicted on blacks in each episode built
the series' audience, much in the style of such
movies as Mandingo which had been exploiting the
sufferings of slavery without improving Americans'
understanding of the subject.(422)

In casting blacks solely as heroes and whites
entirely as villains Roots undercut its credi-
bility--a fact producer David Wolper acknowledged
and sought to remedy in the sequel by introducing
several sensitive white characters. In their un-
requited parade of evil, heartless slave merchants
and slaveowners, the series' creators put the antagonists beyond any identification with white
viewers. White viewers could absolve themselves of
complicity in oppressing blacks by measuring their
prejudices and behavior against the whites shown in
the series. As studies of the effects of Roots and
its sequel suggest, black viewers felt pride in
their own history while white viewers were largely
disassociated from the events in the series, even
though they may have felt twinges of guilt about
racism in America.(271, 326, 333, 581) And whites
also drew the conclusion from Haley's example and
his subtheme of individual success in the face of
poverty and prejudice that blacks could achieve the
American Dream if they worked hard enough. Some
white viewers came away from the series with their
own prejudices reconfirmed, convinced that poor
blacks had only themselves to blame for not ad-
vancing in America.(64) These were hardly messages
on which to build a black television genre or a
drama of realism. Roots, then, had only slight
effect on dramatic opportunities for blacks in
television.(16, 413)

Beyond crime/police dramas and situation comedies contemporary black problems and personalities
have faded from the home screen. The regular contributions of blacks to network news programs
(e.g., Bryant Gumbel on Today and Ed Bradley on 60
Minutes) actually belies the slight presence of
blacks on prime-time television who are connected

ntemporary settings and subjects. Adver-
do not want to buy time on shows the net-
ill not promote and support, and, of late,
with a few exceptions, audiences have shown little
interest in sustaining dramatic series in which
black stars and subject matter happen to play a
significant part. The miniseries King, about Martin
Luther King, Jr., did not do well in the ratings
and probably discouraged other ventures focusing on
important black figures. A show about a black car-
diologist (The Lazarus Syndrome [1979]) lasted one
season, despite the supposed star-quality of Lou
Gossett in the lead role.(413)

Networks have quietly reverted to older
patterns of whitewashing controversial issues,
which often means avoiding the subject of race
whenever treating contemporary life. In the current
structure of television, with its intense counter-
programming pressures, networks are unwilling to
support a new show over more than one season until
it can build a following. Network program executives eschew controversy or any subject that might
split the market and seek out proven formulas and
popular stars capable of appealing to the desired
target audience (i.e., upwardly-mobile, consumer-
oriented Americans with considerable disposable
incomes) who now seem to favor action shows over
social commentary. The networks are content to
leave serious contemporary subjects to the expanding evening news programs. Under such circumstances, black dramatic options remain con-
stricted.(259, 260, 413, 579)

Despite a long list of titles on Afro-Americans
in film and television, the subject of black
imagery in the American mass media has not occasioned a systematic, sustained analysis or even
experimentation with new critical methodologies.
Much of the literature is redundant; too much of it
is polemical or personal rather than objective and
scholarly. Only recently has a critical tradition
emerged to set the black film and television experience in historical context and to introduce recognized aesthetic standards for assessing black
film and television genres.

Most important in offering both an in-depth
study of the contents and sources of black images
in American cinema, and comparing those images with
representations of other groups, is the work of
Thomas Cripps. In Slow Fade to Black(181) and a
series of articles,(160, 162, 163, 172, 177, 178,
183) Cripps demonstrates the interplay between
black aspiration and the politics and sociology of
film expression. Cripps also assays the emergence,
and limits, of a black film tradition, noting not
only the cultural roots but artistic, technological
constraints of a black film genre,(157, 158, 160,
162, 167-170, 177, 178, 180-182) and providing a
detailed analysis of six black film genres and an
essay on the black critical tradition as it relates
to film.(159) Cripps sees an evolving liberal tradition in the film industry which, over time, has
accorded blacks more and better roles and respect.
He especially credits World War II with effecting
changes in blacks' film images and fortunes, arguing that the government-sponsored film, The Negro
Soldier, served as a catalyst for improved racial
understanding within the film industry and for
using film as a medium of protest by blacks.(159,
161, 171, 185). Cripps also has observed how the
poses and styles of black actors work undertones of
black autonomy into their roles.
    Second only to Cripps in scholarly importance
is the work of Daniel Leab, who has surveyed the
black film experience from the early silent film
days through the era of blaxploitation,(387-389,
392, 393), with particular attention to the early
films.(384, 390, 391). Leab, however, finds that
from the beginnings of film blacks suffered from
misrepresentation and exclusion in film and
suggests that, for all their imitation of Hollywood
formulas, black filmmakers offered the only legitimate black film expression. In viewing post-World
War II developments, Leab concludes that the brief
post-war liberalism in film did not eliminate the
use of older stereotypes by Hollywood or independent black film studios,(392, 393), although he
points to the emergence of black stars like Sidney
Poitier and the box-office punch of blaxploitation
films as forcing new images into film.(387)
    Other useful overviews of blacks in American
film include those by Charlotte Ashton, who identifies changing patterns of post-World War II

imagery(59); Donald Bogle, who argues that black
actors, not stereotypes, reveal the essence of
black film history(90, 91); William Burke, who
traces black images from ones of savages to socialized Christians in post-World War II
films(115); Madubuko Diakite, who studies black
filmmaking from the early race movies through the
1970s as a cultural lens through which black
artists see their world(206); Mary Ellison, who
charts Hollywood's responsiveness to social and
political changes as they affect black images(223);
Victor Jerome, who adopts a Marxist perspective and
criticizes the post-World War II liberalism in
Hollywood films for failing to capture social
detail and black purpose(343, 344); Edward Mapp,
who focuses largely on the 1960s(423, 427); James
P. Murray, who looks closely at black filmmaking in
his call for a "new black cinema" free of white
distortions and sensitive to black "realities"
(459); James R. Nesteby, who tries to link film
images to civil rights consciousness(466); Peter
Noble, who presents an English point-of-view in his
surveys of American films and filmography in an
influential, if limited, early treatment of blacks
in film(472); Jim Pines, who provides an expatriate
perspective in his criticism of the social conservatism of Hollywood relating to blacks(494, 495);
and Stephen Zito, who sketches the contours of a
black film criticism and suggests that black movies
must be evaluated by their social intentions rather
than by artistic standards.(652) The black presence
in film has occasioned a pictorial history,(476)
and even a celebration of black film stars.(378)
Anthologies by Richard Maynard,(433) Lindsay Patterson,(488) and Gladstone Yearwood(649) collect
essays, some previously published, on aspects of
black filmmaking and images of blacks, but like so
much of the critical literature, they assume advocacy positions calling for a distinct black film
aesthetic, which, many writers contend, is possible
only in an independent black cinema.

    Missing in the general studies, save that by
Cripps,(181) and, indeed, absent in virtually all
the special studies listed in the bibliography as
well, is an explicit comparative framework to appreciate how the black experience and images in
movies relate to the histories and depictions of
other groups in American film. In their general

studies of film, Garth Jowett(355) and Robert
Sklar(559) place black images and participation in
American film within the context of the industry's
sociological and cultural development. James Monaco
identifies key personalities and styles among black
filmmakers while discussing recent American film
production and the industry's development.(446)
Robert Toll(591) weaves examples of Afro-American
art and popular culture and the uses of black
imagery into his general survey of American entertainment. Emma Lapsansky(381) and J. Stanley Lemons
(400), along with Cripps and Leab, among others,
locate the roots of Afro-American film images in
nineteenth-century popular culture. But only
William Van Deburg has widely excavated the myriad
popular cultural sources from which black images in
American film and television developed.(601)

Useful research tools to locate patterns of
scholarship and commentary on blacks in film
include the annotated bibliography and filmography
by Marshall Hyatt(338); the bibliographies by
Ernest Kaiser(361, 361a); the detailed filmography
by Phyllis Klotman(373); the annotated bibliography
by Daniel Leab(385); the listing of blacks on film
by James L. Limbacher(404a); the selected bibliography by Anne Powers(510); and the source book on
all-black films, with synopses, casts, and mini-
biographies, by Henry Sampson(536). Access to un-
published primary sources on blacks in film and to
prints of films made by and/or about blacks will be
immensely aided with the forthcoming publication of
Thomas Cripps's bibliography by Garland Publishing.

Black images in film date back to the origins
of the medium, and works on early film often took
notice of the black presence. Critical assessments
of blacks in early film awaited recent scholarship,
however. Few black critics covered movies with any
regularity, and even amid the emergence of an independent black cinema in the 1910s through the
1920s, black writers failed to develop a tradition
of film criticism. Afro-American newspapers tended
to recognize only those films in which they had an
interest because of advertising or investment in
film properties. Much of the early criticism was
little more than editorial condemnation of images
of blacks in white movies. White critics and newspapers almost wholly ignored black contributions.

The appearance of Hallelujah! and Hearts in
Dixie in 1929 excited critical interest in black
images in film, especially among civil rights organizations. Robert Benchley, for example, wrote a
piece for Opportunity Magazine weighing Hearts in
Dixie against the history of black roles in
film,(77) and W.E.B. DuBois, writing in Crisis,
believed that the two films broke the white-black
complex which had cast blacks solely in white
terms.(216) The August 1929 issue of Close Up offered the first sustained critical assessment of
blacks in American films, with contributors arguing
that prejudice prevented the film industry from
depicting "real" Afro-Americans on the screen,(129)
that whites "learned" about blacks through
film,(207) that no "serious" black films then
existed,(311) and that Hollywood's belated interest
in blacks as film subjects derived from the "New
Negro" movement of song and stage but failed to
address the aesthetic and cultural issues surrounding blacks' physical appearance.(507) All
contributors called for a black cinema.

Early critics tended to home in on particular
movies to assess blacks' place in cinema. No film
generated more commentary than Birth of a Nation.
Indeed, almost every discussion of blacks in cinema
uses the film as the touchstone for black images in
film. As noted in the text above, the film set off
a furious debate about prejudice and film art and
even calls for censorship and boycotts.(See citations in text.) Critic after critic echoed the
chorus of complaints about distortion and about the
social damage caused by the film, so much so that a
dispassionate, critical review of the film's
symbols and themes became impossible until recently. Even so important an issue as the film's
derivation from "reform" impulses of the Progressive era has only recently received extended
treatment.(See X-59a)

Reviews of other early films measured black
"progress" in film imagery and representation, but
no critical consensus was forthcoming on the aesthetic or social tests for that "progress." Thus,
Imitation of Life (1934) received both cuffs for
perpetuating the mammy stereotype(109) and faint
praise for attempting to address a social problem.
(571) Until the sound era few critics had held out
hope for an enlarged role for blacks in Hollywood.

Most critics looked to a vigorous black cinema
drawing on Afro-American musical and spiritual
resources as the surest road to black liberation on
the screen (e.g., 443, 444),although William Harrison criticized both Hollywood and black filmmakers for casting blacks in unrealistic
roles.(299) Historical surveys of blacks in film
eschewed critical evaluations in favor of ritual
condemnations about racism in Hollywood productions (e.g., 58, 293).

The wartime and post-war liberalism of the
1940s deflected interest away from black movies and
shifted it toward Hollywood films as an instrument
for inter-racial understanding and integration.
Contemporaries applauded the film industry's
efforts to dignify Afro-Americans during World War
II,(238, 297, 418, 419) discounted the influence of
the southern box office,(351, 441) forecast a new
era of fairness in Hollywood productions,(248) and
even condemned all-black films for creating their
own segregationist images.(238) In an influential
scholarly study published in 1944 amid the U.S.
government's growing interest in projecting images
of a united American homefront, Lawrence Reddick of
the Schomburg Collection in New York built on an
earlier study done at Schomburg(192) to review the
Afro-American contribution to American popular
culture. Although he counted 75 percent of Hollywood films as having been "anti-Negro" in some
ways, he believed that Hollywood films, not race
movies, promised the best means of improving
blacks' images in society.(517). Reddick brought
scholarly detachment to the issue of blacks in
film, but he kept the discussion imprisoned in
categories of positive versus negative images and
Hollywood versus independent black cinema.

Only a few critics demurred from the 1940s
optimism. Charles Metzger, for one,(441) revealed
the limits of white "liberal" support for black
aspirations relating to film when he charged that
black protests against what Afro-Americans perceived as negative portrayals in such films as Song
of the South(e.g.,30) would only hurt them in the
industry. William Still did not share Reddick's
faith in Hollywood,(576, 577) and by 1950 Gerald
Weales was reporting that "message" movies had no
effect on audiences' racial attitudes.(619)
Likewise, two social scientists maintained that an

ostensibly anti-prejudice message movie like No Way
Out actually carried hidden anti-black biases.(638)
And also in 1950 Arthur Knight recorded the industry's growing concern over anti-Communist purges
and their effects on treating racial issues in
"social problem" films.(375)

By the 1950s several critics expressed concern
about the social isolation of blacks in "liberal"
films. Ralph Ellison, writing in 1949 about
Intruder in the Dust and Pinky, warned against
sentimentality and self-congratulation regarding
"progress" in film images and insisted that blacks
and whites must keep their own conscience in
film.(224) In 1955 James Baldwin charged that all-
black casts, as in Carmen Jones, insulated film
from the "danger" of forthright black-white interaction.(62) Henry Popkin claimed that the producers
of Island in the Sun and Band of Angels feared
losing the southern box office and so tempered
their professed liberalism by refusing to entrust
blacks with powerful, dominant screen roles.(506)
In reviewing the film fare relating to blacks from
the 1940s through 1959, both Martin Dworkin(217)
and Albert Johnson(346) echoed such reservations
about the reality of Hollywood's liberalism, even
while observing the first glimmers of a renewed
industry willingness to approach such themes as
miscegenation and to risk capital in promoting such
black film stars as Sidney Poitier.

In the 1960s critical attention continued to
focus on individual films and to seek out evidence
of progress, which generally meant evidence of
integrationist themes. During the 1960s several
general surveys of blacks in film recorded the
evolution of black images, and a few critics still
declaimed on the need for an independent black
cinema. Much of the literature fastened on a few
screen personalities and films, which served as the
litmus tests of cinema's social conscience and
relevance. Sidney Poitier, as actor and symbol,
became a principal topic of discussion.(See discussion and citations in text.) While several black
actors and critics maintained that Poitier's
success created its own stereotype and distorted
the genuine opportunities for blacks in film during
the 1960s,(e.g., 74, 431, 511) other writers, such
as Albert Johnson,(347) argued that Poitier's persona opened up new roles for blacks.   Bosley

Crowther, however, measured progress in noting that
Poitier got roles that could have just as easily
been played by whites.(188-89) It was just that
interchangeability of Poitier with whites that
angered those critics who sought a distinct black
film presence rooted in the black urban ethos.

In 1963 William Barrow claimed black actors
stood at the threshold of "realistic" roles in
Hollywood productions.(70) Although less sanguine
than Barrow, Renata Adler, in an influential essay
critical of the false promise of Guess Who's Coming
to Dinner?, forecast the emergence of "real" blacks
of soul and courage who played characters audiences
could believe in because the roles were like the
actors in real life--e.g., the cool, collected
Poitier in In the Heat of the Night and the rugged
Jim Brown in The Dirty Dozen.(38) At least one
black critic insisted Hollywood would never permit
a real black persona to emerge. In perhaps the
angriest attack on Hollywood in the 1960s, John O.
Killens labeled Hollywood as the "most anti-Negro
influence" of the century. Hollywood, said Killens,
invariably transmuted black characters into loyal
blacks supporting the white master's "big house"
and neither understood nor sought any independent
black existence or identity outside the white man's
dominion.(368) Lindsay Patterson added that "liberal" messages disguised Hollywood's reluctance to
accept America's multiracial reality(484) and that
in drawing the color line in films set in Africa or
England the industry conveyed segregationist themes
to the world.(485) As recently as 1976 another
critic echoed Killens' argument, insisting that the
industry consciously used stereotypes to keep minorities in their place.(41)

The emergence of the "blaxploitation" films in
the late 1960s and 1970s revived issues of black
cinema as a tool for social and artistic liberation
and as an authentic mirror for black experience. It
also created two separate markets for black images
--what Ted Angelus identified as the liberal or
intellectual market for the Poitier-like images of
assimilation and repressed anger and the blue-
collar market for the violent language and action
of the blaxploitation films.(49) Pauline Kael provided the fullest explication of the genre, noting
its sociology and cosmology within the American
film tradition.(356) In his useful 1972 assessment

of the blaxploitation phenomenon, in which he contended that box-office receipts rather than politics would shape black images, Charles Michener
speculated on the genre's social effects, but
brought no new or hard data to the case.(442)
Charles Peavy, in an important study of black films
and filmmaking in the late 1960s through the early
1970s, especially black films funded by foundations, identified how blacks tried to use film as
a vehicle for social rehabilitation, self-
expression, and social change.(489) In their
efforts to promote an independent black cinema,
James Murray and others used the pages of Black
Creation to describe the phenomenon and let black
filmmakers express their artistic, commercial, and
social concerns.(e.g., 107, 456-58) In his survey
of black images in film, black actor and filmmaker
Carlton Moss conceded that, their distortions notwithstanding, black films in the 1960s and early
1970s were preferable to the stereotypical offerings of Hollywood from 1915 onward.(452)

Despite the controversies surrounding the authorship and authenticity of blaxploitation images,
surprisingly few black directors received extensive
interviews and scholarly attention. Melvin Van
Peebles vented his anger in a book relating the
production history and purpose of his Sweet
Sweetback,(610a) but few others sought such
outlets. In responding to criticism about blaxploitation films as providing negative role models for
black youth or misrepresenting black urban culture,
Ossie Davis charged Hollywood with ignoring decency
in its rush to exploit the black market and concluded that blacks had to entrust their artistic
future to blacks alone(199); D'Urville Martin insisted that blacks were too smart to emulate the
genre's heroes(18); and Gordon Parks compared his
work, including Sounder which did not fall into the
blaxploitation category, favorably with Hollywood's
presentation of black themes and characters.(551)
Rachel Birtha, in her study of the content and
audience response to one black-directed, black-
oriented film, included interviews with J. E.
Franklin and Ossie Davis,(85) and in his surveys of
black film Oliver Franklin excerpted interviews
with several black filmmakers.(239, 240) Revealing
treatments of contemporary black filmmakers appear
in works by Cripps,(159) Diakite,(206) Mapp,(423)

Monaco,(446), Murray,(459), and Yearwood,(649), to name several examples.

The blaxploitation movies led to considerable soul-searching among blacks about the uses and abuses of the film medium. Indeed, several critics even called for censorship to stem the flow of macho images and end the cult of violence they saw in such movies.(See discussion and citations in text.) Civil rights advocates especially divided over the validity and political value of the genre's messages, with their criticism reflecting their own strategies for achieving social justice. Vernon Jordan, for example, condemned the films for their stereotypes of blacks as criminal and anti-intellectual, among other faults,(352) while Huey P. Newton lavished praise on Van Peebles' Sweet Sweetback's Baadasssss Song, the film that generated the most heated arguments among critics, for its "revolutionary" qualities.(469) More recently, such films have served as touchstones for discussions of the emergence, and need for, a black film aesthetic.(97)

How black moviegoers in fact received the films' messages largely went untested. Rachel Birtha, for one example, surveyed black, white, and Indian responses to Black Girl.(85) Herbert Coverdale, writing for Equal Opportunity in 1976, provided the fullest summary of impressionistic data, reporting that, even as they recognized such fare exploited them, Afro-Americans supported the genre with paid admissions because the films catered to inner-city blacks' need for racial cohesion and cultural references to their own community.(154) During the 1960s and 1970s, however, the genre's effects on audiences did not undergo systematic surveys using acceptable, modern techniques of communications research. So little audience research relating to film's effects on viewers' attitudes (excepting 88, 269), or even critical reception (excepting 114), existed before the heyday of blaxploitation films that comparable data was not available anyway. What early research was available suffered from an underlying assumption, amounting to wishful thinking in one case, that film could effect social change. Sidney Kraus, writing in 1962, for example, optimistically argued that simple dramatic films with a mixed cast of blacks and whites could change racial attitudes of high

school students who had little previous exposure to
blacks(377)--an argument not born out by subsequent
research.

Blaxploitation films did bring issues of black
sexuality into both critical and scholarly circles.
Typical of several early commentators was
Theophilus Green, who, in 1972, thought that the
blaxploitation macho superhero offered a necessary
corrective to the emasculated, cowardly, Stepin'
Fetchit black male screen type.(277)   Loyle
Hairston concurred, although he warned that the
genre's themes would make money the talisman of
power, thereby locking black men in the grips of
American materialism. Hairston also predicted that
the blaxploitation superhero would free Poitier
from his unnatural assimilationist screen persona
by making him (and it) irrelevant, for the new
superheroes would force "liberal" whites to grapple
with their own fears of black masculinity.(292)
Ellen Holly argued that the macho men lacked human
stature so that audiences could not take them
seriously.(324) Francis Ward, however, viewed the
black superheroes as recastings of the "John Wayne
type," but she warned that black macho men had such
"insatiable sexual appetites" and thrived on
action so much in blaxploitation films that they
revived old stereotypes of the black man as virile,
strong, but lacking in cognitive skills.(612-613)
Gladstone Yearwood argued that heroes embody society's traditions, but black film historically had
failed to define its purpose and so to develop
viable heroes--thus Paul Robeson's real life politics clashed with the restraint he exercised in
film roles.(647) In her scholarly treatments, Joan
Mellen set the black male image in the context of
masculinity in American film, noting how the blaxploitation films revived the image of the black as
a sexual being, an attribute of masculinity absent
in Poitier's roles.(435-436) Recent commentary on
black images has largely focused on the limited
screen roles available to blacks in screen drama
and blacks' relative powerlessness in the industry
and moved away from observations on male sexuality.(e.g., 106, 151, 204, 529)

Discussions of female sexuality also gained
fresh interest and insight in the 1960s and 1970s.
Complaints from black actors and critics have
ranged from the lack of leading roles for black

women to the perpetuation of the mammy stereotype
to the creation of over-sexed temptresses,(e.g.,
424-425, 586) although at least two commentators
dared filmmakers to present and promote "sexy"
black actresses.(22, 25) The stereotypes, which in
various forms date back to the silent era, include
the tragic mulatto, the mammy or earth mother, the
innocent, and the siren or seductress.(116, 210,
275, 572) Particularly frustrating to critics has
been the intractability of the female stereotypes,
(e.g., 303, 533) which they largely attribute to
the white- and male-dominated nature of the film
industry, and which have burdened other minority
women as well.(See I-21) One feminist sniffed a
conspiracy in both Hollywood and independent black
cinema to keep "black women in their place" by
casting them solely as supporters of men.(561) In
1974 several black actresses complained that black
women especially suffered from a limited range of
movie roles and sexist characterizations.(291) In
1982 Pearl Bowser recorded little improvement in
opportunities or images and argued that in black
cinema, too, women characters lacked credibility,
for they were variously set on a pedestal, employed
as metaphors for the race's social ills, or offered
up as love goddesses.(101) Despite the periodic
appearance of the other images, especially the
sexually aggressive black women of much 1960s and
1970s fare,(116) the mammy stereotype remained the
dominant black female image in American film, as in
popular culture generally.(345) Even during periods
of racial consciousness when the film industry has
attempted to present favorable images of blacks,
the mammy image persisted--in World War II produc-
tions(60), in post-war message movies(29, 34) and
in depictions of southern or black life, where,
says one writer, the image has sustained the "per-
nicious myth of black matriarchy" in a supposedly
fragmented black family.(203)

     The durability of the mammy stereotype derived
in part from its association with popular images of
regions and lifestyles. As Edward Campbell has
suggested, the "southern" genre from Birth of a
Nation through Gone With the Wind to Mandingo all
used the mammy, among other symbols, to establish
setting and the planter credentials of the white
characters.(119-121) The mammy stereotype, because
of its function, became the victim of the plan-

tation stereotype in film, and not even the black-
over-white worlds of Mandingo and Passion Plantation with their lurid themes of miscegenation
between "comely" young black slaves and lecherous
white planters eliminated the presence of the full-
busted mammy. Less appreciated in the literature
has been the mammy stereotype's function in demar-
cating the class boundaries in films about the
upper class, a favorite subject of Hollywood productions. Indeed, the entire issue of the need for
particular stereotypes, such as the mammy, as reference points in creating mood, setting, and social
relationships has been neglected in treatments of
black images in film, or television too for that
matter.

Scholarly assessments of blacks in film have
followed the principal concerns of film critics.
The silent era has received considerable attention
from scholars, but, like the critics, few have
looked beyond Birth of a Nation to understand the
origin and evolution of screen images within the
social and cultural contexts of early film production, distribution, and exhibition. Notable
exceptions include Bogle,(91) Cripps,(180-82)
Jowett,(355) Leab(384, 387, 390), and William
Everson, who also addresses issues of early film
aesthetics.(226) Hannah Andrews offers an instructive way to track the evolution in depiction
and function of black-related themes and images by
following the various renditions of Uncle Tom's
Cabin in book, play, and film,(48) and Joseph
Boskin,(96) Leslie Fiedler,(230) and Willie Lee
Rose,(532) among others, have charted the movement
of specific racial themes and images across several
media over time. Likewise, William Slout suggests
the interplay of culture and film content by describing the several remakes of Uncle Tom's
Cabin.(563) The southern antecedents to negative
images of blacks have received ample attention,
(e.g., 55, 120-121, 181, 370, 439) as have the
contributions of D.W. Griffith to broadening and
popularizing those images.(See discussion and citations in text.) Early black-made films remain
understudied, however, partly for want of extant
prints--a situation recently being remedied by the
discovery and analysis of several early black films
(e.g., 158, 167, 539). Work on silent film production involving blacks in particular settings--

e.g., early filmmaking in Chicago,(289) in Florida, (465) and in Virginia(234)--awaits further exploration on how locality shaped themes and images. So, too, scholars need to build on the Cripps and Leab foundations in studying specific film companies and films. Surprisingly, even so important a figure as Oscar Micheaux has received only preliminary critical analysis.(e.g., 319, 492)

The advent of sound occasioned new, if temporary, interest in Afro-American subjects in the film industry. Save for discussions in the general surveys of blacks in film and Peter Noble's brief argument on the generally salutary effects the coming of sound had on black imagery and participation in film,(472) and such off-hand assertions as Alexander Walker's suggestion that black music increased moviegoers' interest in sound film,(605) however, the subject of the talkies' significance for blacks cries out for treatment. So, too, does the role of language in affecting screen imagery. The relationship of blacks and black music to film has hardly been heard. An important exception is Charles Berg, whose discussion of jazz and film shows how Hollywood "picked up the beat" from black musicians, even as it cut blacks from scenes in preparing films for distribution in the southern market.(79) Likewise, black musicals as a genre demand scholarly attention from others besides Cripps. Suggestive of possibilities in setting the genre within American social history, Allen Woll has shown how all-black musicals were enlisted in America's cause during World War II.(639)

The relationship of black images to social problem films has occasioned intermittent discussion but insufficient longitudinal study. Too many scholars tend to look at specific films in specific time periods and to neglect the historical development of the social problem genre and its connection to changing social norms. Few studies offer extensive or intensive analysis of black-related themes and issues. In the fullest treatments of 1930s-era films, for example, Andrew Bergman(80) and Nick Roddick(527) both identify instances where racial issues entered the social problem films, without focusing particularly on black images or subjects. Roddick does observe that racism was a hidden feature rather than an explicit theme in Depression-era films until Warner Brothers

directly addressed the subject in several films,
suggesting that racism, like fascism, was a home-
grown product as well as a foreign threat to American values and institutions, but Roddick's
emphasis on film stars as the principal vehicles
within studios for raising ideological issues in
films necessarily discounts black influence or
interest, for blacks had little visibility or power
in the industry. Several scholars have credited
World War II with bringing racial issues to the
surface, and they have attributed the film industry's growing willingness to tackle racial and
social issues involving blacks to the federal government's involvement in making such films as The
Negro Soldier, which demonstrated the political
potential of the film medium.(See discussion and
citations in text.) Scholars have also discussed
black images and issues in relationship to the
post-war message movies, although only Peter
Roffman and Jim Purdy have set the discussion in a
broad comparative framework.(528) Regarding Afro-
American images, they conclude that from the 1930s
through the 1950s film mirrored liberal wishful
thinking in developing the image of the "noble
Negro" patiently waiting for civil rights due him.
Peter Biskind(86) and Richard Maltby(421) comment
on the exclusion of controversial subject matter in
Hollywood fare during the 1950s age of consensus--a
development that locked black-related issues in
obscurity. Neither Biskind nor Maltby, or others,
say much about black responses to such exclusion.

One recent shift in scholarly focus is the
relationship of blacks (and minority and ethnic
groups generally) to cinematic depictions of
working-class life and values. Discussion of movies
such as Blue Collar(186) and Car Wash(535) have
grappled with blue-collar workers' ambivalent identities in films, viewing the films' intimations of
how racial segregation off the job threatens worker
solidarity on the line or messages of alienation
among workers.(651) Such films have elicited similar ambivalent responses from moviegoers, as in
one Detroit sample.(12) Such films derive their
power from contemporary social issues. Thus, as
Daniel Leab has observed, a film like Rocky actually exploits white, "ethnic" working-class hostility toward blacks.(386)

Film scholarship explores other issues as well. But recurring throughout the literature on blacks in film is the assumption that film exercises social and political power--that its images, which function as indices of cultural ascription, can affect social processes. Thus, as recently as 1982, two writers still expected film to make some adjustments in black imagery to adhere to blacks' perceptions of social reality.(204) Similarly, as Hanes Walton,(608) among others, has recently argued, American movies have failed to appreciate the range and diversity of black culture. Whether film ought to be (or even can be) an instrument of social change will no doubt continue to concern film critics and commentators. Whether scholarship on film will move beyond political categories is not so clear.

Although blacks have been visible in commercial television for more than thirty years and have "used" the medium for political and social purposes, surprisingly little work has been done on the history of black involvement in television. Where scholarship on film is strong (e.g., in cataloguing black roles and involvement in film), scholarship on television is weak. Contrariwise, where scholarship on film is not well developed (e.g., studies on the social or political effects that particular black images have on black and white audiences), scholarship on television is more mature. Still, in assaying the relationships between Afro-Americans and television over time, scholars' relative inattention to the early years of television and commentators' preoccupation with the politics of the medium (i.e., hiring policies, regulation, and equal representation) have provided only a partial portrait of the black image in television.

The only extended treatment of blacks in television is J. Fred MacDonald's recent book, Blacks and White TV, which offers a substantial interpretive history of blacks in (and on) television from 1948 through the 1970s.(413) MacDonald brings together much popular and serious writing on television, from the pages of TV Guide to special university-sponsored studies, in showing how blacks historically have looked to the medium to promote civil rights, to weaken racial prejudice, and to provide positive role models for black youth.

MacDonald's work observes the "totality" of television, appreciating, for example, how images and
interests in advertising or in the newsroom affect
entertainment. Critical of the failed promise of
television, which he partly blames on the industry's abandonment of "social relevancy" for
entertainment in the 1970s and the complicity of a
few black stars (e.g., Flip Wilson) in that
process, MacDonald concludes with a call for a new
social commitment within the industry--a plea
echoed throughout the literature.

The few studies of the early years of television have touched on several concerns from
content analyses of particular images to the political and social promise of television. Examples of
such studies include Sydney Head's content analysis
of 1952 drama programs, which revealed that minorities were portrayed as benign types, generally
employed in domestic or service occupations, and
posed no threat to society(305); J. Fred
MacDonald's discussion of NBC's barring of Paul
Robeson and Nat King Cole's difficulties getting a
sponsor, which suggested the failed promise of a
bias-free medium in the 1950s(412); and Marilyn
Rife's survey of the 1950s and 1960s, which indicated the persistence of stereotypes and racism in
television through the 1960s, even as black visibility increased.(519) Also useful are Thomas
Cripps's account of the debate over racial integration that was ignited by the airing of the Amos
'n' Andy show(156); Harold Jackson's chronology of
blacks in prime-time network programming from Amos
'n' Andy to I Spy, which focuses on the particular
roles of black actors(340); Richard Koiner's survey
of black images from the 1950s through the 1970s,
which emphasizes the importance of I Spy in making
black actors marketable in television dramas(376);
and Richard Gehman's 1964 overview of blacks in
television in the 1950s through the early
1960s.(250)

Two suggestions will suffice to show how much
elementary work on the early years of television
still awaits analysis. Aside from promotional biographies and interviews in such magazines as Ebony,
little attention to black performers' interest in
and influence upon television has been recorded.
The connections between Hollywood and television,
and how such connections affected particular images

and television content, have not been explored in relationship to blacks.

The 1960s and 1970s have drawn considerable critical notice. Controversies swirl on such issues as revived stereotypes in the "black" situation comedies spawned by Norman Lear and the confrontational humor in such shows as All in the Family and The Jeffersons. The deleterious effects of "realistic" comedy especially caused concern and generated measurements of how such shows as All in the Family colored viewers' attitudes toward blacks and other minorities.(See discussion and citations in the text.) Also of interest in the 1970s was the powerful immediate impact of Roots on American (and even foreign) viewers, but the very slight long-term effect the Roots phenomenon had on television content or even the careers of some of the principal actors in the mini-series.(See discussion and citations in the text.)

The issues related to the sit-coms and Roots have so consumed critical and scholarly interest that other developments in recent television have been neglected. The role of blacks in daytime television, for example, awaits attention. Sherry Johnson has made the interesting point that blacks are absent from soap operas because they are boring. Nobody wants to offend blacks by portraying them as over-sexed, vulgar, and material--those qualities common to soap opera characters.(348) In that way blacks are victims of white producers' "liberal" good intentions, which, in effect, means blacks are absent from some genres.

Surveys of blacks in television generally focus on head counts of blacks in the medium and on the roles available to blacks. Several studies have enumerated the black presence in various roles (e.g., as servants or domestics), with particular attention to developments in the 1970s.(e.g., 317, 475, 523, 544-46) Black critics have decried the persistent exclusion of blacks from television production and have charged that during the late 1960s and early 1970s white-produced television polarized the races by creating false images,(315) failed to develop realistic black male characters, (94) and generally "distorted, mishandled, and exploited" black subjects.(221) But the program context must be taken into account in identifying stereotypes, for, according to Cherry Banks's 1974 sample of network prime-time programs, regularly-appearing black characters in integrated casts exhibited less stereotypical behavior than did black characters in shows with predominantly black casts.(67) In the early 1970s critics complained that blacks were not allowed to tell their own story(e.g., 321)--a charge repeated in governmental reports(e.g., 596, 597, 600) and virtually every study of the medium. A few commentators have observed a trend toward more "favorable" and diverse roles for blacks during the 1970s,(e.g., 316, 364) while others, including several black actors, have insisted that black images in the 1970s were not substantially different from earlier stereotypes. (e.g., 106, 108, 215, 448) Responding to so much criticism of television's images at a time when television producers were hiring blacks in increasing numbers and casting "all-black" comedies, several producers and critics asked in 1982 what images represent the "real" black experience anyway and who, in fact, spoke for the group.(131)

The authors of the Commission on Civil Rights 1977 and 1979 reports on women and minorities in television(596, 597) also provided histories of black images in television, along with statistics on black participation in various kinds of programming and in production. The reports, like the testimony from black civil rights leaders and scholars before Congress in 1983,(600) repeat the widely-held assumption that the images of blacks (or any group) are intimately related to blacks' (or any group's) representation in and control of the production process. Indeed, perhaps no theme has been more persistent than the one of increasing black involvement in the industry in order to change the images of blacks in the medium.

The issue is power. In 1982 Ossie Davis urged blacks to assert their own image.(201) But how to do so? Pamela Douglas, for one, has suggested that blacks look to cable and public television for outlets and that they purchase stations and exercise their market power more directly to control program content.(212) In the absence of a black-controlled medium, blacks have struggled for a share of the production process and, in some instances, have reminded blacks that they must use television for political/social purposes every chance they get.(e.g., 104)

Critics have charged the industry and the federal government with neglect, or even conspiracy, in denying blacks access to production and allowing stereotypes to persist.(e.g., 99, 569) Several critics have urged a larger federal governmental regulatory role to encourage (and, if necessary to compel) the industry to hire more blacks in all phases of television production and to improve black images on the screen.(e.g., 569, 645) Such critics seem to accept Herbert Schiller's argument, presented in 1969, that only massive minority access to mass media production can undo past stereotypes,(541) but the theoretical scaffolding for arguments urging increased public intrusion into industry policies and production remains incomplete. Other critics have endorsed boycotts and protests against particular shows, series, and stations guilty of presenting unfavorable black images.(e.g., 204, 428) Manifestos and journalistic descriptions of such actions are available,(e.g., 50, 462, 583) but, save for a study of a black pressure group in Ohio,(437) the internal structure and social dynamic controlling boycotts and protests remain unsketched.

Studies on the development, structure, and character of the television industry reveal some of the economic and political decisions behind program content and even specific images. In his important article on the politics of television art, Thomas Cripps notes that Hollywood had abandoned many demeaning stereotypes by the time commercial television developed, so that the real issue was how and by whom the black image in television would be formed. As blacks struggled among themselves to define that image, the industry resorted to fads, cycles, and cardboard types in depicting blacks and, in the wake of the 1967-68 urban riots was unprepared to treat blacks in any way but as angry or flamboyant types.(176)

Others have emphasized the conservatism of industry executives, who respond to the market by producing homogenized goods. The principle of formula production, these critics argue, rules television more ruthlessly than it ever governed film. Be they sponsors/advertisers, as Erik Barnouw emphasizes,(69) or wary, in-bred network executives, as Todd Gitlin emphasizes,(259, 260) they seek to avoid controversy and play to the largest

target audiences. In such an environment blacks,
and social issues, have little place unless they
can be safely adapted to the industry's inherent
conservatism and market needs. Critics have
attacked the false liberalism of recent television
fare, suggesting that programming continues to
perpetuate class and cultural bias and leaves the
"real black" out because entertainment supersedes
social purpose.(e.g., 52, 54, 81, 579) Kwame
Bowmani revealed the frustration blacks felt toward
television when, in 1977, he warned that television
could never serve as a tool for "decolonization"
because the industry's drive for profits inevitably
denied black cultural integrity and sought to encourage blacks to behave, and consume, like
whites.(99) During the 1970s and 1980s critical
attention shifted to the "ethnic" situation comedies, especially the Norman Lear productions and
their imitations, echoing complaints registered
since the early days of television about whites
manipulating black images for commercial purposes
and black actors selling out to a white-controlled
industry by singing, dancing, and jiving for the
white man.(See discussion and citations in text.)

The preoccupation with numbers and calls for
proportionate representation of blacks in television, however, sometimes slight discussions
related to the social, political, and economic contexts, both within and outside of the industry, in
which blacks do or do not appear. To take one
example: Critics and scholars have acknowledged the
influence of the civil rights movement on television images, even as they have noted the resiliency of several stereotypes (e.g., 229, 526). The
increased visibility of blacks in advertisements
and in television journalism bears out such influence. But it is not so clear whether the number
and nature of black faces on television was a
response to external political, social, and/or
economic pressures, to internal decisions rooted in
social justice or market considerations (or whatever), or, as is most likely, to various combi-
nations of external and internal factors.

Even in discussions of blacks in television
advertising (an area where market decisions would
seem to be almost the sole determinants of black
visibility and characterization) authors disagree
about how much sponsors used advertising to attack

stereotypes(e.g., 478) or simply used blacks proportionate to their numbers in America and their
supposed buying power, with social consciousness in
no way figuring in advertising strategies.(e.g.,
117, 480) One study has even implied that television commercials in the mid-1970s were blind to
real social changes occurring in .America, as
evinced in the proliferation of commercials depicting blacks as low achievers.(493)

The inner mechanics of television production
(on the tension between the art and commerce in developing a show, or even a commercial, for example)
require study as they relate to questions of television's social content. This subject is addressed
in larger works on television,(e.g., 259, 413, 468)
but neglected in particular studies of blacks and
television. Indicative of the possibilities of
understanding the subtle cultural prejudices
entering television content is Larry Gross's discussion of how habits of intolerance toward specific groups such as gays and blacks have in-
sinuated themselves so deeply into the popular
culture that television, as a mirror and lens of
that culture, reflects or magnifies those prejudices.(290)

In the interests of social science and policy
many researchers have examined television as a
socializing agent, transmitting information,
values, and roles to its viewers. A significant
literature exists on the processes whereby the
medium conveys social messages, with some observers
arguing that television compares with such other
socializing agents as the family and schools in
establishing role models and beliefs. Children, the
studies agree, are particularly susceptible to such
messages. (See discussion and citations in chapter
I.)

Perhaps more than any other group, Afro-Americans have been concerned about the socializing
functions of television because, statistically,
black children watch more television than do whites
and poor blacks especially have fewer opportunities
to gain alternative images and information than do
more affluent whites. Blacks, and scholars, have
focused particularly on television's effects on
black children's self-perceptions, which supposedly
have been (and are) threatened by negative stereotypes of blacks in the mass media and by value

systems at odds with those taught in black families. Much of the work relating to the socializing
effects of television on black children draws from
several key studies in communications theory, such
as those by A. Bandura and Raymond Williams. Those
studies and the undergirding assumptions about
television's power to influence human attitudes and
behavior are surveyed and examined in the Columbia
University studies headed up by George Comstock,
which provide a convenient introduction to the
subject.(146-48) Also instructive for general
trends are articles by Paula Poindexter and Carolyn
Stroman in 1981(503) and by Stroman in 1984(578)
reviewing the major research findings of the previous ten to sixteen years.

The Bradley Greenberg study teams at Michigan
State University, among others, have monitored
viewing habits regularly beginning in the 1970s and
have documented that black children and adolescents
view more television than white children, and
lower-class black children's viewing time exceeds
that of middle-class white children by three hours
per day. Variables such as age and family-income
affect viewing patterns, but, on average, black
children are heavy consumers of television
fare.(45, 237, 279-81, 285, 408)

Studies of program preferences reveal that
black, and other minority, children express distinctive viewing patterns.(e.g., 219, 280) One 1969
study, for example, indicated that black and white
children and adolescents preferred different kinds
of situation comedies.(236) A rare contradictory
finding for teenage viewing habits was reported in
1974.(408) More significant are black children's
preferences for shows with black characters,(e.g.,
276, 278) a viewing habit seemingly consistent with
black adult preferences,(e.g., 281) and blacks'
responsiveness to commercials that include a black
character.(e.g., 110)

Longitudinal studies tracking the evolution of
black viewers' habits over time (from childhood to
adulthood, for example) are not available, however,
to determine how maturity affects program selection
and influence, although the Comstock group has
broached the subject.(146-48) Two studies conducted
in the 1960s concluded that black viewers preferred
shows involving conflict because blacks were not
able to appreciate television sit-coms or other

genres which focused on white middle-class families,(126, 236) but no follow-up studies have been completed with those, or similar audiences, to determine how the changed color and content of television in the 1970s and 1980s, including "black" sit-coms and a wider range of socioeconomic profiles represented in programs, may have affected viewer choices.

Content analyses of prime-time and children's programming suggest that blacks have had few "positive" (the term is elusive among commentators) role models with which to identify.(596, 597) Samples for television seasons in the mid-1970s, for example, show that black characters are underrepresented in all kinds of television fare and that black characters generally appear in comedic roles.(68, 208, 278, 279) Related to such representation has been the tendency to portray black characters as poor, unemployed, or in low-status occupations, a tendency, some researchers argue, that reinforces negative self-images among young black viewers. When recurring, such representations can constrict the career horizons of young black viewers.(51, 66, 306, 342, 585, 588) Contrariwise, Steven McDermott points out in a 1982 dissertation on television and black children's self-concept, regular exposure to wholesome "family" fare on television can promote self-esteem.(411)

What constitutes wholesome family fare remains open to question. Criticism of depictions of the black family (especially as presented in the black sit-coms of the 1970s) abounds.(e.g., 83, 449) Related to such concerns are the specific images of black men and women, which often perpetuate images drawn from popular culture. Critics have noted the emasculation of black men, by their absence or by their irresponsible, comedic poses in much television fare, or, as George Sweeper concludes in his recent comparative study of black and white family images in prime-time programming,(582) by their abandonment of their families, their low-paying jobs, their hostility, and their vanity. Where black women fit into the schema is less clear. No consensus on the images of black women exists. Karen Jewell, for example, has stressed the persistence of the mammy image in popular culture and television(345); Diana Meehan has argued that black women in television series conform to white models

of "good wives"(434); while Jean Bond has commented
that the strength and "soulfulness" of black women
characters in such shows as Good Times keeps black
men down.(95) Scholars are only beginning to sort
out such contradictory and confusing images and
speculate as to their meaning.

In assaying the effects of black (or any
group's) media images the issue, as Peggy Charren
and Martin Sandler,(136) among others, put it, is
not so much the presentation of particular values,
attitudes, and behaviors as it is their repetition
that invests them with meaning and reality. The
issue is also the expectations raised by the increasing and changing visibility of blacks in
television, from news broadcasting to situation
comedies. Those who believe integrated television
is more important than integrated classrooms in
affecting racial attitudes have, such as Frank
Mankiewicz and Joel Swerdlow, conceded to television a primary role in defining American
values.(422)

Perhaps the worst potential effect of television, say critics, is that, with so many programs
depicting antisocial behavior and violence, television exposes black children (heavy consumers of
television) to values, attitudes, and behavior
harmful to their social development.(e.g., 251) The
exact relationships and effects of media violence
are in dispute. The place of blacks as television
characters or as viewers in creating or responding
to messages of violence is not at all established,
despite a very large literature on television and
violence.(e.g., 380) The tendency of network television to focus on "upper-class crime," in effect
to distort and deny real crime statistics in favor
of the dramatic potential, has excluded blacks from
explicit involvement in much criminal and violent
action, except as victims or law enforcement
agents.(312) While such exclusion might alter
viewers' world view, as at least one scholar has
suggested,(482) it does not exclude blacks from
identification with violence. As the 1977 Brookdale
Institute study of four television diets revealed,
blacks during the 1970s were increasingly shown in
aggressive situations.(566) The very nature of
television, argue George Gerbner and Larry Gross,
creates among heavy consumers of television a tendency to believe that the real world is more

violent than it really is,(251) which may exac-
erbate already existing suspicions between different groups. Television violence, insist Henry
Taylor and Carol Dozier, can be an instrument of
social control.(587) It can keep blacks in their
place by presenting blacks as victims needful of
white protection, or it can insinuate into viewers'
thinking an association between blacks and a crime-
ridden urban world that must be contained (in television and in reality).(414)

Black children are vulnerable to television's
messages because, more than their white counterparts, they identify closely with television characters and accept television's images as reality.
The Greenberg group, working from Bandura's social
learning theory, discovered that black children
thought that blacks on television were like blacks
in real life (even when their own real-life experiences conflicted with the portrayals on television) and that the jobs people performed on
television were like the jobs men and women did in
real life.(278, 279, 283) Jannette Dates learned in
her research that, although youngsters with
positive racial attitudes were critical of black
portrayals on television, many poor black children
regarded television characters as real, so much so
that some children believed certain television
characters lived on in real life as those same
characters even when the television show was off
the air.(195-96)

Black children and adolescents look to television for information as well as entertainment.
(23, 128, 253, 279, 285) Various studies have found
that blacks watch television to learn elementary
social facts about other people (even how they look
and talk), as well as getting information about
jobs and interpersonal relations.(e.g., 279) According to an early report by Bradley Greenberg,
white youths also used television to learn about
blacks, even more so than black children in
Greenberg's sample confessed to using television to
learn about whites.(278)

It is not clear, however, to what extent black
(or any other) children or adolescents in fact
imitate behaviors from television. At least one
study, measuring the effect of television on the
linguistic habits of viewers, concluded that black
children distinguished between language spoken by

television characters and their own real-life
language--a finding challenging the assumption that
black children accept television as reality.(84)
Indicative of the difficulty in sorting out television's influence is a 1980 study suggesting that
learning the contents of television "reality" did
not necessarily mediate television's impact on
children's social attitudes.(211) The welter of
incomplete and sometimes confusing data has led
Richard Allen, among others, to assert that researchers know very little about the uses and
effects of television because too many basic questions remain untested, even unasked.(44) Measuring
what viewers brought to the viewing experience, for
example, requires study before scholars can achieve
any consensus regarding television's "educational"
effects on any audience. In that regard, Leo
Bogart's caveat that blacks do not live isolated in
a media subculture, that significant distinctions
in media habits and values separate blacks from
different geographical regions and classes,(89) is
worth remembering, for no single black or white
audience exists. Until we know the audiences of
television, and film, it will not be possible to
know the effects and meaning of black images on the
screen.

     Major discussions of films and/or television
shows include: All in the Family (39, 53, 81, 103,
259, 395, 396, 413, 422, 514, 582, 603), Amos 'n'
Andy (96, 145, 156, 340, 413, 519), The Autobiography of Miss Jane Pittman (95, 623), Band of
Angels (506), Beulah Land (106, 462), The Bill
Cosby Show (402, 413), The Bingo Long Travelling
All-Stars and Motor Kings (150), The Birth of a
Nation (40, 50, 55, 61, 71, 90, 91, 112, 120, 121,
130, 140, 180, 181, 187, 210, 223, 235, 246, 258,
288, 308, 328, 337, 343, 355, 369, 374, 387, 435,
439, 461, 464, 473, 479, 494, 495, 516, 537, 540,
556, 559, 573, 604, 631), The Birth of a Race (157,
158, 168a, 181, 206, 387), The Biscuit Eater (372),
Black Girl (85, 335), The Blood of Jesus (159),
Blue Collar (186, 651), Body and Soul (177, 181),
Brian's Song (273), The Bronze Buckaroo (359), Buck
and the Preacher (366, 471), Cabin in the Cotton
(181), Cabin in the Sky (314), Carmen Jones (62,

387), Car Wash (535), Casablanca (161, 181),
Conrack (36), Cotton Comes to Harlem (292, 387),
The Defiant Ones (366, 504), Diff'rent Strokes
(413), The Dirty Dozen (38), Drum (120), East
Side/West Side (413), Edge of the City (310, 346),
The Emperor Jones (327, 360, 547), The Final War of
Olly Winter (52), The Flip Wilson Show (94, 413),
For Love of Ivy (225), The Foxes of Harrow (120,
121), Ganja & Hess (446), Get Christy Love (95),
Gone With the Wind (90, 91, 120, 121, 140, 181,
183, 210, 223, 233, 302, 345, 370, 472, 473, 513,
532, 574, 634, 641), Good Times (95, 142, 145, 422,
514, 582), The Great White Hope (363, 538), Green
Pastures (181, 183), Guess Who's Coming to Dinner?
(38, 225, 366, 421, 504, 552), Hallelujah! (181,
216, 311, 314, 473, 605), Harlem Rides the Range
(391), Hearts in Dixie (77, 120, 121, 181, 387,
472, 473), Hill Street Blues (259, 316), Home of
the Brave (375, 387, 619), A House Divided: Denmark
Vesey's Rebellion (241, 592), Hurry Sundown (464),
I Am a Fugitive from a Chain Gang (80, 527), I Spy
(340, 376, 519), Imitation of Life (90, 91, 109,
181, 210, 294, 387, 553), In the Heat of the Night
(38, 366, 387, 504, 650), Intruder in the Dust
(224, 375, 387, 392, 619), Ironside (468), Island
in the Sun (346, 387, 506), The Jazz Singer (181),
The Jeffersons (53, 145, 309, 413, 422, 449, 514,
582, 617), Jezebel (120, 121), Julia (315, 376,
403, 519, 543), King (417), King Kong (307), Lady
Sings the Blues (61), Leadbelly (446), The Learning
Tree (6, 366), Lifeboat (450), Lilies of the Field
(310, 366, 504, 552), Lying Lips (181), Mandingo
(119-21), Mission Impossible (94), Mississippi
(120, 121), The Mod Squad (94, 468), Moon Over
Harlem (181), My Sweet Charlie (401), The Nat King
Cole Show (138, 412, 413, 519), Native Son (113,
173, 307), The Negro Soldier (159, 161, 181, 185,
508, 616), The New Era (234), Norma Rae (36, 651),
Nothing But a Man (159), No Way Out (638), The
Outcasts (376), Pinky (224, 349, 375, 392, 619),
Porgy and Bess (589), Realization of a Negro's
Ambition (181), Richard Pryor Live on the Sunset
Strip (287), Rocky (386), The Rookies (468), Roots
(16, 65, 232, 241, 326, 332, 333, 413, 415, 447,
512, 581, 601, 610, 630, 640, 653), Roots: The Next
Generation (64, 271, 413), St. Louis Blues (159),
Sanders of the River (177, 181), Sanford and Son
(53, 396, 413, 514), The Sante Fe Trail (218, 451),

The Scar of Shame (159, 272), Shaft ([film] 356, 456, 459, [television] 413), Since You Went Away (60), So Red the Rose (120, 121), Sounder (36, 387), Steamboat 'Round the Bend (530), Superfly (356, 613), Sweet Sweetback's Baadasssss Song (78, 124, 159, 206, 292, 397, 435, 436, 446, 458, 459, 469, 522, 601a, 612, 648), Tarzan series (181, 466, 467), Tennessee Johnson (161, 171), To Sir, With Love (552), Uncle Tom's Cabin (48, 96, 119-21, 181, 563), Uptown Saturday Night (93), A Warm December (33), What's Happening? (413), and The World, the Flesh, and the Devil (310, 346).

1. _____. "Appeals Court Backs CBS in Fetchit Defamation Suit." BROADCASTING 86 (March 25, 1974): 31.

2. _____. "Belafonte Plays Angel On and Off Screen." EBONY 24 (October 1969): 76-78ff.

3. _____. "Black Films: Boom or Bust?" JET June 8, 1972, pp. 52-59.

4. _____. "Black Market." TIME 99 (April 10, 1972): 53.

5. _____. "Black-Oriented Films Seen Losing Ground." JET, January 17, 1974, p. 88.

6. _____. "The Black Path to Hollywood." SEPIA 19 (April 1970): 50-54.

7. _____. "The Black Screen Image: Where Is It Going in the Seventies?" SOUL ILLUSTRATED 2 (no. 3. 1970): 18-20.

8. _____. "Black Teenage Conference: 'Does TV Serve the Needs of Black Youth?'" TELEVISION TODAY (item II-570), pp. 199-239.

9. _____. "Blacks Form Film Distribution Company." JET, November 2, 1972, p. 53.

10. _____. "Black TV: Its Problems and Promises." EBONY 24 (September 1969): 88-94.

11. _____. "Blacks vs. Shaft: Formation of Coalition Against Blaxploitation." NEWSWEEK 80 (August 28, 1972): 88.

12. _____. "Blue Collar: Detroit Moviegoers Have Their Say." CINEASTE 8 (no. 4 [1978]): 28-31.

13. _____. "Civil Rights Groups Attack Films." JET, September 14, 1972, p. 50.

14. _____. "Criticism Mounts Over Superfly." JET, September 28, 1972, p. 55.

15. _____. "Dialogue on Film: Sidney Poitier."

AMERICAN FILM 1 (September 1976): 33-48.

16.   _____. "Did Roots Change Anything for Blacks?" SEPIA 28 (May 1979): 18-27.

17.   _____. "Do Negroes Have a Future in Hollywood?" EBONY 11 (December 1955): 24-30.

18.   _____. "D'Urville Martin: Actor, Producer, Angry Black Man." SEPIA 22 (October 1973): 69-80.

19.   _____. "51 Black-Oriented Films Produced Since Mid-1970." JET, September 21, 1972, pp. 58-59.

20.   _____. "Football Heroes Invade Hollywood." EBONY 24 (October 1969): 195-96ff.

21.   _____. "Hollywood Draws Slow Curtain of Mental Death Across the Ghettos." MUHAMMAD SPEAKS, August 25, 1972, pp. 28-29.

22.   _____. "Hollywood's New Black Beauties." SEPIA 22 (March 1973): 37-44.

23.   _____. HOW BLACKS USE TELEVISION FOR ENTERTAINMENT AND INFORMATION. Washington, D.C.: NTIS, 1978.

24.   _____. "The Image of the Black and the Media." J OF THE NATIONAL MEDICAL ASSOCIATION 62 (March 1970): 129-33.

25.   _____. "Is Hollywood Afraid to Star a Sexy Actress?" SEPIA 18 (June 1969): 10-15.

26.   _____. "Julia." EBONY 24 (November 1968): 56-58ff.

27.   _____. "Mission Impossible's Greg Morris: He Keeps His Cool Despite Grueling Competition Both On and Off the Screen." EBONY 23 (December 1967): 99-104.

28.   _____. "More Black Movies Will Deal with Drugs." JET, October 12, 1972, p. 58.

29. _____. "Movie Maids: Eight New Hollywood
Films Backtrack to Hack Racial Stereotypes
in Casting Negro Actors as Usual Maids and
Menials." EBONY 3 (August 1948): 56-59.

30. _____. "Needed: A Negro Legion of Decency."
EBONY 2 (February 1947): 36-37.

31. _____. "Negroes and Film." FILM COMMENT 1
(no. 3 1962): 29.

32. _____. PAUL ROBESON IN FILM. New Brunswick,
N.J.: Paul Robeson Film Retrospective,
Department of Africana Studies, Rutgers
University, [1974].

33. _____. "Poitier's New Film Makes Black Beautiful." JET, May 3, 1973, pp. 56-60.

34. _____. "Secret of a Movie Maid." EBONY 5
(November 1949): 52-56.

35. _____. "Whatever Happened to Lincoln (Stepin
Fetchit) Perry?" EBONY 26 (November 1971):
202.

36. Adams, Michael. "How Come Everybody Down Here
Has Three Names?: Martin Ritt's Southern
Films." SOUTHERN Q 19 (Spring-Summer,
1981): 143-55.

37. Adler, Renata. "Critic Keeps Her Cool on Up
Tight." NEW YORK TIMES, December 29, 1968,
II, p. 1.

38. _____. "The Negro That Movies Overlook." NEW
YORK TIMES, March 3, 1968, II, pp. 1, 10.

39. Adler, Richard P., ed. ALL IN THE FAMILY: A
CRITICAL APPRAISAL (item I-5).

40. Aitken, Roy E., and Al P. Nelson. THE BIRTH OF
A NATION STORY. Middleburg, Va.: William W.
Denlinger, 1965.

41. Alexander, Francis W. "Stereotyping as a
Method of Exploitation in Film." BLACK
SCHOLAR 7 (May 1976): 26-29.

42. Allen, Bonnie. "Blax, Smax, Was It Something
     We Said?" ESSENCE 9 (December 1978): 44,
     47.

43. _____. "The Macho Men: Whatever Happened to
     Them?" ESSENCE 9 (February 1979): 62-63ff.

44. Allen, Richard L. "Communication Research on
     Black Americans." IN SEARCH OF DIVERSITY
     (item I-2), pp. 47-63.

45. _____, and David E. Clarke. "Ethnicity and
     Mass Media Behavior: A Study of Blacks and
     Latinos." J OF BROADCASTING 24 (Winter
     1980): 23-34.

46. Allsopp, Ralph Norman. "Portrayals of Black
     People on Network Television and the Racial
     Attitudes of Elementary School Children: An
     Experimental Study." Ph.D. diss., New York
     University, 1982.

47. Alvarez, Michael. "No Way Out and The Defiant
     Ones." RACE AND ETHNICITY IN THE HISTORY OF
     THE AMERICAS (item I-36), pp. 45-46.

48. Andrews, Hannah Page Wheeler. "Theme and Vari-
     ations: Uncle Tom's Cabin as Book, Play and
     Film." Ph.D. diss., University of North
     Carolina at Chapel Hill, 1979.

49. Angelus, Ted. "Black Film Explosion Uncovers
     an Untapped, Rich Market." ADVERTISING AGE
     43 (July 24, 1972): 51-52.

50. Archer, Leonard C. BLACK IMAGES IN THE AMERI-
     CAN THEATRE: NAACP PROTEST CAMPAIGNS--
     STAGE, SCREEN, RADIO & TELEVISION. Brook-
     lyn, N.Y.: Pageant-Poseidon, Ltd., 1973.

51. Arenstein, Howard L. "The Effect of Television
     on Children's Stereotyping of Occupational
     Roles." M.A. thesis, Annenberg School of
     Communications, University of Pennsylvania,
     1974.

52. Arlen, Michael. THE LIVING-ROOM WAR. New York:
     Penguin, 1982.

53.   _____. "The Media Dreams of Norman Lear." THE
       NEW YORKER 51 (March 10, 1975), 89-94.

54.   _____. THE VIEW FROM HIGHWAY 1 (item I-6).

55.   Armour, Robert A. "History Written in Jagged
       Lightning: Realistic South vs. Romantic
       South in The Birth of a Nation." SOUTHERN Q
       19 (Spring-Summer 1981): 14-21.

56.   Arvey, Verna. "Worth While Music in the
       Movies." THE ETUDE MUSIC MAGAZINE 57 (March
       1939): 152ff.

57.   Asante, Molefi Kete [Arthur L. Smith]. "Tele-
       vision and Black Consciousness." J OF COM-
       MUNICATION 26 (Autumn 1976): 137-41.

58.   Asendio, James. "History of Negro Motion Pic-
       tures." INTERNATIONAL PHOTOGRAPHER 2 (Jan-
       uary 1940): 16-17.

59.   Ashton, Charlotte R. "The Changing Image of
       Blacks in American Film: 1944-1973." Ph.D.
       diss., Princeton University, 1981.

60.   Baker, Melva Joyce. "Images of Women in Film:
       The War Years, 1941-1945." Ph.D. diss.,
       University of California, Santa Barbara,
       1978; Ann Arbor: UMI Research Press, 1980.

61.   Baldwin, James. THE DEVIL FINDS WORK: AN ES-
       SAY. New York: Dial Press, 1976.

62.   _____. "Life Straight in De Eye." COMMENTARY
       19 (January 1955): 74-77.

63.   _____. "Sidney Poitier." LOOK 32 (July 23,
       1968): 50-54.

64.   Ball-Rokeach, Sandra J., and Joel W. Grube,
       and Milton Rokeach. "'Roots: The Next Gen-
       eration': Who Watched and with What Ef-
       fect?" PUBLIC OPINION Q 45 (Spring 1981):
       56-68.

65.   Balon, Robert E. "The Impact of 'Roots' on a
       Racially Heterogeneous Southern Community:

An Exploratory Study." J OF BROADCASTING 22 (Summer 1978): 299-307.

66. Balsley, Daisy F. "A Descriptive Study of References Made to Negroes and Occupational Roles Represented by Negroes in Selected Mass Media." Ph.D. diss., University of Denver, 1959.

67. Banks, Cherry A. McGee. "A Content Analysis of the Treatment of Black Americans on Television." SOCIAL EDUCATION 41 (April 1977): 336-39ff.

68. Barcus, F. Earle. IMAGES OF LIFE ON CHILDREN'S TELEVISION: SEX ROLES, MINORITIES, AND FAMILIES. New York: Praeger, 1983.

69. Barnouw, Erik. TUBE OF PLENTY (item I-10).

70. Barrow, William. "A Gallery of Leading Men." NEGRO DIGEST 12 (October 1963): 45-48.

71. Barry, Iris. D.W. GRIFFITH: AMERICAN FILM MASTER. New York: Museum of Modern Art, 1940.

72. Bart, Peter. "The Still Invisible Man." NEW YORK TIMES, July 17, 1966, II, p. 13.

73. Barthel, Joan. "He Doesn't Want to Be Sexless Sidney." NEW YORK TIMES, August 6, 1967, II, p. 9.

74. Beaupree, Lee. "Brock Peters on Negro Skepticism: One Colored Star Hardly a Trend." VARIETY, December 20, 1967, pp. 1, 54.

75. _____. "One-Third Film Public Negro." VARIETY November 29, 1967, pp. 3, 61.

76. Belafonte, Harry. "Belafonte: 'Look, They Tell Me, Don't Rock the Boat.'" NEW YORK TIMES, April 21, 1968, II, p. 21.

77. Benchley, Robert. "Hearts in Dixie (The First Real Talking Picture)." OPPORTUNITY MAGAZINE 7 (April 1929): 122-23.

78.   Bennett, Lerone, Jr. "The Emancipation Orgasm:
       Sweetback in Wonderland." EBONY 26 (Septem-
       ber 1971): 106-108ff.

79.   Berg, Charles M. "Cinema Sings the Blues."
       CINEMA J 17 (Spring 1978): 1-12.

80.   Bergman, Andrew. WE'RE IN THE MONEY (item I-
       14).

81.   Berk, Lynn M. "The Great Middle American Dream
       Machine." J OF COMMUNICATION 27 (Summer
       1977): 27-31.

82.   Berkman, Dave. "Minorities in Public Broad-
       casting." J OF COMMUNICATION 30 (Summer
       1980): 179-88.

83.   Berry, Gordon L. "Research Perspectives on the
       Portrayals of Afro-American Families on
       Television." BLACK FAMILIES AND THE MEDIUM
       OF TELEVISION (item II-339), pp. 47-59.

84.   _____, and Claudia Mitchell-Kernan, eds.
       TELEVISION AND THE SOCIALIZATION OF THE
       MINORITY CHILD (item I-18).

85.   Birtha, Rachel R. "Pluralistic Perspectives on
       the Black-Directed, Black-Oriented Feature
       Film: A Study of Content, Intent, and Audi-
       ence Response." 2 vols. Ph.D. diss., Uni-
       versity of Minnesota, 1977.

86.   Biskind, Peter. SEEING IS BELIEVING (item I-
       19).

87.   Black, Doris. "Hollywood's New King of Ego."
       SEPIA 22 (August 1973): 37-43.

88.   Bloom,Samuel W. "A Social Psychological Study
       of Motion Picture Audience Behavior: A Case
       Study of the Negro Image in Mass Communica-
       tion." Ph.D. diss., University of Wiscon-
       sin, 1956.

89.   Bogart, Leo. "Black Is Often White." MEDIA/
       SCOPE 12 (November 1968): 53-54ff.

90. Bogle, Donald. "Blacks in Film." DOLLARS & SENSE 7 (August-September 1981): 14-18; (October-November 1981): 14-18; (December 1981-January 1982): 40-45; (February-March 1982): 54-57.

91. _____. TOMS, COONS, MULATTOES, MAMMIES, AND BUCKS: AN INTERPRETIVE HISTORY OF BLACKS IN AMERICAN FILMS. New York: Viking Press, 1973.

92. _____. "Transcending Racist Trash: A Legacy of the First Black Movie Stars." SATURDAY R OF THE ARTS 1 (February 3, 1973): 25-29.

93. _____. "Uptown Saturday Night: A Look at Its Place in Black Film History." FREEDOMWAYS 14 (Fourth Quarter 1974): 320-30.

94. Bond, Jean Carey. "Flip Wilson, The Mod Squad, Mission Impossible: Is This What It's Really Like to Be Black?" REDBOOK 138 (February 1972): 82-83ff.

95. _____. "The Media Image of Black Women." FREEDOMWAYS 15 (First Quarter 1975): 34-37.

96. Boskin, Joseph. "Sambo: The National Jester in the Popular Culture." THE GREAT FEAR: RACE IN THE AMERICAN MIND. Edited by Gary B. Nash and Richard Weiss. New York: Holt, Rinehart & Winston, 1970, pp. 165-85.

97. Bourne, St. Clair. "The Development of the Contemporary Black Film Movement." BLACK CINEMA AESTHETICS (item II-649), pp. 93-105.

98. Bower, Robert T. TELEVISION AND THE PUBLIC. New York: Holt, Rinehart & Winston, 1973.

99. Bowmani, Kwame Nyerere. "Black Television and Domestic Colonialism." Ph.D. diss., Stanford University, 1977.

100. Bowser, Pearl. "History Lesson: The Boom is Really an Echo." BLACK CREATION 4 (Winter 1973): 32-34.

101. _____. "Sexual Imagery and the Black Woman in American Cinema." BLACK CINEMA AESTHETICS (item II-649), pp. 42-51.

102. Boyd, Malcolm. "The Hollywood Negro: Changing Image." THE CHRISTIAN CENTURY 84 (December 6, 1967): 1560-61.

103. Brigham, John C., and Linda W. Giesbrecht. "'All in the Family': Racial Attitudes." J OF COMMUNICATION 26 (Autumn 1976): 69-74.

104. Bright, Hazel V. "TV Versus Black Survival." BLACK WORLD 23 (December 1973): 30-42.

105. Broun, Heywood Hale. "Is It Better To Be Shaft than Uncle Tom?" NEW YORK TIMES, August 26, 1973, II, p. 11.

106. Brown, Cecil. "Blues for Blacks in Hollywood." MOTHER JONES 6 (January 1981): 20-28, 59.

107. Brown, Roscoe C., Jr. "Film as a Tool for Liberation?" BLACK CREATION 4 (Winter 1973): 36-37.

108. _____. "Let's Uproot TV's Image of Blacks." NEW YORK TIMES, February 18, 1979, II, p. 35.

109. Brown, Sterling A. "Imitation of Life: Once a Pancake." OPPORTUNITY MAGAZINE 13 (March 1935): 87-88.

110. Browne, Louis Alban. "Monoethnicity, Multi-ethnicity, and the Television Commercial: A Critical Assessment." Ph.D. diss., State University of New York at Buffalo, 1979.

111. Brownfeld, Allan C. "New Films Degrade Blacks, Stimulate Violence." HUMAN EVENTS 34 (March 2, 1974): 17.

112. Brownlow, Kevin. THE PARADE'S GONE BY. New York: Knopf, 1969.

113. Brunette, Peter. "Two Wrights, One Wrong." THE MODERN AMERICAN NOVEL AND THE MOVIES.

Edited by Gerald Peary and Roger Shatzkin.
New York: Frederick Ungar, 1978, pp. 131-
42.

114. Buchanan, Singer A. "A Study of the Attitudes
of the Writers of the Negro Press Toward
the Depiction of the Negro in Plays and
Films, 1930-1965." Ph.D. diss., University
of Michigan, 1968.

115. Burke, William Lee. "The Presentation of the
American Negro in Hollywood Films, 1946-
1961: Analysis of a Selected Sample of
Feature Films." Ph.D. diss., Northwestern
University, 1965.

116. Burrell, Walter. "The Black Woman as a Sex
Image in Films." BLACK STARS 2 (December
1972): 32-39.

117. Bush, Ronald F., and Paul J. Solomon, and
Joseph F. Hair, Jr. "There Are More Blacks
in TV Commercials." J OF ADVERTISING RE-
SEARCH 17 (February 1977): 21-25.

118. Cameron, Earl. "The Negro in Cinema." FILMS
AND FILMING 3 (May 1957): 9-11.

119. Campbell, Edward D.C., Jr. "'Burn Mandingo
Burn': The Plantation South in Film, 1958-
1978." SOUTHERN Q 19 (Spring-Summer 1981):
107-16.

120. _____. THE CELLULOID SOUTH: HOLLYWOOD AND THE
SOUTHERN MYTH. Knoxville: University of
Tennessee Press, 1981.

121. _____. "The Celluloid South: The Image of the
Old South in American Film, 1903-1978."
Ph.D. diss., University of South Carolina,
1979.

122. _____. "Films in the Classroom: 'The Southern.'" ORGANIZATION OF AMERICAN HISTORIANS
NEWSLETTER 10 (November 1982): 9-10.

123. Canby, Vincent. "Milestones Can Be Mill-

stones." NEW YORK TIMES, July 19, 1970, II, pp. 1ff.

124. _____. "'Sweetback': Does It Exploit Injustice?" NEW YORK TIMES, May 9, 1971, II, pp. 1, 18.

125. Capra, Frank. THE NAME ABOVE THE TITLE: AN AUTOBIOGRAPHY. New York: MacMillan, 1971.

126. Carey, James W. "Variations in Negro/White Television Preferences." J OF BROADCASTING 10 (Summer 1966): 199-212.

127. Carpenter, Sandra. "TWC--The Movie Company Behind 'Claudine.'" ENCORE 4 (June 9, 1975): 40-45.

128. Carter, Earl, ed. HOW BLACKS USE TELEVISION FOR ENTERTAINMENT AND INFORMATION: A SURVEY RESEARCH PROJECT. Washington, D.C.: Booker T. Washington Foundation, 1978.

129. Carter, Elmer, A. "Of Negro Motion Pictures." CLOSE UP 5 (August 1929): 118-22.

130. Carter, Everett. "Cultural History Written with Lightning: The Significance of The Birth of a Nation." AMERICAN Q 12 (Fall 1960): 347-57.

131. Carter, Virginia, and Tony Brown, Wade Nobles, and Stanley Robertson. "Black Families and Television: Current Problems, Future Solutions." BLACK FAMILIES AND THE MEDIUM OF TELEVISION (item II-339), pp. 81-96.

132. Cawelti, John G. "Reflections on the New Western Films: The Jewish Cowboy, the Black Avengers, and the Return of the Vanishing American." THE UNIVERSITY OF CHICAGO MAGAZINE 65 (January-February 1973): 25-32.

133. Champlin, Charles. THE FLICKS, OR WHATEVER BECAME OF ANDY HARDY? (item I-28).

134. _____. "Re-evaluation Needed in Film Industry." LOS ANGELES TIMES, April 9, 1968.

135. Chappell, Fred. "The Image of the South in
      Film." SOUTHERN HUMANITIES R 12 (no. 4
      1978): 303-11.

136. Charren, Peggy, and Martin W. Sandler. CHANG-
      ING CHANNELS: LIVING (SENSIBLY) WITH TELE-
      VISION. Reading, Mass.: Addison-Wesley
      Publishing Company, 1983.

137. Chaudhuri, Arun Kumar. "A Study of the Negro
      Problem in Motion Pictures." M.A.thesis,
      University of Southern California, 1951.

138. Cole, Nat King. "Why I Quit My TV Show." EBONY
      13 (February 1958): 29-34.

139. Coleman, Willette. "Crying at the Movies."
      BLACK COLLEGIAN 5 (January-February 1975):
      30-32.

140. Colle, Royal D. "The Negro Image and the Mass
      Media." Ph.D. diss., Cornell University,
      1967.

141. _____. "Negro Image in the Mass Media: A Case
      Study in Social Change." JOURNALISM Q 45
      (Spring 1968): 55-60.

142. Collier, Eugenia. "'Black' Shows for White
      Viewers." FREEDOMWAYS 14 (Third Quarter
      1974): 209-17.

143. _____. "A House of Twisted Mirrors: The Black
      Reflection in the Media." CURRENT HISTORY
      67 (1974): 228-31, 234.

144. _____. "New Black TV Shows Still Evade the
      Truth." TV GUIDE 22 (January 12,1974): 6-
      8, 10.

145. Comer, James. "The Importance of Television
      Images of Black Families." BLACK FAMILIES
      AND THE MEDIUM OF TELEVISION (item II-339),
      pp. 19-25.

146. Comstock, George, and Steven Chaffee, Natan
      Katzman, Maxwell McCombs, and Donald Rob-

erts. TELEVISION AND HUMAN BEHAVIOR (item I-31).

147. _____, and Robin E. Cobbey. "Television and the Children of Ethnic Minorities." J OF COMMUNICATION 29 (Winter 1979): 104-15.

148. _____. TELEVISION AND THE CHILDREN OF ETHNIC MINORITIES (item I-32).

149. Congressional Black Caucus. "A Position on the Mass Communications Media." [mimeographed report] Washington: Congressional Black Caucus, 1972.

150. Cook, Bruce. "The Saga of Bingo Long and the Traveling All-Stars." AMERICAN FILM 1 (July-August 1979): 9-13.

151. Corliss, Richard. "Blues for Black Actors." TIME 124 (October 1, 1984): 75-76.

152. Corporation for Public Broadcasting. BLACK PARTICIPATION IN PUBLIC TELEVISION: AWARENESS AND AUDIENCE DEVELOPMENT; REPORT OF A DEMONSTRATION PROJECT. Washington, D.C.: Corporation for Public Broadcasting, [1978].

153. Couch, William, Jr. "The Problem of Negro Character and Dramatic Incident." PHYLON 11 (June 1950): 127-33.

154. Coverdale, Herbert L. "The Black Film Experience: Revolution or Rip-Off?" EQUAL OPPORTUNITY 6 (Spring 1976): 17-18ff.

155. Cowan, Geoffrey. SEE NO EVIL: THE BACKSTAGE BATTLE OVER SEX AND VIOLENCE IN TELEVISION. New York: Simon & Schuster, 1979.

156. Cripps, Thomas R. "Amos 'n' Andy and the Debate Over American Racial Integration." AMERICAN HISTORY/AMERICAN TELEVISION (item I-112), pp. 33-54.

157. _____. "The Birth of a Race Company: An Early

Stride Toward a Black Cinema." J OF NEGRO
HISTORY 59 (Janury 1974): 28-37.

158. _____. "The Birth of a Race: A Lost Film
Rediscovered in Texas." TEXAS HUMANIST: A
REVIEW OF IDEAS, HISTORY AND CULTURE 5
(March-April 1983): 10-11.

159. _____. BLACK FILM AS GENRE. Bloomington:
Indiana University Press, 1978.

160. _____. "Black Stereotypes on Film." ETHNIC
IMAGES IN AMERICAN FILM AND TELEVISION
(item I-105), pp. 5-10.

161. _____. "Casablanca, Tennessee Johnson and The
Negro Soldier--Hollywood Liberals and World
War II." FEATURE FILMS AS HISTORY. Edited
by K.R.M. Short. Knoxville: University of
Tennessee Press, 1981, pp. 138-56.

162. _____. "The Dark Spot in the Kaleidoscope:
Black Images in American Film." THE KALEI-
DOSCOPIC LENS (item I-106), pp. 15-35.

163. _____. "The Death of Rastus: Negroes in American Films Since 1945." PHYLON 28 (Fall
1967): 267-75.

164. _____. "Early Films and Television: With
Special Reference to Urban, Ethnic, and
Black Studies" (item I-37).

165. _____. "Films for the Classroom: The Afro-
American Case." ORGANIZATION OF AMERICAN
HISTORIANS NEWSLETTER 11 (February 1983):
8-9.

166. _____. "The Films of Spencer Williams." BLACK
AMERICAN LITERATURE FORUM 12 (Winter 1978):
128-34.

167. _____. "A Generation of Rediscovered Black
Films." OPHELIA: A JOURNAL OF CONTEMPORARY
AFRICAN CULTURE AND LIFE 1 (March 1981):
71-75.

168. _____. "Historical Overview." BLACK IMAGES IN

FILMS, STEREOTYPING, AND SELF-PERCEPTION
(item II-291), pp. 9-19.

169. _____. "Motion Pictures." ENCYCLOPEDIA OF
BLACK AMERICA (item II-405), pp. 571-82.

170. _____. "Movies in the Ghetto, B.P. (Before
Poitier)." NEGRO DIGEST 18 (February 1969):
21-27, 45-48.

171. _____. "Movies, Race, and World War II: Ten-
nessee Johnson as an Anticipation of the
Strategies of the Civil Rights Movement."
PROLOGUE 14 (Summer 1982): 49-67.

172. _____. "The Myth of the Southern Box Office:
A Factor in Racial Stereotyping in American
Movies, 1920-1940." THE BLACK EXPERIENCE IN
AMERICA: SELECTED ESSAYS. Edited by James
C. Curtis and Louis L. Gould. Austin: Uni-
versity of Texas Press, 1970, pp. 116-44.

173. _____. "Native Son in the Movies." NEW LET-
TERS 38 (Winter 1971): 49-63.

174. _____. "Negroes in Movies: Some Reconsidera-
tions." NEGRO AMERICAN LITERATURE FORUM 2
(Spring 1968): 6-7.

175. _____. "New Black Cinema and Uses of the
Past." BLACK CINEMA AESTHETICS (item II-
649), pp. 19-26.

176. _____. "The Noble Black Savage: A Problem in
the Politics of Television Art." J OF POPU-
LAR CULTURE 8 (Spring 1975): 687-95.

177. _____. "Paul Robeson and Black Identity in
American Movies." THE MASSACHUSETTS REVIEW
11 (Summer 1970): 468-85.

178. _____. "'Race Movies' As Voices of the Black
Bourgeoise: The Scar of Shame." AMERICAN
HISTORY/AMERICAN FILM (item I-113), pp. 39-
55.

179. _____. "Racial Ambiguities in American Propaganda Movies." FILM & RADIO PROPAGANDA IN

WORLD WAR II. Edited by K.R.M. Short. Knoxville: University of Texas Press, 1983, pp.
125-45.

180. _____. "The Reaction of the Negro to the
Motion Picture Birth of a Nation." THE
HISTORIAN 25 (May 1963): 344-62.

181. _____. SLOW FADE TO BLACK: THE NEGRO IN AMER-
ICAN FILM, 1900-1942. New York: Oxford
University Press, 1977.

182. _____. "The Unformed Image: The Negro in the
Movies Before Birth of a Nation." MARYLAND
HISTORIAN 2 (Spring 1971): 13-26.

183. _____. "Winds of Change: Gone with the Wind
and Racism as a National Issue." RECASTING:
GONE WITH THE WIND IN AMERICAN CULTURE
(item II-513), pp. 137-52.

184. _____, ed. THE GREEN PASTURES. Madison: University of Wisconsin Press, 1979.

185. _____, and David Culbert. "The Negro Soldier
(1944): Film Propaganda in Black and
White." AMERICAN Q 31 (Winter 1979): 616-
40.

186. Crowdus, Gary, and Dan Georgakas. "Blue Collar: An Interview with Paul Schrader."
CINEASTE 8 (no. 3 [1978]): 34-37, 59.

187. Crowther, Bosley. "The Birth of 'Birth of a
Nation.'" NEW YORK TIMES MAGAZINE, February
7, 1965, pp. 24-25, 83-85.

188. _____. "The Negro in Films." NEW YORK TIMES,
October 6, 1963, II, pp. 1, 10.

189. _____. "The Significance of Sidney [Poi-
tier]." NEW YORK TIMES, August 6, 1967, II,
p. 1ff.

190. Cruse, Harold. THE CRISIS OF THE NEGRO INTEL-
LECTUAL. New York: William Morrow, 1967.

191. Culley, James D., and Rex Bennett. "Selling

Women, Selling Blacks." J OF COMMUNICATION 26 (Autumn 1976): 160-74.

192. Curtwright, Wesley. "Motion Pictures of Negroes." [mimeographed report] New York: Schomburg Collection, New York Public Library, 1939.

193. Damon, Susan. "Love at First Bite." RACE AND ETHNICITY IN THE HISTORY OF THE AMERICAS (item I-36), pp. 41-42.

194. Darrach, Brad. "Hollywood's Second Coming." PLAYBOY 19 (June 1972): 115, 124.

195. Dates, Jannette. "Race, Racial Attitudes and Adolescent Perceptions of Black Television Characters." J OF BROADCASTING 24 (Fall 1980): 549-60.

196. _____. "The Relationship of Demographic Variables and Racial Attitudes to Adolescent Perceptions of Black Television Characters." Ph.D. diss., University of Maryland, 1979.

197. _____. "Thoughts on Black Stereotypes in Television." ETHNIC IMAGES IN AMERICAN FILM AND TELEVISION (item I-105), pp. 17-19.

198. Davis, George. "Black Motion Pictures: The Past." NEW YORK AMSTERDAM NEWS, September 18, 1971, D, pp. 13-14.

199. Davis, Ossie. "The Power of Black Movies." FREEDOMWAYS 14 (Third Quarter 1974): 230-32.

200. _____. "Stepin' Fetchit." THE BLACK MAN ON FILM (item II-433), pp. 1-2.

201. _____. "Where Are the Black Image-Makers Hiding?" BLACK FAMILIES AND THE MEDIUM OF TELEVISION (item II-339), pp. 61-69.

202. de Grazia, Edward, and Roger K. Newman. BANNED FILMS (item I-40).

203. DelGaudio, Sybil. "The Mammy in Hollywood
      Film: I'd Walk a Mile for One of Her
      Smiles." JUMP CUT no. 28 (1983): 23-25.

204. Dempsey, Michael, and Udayan Gupta. "Holly-
      wood's Color Problem." AMERICAN FILM 7
      (April 1982): 67-70.

205. Dent, Tom. "The Negro in Recent Films: Reality
      or Illusion?" RIGHTS AND REVIEWS 2 (Winter
      1965): 19-21.

206. Diakite, Madubuko. "Film, Culture, and the
      Black Filmmaker: A Study of Functional
      Relationships and Parallel Developments."
      Ph.D. diss., University of Stockholm,
      Sweden, 1978; New York: Arno Press, 1980.

207. Dismond, Geraldyn. "The Negro Actor and the
      American Movies." CLOSE UP 5 (August 1929):
      90-97.

208. Dominick, Joseph R., and Bradley S. Greenberg.
      "Three Seasons of Blacks on Television." J
      OF ADVERTISING RESEARCH 10 (July 1970): 21-
      27.

209. Donagher, Patricia C., and Rita W. Poulos,
      Robert M. Liebert, and Emily S. Davidson.
      "Race, Sex and Social Example: An Analysis
      of Character Portrayals on Inter-racial
      Television Entertainment." PSYCHOLOGICAL
      REPORTS 37 (December 1975): 1023-34.

210. Donalson, Melvin B. "The Representation of
      Afro-American Women in the Hollywood Fea-
      ture Film, 1915-1949." Ph.D. diss., Brown
      University, 1981.

211. Dorr, Aimee, and Sherryl Browne, and Erin
      Phelps. "Television Literacy for Young
      Children." J OF COMMUNICATION 30 (Summer
      1980): 71-83.

212. Douglas, Pamela. "Black Television: Avenues of
      Power." BLACK SCHOLAR 5 (September 1973):
      23-31.

213. _____. "The Bleached World of Black TV."
     HUMAN BEHAVIOR 7 (December 1978): 63-66.

214. Drake, Ross. "Ellen Holly Is Not Black
     Enough." TV GUIDE 20 (March 18, 1972): 38-
     40.

215. Dreyfuss, Joel. "Blacks and Television: [part
     I] Television Controversy, Covering the
     Black Experience." WASHINGTON POST, Septem-
     ber 1, 1974, K, pp. 1, 5.

216. [DuBois, W.E.B..] "Dramatis Personae--Hallelu-
     jah!" THE CRISIS   36 (October 1929):342,
     355-56.

217. Dworkin, Martin S. "THE NEW NEGRO on Screen."
     THE PROGRESSIVE 24 (October 1960): 39-41;
     24 (November 1960): 33-36; 24 (December
     1960): 34-36; 25 (January 1961): 36-38; 25
     (February 1961): 38-41.

218. Easley, Larry J. "The Sante Fe Trail, John
     Brown, and the Coming of the Civil War."
     FILM & HISTORY 13 (May 1983): 25-33.

219. Eastman, Harvey A., and Marsha B. Liss. "Eth-
     nicity and Children's TV Preferences."
     JOURNALISM Q   57 (Summer 1980): 277-80.

220. Ebert, Alan. "How Sammy Davis, Jr., Met Dis-
     aster [part 1]." TV GUIDE   14 (July 9,
     1966): 4-9; [part 2] (July 16, 1966): 22-
     26.

221. Efron, Edith. "'Excluded, Distorted, Mis-
     handled and Exploited': What Is Happening
     to Blacks in Media?" TV GUIDE 20 (August
     26, 1972): 44-49.

222. _____. "Report on Minorities: Minority Com-
     plaints about Television" (item I-42).

223. Ellison, Mary. "Blacks in American Film."
     CINEMA, POLITICS AND SOCIETY (item I-39),
     pp. 176-94.

224. Ellison, Ralph. "The Shadow and the Act." THE
     REPORTER 1 (December 6, 1949): 17-19.

225. Elliston, Maxine Hall. "Two Sidney Poitier
     Films." FILM COMMENT 5 (Winter 1969): 26-
     33.

226. Everson, William K. AMERICAN SILENT FILM (item
     I-45).

227. Fabre, Michel. "The Reception of Roots in
     France." AMERICAN STUDIES INTERNATIONAL 17
     (no. 3 1979): 37-39.

228. Fay, Stephen. "The Era of Dummies and
     Darkies." COMMONWEAL 93 (October 30, 1970):
     125-28.

229. Ferguson, Richard D., Jr., and George A. Git-
     ter. BLACKS IN MAGAZINE AND TELEVISION
     ADVERTISING (Communication Research Center
     Report, no. 56). Boston: Communication
     Research Center, Boston University, 1971.

230. Fiedler, Leslie A. THE INADVERTENT EPIC: FROM
     UNCLE TOM'S CABIN TO ROOTS. New York: Simon
     & Schuster, 1979.

231. Fine, Marlene G., and Carolyn Anderson, and
     Gary Eckles. "Black English on Black Situa-
     tion Comedies." J OF COMMUNICATION 29
     (Summer 1979): 21-29.

232. Fishbein, Leslie. "Roots: Docudrama and the
     Interpretation of History." AMERICAN
     HISTORY/AMERICAN TELEVISION (item I-112),
     pp. 279-305.

233. Flamini, Roland. SCARLETT, RHETT, AND A CAST
     OF THOUSANDS: THE FILMING OF GONE WITH THE
     WIND. New York: MacMillan, 1975.

234. Fleener, Nickie. "Answering Film with Film:
     The Hampton Epilogue, A Positive Alterna-
     tive to the Negative Black Stereotypes
     Presented in The Birth of a Nation." J OF
     POPULAR FILM & TELEVISION 7 (no.4 1980):
     400-425.

235. Fleener-Marzec, Nickieann. "D.W. Griffith's The Birth of a Nation: Controversy, Suppression, and the First Amendment As It Applies to Filmic Expression, 1915-1973." Ph.D. diss., University of Wisconsin, 1977; New York: Arno, 1980.

236. Fletcher, Alan D. "Negro and White Children's Television Preferences." J OF BROADCASTING 13 (Fall 1969): 359-66.

237. _____. "Television Viewing Behavior of Negro and White Children in Athens, Georgia." Ph.D. diss., University of Illinois at Urbana-Champaign, 1969.

238. Foster, Joseph. "Hollywood and the Negro." NEW MASSES 53 (October 24, 1944): 28-29.

239. Franklin, Oliver. BLACK FILMS AND FILM MAKERS. Philadelphia: Afro-American Historical and Cultural Museum, 1980.

240. _____. ON BLACK FILM: A FILM AND LECTURE SERIES. Philadelphia: University of Pennsylvania, 1973.

241. Freehling, William W. "History and Television." SOUTHERN STUDIES 22 (Spring 1983): 76-81.

242. French, Philip. WESTERNS: ASPECTS OF A GENRE. New York: Oxford University Press, 1977.

243. French, Warren, ed. THE SOUTH AND FILM. Jackson: University Press of Mississippi, 1981.

244. Friedman, Lawrence J. THE WHITE SAVAGE: RACIAL FANTASIES IN THE POSTBELLUM SOUTH. Englewood Cliffs, N.J.: Prentice-Hall, 1970.

245. Friedman, Norman L. "Responses of Blacks and Other Minorities to Television Shows of the 1970s About Their Groups." J OF POPULAR FILM & TELEVISION 7 (no. 1 1978): 85-102.

246. Gallagher, Brian. "Racist Ideology and Black

Abnormality in the Birth of a Nation."
PHYLON 43 (March 1982): 68-76.

247. Gans, Herbert J. "The Mass Media as an Educational Institution." TELEVISION Q 6 (Spring 1967): 20-37.

248. Garfield, John. "How Hollywood Can Better Race Relations." NEGRO DIGEST 6 (November 1947): 4-8.

249. Garland, Phyl. "Blacks Challenge the Airwaves." EBONY 26 (November 1970): 35-40.

250. Gehman, Richard. "The Negro in Television [part 1]." TV GUIDE 12 (June 20, 1964): 15-23; [part 2] 12 (June 27, 1964): 15-22.

251. Gerbner, George, and Larry Gross. "The Violent Fate of Television and Its Lessons." CHILDREN AND THE FACES OF TELEVISION (item I-115), pp. 149-62.

252. Gerima, Haile. "On Independent Black Cinema." BLACK CINEMA AESTHETICS (item II-649), pp. 106-13.

253. Gerson, Walter. "Mass Media Socialization Behavior: Negro-White Differences." SOCIAL FORCES 45 (September 1966): 40-50.

254. Gibbs, Vernon. "Soul Man." CRAWDADDY   No. 24 (May 1973): 16.

255. Gill, Glenda E. "Careerist and Casualty: The Rise and Fall of Canada Lee." FREEDOMWAYS 21 (no. 1 1981): 15-27.

256. Gillespie, Marcia Ann. "Getting Down." ESSENCE 6 (August 1975): 41.

257. Gipson, D. Parke. $70 BILLION IN THE BLACK: AMERICA'S BLACK CONSUMERS. New York: MacMillan, 1978.

258. Gish, Lillian, with Ann Pinchot. THE MOVIES, MR. GRIFFITH AND ME. Englewood Cliffs, N.J.: Prentice-Hall, 1969.

259. Gitlin, Todd. INSIDE PRIME TIME (item I-59).

260. _____. "Prime-Time Whitewash." AMERICAN FILM
     9 (November 1983): 36-38.

261. Gittens, Tony. "Cultural Restitution and Inde-
     pendent Black Cinema." BLACK CINEMA AES-
     THETICS(itemII-649),pp.115-18.

262. Glaessner, Verina. "The Negro in Contemporary
     Cinema." FILM (G.B.) no. 61 (Spring 1971):
     12-16.

267. Glatzer, Richard, and John Raeburn, eds.,
     FRANK CAPRA: THE MAN AND HIS FILMS. Ann
     Arbor: University of Michigan Press, 1975.

268. Glenn, Larry. "Hollywood Change: Negroes Gain
     in a New Movie and Elsewhere." NEW YORK
     TIMES, September 22, 1963, II, p. 9.

269. Goldberg, Albert L. "The Effects of Two Types
     of Sound Motion Pictures on the Attitudes
     of Adults Toward Minorities." J OF EDUCA-
     TIONAL SOCIOLOGY 29 (May 1956): 386-91.

270. _____. "The Effects of Two Types of Sound
     Motion Pictures on the Attitudes of Adults
     Toward Minority Groups." Ed.D. diss., Indi-
     ana University, 1956.

271. Goldberg, Melvin A. "'Roots: The Next Genera-
     tions'--A Study of Attitude and Behavior."
     TELEVISION Q 16 (Fall 1979): 71-74.

272. Goldwyn, Ronald. "The Scar of Shame." [Phila-
     delphia Sunday Bulletin] DISCOVER MAGAZINE,
     November 17, 1974, pp. 14-16ff.

273. Gomery, Douglas. "Brian's Song: Television,
     Hollywood, and the Evolution of the Movie
     Made for Television." AMERICAN HISTORY/
     AMERICAN TELEVISION (item I-112), pp. 208-
     31.

274. Gow, Gordon. HOLLYWOOD IN THE FIFTIES. New
     York: A.S. Barnes & Company, 1971.

275. Grant, Liz. "Ain't Beulah Dead Yet? Or Images
     of the Black Woman in Film." ESSENCE 4 (May
     1973): 60-61ff.

276. Graves, Sherryl Denise Browne. "Racial Diver-
     sity in Children's Television: Its Impact
     on Racial Attitudes and Stated Program
     Preferences in Young Children." Ph.D.
     diss., Harvard University, 1975.

277. Green, Theophilus. "The Black Man as Movie
     Hero: New Films Offer a Different Male
     Image." EBONY 27 (August 1972): 144-48.

278. Greenberg, Bradley S. "Children's Reactions to
     TV Blacks." JOURNALISM Q 49 (Spring 1972):
     5-14.

279. _____. LIFE ON TELEVISION: CONTENT ANALYSIS
     OF U.S. TV DRAMA. Norwood, N.J: Ablex Pub-
     lishing Corporation, 1980.

280. _____, and Thomas F. Gordon. SOCIAL CLASS AND
     RACIAL DIFFERENCES IN CHILDREN'S PERCEP-
     TIONS OF TELEVISION VIOLENCE (Project Vio-
     lence in the Media, Report no. 3). East
     Lansing, Mich.: Department of Communica-
     tion, Michigan State University, 1971.

281. _____, and Gerhard J. Hanneman. "Racial Atti-
     tudes and the Impact of TV Blacks." EDUCA-
     TIONAL BROADCASTING R 4 (April 1970): 27-
     34.

282. _____, and Sherrie L. Mazingo. RACIAL ISSUES
     IN MASS MEDIA INSTITUTIONS (item I-61).

283. _____, and Byron Reeves. "Children and the
     Perceived Reality of Television." J OF
     SOCIAL ISSUES 32 (Fall 1976): 86-97.

284. _____, and Katrina W. Simmons, Linda Hogan,
     and Charles Atkin. "Three Seasons of Tele-
     vision Characters: A Demographic Analysis."
     J OF BROADCASTING 24 (Winter 1980): 49-60.

285. _____, and Brenda Dervin, eds. USE OF THE
     MASS MEDIA BY THE URBAN POOR: FINDINGS OF

THREE RESEARCH PROJECTS, WITH AN ANNOTATED
BIBLIOGRAPHY. New York: Praeger, 1970.

286. Greene, Laura. "A Bad Black Image in Film."
ESSENCE 4 (May 1973): 70.

287. Grenier, Richard. "Black Comedy." COMMENTARY
73 (no. 6 1982): 54-58.

288. Griffith, D.W. THE RISE AND FALL OF FREE
SPEECH IN AMERICA. Los Angeles: privately
printed, 1916.

289. Grisham, William F. "Modes, Movies, and Mag-
nates: Early Filmmaking in Chicago." Ph.D.
diss., Northwestern University, 1982.

290. Gross, Larry. "The Cultivation of Intolerance:
Television, Blacks and Gays." CULTURAL
INDICATORS: AN INTERNATIONAL SYMPOSIUM.
Edited by Gabriele Melischek, Karl Erik
Rosengren, and James Stappers. Vienna,
Austria: Verlag der Osterreichischen Akade-
mie der Wissenschaften, 1984, pp. 345-63.

291. [Gulliver, Adelaide Cromwell, ed.]. BLACK
IMAGES IN FILMS, STEREOTYPING, AND SELF-
PERCEPTION AS VIEWED BY BLACK ACTRESSES.
Boston: Afro-American Studies Program, Bos-
ton University, 1974.

292. Hairston, Loyle. "The Black Film--'Supernig-
ger' as Folk Hero." FREEDOMWAYS 14 (Third
Quarter 1974): 218-22.

293. Halliburton, Cecil D. "Hollywood Presents Us:
The Movies and Racial Attitudes." OPPOR-
TUNITY 13 (October 1935): 296-97.

294. Halliday, Jon, ed. SIRK ON SIRK: INTERVIEW
WITH JON HALLIDAY. London: Secker & War-
burg, 1971.

295. Hammond, Allen Steward. "Mammies, Coons, Bucks
and 'Good Times': The Evidence of Negative
Black Stereotypes in Prime Time Television:
Implications for Public Policy." M.A.the-

sis, Annenberg School of Communications, University of Pennsylvania, 1977.

296. Hammond, John. "South Carolina's Reaction to the Photoplay, 'The Birth of a Nation.'" PROCEEDINGS OF THE SOUTH CAROLINA HISTORI-CAL ASSOCIATION. Columbia: South Carolina Historical Association, 1963, pp. 30-40.

297. Hardwick, Leon H. "Negro Stereotypes on the Screen." HOLLYWOOD Q 1 (1945-46): 234-36.

298. Harmon, Sidney. "How Hollywood Is Smashing the Colour Bar." FILMS AND FILMING 5 (March 1959): 7ff.

299. Harrison, William. "The Negro in the Cinema." SIGHT AND SOUND 9 (Spring 1939): 16-17.

300. Hart, James, ed. THE MAN WHO INVENTED HOLLY-WOOD: THE AUTOBIOGRAPHY OF D.W. GRIFFITH. Louisville, Ky.: Touchstone, 1972.

301. Hartung, Philip T. "Trillions for Brewster." COMMONWEAL 42 (May 11, 1945): 94-95.

302. Harwell, Richard ,ed. GONE WITH THE WIND AS BOOK AND FILM. Columbia: University of South Carolina Press, 1983.

303. Haskell, Molly. FROM REVERENCE TO RAPE: THE TREATMENT OF WOMEN IN THE MOVIES. Balti-more: Penguin, 1974.

304. Hayakawa, S.I. "Television and the American Negro." ETC: A REVIEW OF GENERAL SEMANTICS 20 (no. 4 1963): 395-410.

305. Head, Sydney. "Content Analysis of Television Drama Programs" (item I-67).

306. Heald, Gary Robert. "Television and Children's Images of Occupations." Ph.D. diss., Michi-gan State University, 1977.

307. Hellenbrand, Harold. "Bigger Thomas Recon-sidered: Native Son, Film and King Kong." J OF AMERICAN CULTURE 6 (no. 1 1983): 84-95.

308. Henderson, Robert M. D.W. GRIFFITH: HIS LIFE
     AND WORK. New York: Oxford University
     Press, 1972.

309. Henry, William A., III. "The Jeffersons: Black
     Like Nobody." CHANNELS OF COMMUNICATION 2
     (March/April 1983): 62-63.

310. Hernton, Calvin C. "And You, Too, Sidney Poi-
     tier!" WHITE PAPERS FOR WHITE AMERICANS.
     Edited by Calvin C. Hernton. New York:
     Doubleday, 1966, pp. 53-70.

311. Herring, Robert. "Black Shadows." CLOSE UP 5
     (August 1929): 97-104.

312. Higgins, Patricia Beaulieu, and Marla Wilson
     Ray. TELEVISION'S ACTION ARSENAL: WEAPON
     USE IN PRIME TIME. [Washington, D.C.]: U.S.
     Conference of Mayors, 1978.

313. Higham, Charles, and Joel Greenberg. HOLLYWOOD
     IN THE FORTIES (item I-69).

314. _____. THE HOLLYWOOD MUSE: HOLLYWOOD DIREC-
     TORS SPEAK. Chicago: Henry Regnery Company,
     1969.

315. Hill, Donald K. "The Broadcast Industry and
     Black Cultural Restitution." R OF BLACK
     POLITICAL ECONOMY 1 (Autumn 1970): 83-98.

316. Hill-Scott, Karen. "Moving Beyond Ethnic Ster-
     eotypes: Black Americans." TELEVISION &
     CHILDREN 7 (Winter 1984): 20-24.

317. Hinton, James L., and John F. Seggar, Herbert
     C. Northcott, and Brian F. Fontes. "Token-
     ism and Improving Imagery of Blacks in TV
     Drama and Comedy: 1973." J OF BROADCASTING
     18 (Fall 1974): 423-32.

318. Hirsch, Foster. "Uncle Tom Is Becoming a
     Superhero." READERS AND WRITERS 3 (November
     1968): 12-14.

319. Hoberman, J[im]. "Bad Movies." FILM COMMENT 16
     (July-August 1980): 7-12.

320. Hobson, Dick. "The Odyssey of Otis Young." TV
     GUIDE 17 (March 1, 1969): 18-22.

321. Hobson, Sheila Smith. "The Rise and Fall of
     Blacks in Serious Television." FREEDOMWAYS
     14 (Third Quarter 1974): 185-99.

322. Hoffman, William. SIDNEY. New York: Lyle
     Stuart, 1971.

323. Holly, Ellen. "How Black Do You Have To Be?"
     NEW YORK TIMES, September 15, 1968, II, pp.
     1, 5.

324. _____. "Where Are the Films About Real Black
     Men and Women?" NEW YORK TIMES, June 2,
     1974, II, p. 11.

325. Hough, Arthur. "Trials and Tribulations: Thir-
     ty Years of Sitcom." UNDERSTANDING TELEVI-
     SION: ESSAYS ON TELEVISION AS A SOCIAL AND
     CULTURAL FORCE. Edited by Richard P. Adler.
     New York: Praeger, 1981, pp. 201-23.

326. Howard, John, and George Rothbart and Lee
     Sloan. "The Response to 'Roots': A National
     Survey." J OF BROADCASTING 22 (Summer
     1978): 279-87.

327. Hoyt, Edwin P. PAUL ROBESON: THE AMERICAN
     OTHELLO. Cleveland: World Publishing, 1967.

328. Huff, Theodore. A SHORT ANALYSIS OF D.W.
     GRIFFITH'S "THE BIRTH OF A NATION." New
     York: Museum of Modern Art, 1961.

329. Hughes, Langston. "Is Hollywood Fair to Ne-
     groes?" NEGRO DIGEST 1 (April 1943): 19-21.

330. _____, and Milton Meltzer. BLACK MAGIC: A
     PICTORIAL HISTORY OF THE NEGRO IN AMERICAN
     ENTERTAINMENT. Englewood Cliffs, N.J.:
     Prentice-Hall, 1967.

331. Hunter, Robert G. "Hollywood and the Negro."
     NEGRO DIGEST 15 (May 1966): 37-41.

332. Hur, K. Kyoon. "Impact of 'Roots' on Black and

White Teenagers." J OF BROADCASTING 22 (Summer 1978): 289-98.

333. _____, and John P. Robinson. "The Social Impact of 'Roots.'" JOURNALISM Q 55 (Spring 1978): 19-24, 83.

334. _____. "A Uses and Gratifications Analysis of Viewing 'Roots' in Britain." JOURNALISM Q 58 (Winter 1981): 582-88.

335. Hurd, Laura E. "Director Ossie Davis Talks About 'Black Girl.'" BLACK CREATION 4 (Winter 1973): 38-39.

336. Hurley, Neil P., S.J. "Using Motion Pictures to Aid Inter-Cultural Communication." J OF COMMUNICATION 18 (June 1968): 97-108.

337. Hutchins, Charles, L. "A Critical Evaluation of the Controversies Engendered by D.W. Griffith's 'The Birth of a Nation.'" M.A. thesis, University of Iowa, 1961.

338. Hyatt, Marshall, ed. THE AFRO-AMERICAN CINE-MATIC EXPERIENCE: AN ANNOTATED BIBLIOGRAPHY & FILMOGRAPHY. Wilmington, Del.: Scholarly Resources, 1983.

339. Jackson, Anthony W., ed., BLACK FAMILIES AND THE MEDIUM OF TELEVISION. Ann Arbor: Bush Program in Child Development & Social Policy, University of Michigan, 1982.

340. Jackson, Harold. "From 'Amos 'n' Andy' to 'I Spy': Chronology of Blacks in Prime Time Network Television Programming, 1950-1964." Ph.D. diss., University of Michigan, 1982.

341. Jarvie, I.C. MOVIES AS SOCIAL CRITICISM (item I-71).

342. Jeffries-Fox, Suzanne Kuulei. "Television's Contribution to Young People's Conceptions About Occupations." Ph.D. diss., Annenberg School of Communications, University of Pennsylvania, 1978.

343. Jerome, Victor Jeremy. THE NEGRO IN HOLLYWOOD
     FILMS. New York: Masses & Mainstream, 1950.

344. _____. "The Negro in Hollywood Films." POLI-
     TICAL AFFAIRS 29 (June 1950): 58-92.

345. Jewell, Karen Sue Warren. "An Analysis of the
     Visual Development of a Stereotype: The
     Media's Portrayal of Mammy and Aunt Jemima
     as Symbols of Black Womanhood." Ph.D.
     diss., Ohio State University, 1976.

346. Johnson, Albert. "Beige, Brown, or Black."
     FILM Q 13 (Fall 1959): 38-43.

347. _____. "The Negro in American Films: Some
     Recent Works." FILM Q 18 (Summer 1965):
     14-30.

348. Johnson, Sherry. "How Soaps Whitewash Blacks."
     AMERICAN FILM 7 (March 1982): 36-37.

349. Jones, Christopher John. "Image and Ideology
     in Kazan's Pinky." LITERATURE/FILM Q 9
     (no. 2 1981): 110-20.

350. Jones, Marquita. "Racism in Television." BLACK
     WORLD 20 (March 1971): 72-78.

351. Jones, Robert. "How Hollywood Feels About
     Negroes." NEGRO DIGEST 5 (August 1947): 4-
     8.

352. Jordan, Vernon E., Jr. "How Hollywood Degrades
     Blacks." NEW YORK AMSTERDAM NEWS, October
     14, 1972, D, p. 1.

353. Joseph, Gloria I., and Jill Lewis. COMMON
     DIFFERENCES: CONFLICTS IN BLACK AND WHITE
     FEMINIST PERSPECTIVES. Garden City, N.Y.:
     Anchor Press/Doubleday, 1981.

354. Jouhaud, C. "Black African Themes in European,
     American, Japanese and African Films from
     the Standpoint of Social History." MOUVE-
     MENT SOCIAL (France) no. 126 (1984): 83-89.

355. Jowett, Garth. FILM: THE DEMOCRATIC ART (item I-74).

356. Kael, Pauline. "Notes on Black Movies." THE NEW YORKER 48 (December 2, 1972): 159-65.

357. Kagan, Norman. "Amos 'n' Andy: Twenty Years Late, or Two Decades Early?" J OF POPULAR CULTURE 6 (Summer 1972): 71-75.

358. _____. "Black American Cinema: A Primer." CINEMA 6 (Fall 1970): 2-7.

359. _____. "The Dark Horse Operas: A Film Article." NEGRO HISTORY BULLETIN 36 (January 1973): 13-14.

360. _____. "The Return of the Emperor Jones." NEGRO HISTORY BULLETIN 34 (November 1971): 160-62.

361. Kaiser, Ernest. "Black Images in the Mass Media: A Bibliography." FREEDOMWAYS 14 (Third Quarter 1974): 274-87.

362. _____, ed. A FREEDOMWAYS READER: AFRO-AMERICA IN THE SEVENTIES. New York: International Publishers, 1977.

363. Kalson, Alfred E. "Animal Man Meets the Human Animal." J OF POPULAR CULTURE 5 (Fall 1971): 469-75.

364. Kassarjian, Waltraud M. "Blacks as Communicators and Interpreters of Mass Communication." JOURNALISM Q 50 (Summer 1973): 285-91, 305.

365. Kauffman, Stanley. "The Mack." THE NEW REPUBLIC 168 (April 28, 1973): 20ff.

366. Kelley, Samuel Lawrence. "The Evolution of Character Portrayals in the Films of Sidney Poitier, 1950-1978." Ph.D. diss., University of Michigan, 1980; New York: Garland Press, 1983.

367. Killens, John Oliver. "A Black Writer Views

TV." TV GUIDE 18 (July 25, 1970): 6-9.

368. _____. "Hollywood in Black and White." THE
     NATION 201 (September 20, 1965): 157-60.

369. Kirby, Jack Temple. "D.W. Griffith's Racial
     Portraiture" (item I-80).

370. _____. MEDIA-MADE DIXIE: THE SOUTH IN THE
     AMERICAN IMAGINATION. Baton Rouge: Louisi-
     ana State University Press, 1978.

371. Kisner, Ronald E. "What Films Are Doing to the
     Image of Black Women." JET, June 29, 1972,
     pp. 56-61.

372. Kliman, Bernice W. "The Biscuit Eater: Racial
     Stereotypes, 1939-1972." PHYLON 39 (March
     1978): 87-96.

373. Klotman, Phyllis Rauch. FRAME BY FRAME--A
     BLACK FILMOGRAPHY. Bloomington: Indiana
     University Press, 1979.

374. Knight, Arthur. THE LIVELIEST ART: A PANORAMIC
     HISTORY OF THE MOVIES. New York: MacMillan,
     1957.

375. _____. "The Negro in Films Today: Hollywood's
     New Cycle." FILMS IN REVIEW 1 (February
     1950): 14-19.

376. Koiner, Richard B. "The Black Image on TV."
     TELEVISION Q 17 (Summer 1980): 39-46.

377. Kraus, Sidney. "Modifying Prejudice: Attitude
     Change As a Function of the Race of the
     Communicator." AUDIO VISUAL COMMUNICATION R
     10 (January-February 1962): 14-22.

378. Landay, Eileen [Eileen Rosenbaum]. BLACK FILM
     STARS. New York: Drake Publishers, 1973.

379. Landry, Robert J. "Films, Poitier and Race
     Riots." VARIETY, January 3, 1968, p. 12.

380. Lange, David L., and Robert K. Baker, and
     Sandra J. Ball, eds. MASS MEDIA AND VIO-

LENCE: A REPORT TO THE NATIONAL COMMISSION
ON THE CAUSES AND PREVENTION OF VIOLENCE.
Washington, D.C.:   G.P.O., November 1969.

381. Lapsansky, Emma Jones. "Distorted Reflections:
     Thoughts on Afro-Americans and American
     Visual Imagery." ETHNIC IMAGES IN AMERICAN
     FILM AND TELEVISION (item I-105), pp. 11-
     15.

382. Lawson, John Howard. FILM: THE CREATIVE PRO-
     CESS, THE SEARCH FOR AN AUDIO-VISUAL LAN-
     GUAGE AND STRUCTURE. New York: Hill & Wang,
     1967.

383. _____. FILM IN THE BATTLE OF IDEAS. New York:
     Masses & Mainstream, 1953.

384. Leab, Daniel J. "'All-Colored'--But Not Much
     Different: Films Made for Negro Ghetto
     Audiences, 1913-1928." PHYLON 36 (September
     1975): 321-39.

385. _____. "The Black in Films: An Annotated
     Bibliography." J OF POPULAR FILM 4 (no. 4
     1975): 345-56.

386. _____. "The Blue Collar Ethnic in Bicenten-
     nial America: Rocky." AMERICAN HISTORY/
     AMERICAN FILM (item I-113), pp. 257-72.

387. _____. FROM SAMBO TO SUPERSPADE: THE BLACK
     EXPERIENCE IN MOTION PICTURES. Boston:
     Houghton Mifflin, 1975.

388. _____. "From 'Sambo' to 'Superspade': The
     Black in Film." FILM & HISTORY 2 (September
     1972): 1-6.

389. _____. "From Sambo to Superspade: The Black
     Man in American Film--The Historical Devel-
     opment of an Image." ZEITGESCHICHTE IN FILM
     UND FERNSEHEN. Edited by K.F. Reimers and
     H. Frierich. Munich, West Germany: Verlag
     Olschlager, 1982, pp. 249-61.

390. _____. "The Gamut from A to B: The Image of
     the Black in Pre-1915 Movies." POLITICAL

SCIENCE Q 88 (March 1973): 53-70.

391. _____. "Harlem Rides the Range." CULTURAL
AFFAIRS no. 5 (1969): 29-31.

392. _____. "The Negro in American Film, 1945-
1955." FILMS OF SOCIAL COMMENT: BACKGROUND
MATERIAL FOR A STUDY SEMINAR ON SOCIAL
REALISM AND CRITICISM IN THE AMERICAN CINE-
MA, SPONSORED BY THE AMERICAN HOUSES IN
HAMBURG AND FRANKFURT, FEBRUARY, 1973.
Edited by Herbert Graf. Bonn, West Germany:
Cultural Program Office, United States
Embassy, 1973, appendix (52pp.).

393. _____. "A Pale Black Imitation: All-Colored
Films, 1930-60." J OF POPULAR FILM 4 (no. 1
1975): 56-76.

394. Leahy, Michael, and Wallis Annenberg. "Discrimination in Hollywood: How Bad Is It?"
(item I-87).

395. Leckenby, John D. "Attribution of Dogmatism to
TV Characters." JOURNALISM Q 54 (Spring
1977): 14-19.

396. _____, and Stuart H. Surlin. "Incidental
Social Learning and Viewer Race: 'All in
the Family' and 'Sanford and Son.'" J OF
BROADCASTING 20 (Fall 1976): 481-94.

397. Lee, Don L. "The Bittersweet of Sweetback: Or,
Shake Yo Money Maker." BLACK WORLD 21 (November 1971): 43-48.

398. Lemon, Judith. "Women and Blacks on Prime-Time
Television." J OF COMMUNICATION 27 (Autumn
1977): 70-79.

399. Lemon, Richard. "Black Is the Color of TV's
Newest Stars." SATURDAY EVENING POST 241
(November 30, 1968): 42-44.

400. Lemons, J. Stanley. "Black Stereotypes as
Reflected in Popular Culture, 1880-1920."
AMERICAN Q 29 (Spring 1977): 102-16.

401. Levinson, Richard, and William Link. STAY
     TUNED (item I-89).

402. Lewis, Richard Warren. "Cosby Takes Over."TV
     GUIDE 17 (October 4, 1969): 12-15.

403. _____. "The Importance of Being Julia." TV
     GUIDE 16 (December 14, 1968): 24-28.

404. Liebert, Robert M., and John M. Neale, and
     Emily S. Davidson. THE EARLY WINDOW: EF-
     FECTS OF TELEVISION ON CHILDREN AND YOUTH.
     New York: Pergamon Press, 1973.

405. Low, W. Augustus, and Virgil A. Clift, eds.
     ENCYCLOPEDIA OF BLACK AMERICA. New York:
     McGraw-Hill, 1981.

406. McBride, Joseph. "Stepin' Fetchit Talks Back."
     FILM Q 24 (Summer 1971): 20-26.

407. McCabe, Bruce. "On and Off Camera, Blacks Get
     Few Roles." BOSTON GLOBE, April 18, 1982.

408. MacConkey, Dorothy Ingling. "Teens and the
     Mass Media: A Study of Black and White
     Adolescents and Their Use of Mass Media."
     Ph.D. diss., University of Maryland, 1974.

409. McClure, Arthur F. "Hollywood at War: The
     American Motion Picture and World War II"
     (item I-91).

410. McCray, Charles, Jr. "Blue Collar and The
     Traitors." RACE AND ETHNICITY IN THE HIS-
     TORY OF THE AMERICAS (item I-36), 26-28.

411. McDermott, Steven Thomas. "The Influence of
     Communication on Black Children's Self-
     Concept." Ph.D. diss., Michigan State Uni-
     versity, 1982.

412. MacDonald, J. Fred. "Black Perimeters--Paul
     Robeson, Nat King Cole and the Role of
     Blacks in American TV." J OF POPULAR FILM
     & TELEVISION 7 (no. 3 1979): 246-64.

413. _____. BLACKS AND WHITE TV: AFRO-AMERICANS IN

TELEVISION SINCE 1948. Chicago: Nelson-Hall, 1983.

414. MacDonald Susan Schwartz. "Learning About Crime: Conceptions of Crime and Law Enforcement as They Relate to Use of Television and Other Information Sources." Ph.D. diss., Annenberg School of Communications, University of Pennsylvania, 1977.

415. McFarland, Ronald-Bryant. "A Critique of the TV Presentation of Roots I." FREEDOMWAYS 19 (Second Quarter 1979): 87-94.

416. McGilligan, Patrick. "Summing Up the Seventies: Transitions." AMERICAN FILM 5 (December 1979): 26, 50-52.

417. McKerns, Joseph P. "Television Docudramas: The Image as History." JOURNALISM HISTORY 7 (Spring 1980): 24-25, 40.

418. McManus, John T., and Louis Kronenberger. "Motion Pictures, the Theater, and Race Relations." ANNALS OF THE AMERICAN ACADEMY OF POLITICAL AND SOCIAL SCIENCE 244 (March 1946): 152-58.

419. _____. "Hollywood's New Deal for Negroes." NEGRO DIGEST 4 (June 1946): 77-80.

420. Maloney, Martin. "Black Is the Color of Our New TV." TV GUIDE 16 (November 16, 1968): 7-10.

421. Maltby, Richard. HARMLESS ENTERTAINMENT: HOLLYWOOD AND THE IDEOLOGY OF CONSENSUS (item I-95).

422. Mankiewicz, Frank, and Joel Swerdlow. REMOTE CONTROL: TELEVISION AND THE MANIPULATION OF AMERICAN LIFE. New York: Times Books, 1978.

423. Mapp, Edward. BLACKS IN AMERICAN FILMS: TODAY AND YESTERDAY. Metuchen, N.J.: Scarecrow Press, 1972.

424. _____. "Black Women in Films." BLACK SCHOLAR 13 (Summer 1982): 36-40.

425. _____. "Black Women in Films: A Mixed Bag of Tricks." BLACK FILMS AND FILM-MAKERS (item II-488), pp. 196-205.

426. _____. "The Image Makers." NEGRO HISTORY BULLETIN 26 (December 1962): 127-28.

427. _____. "The Portrayal of the Negro in American Motion Pictures, 1962-1968." Ph.D. diss., New York University, 1970.

428. Marshall, Pluria. "The Role of Advocacy Groups." BLACK FAMILIES AND THE MEDIUM OF TELEVISION (item II-339), pp. 71-74.

429. Martin, Bruce A. "An Investigation of the Image of American Men as Portrayed in Selected Commercial Prime Time Television Programs, TV Seasons 1950-51 Through 1975-76." Ph.D. diss., New York University, 1980.

430. Mason, B.J. "The New Films: Culture or Con Game?" EBONY 28 (December 1972): 60-62ff.

431. Mason, Clifford. "Why Does White America Love Sidney So?" NEW YORK TIMES, September 10, 1967, II, p. 1ff.

432. Maynard, Richard. "Everything But a Man: The Black Man in the Movies." THE CELLULOID CURRICULUM: HOW TO USE MOVIES IN THE CLASSROOM. Edited by Richard A. Maynard. New York: Hayden Book Company, 1971, pp. 148-64.

433. _____, ed. THE BLACK MAN ON FILM: RACIAL STEREOTYPING. Rochelle Park, N.J.: Hayden Book Company, 1974.

434. Meehan, Diana M. LADIES OF THE EVENING: WOMEN CHARACTERS OF PRIME-TIME TELEVISION. Metuchen, N.J.: Scarecrow Press, 1983.

435. Mellen, Joan. BIG BAD WOLVES: MASCULINITY IN

THE AMERICAN FILM. New York: Pantheon,
      1977.

436. _____. "Hollywood's 'Political' Cinema." CI-
      NEASTE 5 (Spring 1972): 26-31.

437. Merritt, Bishetta D. "A Historical-Critical
      Study of a Pressure Group in Broadcasting--
      Black Efforts for Soul in Television."
      Ph.D. diss., Ohio State University, 1974.

438. Merritt, M. "A Giant Step Sideways from 'Sap-
      phire' to 'Billie.'" VILLAGE VOICE 18
      (February 1, 1973): 65.

439. Merritt, Russell. "Dixon, Griffith, and the
      Southern Legend." CINEMA J 12 (Fall 1972):
      26-45.

440. _____. "The Impact of D.W. Griffith's Motion
      Pictures from 1908 to 1914 on Contemporary
      American Culture." Ph.D. diss., Harvard
      University, 1970.

441. Metzger, Charles R. "Pressure Groups and the
      Motion Picture Industry." ANNALS OF THE
      AMERICAN ACADEMY OF POLITICAL AND SOCIAL
      SCIENCE 254 (November 1947): 110-15.

442. Michener, Charles. "Black Movies: Renaissance
      or Ripoff?" NEWSWEEK 80 (October 23, 1972):
      74-79ff.

443. Miller, Loren. "Hollywood's New Negro Films."
      THE CRISIS 45 (January 1938): 8-9.

444. _____. "Uncle Tom in Hollywood." THE CRISIS
      41 (November 1934): 329, 336.

445. Mills, Jon, II. "Blackness in Televisionland."
      ESSENCE 6 (April 1976): 15.

446. Monaco, James. AMERICAN FILM NOW (item I-107).

447. _____. "Roots and Angels: U.S. Television,
      1976-77." SIGHT AND SOUND 46 (Summer 1977):
      158-61.

448. Moore, Melvin M., Jr. "Blackface in Prime Time." SMALL VOICES AND GREAT TRUMPETS (item I-129), pp. 117-40.

449. Morrow, Lance. "Blacks on TV: A Disturbing Image." TIME 111 (March 27, 1978): 101-102.

450. Morseberger, Robert. "Adrift in Steinbeck's Lifeboat." LITERATURE/FILM Q 4 (Fall 1976): 325-38.

451. _____. "Slavery and The Sante Fe Trail, or, John Brown on Hollywood's Sour Apple Tree." AMERICAN STUDIES 18 (Fall 1977): 87-98.

452. Moss, Carlton. "The Negro in American Films." FREEDOMWAYS 3 (Spring 1963): 134-42.

453. _____. "Problems Facing Blacks in Film." BLACK IMAGES IN FILMS, STEREOTYPING, AND SELF-PERCEPTION (item II-291), pp. 21-27.

454. Muccigrosso, Robert. "Television and the Urban Crisis." SCREEN AND SOCIETY: THE IMPACT OF TELEVISION UPON ASPECTS OF CONTEMPORARY CIVILIZATION. Edited by Frank J. Coppa. Chicago: Nelson-Hall, 1979, pp. 31-57.

455. Murray, James P. "Black Movies and Music in Harmony." BLACK CREATION 5 (Fall 1973): 9-11.

456. _____. "Do We Really Have Time for a 'Shaft?'" BLACK CREATION 3 (Winter 1972): 12-14.

457. _____. "The Independents: Hard Road for the Old and New." BLACK CREATION 3 (Spring 1972): 8-11.

458. _____. "Running with Sweetback." BLACK CREATION 3 (Fall 1971): 10-12.

459. _____. TO FIND AN IMAGE: BLACK FILMS FROM UNCLE TOM TO SUPER FLY. Indianapolis: Bobbs-Merrill Company, 1973.

460. Murray, John P., and Eli A. Rubinstein, and

George A. Comstock, eds. TELEVISION AND
SOCIAL BEHAVIOR: REPORTS AND PAPERS. A
TECHNICAL REPORT TO THE SURGEON GENERAL'S
SCIENTIFIC ADVISORY COMMITTEE ON TELEVISION
AND SOCIAL BEHAVIOR. Rockville, Md.: Na-
tional Institute of Mental Health, 1972.

461. National Association for the Advancement of
Colored People. FIGHTING A VICIOUS FILM:
PROTEST AGAINST "THE BIRTH OF A NATION."
Boston: Boston Branch, NAACP, 1915.

462. _____. A POSITION PAPER AGAINST THE AIRING OF
BEULAH LAND: A CALL TO CREATE, NURTURE AND
PROTECT POSITIVE BLACK IMAGES. New York:
NAACP, 1980.

463. Neal, Larry. "Beware of the Tar Baby." NEW
YORK TIMES, August 3, 1969, II, p. 13.

464. Nelsen, Anne K., and Hart M. Nelsen. "The
Prejudicial Film: Progress and Stalemate,
1915-1967." PHYLON 31 (Summer 1970): 142-
47.

465. Nelson, Richard Alan. "Florida and the American Motion Picture Industry, 1898-1930." 2
vols. Ph.D. diss., Florida State University, 1980; New York: Garland Press, 1983.

466. Nesteby, James R. BLACK IMAGES IN AMERICAN
FILMS, 1896-1954. Washington, D.C.: University Press of America, 1982.

467. _____. "The Tarzan Series of Edgar Rice Bur-
roughs: Lost Races and Racism in American
Popular Culture." Ph.D. diss., Bowling
Green State University, 1978.

468. Newcomb, Horace. TV: THE MOST POPULAR ART.
Garden City, N.Y.: Anchor Press, 1974.

469. Newton, Huey P. "He Won't Bleed Me: A Revolu-
tionary Analysis of 'Sweet Sweetback's
Baadasssss Song.'" THE BLACK PANTHER 6
(June 19, 1971): A-L.

470. Noble, Gil. BLACK IS THE COLOR OF MY TV TUBE.
Secaucus, N.J.: Lyle Stuart, 1981.

471. _____. "Entertainment, Politics, and the Movie Business: An Interview with Sidney Poitier." CINEASTE 8 (no. 3 [1978]): 17-23.

472. Noble, Peter. "The Coming of Sound Film." ANTHOLOGY OF THE NEGRO IN THE THEATRE (item II-487), pp. 247-66.

473. _____. THE NEGRO IN FILMS. London: Skelton Robinson, 1948.

474. Nolan, William F. "Southern Pride: When Holly-wood Intrudes into the Race Problem." FILMS AND FILMING 8 (April 1962): 21ff.

475. Northcott, Herbert C., and John F. Seggar, and James L. Hinton. "Trends in TV Portrayal of Blacks and Women." JOURNALISM Q 52 (Winter 1975): 741-44.

476. Null, Gary. BLACK HOLLYWOOD: THE NEGRO IN MOTION PICTURES. Secaucus, N.J.: Citadel Press, 1975.

477. Obatala, J.K. "Blacks on TV: A Replay of Amos 'n' Andy?" LOS ANGELES TIMES, November 26, 1974, V, p. 5.

478. O'Brien, Adrienne. "Public Relations of Anti-Stereotype Television Spots." PUBLIC RELA-TIONS REVIEW 6 (Fall 1980): 14-22.

479. O'Dell, Paul. GRIFFITH AND THE RISE OF HOLLY-WOOD (item I-114).

480. O'Kelly, Charlotte G., and Linda Edwards Bloomquist. "Women and Blacks on TV." J OF COMMUNICATION 26 (Autumn 1976): 179-84.

481. O'Neal, Mary. "Tricked by Flicks." ESSENCE 5 (October 1974): 17.

482. Pandiani, John A. "Crime Time TV: If All We Knew Is What We Saw." CONTEMPORARY CRISES 2 (October 1978): 437-58.

483. Paperny, David Charles. "Race, Social Class, and Children's Interpretations of Televi-

sion." M.A. thesis, Annenberg School of
Communications, University of Pennsylvania,
1982.

484. Patterson, Lindsay. "Hollywood's Boy and Girl
Next Door--Color Them White." NEW YORK
TIMES, June 16, 1968, II, p. 8.

485. _____. "In Movies, Whitey Is Still King." NEW
YORK TIMES, December 13, 1970, II, p. 17.

486. _____. "The Negro in the Performing Arts." IN
BLACK AMERICA 1968: THE YEAR OF AWAKENING.
Edited by Patricia W. Romero. New York:
Publishers Company, 1969, pp. 247-55.

487. _____, ed. ANTHOLOGY OF THE NEGRO IN THE
THEATRE: A CRITICAL APPROACH. New York:
Publishers Company, Inc., 1967.

488. _____. BLACK FILMS AND FILM-MAKERS: A COMPRE-
HENSIVE ANTHOLOGY FROM STEREOTYPE TO SUPER-
HERO. New York: Dodd, Mead & Company, 1975.

489. Peavy, Charles D. "Black Consciousness and the
Contemporary Cinema." POPULAR CULTURE AND
THE EXPANDING CONSCIOUSNESS. Edited by Ray
B. Browne. New York: Wiley, 1973, pp. 178-
200.

490. [Perry, Lincoln]. "'I'm No Derogatory Black
Image': Stepin' Fetchit." JET, May 3, 1973,
p. 61.

491. Peters, Art. "What the Negro Wants from TV."
TV GUIDE 16 (January 20, 1968): 6-10.

492. Peterson, Bernard L., Jr. "The Films of Oscar
Micheaux: America's First Fabulous Black
Filmmaker." THE CRISIS 86 (no.4 1979):
136-41.

493. Pierce, Chester M., and Jean V. Carew, Diane
Pierce-Gonzalez, and Deborah Wills. "An
Experiment in Racism: TV Commercials."
EDUCATIONAL AND URBAN SOCIOLOGY 10 (no. 1
1977): 61-87.

494. Pines, Jim. BLACKS IN THE CINEMA: THE CHANGING IMAGE. London: British Film Institute, 1971.

495. _____. BLACKS IN FILMS: A SURVEY OF RACIAL THEMES AND IMAGES IN THE AMERICAN FILM. London: Studio Vista, 1975.

496. _____. "Coon Show." IT (G.B.) no. 79 (May 8-21, 1970): 3.

497. Pinsky, Mark T. "Racism, History and Mass Media." JUMP CUT no. 28 (1983): 66-67.

498. Ploski, Harry A., and Ernest Kaiser, comps. and eds. THE NEGRO ALMANAC. New York: The Bellwether Company, 1971.

499. Plotkin, Lawrence. THE FREQUENCY OF NEGRO APPEARANCE IN TELEVISED COMMERCIALS. New York: NAACP Legal Defense Fund, 1967.

500. _____. THE FREQUENCY OF NEGRO APPEARANCE ON TELEVISED COMMERCIALS. New York: NAACP Legal Defense & Educational Fund, 1970.

501. _____, and D. Pugh. THE FREQUENCY OF APPEARANCE OF NEGROES IN TELEVISION. New York: New York Society for Ethical Culture, 1962.

502. _____. THE FREQUENCY OF APPEARANCE OF NEGROES IN TELEVISION. New York: New York Society for Ethical Culture, 1964.

503. Poindexter, Paula M., and Carolyn A. Stroman. "Blacks and Television: A Review of the Research Literature." J OF BROADCASTING 25 (Spring 1981): 103-22.

504. Poitier, Sidney. THIS LIFE. New York: Ballantine Books, 1981.

505. _____. "Walking the Hollywood Color Line." AMERICAN FILM 5 (April 1980): 24-29.

506. Popkin, Henry. "Hollywood Tackles the Race Issue." COMMENTARY 24 (October 1957): 354-57.

507. Potamkin, Harry A. "The Aframerican Cinema."
     CLOSE UP 5 (August 1929): 107-17.

508. Pounds, Michael C. "Details in Black: A Case
     Study Investigation and Analysis of the
     Content of the United States War Department
     Non-Fiction Motion Picture, The Negro Sol-
     dier." 2 vols. Ph.D. diss., New York Uni-
     versity, 1982.

509. Poussaint, Alvin F. "Blaxploitation Movies:
     Cheap Thrills That Degrade Blacks." PSY-
     CHOLOGY TODAY 7 (February 1974): 22, 26-
     27ff.

510. Powers, Anne, comp. and ed. BLACKS IN AMERICAN
     MOVIES: A SELECTED BIBLIOGRAPHY. Metuchen,
     N.J.: Scarecrow Press, 1974.

511. Prelutsky, Burt. "Hollywood's Negroes Mired in
     Stereotypes." LOS ANGELES TIMES, February
     19, 1967.

512. Protinsky, Ruth A., and Terry M. Wildman.
     "Roots: Reflections from the Classroom." J
     OF NEGRO EDUCATION 48 (no. 2 1979): 171-81.

513. Pyron, Darden Asbury, ed., RECASTING: GONE
     WITH THE WIND IN AMERICAN CULTURE. Miami:
     University Presses of Florida, 1983.

514. Rabinowitz, Dorothy. "Watching the Sit-coms."
     COMMENTARY 60 (October 1975): 69-71.

515. Raddatz, Leslie. "Mama." TV GUIDE 23 (January
     18, 1975): 20-22.

516. Ramsaye, Terry. A MILLION AND ONE NIGHTS (item
     I-121).

517. Reddick, Lawrence D. "Educational Programs for
     the Improvement of Race Relations: Motion
     Pictures, Radio, the Press and Libraries."
     J OF NEGRO EDUCATION 13 (Summer 1944): 367-
     89.

518. Reid, P.M. "Racial Stereotyping on TV: A Com-
     parison of the Behavior of Both Black and

White Television Characters." J OF APPLIED PSYCHOLOGY 64 (October 1979): 465-71.

519. Rife, Marilyn Diane. "The Black Image in American TV: The First Two Decades." BLACK SCHOLAR 6 (November 1974): 7-15.

520. Riley, Clayton. "The Black Critic-Theater and Film." NEW YORK AMSTERDAM NEWS, September 18, 1971, D, p. 18.

521. _____. "John Wayne Dethroned: On and Off Screen Racism." EBONY 27 (September 1972): 127-28.

522. _____. "What Makes Sweetback Run?" NEW YORK TIMES, May 9, 1971, II, p. 11.

523. Roberts, Churchill. "The Portrayal of Blacks on Network Television." J OF BROADCASTING 15 (Winter 1970-71): 45-53.

524. Robertson, Stanley. "The Creative Process in Television Production." BLACK FAMILIES AND THE MEDIUM OF TELEVISION (item II-339), pp. 33-37.

525. Robinson, Louie. "TV Discovers the Black Man." EBONY 24 (February 1969): 30ff.

526. Robinson, Matt. "Images and Other Illusions." ESSENCE 9 (March 1979): 70-71ff.

527. Roddick, Nick. A NEW DEAL IN ENTERTAINMENT (item I-124).

528. Roffman, Peter, and Jim Purdy. THE HOLLYWOOD SOCIAL PROBLEM FILM (item I-125).

529. _____, and Bev Simpson. "Black Images on White Screens." CINEASTE 13 (no. 3 1984): 14-21.

530. Rollins, Peter C. "Will Rogers and the Relevance of Nostalgia.: Steamboat 'Round the Bend." AMERICAN HISTORY/AMERICAN FILM (item I-113), pp. 77-96.

531. Ronan, Margaret. "Black Films: Rip Off or
     Right On?" SENIOR SCHOLASTIC   101(December
     11, 1972): 8-9.

532. Rose, Willie Lee. RACE AND REGION IN AMERICAN
     HISTORICAL FICTION: FOUR EPISODES IN AMERI-
     CAN POPULAR CULTURE, AN INAUGURAL LECTURE
     DELIVERED BEFORE THE UNIVERSITY OF OXFORD
     ON 4 MAY 1978. Oxford, England: Clarendon
     Press, 1979.

533. Rosen, Marjorie. POPCORN VENUS: WOMEN, MOVIES,
     AND THE AMERICAN DREAM. New York: Avon,
     1974.

534. Rosenberg, Elaine. "Radio and Television."
     ENCYCLOPEDIA OF BLACK AMERICA (item II-
     405), pp. 723-26.

535. Ryan, Michael. "Working Class Film." TABLOID:
     A REVIEW OF MASS CULTURE AND EVERYDAY LIFE
     no. 5 (Winter 1982): 2-10.

536. Sampson, Henry T. BLACKS IN BLACK AND WHITE: A
     SOURCE BOOK ON BLACK FILMS. Metuchen, N.J.:
     Scarecrow Press, 1977.

537. Sarris, Andrew. "The Birth of a Nation, or
     White Power Back When." THE VILLAGE VOICE,
     July 17,1969, p.45;   July 24, 1969,   pp.
     37, 45.

538. _____. THE PRIMAL SCREEN: ESSAYS ON FILM AND
     RELATED SUBJECTS. New York: Simon & Schus-
     ter, 1973.

539. Schickel, Richard. "Artifacts of a Lost Cul-
     ture." TIME 123 (February 27, 1984): 102-
     103.

540. _____. D.W. GRIFFITH: AN AMERICAN LIFE. New
     York: Simon & Schuster, 1984.

541. Schiller, Herbert I. "The Mass Media and the
     Public Interest." TELEVISION TODAY (item
     II-570), pp. 53-69.

542. Schlinger, Mary Jane, and Joseph T. Plummer.

"Advertising in Black and White." J OF
MARKETING RESEARCH 9 (May 1972): 149-53.

543. See, Carolyn. "Diahann Carroll's Image." TV
GUIDE 18 (March 14, 1970): 26-28, 30.

544. Seggar, John F. "Television's Portrayal of
Minorities and Women, 1971-75." J OF BROAD-
CASTING 21 (Fall 1977): 435-46.

545. _____, and Jeffrey Hafen, and Helena Han-
nonen-Gladden. "Television's Portrayal of
Minorities and Women in Drama and Comedy
Drama, 1971-80." J OF BROADCASTING 25
(Summer 1981): 277-88.

546. _____, and Penny Wheeler. "The World of Work
on TV: Ethnic and Sex Representation in TV
Drama" (item I-133).

547. Shales, Tom. "The Emperor Jones." THE AMERI-
CAN FILM HERITAGE (item II-548), pp. 70-74.

548. _____, ed. THE AMERICAN FILM HERITAGE: IM-
PRESSIONS FROM THE AMERICAN FILM INSTITUTE.
Washington, D.C.: Acropolis Books, 1972.

549. Shaw, Ellen Torgeson. "Roxie Roker of The
Jeffersons." TV GUIDE 29 (April 4, 1981):
12-14.

550. Shayon, Robert Lewis. "Same Old Tunnel." SAT-
URDAY R 54 (September 4, 1971): 46.

551. Shepard, Thom, ed. "Beyond the 'Black Film':
An Interview with Gordon Parks." CINEASTE 8
(no. 2 [1977]): 38-40.

552. Shook, Mollie Stell Wiggins. "Changing the
Racial Attitudes of White Students Toward
Blacks Using Commercially Produced Films."
Ed.D. diss., Duke University, 1972.

553. Short, Bobby. BLACK AND WHITE BABY. New York:
Dodd, Mead, 1971.

554. Shosteck, Herschel. "Some Influences of Television on Civil Unrest." J OF BROADCASTING
13 (Fall 1969): 371-86.

168 ETHNIC AND RACIAL IMAGES

555. Sidney, P. Jay. "Anti-Negro Propaganda in Films." VISION: A JOURNAL OF FILM COMMENT 1 (Spring 1962): 22-23.

556. Silverman, Joan L. "The Birth of a Nation: Prohibition Propaganda." SOUTHERN Q 19 (Spring-Summer 1981): 23-30.

557. Simmons, Katrina W., and Bradley S. Greenberg, Charles Atkin, and C. Heeter. "The Demography of Fictional Television Characters in 1975-76." [mimeographed report] East Lansing, Mich.: Department of Communication CASTLE report no. 2, Michigan State University, 1977.

558. Sklar, Robert. "Is Television Taking Blacks Seriously?" AMERICAN FILM 3 (September 1978): 25-29.

559. _____. MOVIE-MADE AMERICA (item I-138).

560. _____. PRIME-TIME AMERICA (item I-139).

561. Sloan, Margaret. "Keeping the Black Woman in Her Place." MS MAGAZINE 2 (January 1974): 30-31.

562. Sloan, William J. "The Documentary Film and the Negro: The Evolution of the Integration Film." CINEMA J 5 (1965): 66-69.

563. Slout, William. "Uncle Tom's Cabin in American Film History." J OF POPULAR FILM 2 (no. 2 1973): 137-51.

564. Smith, Gaines. "Super WASP." NEW GUARD 13 (March 1973): 18-20.

565. Soriano, Michael Esteban. "Minority Activism and Media Access: An Analysis of Community Participation in Policy, Programming, and Production." Ph.D. diss., Stanford University, 1977.

566. Sprafkin, Joyce N., and Eli A. Rubenstein, and Arthur Stone. A CONTENT ANALYSIS OF FOUR TELEVISION DIETS. (Occasional Paper 77-3)

Stony Brook, N.Y.: Brookdale International
Institute for Applied Studies in the Mental
Health Sciences, 1977.

567. Stafford, J.E., and A.E. Birdwell, and C.E.
Van Tassell. "Integrated Advertising--White
Backlash?" J OF ADVERTISING RESEARCH 10
(April 1970): 15-20.

568. Stam, Robert. "Slow Fade to Afro: The Black
Presence in Brazilian Cinema." FILM Q 36
(Winter 1982-83): 16-32.

569. Stavins, Ralph L. "Public Interest: Old and
New." TELEVISION TODAY (item II-570), pp.
70-92.

570. _____, ed. TELEVISION TODAY: THE END OF COM-
MUNICATION AND THE DEATH OF COMMUNITY.
Washington, D.C.: Institute for Policy
Studies, 1969.

571. Stebbins, Robert. "Hollywood's Imitation of
Life." NEW THEATRE 3 (July 1935): 8-10.

572. Stephens, Lenora C. "Black Women in Film."
SOUTHERN Q 19 (Spring-Summer 1981): 164-70.

573. Stern, Seymour. "Griffith: I--The Birth of a
Nation, Part I." FILM CULTURE no. 36
(Spring-Summer 1965): 1-210.

574. Stevens, John D. "The Black Reaction to Gone
with the Wind." J OF POPULAR FILM 2 (Fall
1973): 366-71.

575. Stewart, Ted. "The Black Movie Boom." SEPIA
21 (April 1972): 44-52.

576. Still, William Grant. "How Do We Stand in
Hollywood?" OPPORTUNITY 23 (Spring 1945):
74-77.

577. _____. "The Negro and His Music in Films."
PROCEEDINGS OF THE CONGRESS HELD IN OCTOBER
1943 (item I-173), pp. 277-79.

578. Stroman, Carolyn A. "The Socialization Influ-

ence of Television on Black Children." J OF
BLACK STUDIES 15 (September 1984): 79-100.

579. Strong, Lester. "Blacks, Television, and Ratings." BLACK FAMILIES AND THE MEDIUM OF
TELEVISION (item II-339), pp. 27-32.

580. Sugy, Catherine. "Black Men or Good Niggers?
Race in the New Movies." TAKE ONE 1 (December 1967): 18-21.

581. Surlin, Stuart H. "'Roots' Research: A Summary
of Findings." J OF BROADCASTING 22 (Summer
1978): 309-20.

582. Sweeper, George Wilson. "The Image of the
Black Family and the White Family in American Prime-Time Television Programming, 1970
to 1980." Ph.D. diss., New York University,
1983.

583. Swertlow, Frank. "The Night the Emmy Winners
Didn't Show Up." TV GUIDE 28 (September 20,
1980): A-3, 7.

584. Tan, Alexis S. "Media Use and Political Orien-
tations of Ethnic Groups" (item I-148).

585. _____, and Gerdean Tan. "Television Use and
Self-Esteem of Blacks." J OF COMMUNICATION
29 (Winter 1979): 129-35.

586. Taylor, Clyde. "Shooting the Black Woman."
BLACK COLLEGIAN 9 (May-June 1979): 94-96.

587. Taylor, Henry, and Carol Dozier. "Television
Violence, African-Americans, and Social
Control, 1950-1976." J OF BLACK STUDIES 14
(December 1983): 107-36.

588. Thomer, Penny. "Occupational Portrayals on
Television, with Special Emphasis on Minor-
ity Groups." M.A. thesis, Brigham Young
University, 1971.

589. Thompson, Era Bell. "Why Negroes Don't Like
Porgy and Bess: To Those Who Disliked the
Stage Play, Movie Version Is Same Kettle of
Fish." EBONY 14 (October 1959): 50-54.

590. Thomson, David. AMERICA IN THE DARK: THE IM-
     PACT OF HOLLYWOOD FILMS ON AMERICAN CUL-
     TURE. New York: William Morrow, 1977.

591. Toll, Robert C. THE ENTERTAINMENT MACHINE
     (item I-150).

592. Toplin, Robert Brent. "The Making of Denmark
     Vesey's Rebellion." FILM & HISTORY 12 (Sep-
     tember 1982): 49-56.

593. Trumbo, Dalton. "Blackface, Hollywood Style."
     THE CRISIS 50 (December 1943): 365-67.

594. _____. "Minorities and the Screen." THE PRO-
     CEEDINGS OF THE CONGRESS HELD IN OCTOBER
     1943 (item I-173), pp. 495-501.

595. Tunstall, Jeremy. THE MEDIA ARE AMERICAN (item
     I-151).

596. U.S. Commission on Civil Rights. WINDOW DRES-
     SING ON THE SET: AN UPDATE (item I-156).

597. ------. WINDOW DRESSING ON THE SET: WOMEN AND
     MINORITIES IN TELEVISION (item I-157).

598. _____, California Advisory Committee. BEHIND
     THE SCENES (item I-158).

599. _____, Montana Advisory Committee. THE MEDIA
     IN MONTANA (item I-159).

600. U.S. House of Representatives, MINORITY PARTI-
     CIPATION IN THE MEDIA: HEARINGS BEFORE THE
     SUBCOMMITTEE ON TELECOMMUNICATIONS, CON-
     SUMER PROTECTION, AND FINANCE OF THE COM-
     MITTEE ON ENERGY AND COMMERCE, HOUSE OF
     REPRESENTATIVES, NINETY-EIGHTH CONGRESS,
     FIRST SESSION, SEPTEMBER 19 AND 23, 1983.
     Washington, D.C.: G.P.O., 1984.

601. Van Deburg, William L. SLAVERY & RACE IN AMER-
     ICAN POPULAR CULTURE. Madison: University
     of Wisconsin Press, 1984.

602. Verschuure, Eric Peter. "Stumble, Bumble,

Mumble: TV's Image of the South." J OF
POPULAR CULTURE 16 (no. 3 1982): 92-96.

603. Vidmar, Neil, and Milton Rokeach. "Archie
Bunker's Bigotry: A Study in Selective
Perception and Exposure." J OF COMMUNICA-
TION 24 (Winter 1974): 36-47.

604. Wagenknecht, Edward, and Anthony Slide. THE
FILMS OF D.W. GRIFFITH. New York: Crown,
1975.

605. Walker, Alexander. THE SHATTERED SILENTS: HOW
THE TALKIES CAME TO STAY (item I-163).

606. _____. STARDOM: THE HOLLYWOOD PHENOMENON. New
York: Stein & Day, 1970.

607. Walsh, Moira. "More About Black Films." AMERI-
CA 127 (November 25, 1972): 459-60.

608. Walton, Hanes, Jr. "Black Culture in Films."
PHYLON 42 (June 1981): 194-203.

609. Wander, Brandon. "Black Dreams: The Fantasy
and Ritual of Black Films." FILM Q   29
(Fall 1975): 2-11.

610. Wander, Philip. "On the Meaning of 'Roots.'" J
OF COMMUNICATION 27 (Autumn 1977): 64-69.

611. Wanderer, Aviva. "The Negro Image in Television Advertising--1970." M.A. thesis, University of California, Los Angeles, 1970.

612. Ward, Francis. "Black Male Images in Films."
FREEDOMWAYS 14 (Third Quarter 1974): 223-
29.

613. _____. "Super Fly: The Black Film Ripoff."
THE BLACK POSITION, NO. 2. Detroit: Broad-
side Press, 1972, pp. 37-42.

614. Ward, Renee. "Black Films, White Profits."
BLACK SCHOLAR 7 (May 1976): 13-24.

615. Ward, Robert. "Ossie Davis and Ruby Dee: The
Frustration of Black Actors." TV GUIDE 28
(March 22, 1980): 22-24, 26.

616. Warner, Virgina. "The Negro Soldier: A Chal-
     lenge to Hollywood." THE DOCUMENTARY TRADI-
     TION, FROM NANOOK TO WOODSTOCK. Edited by
     Lewis Jacobs. New York: Hopkinson & Blake,
     Publishers, 1971, pp. 224-25.

617. Washington, Mary Helen. "The Blanding of The
     Jeffersons." TV GUIDE 31 (July· 30, 1983):
     4-6, 8-9.

618. Watkins, Mel. "Beyond the Pale." CHANNELS OF
     COMMUNICATIONS 1 (April/May 1981): 56-60.

619. Weales, Gerald. "Pro-Negro Films in Atlanta:
     Their Educational Effect is Nil." FILMS IN
     REVIEW 3 (November 1952): 455-62.

620. Weaver, Harold D. "Paul Robeson and Film:
     Racism and Anti-Racism in Communication."
     NEGRO HISTORY BULLETIN 37 (January 1974):
     204-206.

621. Weigel, Russell H., and Paul W. Howes. "Race
     Relations on Children's Television." J OF
     PSYCHOLOGY 111 (1982): 109-12.

622. _____, and James W. Loomis, and Matthew J.
     Soja. "Race Relations on Prime Time Televi-
     sion." J OF PERSONALITY AND SOCIAL PSYCHOL-
     OGY 39 (November 1980): 884-93.

623. Weinberg, Sydney. "Jane Pittman's Story." FILM
     & HISTORY 5 (December 1975): 13-16.

624. West, Hollie I. "Makers of Black Films Stand
     at Crossroads." LOS ANGELES TIMES, January
     28, 1973.

625. White, David Manning, and Richard Averson. THE
     CELLULOID WEAPON: SOCIAL COMMENT IN THE
     AMERICAN FILM (item I-166).

626. White, Miriam Betty. "An Extra Body of Refer-
     ence: History in Cinematic Narrative."
     Ph.D. diss., University of Iowa, 1981.

627. Wiggins, H. Curtis. "Media Power and the Black
     American." THE CRISIS 82 (no. 6 1975): 205-
     10.

628. Wilford, Red. "Looking to the '80's: Blacks in the Movies and Television." ST. LOUIS ARGUS, April 24, 1980.

629. Wilkerson, Isabel. "Blacks Left Out of Movie Boom." BOSTON GLOBE, August 29, 1982.

630. Willett, Ralph. "Twisting the Roots: Fiction, 'Faction' and Recent TV Drama." UMOJA 4 (no. 1 1980): 11-20.

631. Williams, Martin. GRIFFITH: FIRST ARTIST OF THE MOVIES. New York: Oxford University Press, 1980.

632. Williams, Robert. "Stereotypes of Negroes in Film." VISION: A JOURNAL OF FILM COMMENT 1 (Summer 1962): 67-69.

633. Williams, Ruthanne. "Love at First Bite." RACE AND ETHNICITY IN THE HISTORY OF THE AMERICAS (item I-36), pp. 43-44.

634. Willis, Ellen. "'War!' said Scarlett. Don't you men think about anything important?" FAVORITE MOVIES: CRITICS' CHOICE (item I-109), pp. 190-95.

635. Winston, Brian. "Escapist Realism." CHANNELS OF COMMUNICATIONS 1 (December 1981/January 1982): 19-20.

636. Withey, Stephen B., and Ronald P. Abeles. TELEVISION AND SOCIAL BEHAVIOR: BEYOND VIOLENCE AND CHILDREN. (Report of the Committee on Television and Social Behavior, Social Science Research Council) Hillsdale, N.J.: Lawrence Erlbaum Associates, 1980.

637. Wolfe, Bernard. "Ecstatic in Blackface: The Negro as a Song-and-Dance Man." THE SCENE BEFORE YOU: A NEW APPROACH TO AMERICAN CULTURE. Edited by Chandler Brossard. New York: Rinehart & Company, 1955, pp. 51-70.

638. Wolfenstein, Martha, and Nathan Leites. "Two Social Scientists View No Way Out: The Unconscious vs. the 'Message' in an Anti-

Bias Film." COMMENTARY 10 (October 1950): 388-91.

639. Woll, Allen L. THE HOLLYWOOD MUSICAL GOES TO WAR (item I-170).

640. Wolper, David L., and Quincy Troupe. THE INSIDE STORY OF TV'S "ROOTS." New York: Warner Books, 1978.

641. Wood, Gerald. "From The Clansman and Birth of a Nation to Gone with the Wind: The Loss of American Innocence." RECASTING: GONE WITH THE WIND IN AMERICAN CULTURE (item II-513), pp. 123-36.

642. Wood, Michael. AMERICA IN THE MOVIES (item I-171).

643. Woodward, Patricia Ann. "The Black-Oriented Movies: A Study of Film as a Confluence of Institutionalized Power Roles and Relationships." M.A. thesis, Annenberg School of Communications, University of Pennsylvania, 1974.

644. Wright, Charles R. MASS COMMUNICATION (item I-172).

645. Wright, Lois. "Television and the Black Family: The Role of Government." BLACK FAMILIES AND THE MEDIUM OF TELEVISION (item II-339), pp. 75-80.

646. Yearwood, Gladstone L. "Black Cinema: Theory and Practice." IN COLOR (item I-21), pp. 20-22.

647. _____. "The Hero in Black Film: An Analysis of the Film Industry and Problems in Black Cinema." WIDE ANGLE 5 (no. 2 1982): 42-50.

648. _____. "Towards a Theory of a Black Cinema Aesthetic." BLACK CINEMA AESTHETICS (item II-649), pp. 67-81.

649. _____, ed. BLACK CINEMA AESTHETICS: ISSUES IN INDEPENDENT BLACK FILMMAKING. Athens, Ohio:

Center for Afro-American Studies, Ohio
University, 1982.

650. Young, Vernon. ON FILM: UNPOPULAR ESSAYS ON A
POPULAR ART. Chicago: Quadrangle, 1972.

651. Zieger, Gay P., and Robert H. Zieger. "Unions
on the Silver Screen: A Review Essay on
F.I.S.T., Blue Collar, and Norma Rae."
LABOR HISTORY 23 (Winter 1982): 67-78.

652. Zito, Stephen F. "The Black Film Experience."
THE AMERICAN FILM HERITAGE (item II-548),
pp. 61-69.

653. _____. "Out of Africa." AMERICAN FILM 2 (October 1976): 8-17.

654. _____. "The Silent Minority." AMERICAN FILM
INSTITUTE EDUCATION NEWSLETTER 4 (May
1971): 2-3.

Addenda:

11a. Beck, Mindy. "Minority Images on T.V.: Up from
Amos 'n' Andy?" ACCESS no. 19 (October 6,
1975): 4-7.

138a. Coleman, Horace W. "Melvin Van Peebles." J OF
POPULAR CULTURE 5 (Fall 1971): 368-84.

168a. Cripps, Thomas. "The Lincoln Motion Picture
Company and the Birth of a Race Company:
Two Early Strides Toward a Black Aes-
thetic." FILM AND AFRICANA POLITICS (mimeo-
graphed report). Edited by Harold Weaver,
Jr. New Brunswick, N.J.: Department of
Africana Studies, Rutgers University, 1973,
pp. 1-26.

331a. Hunter-Lattany, Kristin. "Why Buckwheat Was
Shot." MELUS 11 (Fall 1984): 79-85.

361a. Kaiser, Ernest. "Blacks and the Mass Media: A
Bibliography." FREEDOMWAYS 22 (Third
Quarter 1982): 193-209.

404a. Limbacher, James L. "Blacks on Film: A Se-
       lected List." J OF POPULAR FILM 4 (1975):
       358-78.

560a. Slater, Jack. "The Amos 'n' Andy Show." EMMY 6
       (November/December 1984): 46-49.

601a. Van Peebles, Melvin. SWEET SWEETBACK'S
       BAADASSSSS SONG. New York: Lancer Books,
       1971.

III. ARABS

From the silent era to today the Arab image has stalked the silver screen as a metaphor for anti-Western values. The movie Arabs, and now the television Arabs, have appeared as lustful, criminal, and exotic villains or foils to Western heroes and heroines. They represent a religion, Islam, supposedly at war with Judaism and Christianity and a region at war with Western concepts of political economy and order. Saharan landscapes, Arabian harem rooms, and Baghdad or Casablanca alleyways and cafes have provided the film and television settings wherein the fictive sterile and corrupt "Arab" culture operates. The movie and television Arabs tend no gardens, nurture no families. They live, rather, by sword and intrigue in a world of extremes in climate and character, and function, thereby, as the ultimate un-assimilable aliens to a supposedly more temperate Western nature and behavior.

The Arab stereotype derives from cultural traditions dating back to the Middle Ages. The expansion of Islam into Europe pitted Arab against European and led to Western cultural and political efforts to discredit Islam and Arab culture. In song and literature Westerners portrayed Islam and Arabs as heathenish and dangerous. The Crusades provided further political and cultural reasons to implant anti-Arab images in the Western mind. Western explorers added to the lore about the Arab world, especially making popular the tales of the Arabian Nights. Fantasies about Aladdin and Sinbad the sailor cloaked Arab images in the exotic and mysterious.(8, 11)

In recent years, argue Jack G. Shaheen and others, the Arab stereotype has metamorphosed into a sinister figure of crime and corruption. International events--particularly the continuing Arab-Israeli conflict, Middle Eastern political instability, and the rise of OPEC--have seemingly placed

"Arab" economic and political interests against
American ones, and negative reporting about the
Arab world has spilled over into all forms of
popular culture. From comic books, cartoons, and
children's television to Hollywood motion pictures,
television network programming, and television news
and documentaries, the modern "media" Arab is en-
snarled in a tangle of evil characteristics and
pursuits, some contradictory but all bad. In news
and in commercial film and television, say Arab
critics, media-made Arabs remain of a piece, un-
differentiated by location, religion, politics, or
values. The media-made Arab is at once cunning and
stupid, lustful and impotent, sensual and cold, but
almost invariably dirty, dark, and depraved. (1, 2,
5, 8, 9, 13-18, 20, 22, 23, 25-29)

    Stereotypical Arab images drawn from Western
popular culture transferred to American film as
early as 1893, but the Arab world as backdrop for
tales of romance and adventure did not become popular until the 1920s. More than any other film, The
Sheik (1921), starring Rudolph Valentino, locked
the image of the Arab as exotic and hedonist,
though not quite as lover. The film blurred distinctions among various Arab peoples, making all
Arabs, all Muslims, the same in movie parlance. A
collective Arab emerged from the sands. The film
also fed the mystique of the romantic sheik bent on
seducing Western women, much as Arab culture supposedly tried to corrupt the West, and, so, warned
against the lures of opulence. In the movie, the
sheik holds a beautiful young English women in his
desert tent. She surrenders to the brown prince's
will, but, as it turns out, the sheik is no Arab
at all. To consummate and legitimate any union, he
reveals himself to be a Scottish earl in burnoose,
once abandoned as a baby in the desert. Apparently,
the hot Saharan sun gave him both dark thoughts and
dark skin.(8, 11)

    The success of The Sheik spawned a series of
exotic melodramas associating Arabs with violence
and sexuality, but the charm of Valentino's sheik
quickly played out. Movie Arabs who abducted white
women became increasingly lustful, apparently because they were not Europeans in disguise. The
Arab-as-lover theme vanished from the movie screen
after the 1920s, except as a comedic stereotype.
Arab sexuality, such as it was, survived in the

form of harem girls and belly dancers, ornaments in
the male-dominated world of film Arabs. Modern
movie Arabs seemed more interested in the Westerners' money than their women. The fez and the
interior of the Blue Parrot Cafe first seen in
Casablanca (1942) reappeared in countless films as
symbols for thievery and greed, but even in burnoose and on the sands the movie Arab had become a
trader in flesh, not romance. In The Wind and the
Lion (1975), for example, an Arab kidnaps an American woman in order to get a huge ransom. If the
modern movie Arab acted on his lusts, it was to
ravish and rape, as in Paradise (1982), wherein an
Arab slave trader pursues an English girl. The
current low state of the Arab as lover (and the
changed state of American concepts of Western sexuality) was made apparent in Bolero (1983), when Bo
Derek, portraying a wealthy young virgin in the
1920s, offers herself up to a real sheik only to
find him incapable of satisfying her.(8, 10, 11,
19, 24)
     The second major Arab image coming out of early
films proved more durable. The Arab lovers and
swashbucklers of the Valentino or Douglas Fairbanks
type survived intermittently in adventure movies
such as the Sinbad series and the four versions of
The Thief of Baghdad, but they were largely replaced by Arabs as the dead rising to curse modern
man in the several Mummy films, and especially by
Arabs as banditti or renegades, attacking symbols
of Western rule in the various films about the
Foreign Legion (the three Beau Geste versions, for
example) and the Crusades, produced from the 1920s
on. The clear implication in such movies was that
European colonialism in the Arab world was a good
thing. A few films (Lawrence of Arabia [1962], for
example) partially relieved the uniformly nasty
images of Islamic people, and Omar Sharif rose to
international stardom despite his "Arab" background
and looks, but, say critics, Arab images actually
deteriorated in recent years. After World War II,
films celebrating the creation of modern Israel
(e.g., Exodus [1960] and Cast a Giant Shadow
[1966]) depicted Arabs as brutal soldiers. The
Arab-Israeli conflict colored American news and
popular images of Arabs as the "bad guys," and lent
"credence" to film stereotypes of Arabs as kidnappers, terrorists, and murderers. Despite a

slight shift to more favorable American attitudes
toward "moderate" Arab countries after the Camp
David meetings and the collapse of OPEC, Arab film
images have not improved. Only the tele-movie Sadat
cast a modern Arab leader in a positive light. More
typical are two recent movies, Black Sunday (1977)
and Rollover (1981) in which Arab terrorists plot
to kill innocent spectators and the U.S. president
at the Superbowl and oil-rich sheiks seek to de-
stroy the world financial structure, respectively.
Sacred American institutions, indeed capitalism
itself, remain the targets of the movie Arabs.(4,
6, 8, 12, 21)

The television Arab, argues Jack Shaheen, derives wholly from distorted, negative television
news stories about Arabs and the cartoon and film
stereotypes of Arabs as terrorists or power-hungry
oil sheiks. Playing on American fears of international disorder and foreign investment, and building on resentments spurred by the oil crisis of the
early 1970s, television cartoons, comedy shows, and
prime-time programs and tele-movies have regularly
used the Arab as metaphor for crime, chaos, and
greed. From Scooby Doo to Johnny Carson's Tonight
Show the Arabs have been the butts of jokes about
stupidity and evil. They are ubiquitous in cartoons
as prowling mummies, nomadic thieves, and evil
genies, and they show up in comedy shows as conniving and over-indulgent schemers. In prime-time
dramas, especially in detective series (e.g., Charlie's Angels and The Rockford Files), they appear
only as villains. In docudramas, especially in
Death of a Princess which aired on PBS stations in
1980 despite formal protest from Saudi Arabia, the
Arab world came across as repressive. Such recurrent patterns of negative stereotyping, when added
to the uninformed and negative news reporting about
the Arab world, say Arab critics, continue to mis-
represent Arab culture by making all Arabs appear
to be alike and continue to foster anti-Arab feelings and public policies by making all Arabs appear
to be dangerous.(1, 2, 5, 9, 14-18, 20, 22, 23, 25-
29)

Critics of Arab images have universally condemned the patterns of Arab representations in
American mass media, and they have warned that Arab
stereotypes undermine American foreign policy and
appeal to racism in the United States. They argue

that such negative stereotypes are so deeply rooted in Western popular culture that heroic efforts are necessary to change their shape. They decry the lack of Arab influence in American mass media, noting that, despite supposed Arab wealth, Arabs control no instruments of mass persuasion in the United States. An Arab literature and an Arab intellectual community are not yet available in the United States to draw on for more positive images, but American mass media, Arab critics charge, have been closed to Arab interests and individuals by law and design. Led by Jack Shaheen, such critics have called for American producers to recognize the prevalence of the negative Arab stereotypes and to correct them by becoming more knowledgeable about the Arab world and by looking for positive Arab examples to insert in news and popular programming. They believe that media images are malleable, as the various permutations of the Arab film image suggest, and they believe media images respond to commercial and political pressures. They liken the Arabs' case to that of other ethnic minorities who have suffered from poor treatment in film and television, but they admit that the Arabs lack the numbers and political strength in the United States necessary to gain rights in the film and television industry from which they have been excluded.(1, 2, 5, 9, 16, 22, 25, 26)

The direction of scholarship on Arab images in film and television, perforce, has been almost exclusively to identify the sources and character of stereotypes and to propose alternative visions of Arabs, with scholars as yet devoting little attention to audience surveys, questions of aesthetics, concerns about authorship, or use of comparative models. The focus of this scholarship has been, in one sense, political, for much of it has been in response to the frequent, and recent, appearance of the television Arab as metaphor for anti-Western values. Indeed, only Nasir's dissertation examines the film Arab in depth,(11) and almost the entire literature on Arab images has appeared in the last decade. Similar to Asian and German images, the Arab film and television image has derived from international politics as well as

from Western cultural wellsprings, but as the most
recent symbol of international "villainry," the
media-made Arab remains more sharply etched in
black and less subject to immediate modification
and sophistication than Asian and German images
have been. As such, the critics fear, the media-
made Arab will become even more perverse and un-
just. So, too, will Americans' views of the Arab
world.

     Major discussions of films and/or television
shows include: Ashanti (21), Beau Geste (8, 11),
Best Defense (19), Black Stallion (8, 22), Black
Sunday (8), Bolero (19), Cannonball Run II (19),
Casablanca (8), Cast a Giant Shadow (8), Death of a
Princess (7, 26), Evening in Byzantium (23, 27,
28), Exodus (8), Lawrence of Arabia (8), Rollover
(6, 8, 12), The Sheik (8, 11), The Thief of Baghdad
(8, 11), and The Wind and the Lion (8).

1. Baerg, James R. "Television Programming Prac-
    tice." THE AMERICAN MEDIA AND THE ARABS
    (item III-5), pp. 45-48.

2. Ghareeb, Edmund, ed. SPLIT VISION: THE POR-
    TRAYAL OF ARABS IN THE AMERICAN MEDIA.
    Washington, D.C.: American-Arab Affairs
    Council, 1983.

3. Griffith, Richard, and Arthur Mayer. THE
    MOVIES (item I-62).

4. Harmetz, Aljean. "Hollywood Tackles Hot Is-
    sues." SAN FRANCISCO CHRONICLE, September
    12, 1983, p. 1.

5. Hudson, Michael C., and Ronald G. Wolfe, eds.
    THE AMERICAN MEDIA AND THE ARABS. Washing-
    ton, D.C.: Center for Contemporary Arab
    Studies, Georgetown University, 1980.

6. Johnson, Penny. "Rollover Targets Arabs." AAUG
    NEWSLETTER 15 (January 1982): 3.

7. Levinson, Richard, and William Link. STAY
    TUNED (item I-89).

8. Michalak, Laurence. "Cruel and Unusual: Nega-
    tive Images of Arabs in Popular American
    Culture." ADC ISSUES no. 19 (January 1984):
    3-22.

9. Morsy, Soheir. "Politicization Through the
    Mass Information Media: American Images of
    the Arabs." J OF POPULAR CULTURE 17 (Winter
    1983): 91-97.

10. Nasir, Sari J. "The Arab World in U.S. Movie
    Titles." JOURNALISM Q 40 (Summer 1963):
    351-53.

11. _____. "The Image of the Arab in American
    Popular Culture." Ph.D. diss., University
    of Illinois, 1962.

12. Rainer, Peter. "Rollover Cashes in on Sex,
    Money and Arabs." LOS ANGELES HERALD EXAM-
    INER, December 11, 1981, D, p. 6.

13. Romdhani, Oussama. "The Arab Image in the United States: An Overview." ARAB STUDENT BULLETIN 3 (April-June 1982): 12-18.

14. Shaheen, Jack G. "American Television: Arabs in Dehumanizing Roles." THE AMERICAN MEDIA AND THE ARABS (item III-5), pp. 39-44.

15. _____. "The Arab Image in American Mass Media." AMERICAN-ARAB AFFAIRS no. 2 (Fall 1982): 89-96.

16. _____. "The Arab Image in American Mass Media." SPLIT VISION: THE PORTRAYAL OF ARABS IN THE AMERICAN MEDIA. Edited by Edmund Ghareeb. Washington, D.C.: American-Arab Affairs Council, 1983, pp. 327-36.

17. _____. "The Arab Stereotype on Television." THE LINK 13 (April/May 1980): 1-13.

18. _____. "The Arab: TV's Most Popular Villain." THE CHRISTIAN CENTURY 95 (December 13, 1978): 1213-15.

19. _____. "The Arabs and the Moviemakers." MIDDLE EAST INTERNATIONAL (G.B.) no. 238 (November 1984): 15-16.

20. _____. "Arabs--TV's Villains of Choice." CHANNELS OF COMMUNICATIONS 4 (March-April 1984): 52-53.

21. _____. "'Ashanti': The Arab as Black Slaver." MIDDLE EAST PERSPECTIVE 12 (December 1979): 4-5.

22. _____. "The Influence of the Arab Stereotype on American Children." ARAB PERSPECTIVES 1 (December 1980): 15-20.

23. _____. "Do Television Programs Stereotype the Arabs?" WALL STREET JOURNAL, October 12, 1979, p. S:10.

24. _____. "Movie Arabs: Why the Stereotypes?" ARAB PERSPECTIVES 5 (December 1984): 27-30.

25. _____. "On Prejudice: A Review of Arab Images." ARAB PERSPECTIVES 4 (October 1983): 22-27.

26. _____. THE TV ARAB. Bowling Green, Ohio: Bowling Green State University Popular Press, 1984.

27. _____. "TV Pictures in Our Mind." THE MEDIUM 1 (Fall 1982): 2-4.

28. _____. "TV's Dehumanizing Perception of Arabs." THE MEDIA REPORTER (G.B.) 4 (Summer 1980): 38-39.

29. _____. "The Ugly Arabs: U.S. TV Image." MIDDLE EAST (G.B.) no. 43 (May 1978): 108-10.

IV. ASIANS

Although "Asian" may at first seem an unusual-
ly broad chapter designation, it becomes apparent
to anyone who has analyzed the Asian image on the
American screen that Hollywood's geographical
boundaries are often cast widely. Clear designations of countries or national types have been
fuzzy at best. Also complicating the accurate
characterizations of, say, Chinese, Japanese, or
Koreans has been the practice of casting any Asian
(or even white) in the role of the citizen of any
Asian country. The interchangeability of Chinese
and Japanese actors and their roles has been a
long-standing Hollywood tradition. Sessue Hayakawa,
a Japanese-American actor who began his career in
the 1920s, portrayed Chinese roles with regularity,
while the ever popular Charlie Chan was portrayed
by white or Japanese actors. The result, argue
many, is the broadening of specific national character types into a generalized Oriental or Asian
character.(26)
Three countries and their citizens, however,
do come to the fore, with Chinese, Japanese, and
Indian characters evolving distinct personae as
their filmic roles increased. Added to that list in
recent years has been the Vietnamese as a reflection of American interest in Southeast Asia
during and after the Vietnam War. With these exceptions, the Asian image has remained somewhat blur-
ry, or, as Harold Isaacs suggested, mere "scratches
on our minds."(25)
The earliest silent films revealed an attrac-
tion for the diverse cultures of China, India, and
Japan. In the first documentary thrust of filmmaking, movie producers sent film crews to view the
"oddities" of these three cultures. This early
emphasis on the real faded as these diverse locales
were absorbed into the fictional films of the era.
Eastern locales and their ghetto counterparts (the
Chinatowns of America and the Limehouse district of

189

London) soon became stock settings for the silents. These films accentuated the stark differences between Eastern and Western cultures, a contrast that Westerners were often unable to fathom. The character types which inhabited these mysterious lands or urban ghettoes revealed several common characteristics. More often than not these individuals (both male and female) were considered evil, and tended to be involved in drug or crime-related activities.

Not all characters were of such low esteem. D. W. Griffith, who played a major and controversial role in shaping the film image of blacks during the silent era, also created one of the first major (and sympathetic) Chinese characters in <u>Broken Blossoms</u> (1919). (22, 30, 50, 53) Here, despite a few differences with Oriental culture, Griffith acknowledged the validity of many eastern traditions. Indeed, it seems that Chinese philosophy is painted in a much more favorable light than that of the West. In this film "the Yellow Man" (Richard Barthelmess) becomes a man of peace and honor, while the leading male figure, a pugilist (Donald Crisp), who brutalizes his daughter Lucy (Lillian Gish), is portrayed as evil. "The Yellow Man" ultimately protects and defends young Lucy from her father's fists.

Although "the Yellow Man" is an honorable character, according to Griffith, he still bears that one flaw which became a major concern in the silent era and remained so during the 1930s as well -- the sexual desire for Occidental women. Miscegenation was easily the most horrid crime any Oriental could commit. Although "the Yellow Man's" love was never consummated (or even revealed), it was clear that he had broken a major taboo. The result of such an undesirable interest was often inevitable, as both heroine and hero had to meet their deaths. Here, Gish is killed by her father's blows, and "the Yellow Man" perishes as well.

The success of <u>Broken Blossoms</u> at the box office led to a slew of successors, which copied the film's atmosphere and, in many cases, utilized the miscegenation theme. This subject continued in the sound era as well, with such films as Frank Capra's early success, <u>The Bitter Tea of General Yen</u> (1932), which featured Barbara Stanwyck as the Occidental maiden and Nils Asther (a relatively unknown Swedish actor) as the Chinese warlord who became her lover. Even in the 1930s death remained the only solution for illicit romance.

A survey of some of the "Oriental" characters in these early films reveals that, more often than not, white actors played the leading roles. This was true not only for Orientals in Hollywood's early years, but for Afro-Americans, Jews, and Hispanics as well. Yet, this cultural masquerade continued for a much longer time for Orientals. While secondary roles were often acceptable for "true" Asians, primary roles remained the province of Occidentals. Hence, in the 1930s it is not surpising to see Paul Muni (formerly Warner Brothers' resident minority player) and Luise Rainer reaping the acting honors for Pearl Buck's tale of the Chinese peasantry in MGM's The Good Earth (1937).

The emphasis on the evil character of the Chinese and Japanese in many of these films brought criticism from the Asian governments which realized the powerful message that these films were carrying throughout the world. Their complaints bore some fruit during the 1930s, as positive images were occasionally presented. For example, in contrast to the evil Fu Manchu or villainous Emperor Ming of the Flash Gordon serials, a reverse image began to appear.(6, 18) Here, the extremely clever Oriental was on the side of the law, and he used his wits to bring evil-doers to justice. Charlie Chan, whose films exploits began in the mid-1920s but who became a series regular in the 1930s, emerged as the number one Oriental sleuth, with Mr. Moto a close second. Spouting fortune cookie witticisms, Chan faced the conflicts with Western culture (both with villains as well as his "Number One Son") with a calm demeanor, and proved to audiences that not all Orientals were on the side of evil. Again, Chan was never played by a Chinese actor, although two Japanese received the honors (George Kuwa and Sojin).(2, 11, 14)

Other favorable film portrayals of Chinese during the 1930s included MGM's The Good Earth which attempted to present the difficult lives of the Chinese peasantry. Consultations with the Chinese government brought several useful sugges- tions for the film's screenplay, although China's hope that real Chinese would play major roles went

unfulfilled.
      During the 1930s India often became a locale
for Hollywood features. The image of the Indians
appearing in American films cannot properly be
called a "Hollywood" image. American filmmakers
frequently presented a British view of the events
and personalities of the Indian colony. To a
certain extent this was not surprising since the
British provided a variety of technical assistance
and advice to American filmmakers. As a result, the
image of British omnipotence and Indian weakness is
often apparent, as in Gunga Din (1939), where three
British officers are capable of outwitting and
outfighting thousands of evil Indians who have been
crazed by the excesses of their warlike religion.
      The changing international situation in the
1940s finally allowed for the clear definition of
Chinese and Japanese. The Chinese were portrayed as
heroic and noble (following the model of The Good
Earth) in such wartime films as Dragon Seed (1944)
and Thirty Seconds Over Tokyo (1945). (5, 8, 19, 24,
27, 39, 52) On the other hand, the screen image of
the Japanese borrowed all the evil characteristics
of Ming and Fu Manchu and brought them to bear in
the war effort in such films as Wake Island (1942)
and Objective Burma (1945). Richard Oehling
suggests in his survey on Asian images in film that
the evil Chinese (of the 1920s and early 1930s)
merely donned Japanese uniforms to become the new
villains of the age.(35)
      The post-war situation brought an abrupt shift
in the American definitions of Oriental heroes and
villains, as China's Communist turn and Japan's
growing friendship led to a sharp turnabout in
screen images. The heroic Chinese lost their
beatific glow of the war years and became the enemy
agents in films ranging from The Manchurian Candi-
date (1962) to Dr. No (1963) (the 1960s answer to
Fu Manchu). The Japanese evil streak swiftly faded,
and even the events leading up to World War II
could be presented in a dispassionate manner in
such films as Tora, Tora, Tora (1970), which
provided both the Japanese and the American
versions of the bombing of Pearl Harbor.
      International events have continued to shape
the Oriental image on film and television in recent
years. New national images have been coming to the
fore in response to American wars of the past

thirty years. First Korea assumed a screen presence
in the 1950s, and later Vietnam would take over in
the 1960s and 1970s, and now Cambodia (The Killing
Fields (1984)) in the 1980s.(3, 42, 43, 44, 54) For
the most part, these new nations and their citizens
have been defined as wartime enemies, and as such
have received characteristics similar to those of
the Japanese during World War II. Rarely delineated
as individuals, the Vietnamese, for example, are
often faceless and anonymous people capable of
extreme brutality as demonstrated in such films as
The   Deer   Hunter   (1978) and Apocalypse Now
(1979).(9, 16, 21, 29)
     After a long   respite,   India and Indian
characters have been coming to the fore in recent
years. Interestingly, most of these films are made
by the British, but in many ways they hearken back
to the American versions of Indian life presented
in the 1930s. In Gandhi (1982), A Passage to India
(1984), and Granada Television's The Jewel in the
Crown, images often focus more on the life of the
British in India, rather than the life of Indians
themselves. These films tend to produce a nostalgic
glow for the days of the raj, rather than any
understanding of Indian culture or politics.(40)
     Another trend that has hardly changed from the
early days of film is the tendency to cast
Occidental actors in major roles that are clearly
Oriental. The recent revival of the Charlie Chan
character, Charlie Chan and the Curse of the Dragon
Queen (1981), featured Peter Ustinov as Chan, Angie
Dickinson as the Dragon Queen, and Richard Hatch as
Chan's half-Jewish Number One Grandson.(20)
Similarly, Peter Sellers' last film The Fiendish
Plot of Fu Manchu (1980), revived the Sax Rohmer
villain in the guise of a Caucasian actor. Both
films were greeted by pickets as Chinese Americans
protested Hollywood's hesitance in casting real
Orientals in leading roles. Also of concern was the
fact that Hollywood seemed to be unable to develop
new Oriental characters. As a replacement for
creativity, screenwriters utilized the hackneyed
and stereotyped creations of the 1920s and 1930s.
This was evident as recently as 1984 in Steven
Spielberg's Indiana Jones and the Temple of Doom,
which seemed to borrow its conception of Indian
life from the tribesmen of RKO's Gunga Din.(1, 4)
     One facet of the attempt to deal with this

problem has been the attempt of Asian-American
filmmakers to present non-stereotyped images in
independent films and television dramas (mostly for
PBS). Wayne Wang's Chan Is Missing provides a
modern view of San Francisco's Chinatown in this
reversal of the cliches of the inscrutable Chinese
detective of the 1930s. Chan is therefore missing
in more ways than one.(17)
      Television has continued a notion of Oriental
invisibility with few exceptions.(7, 47, 48, 49,
56) Hawaii Five-0 provided a few Oriental
policemen, but at the same time continued the use
of larger-than-life villains. While Orientals may
fill some secondary roles on television (from Happy
Days to MASH), the leading roles still remain
elusive.

      Harold Isaacs' study, Scratches on Our Minds,
analyzed American attitudes concerning the Orient
utilizing newspaper cartoons, public opinion polls,
and popular literature.(25) As a complement to this
seminal work, one must consider Dorothy B. Jones's
exemplary The Portrayal of China and India on the
American Screen, 1896-1955, which in many ways
remains the model for research in this area.(26)
Jones provides a statistical analysis of films
concerning China and India in order to detect the
frequency of certain generalizations concerning
Oriental life. She also endeavors to discuss the
changing political trends which may have altered
the depiction of Oriental characters on the
American screen. Additionally, she documents the
attempt of the Chinese and Indian (i.e.,British)
governments to alter the filmic image of their citizens. Although published in 1955, this study
remains one of the major works concerning this
issue.
      Since Jones gives the reader only a cursory
look at the Japanese in film, it has become the
task of others to fill this gap. Richard A. Oehling's series of articles on Oriental images offers
excellent insights on the Japanese, as do the works
of Choy, Conroy, and Wong.(34, 35, 12, 15, 55)
      Of the silent films discussed in this section,
Broken Blossoms has received the most attention,
perhaps because it is a D. W. Griffith work. Inter-

esting information on the making of the film, and
Griffith's changes of the original novel on which
it is based can be found in works by Henderson,
Lesage, Wagenknecht, and Williams.(22, 30, 50, 53)
In many ways this Griffith film was the exception
rather than the rule in its treatment of Oriental
life and characters. For this reason, other works
should be considered for a contrast with Griffith's
idealized vision. Barshay and Durgnat provide convincing portraits of Oriental villainy in their
studies of the 1920s and 1930s.(6, 18)

Articles considering the 1930s images tend to
focus primarily on Charlie Chan as the foremost
Oriental character on film during the decade. For
studies of the Oriental detective and the implications of his persona, see works by Chin, Connor,
Goldstein, and Yamada.(11, 14, 20, 58)

World War II brought major reversals in the
film image of Orientals. Kathryn Rose Kane's study,
Visions of War details these changes, as do the
works of Blakefield, Oehling, and Willett.(27, 8,
34, 35, 52) For details concerning the role of
Oriental women in wartime film, see the studies by
Baker and Tajima.(5, 46)

The Vietnam War has brought the most recent
surge of scholarship in this area, as a flurry of
films with Southeast Asian themes have come to the
screen. Studies of these recent films seem to reveal that there has been little change in film
images from the days of World War II, as the
nationalities are different but the characteristics
of the Oriental enemies remain the same. Works of
interest include Adair, Dempsey, Hellman, Lehman,
Suid, and Wilson.(3, 16, 21, 29, 43, 44, 54)

Studies of the Oriental image on television
have been somewhat sparse, perhaps due to the relatively few prominent Asian characters on major network television shows. Kung Fu, as one of the prime
exceptions to television's invisible Orientals, has
provided some commentary.(7, 38) For the effect of
television's lack of Oriental images on the audience, see the works of Chan and Seggar.(10, 41)

Anand A. Yang has provided a thoughtful study
of a course on Oriental images in film and television at the college level in a recent article.
Yang's survey attempts both to identify stereotypes
in American films and to present each country's own
vision of its people and society.(59)

Major   discussions   of films and/or television
shows   include: AfterMASH   (36),   Air   Force (27),
Apocalypse   Now (3, 21),   Bataan   (27), Behind   the
Rising Sun (5, 57),   Bridge on the River Kwai (39),
Broken   Blossoms (22, 30, 50, 53), Chan   Is Missing
(17), Charlie Chan films (2, 11, 14, 20), The Deer
Hunter (9, 16, 21, 29), The Evils of Chinatown
(18), Flash Gordon   (6),   Flower Drum Song (46), Fu
Manchu films (6, 18), Go For Broke (58), The Good
Earth (26, 46), The Green Berets (3), Guadacanal
Diary (27), Gunga Din (26), Indiana Jones and the
Temple of Doom   (1), Know Your Enemy--Japan (8),
Kung Fu (7, 38), Objective Burma (27), The Rains
Came (26), Sixteen Candles (1), The Story of G. I.
Joe (27), The Teahouse of the August Moon (46),
They Were Expendable (27), and You Only Live Twice
(31).

1. ――――. "'Indiana,' 'Candles' Called 'Racist'
    By Two Asian Groups." VARIETY, July 4,
    1984, pp. 4, 36.

2. ――――. "Oriental Detectives on the Screen."
    SCREEN FACTS 2 (1964): 30-39.

3. Adair, Gilbert. VIETNAM ON FILM: FROM "THE
    GREEN BERETS" TO "APOCALYPSE NOW." New
    York: Proteus, 1981.

4. Asian Americans for a Fair Media. "Asian
    Images -- A Message to the Media." BRIDGE 3
    (April 1974): 25-30.

5. Baker, Melva Joyce. "Images of Women in Film:
    The War Years, 1941-1945." (item II-60).

6. Barshay, Robert. "Ethnic Stereotypes in Flash
    Gordon." J OF POPULAR FILM 3 (Spring 1974):
    15-30.

7. Berger, Arthur Asa. THE TV-GUIDED AMERICAN
    (item I-13).

8. Blakefield, William J. "A History and Analysis
    of 'Know Your Enemy -- Japan.'" M. A. the-
    sis, University of Maryland, 1981.

9. Burke, Frank. "In Defense of The Deer Hunter,
    or: The Knee Jerk Is Quicker Than the Eye."
    LITERATURE/FILM Q 11 (no. 1 1983): 22-27.

10. Chan, Kenyon. "Moving Beyond Ethnic Stereo-
    types: Asian and Pacific Americans."
    TELEVISION AND CHILDREN 7 (Winter 1984):
    12-15.

11. Chin, Frank. "Confessions of a Number One Son:
    Charlie Chan and the Hollywood Image of
    Asians." RAMPARTS 11 (March 1973): 41-48.

12. Choy, Christine. "Cinema as a Tool of Assimil-
    ation: Asian Americans, Women, and Holly-
    wood." IN COLOR (item I-21), pp. 23- 25.

13. ――――. "Images of Asian Americans in Films
    and Television." ETHNIC IMAGES IN AMERICAN

       FILM AND   TELEVISION (item I-105), pp. 145-
       55.

14.   Connor, Edward. "The Six Charlie Chans." FILMS
       IN REVIEW 6 (January 1955): 23-27.

15.   Conroy, Hilary. "Concerning the Asian-American
       Experience." ETHNIC IMAGES IN AMERICAN FILM
       AND TELEVISION (item I-105), pp. 157-60.

16.   Dempsey, Michael. "Hellbent for Mystery"
       ("Four Shots at The Deer Hunter").   FILM
       Q 22 (Summer, 1979): 10-13.

17.   Dittus,   Erick.   "'Chan Is Missing': An
       Interview with Wayne Wang."   CINEASTE 12
       ([no. 3] 1983): 16-20.

18.   Durgnat, Raymond.   "The Yellow Peril Rides
       Again."   FILM SOCIETY R 5 (October 1969):
       36-40.

19.   Fyne, Robert. "The Unsung Heroes of World War
       II." LITERATURE/FILM Q 7 (no. 2 1979): 148-
       54.

20.   Goldstein, Richard.   "The   Chan Syndrome."
       VILLAGE VOICE, May 5, 1980, p. 32.

21.   Hellman, John. "Vietnam and the Hollywood
       Genre Film: Inversions of American
       Mythology in 'The Deer Hunter' and
       'Apocalypse Now.'"   AMERICAN Q 34 (Fall
       1982): 418-39.

22.   Henderson, Robert M. D. W. GRIFFITH: HIS LIFE
       AND WORK (item II-308).

23.   Higham, Charles and Joel Greenberg. HOLLYWOOD
       IN THE FORTIES (item I-69).

24.   Horikawa, Herbert. "Psychological Implications
       of Asian Stereotypes in the Media." ETHNIC
       IMAGES IN AMERICAN FILM AND TELEVISION
       (item I-105), pp. 161-165.

25.   Isaacs, Harold R.   SCRATCHES ON OUR MINDS:
       AMERICAN IMAGES OF CHINA AND INDIA. New

York: John Day Company, 1958.

26. Jones, Dorothy B. THE PORTRAYAL OF CHINA AND INDIA ON THE AMERICAN SCREEN, 1896-1955. Cambridge, Mass.: M.I.T. Press, 1955.

27. Kane, Kathryn Rose. VISIONS OF WAR (item I-77).

28. Kim, Elaine H. ASIAN-AMERICAN LITERATURE: AN INTRODUCTION TO THE WRITINGS AND THEIR SOCIAL CONTEXT. Philadelphia: Temple University Press, 1982.

29. Lehman, Peter. "Well, What's It Like Over There? Can You Tell Us Anything?: Looking for Vietnam in The Deer Hunter" NORTH DAKOTA Q 51 (Summer 1983): 131-41.

30. Lesage, Julia. "'Broken Blossoms': Artful Racism, Artful Rape." JUMP CUT 26 (1981): 51-55.

31. Mellen, Joan. BIG BAD WOLVES: MASCULINITY IN THE AMERICAN FILM (item II-435)

32. Moskowitz, Suree. "Some Observations on the Images of Asian Americans in American Popular Visual Media." ETHNIC IMAGES IN AMERICAN FILM AND TELEVISION (item I-105), pp. 167-69.

33. Nahm, Tom Kagy. "Stop Stereotyping Me." NEWSWEEK, January 15, 1979, p. 15.

34. Oehling, Richard A. "Hollywood and the Image of the Oriental, 1910-1950" FILM & HISTORY, Part I, 8 (March 1978): 33-41; Part II, 9 (September 1978): 59-67.

35. ————. "The Yellow Menace: Asian Images in American Film." THE KALEIDOSCOPIC LENS (item I-106), pp. 182-206.

36. O'Hallaren, Bill. "Rosalind Chao of After-MASH." TV GUIDE 32 (January 7, 1984): 12-14.

37. Paik, Irvin. "That Oriental Feeling: A Look at
     the Caricatures of the Asians as Sketched
     in American Movies." Edited by Amy Tachiki,
     et al, ROOTS: AN ASIAN-AMERICAN READER.
     Los Angeles: Continental Graphics, 1971,
     pp. 30-35.

38. Radditz, Leslie. "Introducing the Kung Fu
     Cast." TV GUIDE 21 (June 23, 1973): 27-34.

39. Rubin, Steven Ray. COMBAT FILMS, AMERICAN
     REALISM: 1945-1970. Jefferson, N.C.:
     McFarland & Company, 1981.

40. Rushdie, Salman. "Outside the Whale." AMERICAN
     FILM 10 (January-February 1985): 16, 70,
     72-73.

41. Seggar, John F. and Penny Wheeler. "World of
     Work on TV: Ethnic and Sex Representation
     in TV Dramas." (item I-133).

42. Smith, Julian. LOOKING AWAY: HOLLYWOOD AND
     VIETNAM. New York: Charles Scribner's Sons,
     1975.

43. Suid, Lawrence. "The Film Industry and the
     Vietnam War." Ph. D. diss., Case-Western
     Reserve University, 1980.

44. ————. GUTS AND GLORY: GREAT AMERICAN WAR
     MOVIES. Reading, Mass. Addison-Wesley
     Publishing Co., 1978.

45. Tan, Alexis S. "Television Use and Social
     Stereotypes." JOURNALISM Q 59 (no. 1 1982):
     119-22.

46. Tajima, Renee. "Asian Women's Images in Film:
     The Past Sixty Years." IN COLOR (item
     I-21), pp. 26-29.

47. U. S. Commission on Civil Rights. WINDOW
     DRESSING ON THE SET: AN UPDATE (item
     I-156).

48. ————. WINDOW DRESSING ON THE SET: WOMEN AND
     MINORITIES IN TELEVISION (item I-157).

49. ———. BEHIND THE SCENES: EQUAL EMPLOYMENT OPPORTUNITIES IN THE MOTION PICTURE INDUSTRY (item I-158).

50. Wagenknecht, Edward, and Anthony Slide. THE FILMS OF D. W. GRIFFITH (item II-604).

51. Whang, Paul K. "Boycotting American Movies." WORLD TOMORROW 13 (August 1930): 339-40

52. Willett, Ralph. "The Nation in Crisis: Hollywood's Response to the 1940s." CINEMA, POLITICS AND SOCIETY IN AMERICA (item I-39), pp. 59-75.

53. Williams, Martin. GRIFFITH: FIRST ARTIST OF THE MOVIES (item I-631).

54. Wilson, James. VIETNAM IN PROSE AND FILM. Jefferson, N.C.: McFarland Press, 1982.

55. Wong, Eugene. "On Visual Media Racism: Asians in the American Motion Picture." Ph. D. diss., University of Denver, 1977; New York: Arno Press, 1978.

56. Wright, Charles R. MASS COMMUNICATION: A SOCIOLOGICAL PERSPECTIVE (item I-172).

57. Wright, Virginia and David Hanna. "Motion Picture Survey." THE PROCEEDINGS OF THE CONFERENCE HELD IN OCTOBER 1943 (item I-173), pp. 402-11.

58. Yamada, George. "Old Stereotypes Pattern." THE CRISIS 60 (January 1953): 17-19.

59. Yang, Anand A. "Images of Asia: A Passage Through Fiction and Film." THE HISTORY TEACHER 15 (May 1980): 351-69.

V. EAST EUROPEANS & RUSSIANS

Despite their large numbers in the United States, East Europeans and Russians have had a limited, blurred, and even contradictory image in American film and television. For most of this century an East European screen image hardly existed, while the Russian image has been locked in political categories since (and because of) the Russian Revolution. East European immigrants (consisting principally of Slavs, and among them, Poles) suffered from American social prejudices against and misperceptions of peasant culture, and their screen image became equated with working-class culture in the United States. The Russians, meanwhile, suffered from their association with communism in the American mind, and their screen image hinged on the political imperatives and interests of Hollywood and the federal government. Within the past decade or so, however, East Europeans have appeared more frequently in American film and television—still tied to stereotypes about the working classes and still mainly cast as people of passion rather than intellect, brawn rather than brain, but not wholly so. Russians, too, have continued as the "bad guys" in films and television shows about international events, conspiracies, and intrigue but even in that role they have achieved no monopoly. Ever responsive to shifting political currents and popular mythology, Hollywood in recent years has drafted Asian or ex-Nazi characters to represent enemies of American freedom and values, and it has even introduced the friendly Russian as a screen type.

Russian screen images trace their origins to some of the earliest movies, and from their beginnings they suggested that Russians had no life outside politics. Shorts and documentaries glimpsed life in tsarist Russia, but the upheavals of the Russian Revolution particularly invited film interest. Newsreels and film accounts of events in

Russia were a staple in theaters from the mid-1910s
through the early 1920s.

During the 1920s Russian silent film imports
offered American audiences compelling images of
heroic Russians and explored the complexity and
meaning of the Russian Revolution from a Marxist
perspective. The Soviet films mixed art and politics. The Soviets' film artistry, as displayed in
Sergei Eisenstein's Potemkin (1925), astounded
American filmmakers. So, too, did the undisguised
purpose of the Soviets' juxtapositioning and assembling of shots--which was to achieve a Marxist
vision of social reality. The Soviets introduced an
alternative film aesthetic in their use of montage,
but the political intent of the aesthetic troubled
the American film industry, preoccupied as it was
in the 1920s with satisfying the tastes of its
middle-class audience and with beating back criticism, and threats of regulation, because of its
social "liberalism." The Soviet films failed to
capture a market, in part because of their political content, but their effects on the Russian
screen image were important. As Hollywood hastened
to develop its own apolitical film aesthetic, it
retreated from making movies carrying overt political affiliations, such as it had done during World
War I in its "Hate the Hun" films (see chapter VI)
and in 1919 in response to Attorney General A.
Mitchell Palmer's request for anti-Bolshevik movies
(e.g., Bolshevism on Trial). Russian subjects faded
from the screen by the late 1920s. Hollywood even
abandoned making anti-communist films, leaving that
market to independent filmmakers, who provided only
cheap melodramas, with the Russians, qua communists, cast in forbidding tones and gross stereotype. Along with the print journalism and popular
literature of the 1920s, film imbedded the image of
the Russian as revolutionary in the American imagination.(21, 29, 34. See also 1-45, 70, 138)

During the Depression years Hollywood attracted
writers and intellectuals, especially European
emigres fleeing Nazism, who sought to convert sound
film, the most powerful medium of mass persuasion
available, to political purposes. The Depression
and the fascist menace in Europe stirred Hollywood
from its apolitical slumber, and "social problem"
films became fashionable. Warner Brothers took the
lead, parading Roosevelt's New Deal philosophy in a

host of movies in the 1930s. The federal government
also produced a series of moving documentaries
which suggested that only the collective force of
government could solve problems of poverty, natural
disaster, and social disorder. Some Hollywood
writers and intellectuals flirted with communism,
some few others embraced it.

Surprisingly, the films produced during the
1930s did not signal a pro-communist shift. Anti-
communist messages still echoed in American film,
but the Russian people no longer looked so menacing. It was even possible to consider Russians as
people rather than political metaphors when the
capitalism versus communism dichotomy lost its edge
during the 1930s. In such films as Ninotchka
(1939), for example, emigre filmmaker Ernst
Lubitsch used Russian and East European characters
and settings in sympathetic, and even comic, ways
in stories about American middle-class values. In
the Flash Gordon serials the "Russian-style" scientist Dr. Zarkov fought on the side of good
against Emperor Ming's evil, although, as befitted
the stereotype of the over-zealous scientist, he
could be bought by Ming for the promise of scientific freedom.(2, 10, 25, 26, 33)

World War II forced American movies back into
politics. An awakened political consciousness in
Hollywood and the federal government's intervention
in filmmaking brought a refurbished Russian image
to the screen. The federal government, through the
Bureau of Motion Pictures of the Office of War
Information and through the War Department, made
films about the common interests of the Soviet
Union and the United States as allies in the fight
against fascism (e.g., The Battle of Russia [1943]
made for the United States Army as part of Frank
Capra's Why We Fight series). Needful of convincing
its citizens that American and Soviet interests
converged during the war, the United States government also asked, and coerced, Hollywood to make
pro-Soviet movies.(24)

Operating with almost complete ignorance about
the Soviet Union and not wanting to offend either
its audiences or its government, Hollywood responded with films depicting the Russian people in
heroic terms. The films avoided any intimations of
ideological conflict between communism and capitalism and fixed on the struggle of the Russian

people and nation against the Nazi foe. No film
went as far as did Warner Brothers' 1943 release
Mission to Moscow (based on Joseph E. Davies' book
of the same title recounting his diplomatic experiences in the Soviet Union between 1936 and 1938,
but significantly reworked by Hollywood and government) in exculpating Stalin and the Soviets from
blame in the Stalinist purges and other brutalities
and distorting history to sell an image of a kindly
and trustworthy Stalin, but various Hollywood studios made films glorifying Stalin as a national
leader and praising the fighting capacities of the
Russian people (e.g., RKO's The North Star [1943]
and MGM's Song of Russia [1943]). In films about
American fighting men, soldiers with Russian-
sounding names formed part of the melting-pot units
American filmmakers sent into battle. Americans
(including Russian Americans) and Russians were in
the fight together.(7, 8, 9, 10, 20, 21, 22, 24,
25, 26, 34, 40, 42, 43)

The World War II films were pro-Russian without
being pro-communist, but the distinction was not so
clear to observers then, or later. Hollywood made
films about Russia (i.e., the Soviet Union, but
rarely identified as such in the pro-Russian films)
because Russia was in the news and because the
government demanded it, but the heroic Russian they
created was as overdone as the Russian-as-revolu-
tionary stereotype of the pre-1939 anti-communist
potboilers. Some writers and filmmakers would
later suffer for such excesses during the Cold War,
when anti-communist watchdogs began sniffing about
in Hollywood.

After the war Hollywood dropped the heroic
Russian theme; indeed, it ignored Russian subjects
altogether for a time. Hollywood redirected its
social consciousness to domestic problems in a
series of post-war "message" movies, but communism
was not among the topics treated. Liberalism, in
fact, was fading anyway. Between 1947 and 1951 the
House Un-American Activities Committee (HUAC) conducted hearings about alleged communist influence
in Hollywood. The film industry, suffering from
anti-trust suits threatening the studio system,
declining movie attendance, and the rise of television, capitulated to the Red hunters in Washington by blacklisting suspected and real communists and communist sympathizers and abandoning

its social problem genre. For several years Hollywood also released a spate of anti-communist films,
even though they attracted few patrons. Mostly,
however, Hollywood tried to recover its audience by
returning to entertainment. Russians or communists
had little role to play in the westerns, musicals,
and Bible epics Hollywood offered in the 1950s.

Russians reemerged as the enemy in the real
world but not quite in film. In movies the Russian
as communist assumed no new features and appeared
in many ways as a tired old stereotype. Indeed, in
most of the anti-communist films Hollywood spat
forth from 1948 through the 1950s, the communists
were unseen forces (even alien pods as in Invasion
of the Body Snatchers [1956]), or they were Americans who had sold out their country. Hollywood had
turned inward to examine American society in its
"message" movies after the war, and then it turned
inward to demonstrate its political loyalties in
its anti-communist films. Russians, or East Europeans, still popped up in occasional films as the
communist bad guys, especially in films about
foreign intrigue and conspiracy, but they slipped
from view as Hollywood looked for domestic villains
in such films as I Married a Communist (1949) and
The Enemy Within (1949).(29, 41, 43)

The Russian-as-communist image revived in the
1960s and persisted thereafter in adventure films,
such as the spy thrillers and the James Bond
series. The media-made Russian communist grew
fatter, more self-indulgent, and more fanatical,
but he was also no more believable than earlier
stereotypes. He slurred his speech, dressed badly,
and drank too much. His habits betrayed his purpose, and the agents of the free world usually out-
maneuvered the plodding Russian type on screen.

As the Cold War has thawed, non-threatening
Russian types have appeared, if only in a few
instances. In The Russians Are Coming (1966), for
example, Russian sailors mistakenly land on a New
England beach and occupy the town, but they behave
themselves and get along well with the Americans
once mutual suspicions are allayed, eventually
having the requisite level of romantic involvement
with their hosts to keep audiences interested in
the story. Deep down, the movie implied, Russians
were just like Americans. The recent film Moscow on
the Hudson, starring Robin Williams as a Russian

seeking asylum in the United States, includes the
usual Russian secret police types, easily identified by their dress and manner and eluded by the
energetic Williams, but the Russian refugee protag-
onist adapts readily to American social customs and
tastes. He has a funny accent and does not quite
understand American gadgetry and foods, but he is
an American at heart. The movie shows that Russians
as people are not the same as the Soviets as communists.(43)

Such alternative images of Russians, of course,
remain locked in political categories and present
their own problems as stereotypes. They do suggest,
however, a new softness in tone for Russians on
the screen and the possibility of depicting Russians in roles and stories free of ideological
imperatives.

On television the Russian as communist steals
about as a spy or subversive in late-night movie
reruns, but otherwise the Russian image has not
invaded the home screen. One generation of television viewers grew up with Dr. Zarkov (good guy)
in the Flash Gordon serials broadcast on Saturday
mornings, and the next generation contended with
Boris and Natasha (bad guys) on the cartoon series,
Rocky & His Friends (also aired as The Rocky &
Bullwinkle Show). The Russian screen image largely
remained confined to Hollywood film, and the television Russian remained tied to its film sources.
For that reason, too, television has not developed
a recognizable Russian-American character, despite
the appearance and prominence of several television
characters with East European backgrounds (mostly
Polish).

The most visible Russian-American images occurred in Michael Cimino's The Deer Hunter (1978),
set in the working-class world of Clairton, Pennsylvania, a town ruled by the steel mill and the
Russian and Ukrainian "ethnic" hardhats who worked
and lived there. Cimino conceived his vision of
Russian and Ukrainian working-class life from popular stereotypes about East Europeans as metaphors
for the American working class (see below), and he
used all the cliches about Russians and East Europeans knocking about in the American imagination.
His characters work hard, play hard, and drink hard
(and too much). The men were preoccupied with their
virility and loyalty to one another; the women were

subjected to male tyranny and somewhat sluttish.
Despite their grimy and grim existence, the men
love America and willingly go off to Vietnam to die
for it. Cimino's Russians and Ukrainians are not a
pretty picture. They invite no emulation as character models for family television entertainment.
(1, 6, 13, 14, 16, 30, 31)

They do suggest, however, an effort to assim-
ilate East European and Russian characters into an
unspoken theme of ethnic blurring. As Frank Burke
points out, Cimino's Russians and especially his
Ukrainians surrender their true Old World identities in the film because they prostitute their
heritage to fight for American military "imperialism," opposing Russia by fighting its communist
surrogate in Vietnam. The film's Ukrainians were
"doubly uprooted" in Burke's judgment, for the
Ukraine had been subjected by the Russians, and the
children of the Ukrainians who abandoned the homeland for Clairton, or wherever, must fight for
America against the Soviet Union (of which the
Ukraine was a part).(6)

Cimino's choice of Ukrainians and Russians as
metaphors for the American working class, and his
blurring of their ethnic distinctiveness, mirrored
the basic patterns of popular belief about East
Europeans and their consequent screen imagery. The
East European image is largely a Slavic one, and
within that category largely a Polish one. To the
American mind, East Europeans are interchangeable,
as Slavs or whatever. Although Slavs comprise at
least sixteen different nationalities and although
not all East Europeans are Slavs (Hungarians and
Lithuanians), few Americans have appreciated such
distinctions, if they noticed them at all. From the
beginnings of the influx of East European immigrants in the late nineteenth century to the stereotypes of them in American film and television,
East Europeans (Slavs) have been of a piece in
popular conception and even much scholarly presen-
tation--peasant, lower-class, stolid, and even
stupid. As unskilled laborers, the East European
immigrants became identified with "the working
class," and, as they have remained concentrated in
"blue-collar" occupations, East Europeans (most
visibly by numbers, the Poles) remain the quintessential working-class type, the ethnic hardhat.
Cimino simply borrowed a stereotype for all East

Europeans and applied it to Ukrainians and Russians. He could have made his point about the male-dominated world of ethnic working-class America just as easily by employing Poles (the most common representation in film and television), Czechs, Slovaks, or any East European group.(14)

The East European screen image is of relatively recent vintage and limited in quantity. Caroline Golab estimates that of all the films made in America, "probably less than two dozen contain Slavic-Americans as major or minor characters." Few, if any, East European characters and subjects figured prominently in silent films, and they have almost exclusively appeared in social problem, or "message," movies during spasms of Hollywood social consciousness in the 1930s, the late 1940s, and since the mid-1960s. On the whole, East Europeans have not been attractive subject matter for Hollywood, which has generally preferred to relate the lives and loves of the middle and upper classes and has ignored working-class themes in its films. East European images or subjects only entered film when good stories about them were available from non-film sources--novels, plays, newspaper accounts of specific events. By the time working-class subjects and ethnic identities became popular in the 1970s, the Slavic working-class stereotype was firmly established and translated readily to film and television.(4, 14, 15, 37, 38, 39)

However infrequently seen, the East European, or Slavic, working-class stereotype became a national one through the medium of film. Confined to mining towns and a few industrial cities, East Europeans were not generally in public view, as were other "new immigrant" groups coming in the late nineteenth and early twentieth centuries, such as the Italians and the Jews. Films found the East Europeans in their isolated settings and disseminated the stereotype of the Slavs as unskilled, ignorant laborers across the nation, making it common currency in film from the Warner Brothers' social problem movie about labor racketeering in a mining community (Black Fury [1935]), to Columbia's examination of social despair and bankruptcy in a Pennsylvania mill town (Anna Lucasta [1949]), to Universal's examination of corruption in a Detroit autoworkers' union local (Blue Collar [1978]).(4, 14, 15, 36, 37, 39, 45)

The stereotype was most vividly realized in
Elia Kazan's film version of Tennessee Williams' A
Streetcar Named Desire (1951), which Kazan had
earlier directed on stage. Stanley Kowalski, played
in both the play and the film by Marlon Brando, was
the epitome of the crude, primitive, sensual, and
brutish working-class slob. He was Polish, from his
bowling shirt down to his polka-dot underwear.
Williams chose a Polish image because he sought to
represent through Stanley all the ways the "working
class" threatened civilization. The working class
was anti-intellectual, physical, passionate, and
violent. So was Stanley,"the Polack." The Polish
stereotype succeeded as a metaphor because the
audience equated the working class with the Pole
(the East European, the Slav). In that sense, only
a Kowalski would do. No other ethnic ascriptions
carried the working-class identity so widely in
popular imagination as did the East Europeans, the
Slavs.(14)

On television East Europeans have shared
working-class settings with blacks, Hispanics,
Irish, and Italians. Still, the "dumb Polack" image
persists as the focus of humor about working-class
"ethnics." The Polish joke, which flourished on
television and in magazines during the 1960s, is a
case in point. In situation comedies the Polish
personality is inevitably the slowest of wit and
the butt of much humor. Although they show compassion, dedication, and loyalty, Wojohowicz in
Barney Miller and Renko in the drama series Hill
Street Blues lack the polish and wit of most of the
other ethnically identifiable characters. In All in
the Family Norman Lear inverted the stereotypes,
making Michael Stivic (the Pole) the intellectual,
liberal, and sensitive character and Archie Bunker
(the WASP) the working-class slob. Archie refers to
his son-in-law as the "meathead" and the "dumb
Polack," but Archie is clearly the "dumbest" of all
the characters. Lear's inversion of the ethnic
joke, however, worked only so much as the audience
accepted the original Polish stereotype. George
Peppard's portrayal of the cool, smooth Polish-
American private-eye Thomas Banacek, in the drama
series Banacek, contradicted the stereotype and won
an award from the Polish-American Congress for its
positive image. Banacek, too, was based on an
"ethnic gimmick" of Peppard playing off the Polish

stereotype. The show lasted two seasons. The durable East European television type remained well-
meaning, but blue-collared, uncouth, and not-so-
bright (e.g., Lenny in Laverne and Shirley, the
Marine sergeant Szysznyk in Szysznyk, or Kowalski
in C.P.O. Sharkey).(3, 15, 23, 44)

The scholarship on East European and Russian
screen images largely addresses the working-class
stereotype of the former and the political categories of the latter. Only Caroline Golab and Thaddeus Gromada have taken the long view regarding
East European, or Slavic, film depictions, relating
them to the peculiar social and economic history of
Slavic immigrants.(14, 15) Several authors have
traced the evolution of the Russian-as-communist
image in film, but such discussions have neglected
non-political themes and the Russian American on
screen.(25, 26, 29, 34, 42, 43)
    As yet, the connection between the artistic
influence of Soviet cinema and Russian images in
American film remains unexamined. William Paul
briefly discussed Ernst Lubitsch's use of East
European and Russian settings and subjects, and
Jerzy Kucharski discovered an early Polish-American movie, but East European or Russian authorship
has received almost no attention.(27, 33) So, too,
the influence of audience on screen subject matter
and portrayals awaits study. This neglect is all
the more surprising given the attempts of Polish-
American organizations to block negative Polish
stereotypes by court and legislative action, as,
for example, suits brought against the film The End
(1978) and the television series Rowan and Martin's
Laugh In, both of which fed off Polish jokes.
Similarly, no one has followed up Arthur Berger's
interesting suggestion that Michael Stivic on All
in the Family demonstrates the inversion of the
Polish joke.(3)
    Despite much insistence in the literature (par-
ticularly about Poles) that screen stereotypes
deepen prejudice and weaken the group's self-confi-
dence,(5, 15, 28, 36) scholars still lack a methodology and a significant data base to measure the
meaning or influence of film or television images.
The Peterson/Thurstone test of high school stu-

dents' attitudes toward Russians after viewing one
film, conducted over thirty years ago, remains the
only systematic effort to determine how film images
affect prejudices.(35) The Jeffres/Hur Cleveland
samples are the only scientific gauge of Slavic-
American reactions to television programming.(18,
19) The Vidmar/Rokeach study of United States and
Canadian viewers' responses to All in the Family,
which found that the show may reinforce rather than
reduce ethnic and racial prejudices, is the only
general television audience survey that touches
Slavic images, however tangentially in the case of
the Vidmar/Rokeach research.(44)

     In essaying the development of the Russian film
image, several authors have noted its imprisonment
in political categories. Siegfried Kracauer argues
that the Russian image changed in the 1930s in
response to contemporary interest in communism, but
that after Ninotchka in 1939, the Russians vanished
as screen subjects until World War II.(25, 26) Jeff
Peck charts the "heroic Soviet" course in American
film, noting how American films pitted peasants and
aristocrats against Bolshevik "barbarians" in early
films, found new strength in peasant life in films
of the 1930s, and fused the Soviets with Russian
nationalism during World War II.(34) Melvin Small
emphasizes the wartime needs to create a positive
Russian (Soviet) image,(42, 43) as do Larry Ceplair
and Steven Englund, who maintain that Hollywood
sought profits, avoided controversy, and produced
"Sovietized versions of Mrs. Miniver" as a
result.(7) David Culbert wrote a detailed production history of Mission to Moscow and examined
the post-war political fallout from making the
movie.(8, 9) Several studies identify the wartime
practice of showing Slavic and/or Russian-American
loyalty in films such as An American Romance (1944)
and Bataan (1943).(20, 21, 22, 24, 40) Daniel Leab
mentions the "rotten Russian" images of anti-communist films as background for his discussion of I
Married a Communist,(29) and James Skinner briefly
notes the Russian-as-communist cliches and con-
ventions in Cold War anti-communist Hollywood
fare.(41) The content, purpose, and effects of
post-World War II films with Russian characters,
however, all demand study.

     Michael Cimino's depiction of Russian-American
and Ukrainian-American life in Clairton has occa-

sioned some controversy regarding the validity of
the images and the purpose of the message in The
Deer Hunter. Al Auster and Leonard Quart find
working-class solidarity in the film's characters,
but decry Cimino's superficial treatment of the
ethnic community.(1) Terry Fox briefly surveys the
setting,(13) and Peter Lehman argues that Cimino
was interested in realistic detail in rendering the
steel town, including the Slavs' brutality against
women.(30) Frank Burke charges Cimino with cultural
destruction (see above), in that he makes the
Ukrainians of Clairton deny their former homeland
by fighting a war of American imperialism in Vietnam.(6) Caroline Golab maintains that Cimino's
Slavs represented standard practice in portraying
the hard and mean world of the ethnic hardhat.(14)

Golab's essay on Slavic images provides the key
to understanding why Slavic images have appeared
infrequently on screen but have remained inextricably tied to working-class symbols when they do
show up in American film. Along with Thaddeus
Gromada and Edward Plocha,(15, 36) Golab argues
that the Slavic film image, from Black Fury to The
Deer Hunter, was rooted in the historical linkage
of Slavic immigrants to mining and heavy industrial
settings. The historical circumstance of the Slavs
made them a metaphor for whatever the "working
class" meant in art and popular culture. In explaining the purpose of a stereotype in dramatic
production, she concluded that the the Slav was of
necessity the working-class slob in A Streetcar
Named Desire, or the violent labor organizer in
F.I.S.T. (1978), or the hard-drinking steelworker
in The Deer Hunter.(14)

The East Europeans' identification with blue-
collar occupations and values has been the principal point of scholarly discussion about their
screen images. William Everson discovered a Russian
detective,(12) but East European characters seem to
have been trapped in working-class settings and
characters. Andrew Bergman, Nick Roddick, and Peter
Roffman and Jim Purdy found Slavic stereotypes in
Depression-era films about labor racketeering and
mining towns.(4, 37, 38, 39) Charles Higham and
Joel Greenberg located the Polish-American neighborhoods of Chicago in describing Call Northside
777.(17) Gay and Robert Zieger compare the vigor of
the East European worker, played by Sylvester Stal-

lone, in F.I.S.T. with the "dessicated, crippled
WASP" employer, and also examine the alienation of
the Polish autoworker character in Blue Collar.(45)
     The ethnic resurgence in America since the
1960s has peopled film and television with "ethnic"
types. East European characters currently appear
more frequently than in earlier years, when their
work in mines and steel mills, or wherever, relegated them to obscurity and the film and television
industries were indifferent to ethnic themes and
subjects. Even in their new visibility on screen,
however, East Europeans remain confined to the
limited roles in which historical circumstance and
popular culture found them. They are interchangeable, like the character Latka on Taxi who lacks a
distinct nationality because he stands for all East
Europeans. As the scholarly literature concludes,
the media-made East Europeans lack the clarity,
complexity, and diversity that only a close reading
of history and appreciation of social change can
provide. For the moment, the East Europeans on
screen will still be wearing hardhats.
     The Russians, too, have not yet developed a
screen identity free of shopworn film stereotypes
and politics. Their screen fortunes ebb and flow
with the Cold War, and filmmakers continue to fish
in a deep cinematic reservoir of Russian "heavies"
whenever they cast for spies or secret police.
Gorky Park, not Clairton, is the "reel" home for
Russians. As the scholarly literature has noted,
and as screen images confirm, the media-made Russian bears a striking resemblance to his antecedents in anti-communist propaganda. He is fatter,
better-dressed, and cleaner-shaven than the old
Bolshevik screen types, but he cannot hide his
politics. The "friendly Russian" characters of a
few recent films promise a new direction, but, for
now, the Russian-as-communist character will have
to be watched.

     Major discussions of films and/or television
shows include: All in the Family (3, 44), An American Romance (24), Anna Lucasta (14), Black Fury
(4, 14, 15, 37, 39), Blue Collar (14, 32, 45), The
Caine Mutiny (14), Call Northside 777 (14, 17),
Comrade X (42, 43), The Deer Hunter (1, 6, 13, 14,

16, 30, 31), F.I.S.T. (14, 45), Flash Gordon (2),
Halka (27), I Married a Communist [alternative
title: The Woman on Pier 13] (29), The Man with
the Golden Arm (14), Mission to Moscow (8, 9, 40,
42), Ninotchka (33, 42, 43), The North Star (42,
43), The Russians Are Coming, The Russians Are
Coming (43), Saturday's Hero (14), and A Streetcar
Named Desire (14).

1. Auster, Al, and Leonard Quart. "Hollywood and
    Vietnam: The Triumph of the Will." CINEASTE
    9 (Spring 1979): 4-9.

2. Barshay, Robert. "Ethnic Stereotypes in Flash
    Gordon" (item IV-6).

3. Berger, Arthur Asa. THE TV-GUIDED AMERICAN
    (item I-13).

4. Bergman, Andrew. WE'RE IN THE MONEY (item I-
    14).

5. Brazaitis, Thomas J. "Ethnics Fear Images
    Warped"(item I-23).

6. Burke, Frank. "In Defense of The Deer Hunter"
    (item IV-9).

7. Ceplair, Larry, and Steven Englund. THE INQUI-
    SITION IN HOLLYWOOD: POLITICS IN THE FILM
    COMMUNITY, 1930-1960. Berkeley: University
    of California Press, 1979.

8. Culbert, David. "Our Awkward Ally: Mission to
    Moscow (1943)." AMERICAN HISTORY/AMERICAN
    FILM (item I-113), pp. 121-45.

9. _____, ed., MISSION TO MOSCOW. Madison:
    University of Wisconsin Press, 1980.

10. de Grazia, Edward, and Roger K. Newman. BANNED
    FILMS (item I-40).

11. Dooley, Roger. FROM SCARFACE TO SCARLETT (item
    I-41).

12. Everson, William K. THE DETECTIVE IN FILM
    (item I-46).

13. Fox, Terry Curtis. "Stalking 'The Deer
    Hunter.'" FILM COMMENT 15 (March-April
    1979): 22-24.

14. Golab, Caroline. "Stellaaaaaa. . . . . ! ! !
    ! ! ! ! !: The Slavic Stereotype in Ameri-
    can Film." KALEIDOSCOPIC LENS (item I-106),
    pp. 135-55.

15.   Gromada, Thaddeus V. "The Image of the Poles
      in American Film and Television." ETHNIC
      IMAGES IN AMERICAN FILM AND TELEVISION
      (item I-105), pp. 113-20.

16.   Hellman, John. "Vietnam and the Hollywood
      Genre Film: Inversions of American Mythol-
      ogy in The Deer Hunter and Apocalypse Now"
      (item IV-21).

17.   Higham, Charles, and Joel Greenberg. HOLLYWOOD
      IN THE FORTIES (item I-69).

18.   Jeffres, Leo W., and K. Kyoon Hur. "The For-
      gotten Media Consumer--The American Eth-
      nic." JOURNALISM Q 57 (Spring 1980): 10-
      17.

19.   _____. "White Ethnics and Their Media Images"
      (item I-72).

20.   Jones, Dorothy B. "Tomorrow the Movies IV: Is
      Hollywood Growing Up?" (item I-73).

21.   Jowett, Garth. FILM: THE DEMOCRATIC ART (item
      I-74).

22.   Kane, Kathryn Rose. VISIONS OF WAR (item I-
      76).

23.   Kelly, Katie. MY PRIME TIME: CONFESSIONS OF A
      TV WATCHER (item I-79).

24.   Koppes, Clayton R., and Gregory D. Black.
      "What to Show the World: The Office of War
      Information and Hollywood, 1942-1945" (item
      I-82).

25.   Kracauer, Siegfried. "National Types as Holly-
      wood Presents Them" (item I-83).

26.   _____. "How American Films Portray Foreign
      Types: A Psychological View of the British
      and the Russians." FILMS IN REVIEW 1 (March
      1950): 21-22, 45-47.

27.   Kucharski, Jerzy S. "Halka--Wisconsin's First
      Motion Picture." POLISH AMERICAN STUDIES 33

([no. 1] 1976): 44-47.

28. Kusielewicz, Eugene. "Questions About the Polish Image in American Film and Television." ETHNIC IMAGES IN AMERICAN FILM AND TELEVISION (item I-105), pp. 121-23.

29. Leab, Daniel J. "How Red Was My Valley: Hollywood, the Cold War Film, and I Married a Communist." J OF CONTEMPORARY HISTORY 19 (January 1984): 59-88.

30. Lehman, Peter. "'Well, what's it like over there? Can you tell us anything?': Looking for Vietnam in The Deer Hunter" (item IV-29).

31. McAlpin, Sally T. "The Deer Hunter and Mean Streets." RACE AND ETHNICITY IN THE HISTORY OF THE AMERICAS (item I-36), pp. 39-40.

32. McCray, Charles, Jr. "Blue Collar and The Traitors." RACE AND ETHNICITY IN THE HISTORY OF THE AMERICAS (item I-36), pp.26-28.

33. Paul, William. ERNST LUBITSCH'S AMERICAN COMEDY. New York: Columbia University Press, 1983.

34. Peck, Jeff. "The Heroic Soviet on the American Screen." FILM & HISTORY 9 (September 1979): 54-63.

35. Peterson, Ruth C., and L. L. Thurstone. MOTION PICTURES AND THE SOCIAL ATTITUDES OF CHILDREN (item I-116).

36. Plocha, Edward F. "Polish Stereotypes in American Film and Television: Commentary." ETHNIC IMAGES IN AMERICAN FILM AND TELEVISION (item I-105), pp. 125-28.

37. Roddick, Nick. A NEW DEAL IN ENTERTAINMENT (item I-124).

38. Roffman, Peter, and Jim Purdy. THE HOLLYWOOD SOCIAL PROBLEM FILM (I-125).

39.   _____. "The Worker and Hollywood." CINEASTE 9
       (no. 1 [1978-79]): 8-13.

40.   Shain, Russell Earl. "An Analysis of Motion
       Pictures About War Released by the American
       Film Industry, 1930-1970" (item I-134).

41.   Skinner, James M. "Cliché and Convention in
       Hollywood Cold War Anti-Communist Films."
       NORTH DAKOTA Q 46 (Summer 1978): 35-40.

42.   Small, Melvin. "Buffoons and Brave Hearts:
       Hollywood Portrays the Russians, 1939-
       1944." CALIFORNIA HISTORICAL Q 52 (Winter
       1973): 326-37.

43.   _____. "Hollywood and Teaching About Russian-
       American Relations." FILM & HISTORY 10
       (February 1980): 1-8, 15.

44.   Vidmar, Neil, and Milton Rokeach. "Archie
       Bunker's Bigotry: A Study in Selective
       Perception and Exposure." J OF COMMUNICA-
       TION 24 (Winter 1974): 36-47.

45.   Zieger, Gay P., and Robert H. Zieger. "Unions
       on the Silver Screen: A Review Essay on
       F.I.S.T., Blue Collar, and Norma Rae" (item
       II-651).

VI. GERMANS

More than any other factor, political considerations and international events forged the German
stereotype in American film and television. The
militaristic image of imperial Germany that followed Bismarck's "blood and iron" policy in the
late nineteenth century made accessible and credible the anti-German propaganda of World War I, and
Hollywood's monocled, maniacal German warmonger
survived thereafter as a staple in films about war,
international intrigue, or conspiracy. The Japanese
and Russians, too, suffered deprecating stereotypes
because of their enemy status during World War II
and the Cold War, respectively, but in the German
case the federal government aggressively intervened
to shape the group's screen image, tarring German
government and people alike as bloody Huns during
World War I and then distinguishing between Nazism
and the German people during World War II. Cold War
concerns guided Hollywood's shift to more sympathetic portrayals of Germans in film since the
1950s, as West Germany emerged as an important ally
of and symbol for American capitalism and democratic values in Europe, leaving the Russians, qua
communists, to become the inevitable and ubiquitous
bad guys in Hollywood offerings on political themes
or subjects. But the Germans have never wholly
escaped identification with war themes in film or
television--indeed, so much so that no other role
or function seems possible for media-made Germans.
As such, the German screen image remains one-dimensional, built of the cheapest cardboard and set off
from German-American historical experience or artistic expression.
The lack of alternative German images in film,
and later television, derived from historical circumstance. Before America's entry into World War I,
representations of Germans and German Americans in
American popular culture included the beer-bellied
burgher and the hefty hausfrau, as well as images

drawn from military subjects. The widely-circulated
cartoon series, "The Katzenjammer Kids," lampooned
German authoritarianism and had the German characters murder the English language and their own
sense of propriety, but the characters were likeable and not threatening. A numerically strong and
well-organized group (the second largest immigrant
group in the United States), the Germans seemed to
exude strength and purpose at the turn of the
century, counting their national German-American
associations and press and their concentrations in
important cities and states. In fact, German-American unity and purpose were illusory, for the Germans were divided by religion, class, and culture.
By the time movies developed as an entertainment
form, most people of German background in the
American population were second- or third-generation "German Americans," if they retained any Ger-
manness at all. The German groups rarely spoke with
one voice on any issue, and the assimilation of
most Germans further muted German cultural and
political force in the nation.

Few Americans, however, appreciated such nice-
ties as they surveyed the German day celebrations
in eastern and midwestern cities and watched the
ominous rise of imperial Germany in Europe. Americans admired the Germans' thrift, industry, and
music, but they also linked German immigrants with
political radicalism and social unrest (particularly in labor relations). Depictions of German
Americans as arrogant, stupid, and violent filtered
into early silent films, while positive German
traits often did not.

Confronting rampant anti-German stereotypes
increasingly appearing in print and film, as occurred during World War I, German-American organizations briefly rallied to protest the grossest
distortions, but the fragmentation and weakness of
German America undermined such efforts. The war
hastened the decline of a German America already
fast disappearing anyway. The Germans in the United
States were unprepared and unable to defend themselves against war propaganda and hysteria, and
their thinning ranks ended whatever power they
might have exerted after the war as a lobby to
oppose screen stereotypes or as a market to support
German-American themes. Thus, almost from the beginning of film,   the German screen image was,   and

remained, the product of external forces, events in
Europe, rather than a reflection of German experience in America. The German-American vanished
from the American screen with the war, a casualty
of its film cousin, the German as militarist. The
German soldier survived on screen to fight again--
and again.(38, 51, 52)

During World War I American filmmakers had discovered that war subjects were popular escapist
entertainment. Between 1914 and 1917 Germans in
spiked helmets almost completely monopolized villainy in American films, and even newsreels, about
the war, and American filmmakers warned against an
approaching German menace. In Thomas Dixon's sensational and controversial The Fall of a Nation
(1916), for example, an unprepared America falls
victim to cruel German-looking invaders who miss no
opportunity to inflict humiliation and suffering on
their victims. After the United States entered the
war, the American film industry joined the public
in its anti-German excesses. Just as everything
German was now suspect in America, and renaming
things German was the only means of salvaging them
(thus, sauerkraut became liberty cabbage, dachsunds
became liberty pups, and so on), the German loomed
as evil incarnate in war films and morality plays.
The propaganda-minded film industry made no distinctions between Germans and German Americans, as,
for example, in the widely-exhibited The Little
American (1917), starring Mary Pickford, in which a
German American leaves his love, "the little American," to enlist in the Kaiser's cause and later
assaults the Pickford character, who happens to be
in France during a bloody German invasion.

Many war films made the Kaiser the personification of German arrogance and cruelty. In such potboilers as The Kaiser-The Beast of Berlin (1918)
and To Hell with The Kaiser (1918) the filmmakers,
in concert with the "Hate the Hun" campaigns or-
chestrated by the Creel Commission, encouraged
Americans to "Get the Kaiser" by any means (which,
in the movies, somebody always did). The Armistice
in late 1918 ended audience demand for war films;
indeed, film exhibitors refused war-related films
and, whenever possible, advertised their fare as
"NOT a war film." But the image of the Germans as
warmongers had become firmly lodged in popular
belief, where it would reside to this day.(4, 5,

10, 15, 16, 21, 22, 23, 24, 26, 27, 28, 37, 38, 41, 47, 51, 52, 55, 57, 69, 77)

During the 1920s and 1930s American disillusionment with the Versailles Treaty, indeed with the country's involvement in the war altogether, fostered isolationism in international affairs and disinterest in European subjects. Between 1920 and 1939 American studios released few major films about the war, and between 1921 and 1930, only about 150 American-made films out of more than 6,000 releases in any way treated Germans or Germany. Save for Behind the Door, a box-office hit in 1920, the German American disappeared from the screen. In his place appeared complex, even sympathetically drawn, German figures. Old hostilities toward German militarism remained, as did stereotypes of haughty and over-bearing German aristocrats (an image Erich von Stroheim cultivated profitably in the United States), but post-war filmmakers generally balanced positive and negative images of Germans, associating the former with the common people and the latter with aristocrats and Prussian officers. In the powerful All Quiet on the Western Front (1930), based on Erich Maria Remarque's novel, American audiences saw unflattering German officers and even a professor trumpeting the glories of war, but the film turned on the tragedy of seven German youths who could not escape the war's horrors. All Quiet on the Western Front, and John Ford's earlier Four Sons (1928), reminded Americans that Germans knew pain and gave love and loyalty just as Americans did. Still, the movie-made German remained dressed in military garb.(21, 22, 38, 51, 52, 65, 69)

Between the two world wars another German force invaded American movies and, for a time, deflected attention from the German military stereotype. The growing sophistication of American movie-going audiences by the 1920s had created a demand for mature themes in films. The American filmmakers satisfied the new taste as much as possible, but foreign-made films also found a market in American theaters. More than any other imports, German films influenced American film. The works of Ernst Lubitsch gained favor, especially those starring the earthy Pola Negri,(5-33) and expressionist films like The Cabinet of Dr. Caligari, despite only modest commercial success in the United

States, powerfully affected American directors.
German emigre Erich von Stroheim introduced an
unabashed modernism to film with his Foolish Wives
(1921/1922). The sensuality of Foolish Wives,
throbbing with von Stroheim's usual emphasis on
depravity and glamour, angered critics and shocked
audiences, but fascinated them at the same time.
The film was a huge box-office hit. During the
1920s German film imports increasingly became, in
William Everson's words, "both fashionable and
reasonably profitable." German directors and actors
moved to Hollywood to capitalize on the American
interest in German film, and studios hired German
filmmakers to give the "German" look to American
productions. William Fox signed F.W. Murnau, who
proceeded to make Sunrise (1927), the most widely-
admired and critically acclaimed silent film of the
decade in terms of its artistic expression. Sunrise
succeeded, however, because of its visual techniques and universality in message, not because of
any discernible "German" content and imagery.(10,
24. See also 1-138.)
     More important, in the long run, for the German
image in American film were the players, the German
emigre artists who brought European manners to the
American screen. European women had already received a license for a sexuality in film that few
American actresses could claim, because of social
convention, personality, and studio policies geared
toward cleaning up Hollywood's image. During the
1920s, the era of the female star, the Europeans
made the most of it, cornering the film market on
openly sexual female characters who did not have to
die for their sins on screen. The Polish-born Pola
Negri stepped from her popularity in German imports
to American productions, and her vitality continued
to enthrall American audiences in the age of silent
film. Negri did not survive the transition to sound
films, but Marlene Dietrich had no such trouble. As
the cabaret singer in Josef von Sternberg's dual-
language production of The Blue Angel (1930), she
communicated a power beyond spoken German or
English subtitles. Playing prostitutes or fallen
women, Dietrich, like the Swedish Greta Garbo in
her films, seemed incapable of submission to any
male character. Her screen presence was too powerful. Strong European women in film helped forge
the identification of Europeans, notably Germans,

with sensuality, a trait that, during and after
World War II, would come to characterize German
images.(10, 24)

Erich von Stroheim's posturing, combined with
his grotesque over-acting and make-up, proved even
more potent than female sexuality in shaping German
images. In a host of films, he strutted about as
the corrupt German aristocrat, the cruel Prussian
officer, and his monocled, scar-faced screen personality became synonymous with villainy. Von
Stroheim's characters infuriated audiences. They
also kept alive, vividly so, the stereotype of the
arrogant, militant German. In the major films he
directed--from Blind Husbands (1919) to The Wedding
March (1927) and Queen Kelly (1928)--which, save
for Greed (1925), largely centered on court life in
Vienna, von Stroheim's preoccupation with sexuality
and depravity and his excesses in showing them
reconfirmed the connection between Germans and
degeneracy that World War I propagandists had so
assiduously cultivated.(6, 11, 33, 45, 50)

Adolph Hitler's real excesses and Nazism's
degeneracy redirected attention to German military
themes even before American involvement in World
War II. One of the first effects of Hitler's rise
in Germany was the emigration of German artists,
filmmakers, and writers, many of whom settled in
Hollywood. There the refugees tried to prod America
out of its self-imposed isolationism. The New Deal
had already awakened the social consciousness of
the film industry, and Hitler's masterful manipulation of film and radio had demonstrated the propagandistic power of mass media. The emigres needed
no such education. Whenever possible, they introduced political themes into their work. Americans,
however, resisted entanglement in Europe's troubles
through most of the 1930s, and as late as 1941
isolationists used a Congressional investigation to
criticize Hollywood for promoting intervention by
making any movies about wartime subjects.(28, 37,
58, 59, 73)

With the outbreak of war in Europe in 1939, and
the loss of the lucrative German film market for
export, Hollywood was no longer hesitant to attack
Nazism on screen. In Warner Brothers' Confessions
of a Nazi Spy (1939) Hollywood broke with isolationism. The film featured cruel, deceitful German
subversives threatening the unprepared United

States. In Escape (1940) Nazi brutality received
treatment; in The Mortal Storm (1940) Nazi concentration camps appear. Most film fare, however,
remained bland entertainment, and movies about war
served up old stereotypes about Germans, and other
Europeans.(25, 27, 28, 38, 53, 61, 65)

The industry's willingness to address war subjects did at least provide employment for German
emigre actors, who, from 1940 through the end of
the war, were much in demand for their German
accents to play Nazi characters. Conrad Veidt, for
example, won critical acclaim for his role as Major
Strasser in Casablanca (1942), and von Stroheim
outdid himself as the Prussian officer in The North
Star (1943). Returned to uniform, the German image
tramped once more across the American screen.(73)

From December 1941 through the duration of the
war, movies involving the Nazis abounded. Richard
Oehling estimates that, between 1939 and 1945,
Hollywood produced over fifty feature films in some
way treating the German enemy, but most of those
films were released after the United States had
declared war on the Axis powers. Hollywood films
generally presented three themes in movies about
Germans: Nazis as spies, the Nazis as occupiers of
conquered peoples, or the Nazis in Germany. The
Nazi spies were so overdrawn in their fanaticism
that they were hardly believable as threats; indeed, their fanaticism readily made transparent
their disguises and revealed their designs. In
films about German conquest and occupation, Nazi
officers committed numerous outrages, and in those
movies about Nazi personality types and life in
Germany (e.g., Hotel Berlin [1945], which collected
virtually every Nazi type), they practiced almost
unrelieved cruelty. By Russell Shain's count, the
film Nazis reached their highest "per minute" rate
of evil in Hitler's Children (1943), in which they
violated motherhood, family, love, individual freedom, religion, bodily integrity, and more.(1, 5,
13, 14, 17, 20, 25, 26, 27, 34, 35, 38, 40, 42, 43,
48, 51, 53, 54, 55, 63, 65, 72)

The film Nazis thrived on sadism and brutality,
but the film Germans did not. Recalling the excesses of World War I and attempting to make film
an effective instrument of propaganda, the United
States Office of War Information (OWI) criticized
Hollywood for its early war films, which obscured

the real reasons the United States was fighting the
war by depicting the enemy in simplistic, one-
dimensional terms. Convinced that motion pictures
could convey the complex issues of the war, the
OWI, through its Bureau of Motion Pictures, issued
guidelines in 1942 that Hollywood producers were to
follow and later even reviewed movie scripts to
make sure Hollywood was complying. In its criticism
of many Hollywood releases, the OWI further sought
to manipulate film content, urging Hollywood toward
the production of films on ideological themes.

In the case of German images, the OWI stipulated that filmmakers draw distinctions between
Nazis and Germans. America was fighting an idea, a
political system of totalitarianism, not the German
people. The distinction between Nazis and Germans
often blurred in Hollywood films, and the War Department projected its own documentaries of the
Germans as a warlike people, but the German image
in World War II films was vastly superior to that
of the Japanese who received no sensitivity from
the OWI or Hollywood. The "good German" emerged as
a movie type, generally in films about life in Nazi
Germany. German Americans, too, were absolved of
blame for Nazism and reappeared in World War II
films as loyal Americans (e.g., They Came To Blow
Up America [1943] and The House on 92nd Street
[1945]).(2, 3, 13, 18, 25, 27, 28, 32, 38, 40, 42,
44, 51, 54, 63, 65, 67, 70, 78)

The separation of the "good German" from Nazism
continued after World War II. Allied victory revealed more real horrors and atrocities committed
by the Nazis than were ever imagined in film.   The
Nazi became in fact and film the embodiment of
evil. The good German, meanwhile, assumed a new
life in the post-war world. In rebuilding West
Germany to counter communism during the Cold War,
America also refurbished the German image. German
qualities of loyalty, industry, and organization
were now prized. In films the "good German" now
fought America's fight. By the 1950s the "good
Germans" of Hollywood included even German generals
such as Field Marshal Erwin Rommel. In Rommel--The
Desert Fox (1951) James Mason played Rommel as an
aristocrat who plotted to overthrow his Nazi over-
lords and who fought for country rather than ideology. By the 1970s, in A Bridge Too Far (1977) and
such British productions as Cross of Iron (1977)

and The Eagle Has Landed (1976/1977), American
audiences were, in Daniel Leab's judgment, "manipulated to root for the Germans."(9, 13, 38, 39, 51,
60)

The German military did not come off well in
most post-war American movies about World War II.
The Germans, after all, had been the real enemy.
Movies such as The Guns of Navarone (1961) avoided
ideological questions but clearly showed the Wehr-
macht as threatening to American soldiers. However
presented, the German film image still had not
escaped identification with military themes.

But the real bad guy was the Nazi, who indulged
himself in every deviancy and sensuality possible
on screen. Various films essayed Hitler and his
following (e.g., Hitler [1962] and Hitler: The Last
Ten Days [1972]), and several became, in Andrew
Sarris' words, "sado-masochistic spectacles" (e.g.,
The Night Porter [1974]). The Nazi sometimes lived
on in film as the ex-Nazi, hatching new schemes to
conquer the free world, including a plan to send
forth Hitler clones (The Boys from Brazil [1978]).
The media-made ex-Nazi also resurfaced as the mad
scientist in countless films, from Dr. Strangelove
(1964) to the James Bond series. Whatever the
guise, even as a communist, the film ex-Nazi retained unshakable loyalty to Hitler and belief in
Nazism's ultimate destiny or evinced at least one
perversion.(31, 38, 51, 62, 69)

The German image on television borrows heavily
from Hollywood film constructions. Leering Nazi
spies and Gestapo still lurk in late night television reruns of old movies. Film's recent focus on
Nazi or ex-Nazi threats also appears as prime-time
television movie entertainment or as late night
movie entries.

Television's own image making has oscillated
between the ridiculous and the real. In the popular
long-running (and currently syndicated) comedy
series, Hogan's Heroes, set in a German prisoner-
of-war camp during World War II, Allied prisoners
easily out-foxed their German captors, who were so
vain and stupid they were discredible even as caricatures of German types. Likewise, the German military in Hogan's Heroes and several action series
(e.g., Combat and The Rat Patrol) seemed so inept
as to be harmless. Within the past few years,
however, docudramas about Nazi Germany have brought

television viewers into direct confrontation with
the Holocaust and the seductions of Nazism for
Germans. In Holocaust there is no mincing of Nazi
cruelty, and German complicity in the horrors, at
least by silence, is implied. In making Inside the
Third Reich, a docudrama about Albert Speer, actors
and directors worried that the production was portraying Speer too sympathetically--an indication of
television's sensitivity to historical accuracy in
depicting Nazi Germany. The recent success of the
docudrama as a form, the willingness of artists and
producers to confront the Holocaust in their work,
and America's fascination with World War II--all
suggest that television will attempt additional
essays on Nazi Germany and that the silliness of
Hogan's Heroes is past. Whatever the direction of
television's offerings about Germans, the German
American and the German out of uniform seem unlikely subjects for visual treatment. In that
sense, television has inherited and extended the
film image of the German as almost exclusively a
military creature.(7, 30, 39, 46, 51, 74)

    The scholarship on German images reflects the
preoccupation of film and television with military
subjects. Only Daniel Leab and Richard Oehling have
written overviews charting the evolution of German
images and linking American popular culture with
varying German images and stereotypes. Only they
have included examples of German Americans in film
or attempted to show how images of Germans in
Europe affected Germans in America. Most other
scholarship has examined the German image in the
wartime context alone or has discussed one film or
television production on some aspect of German or
Nazi war activity.(38, 39, 51, 52, 53, 54)
    The German image in World War I has been the
focus of several works. Kevin Brownlow compared the
image-making power of early movies in depicting
Germans, Native Americans, and others.(4) Robert
Henderson noted that D.W. Griffith participated in
smearing the Germans in Hearts of the World (1918)
but, like many Americans during the 1920s, recanted
his earlier views of the war, which showed up in
his 1924 film Isn't Life Wonderful.(16) The development of the "Hate the Hun" campaign during the

war, and its consequences for German images in
film, receives attention from several writers.
Michael Isenberg places the war film, and German
images to a lesser extent, in the context of America's shifting attitudes toward film as a medium
and its view of itself in the world.(21, 22, 23)
Garth Jowett discusses the interplay between government, audience, and film industry.(28) Daniel
Leab connects World War I stereotypes with German
images in American popular culture.(38) Timothy
Lyons surveys the World War I film in Hollywood.(11) Charles Mitchell explores Beware as an
example of wartime propaganda.(47) Richard Oehling
describes the changing film images of Germans at
war from 1914 through the 1930s.(51, 52) Richard
Soderbergh analyzes plot patterns in Hollywood war
films from 1916 to 1930.(69)
    Less successful have been the pictorial his-
tories of war, which generally provide vivid stills
to demonstrate the various stereotypes but accom-
pany the pictures with weak, even contradictory,
texts. Ivan Butler's assertion that Germans were
expected to betray their evil country in World War
I and World War II films is not supported by his
visual examples.(5) Clyde Jeavons does little more
than set American movie images against those of
European filmmakers during both world wars.(26)
Tom Perlmutter, however, gives a detailed pictorial
and historical account of German and other wartime
images, observing how the war movie as a genre came
into its own during World War II. He traces the
origins of propagandistic film in World War I
through World War II, observing that the incidence
of German cruelty in film rose in proportion to
American involvement in European affairs and that
American filmmakers in World War II learned from
the film industry's excesses in World War I and
from the Nazis' hypnotic propaganda films of the
1930s.(55)
    The propaganda function of film has been a
major source of information concerning German images. World War I demonstrated the propaganda power
of film and led to several studies of film's influence on audiences. German images were among
those tested in such studies. By the 1930s American
moviemakers appreciated film's ability to convey
social messages. During the Depression Hollywood
turned its attention to social problems, and in

several films Germans appeared among the Americans
afflicted by bad management, evil employers, or
impersonal economic forces. The new social and
political consciousness of several filmmakers combined with their awe over the propaganda effects of
European, especially German, film productions in
the 1930s to lead them to try their hands at the
form. Early criticism of Nazism came from such
experiments.(28, 56, 58, 59, 61, 65, 75)

Concerning World War II, the Office of War
Information's role in shaping film images has been
the subject of several works. Gregory Black and
Clayton Koppes, especially, relate the OWI's sophisticated approach to film and its disgust with
crude Hollywood varieties of propaganda.(2, 3)
Other writers have described the nature of film
images produced by Hollywood and government filmmakers. The German contributors to Alice Goetz's
collection, for example, comment on America's ability to make distinctions between "good Germans" and
"nasty Nazis," among the several subjects they explore.(13) Charles Higham and Joel Greenberg survey
the cardboard Nazi types in films of the 1940s.(17)
William Hughes describes the techniques of propaganda in World War II films.(18) Lewis Jacobs marks
the shift from escapist entertainment to propaganda
in film.(25) Robert Joseph surveys the treatment
of Germans in war films and notes Hollywood's success in toning down stereotypes of Germans during
World War II.(27) Garth Jowett details the government's role in analyzing and influencing film
content.(28) Kathryn Kane discusses Germans in
combat films.(29) Siegfried Kracauer remarks on the
reemergence of the German military type after
1939.(34) Harold Lavine and James Wechsler explore
the phenonenom of American war propaganda in its
various forms up to 1939.(37) Daniel Leab relates
the OWI's work to Hollywood's failure to present
realistic images.(38, 39) Richard Lingeman places
film in the context of the home front.(40) Arthur
McClure relates the subject matter of World War II
films.(42) Roger Manvell examines films from the
American soldiers' viewpoint as well as discussing
propaganda films.(43) Robert Morseberger argues
that Hitchcock's Lifeboat (1944) implicates all
Germans in evil.(49) Richard Oehling traces the
German image from the 1930s through the war.(51,
53, 54) Harry Sauberli points to the melting-pot

metaphor in American war films, which included
German Americans among the American soldiers united
in a common cause.(63) Russell Shain shows how
United States policy determined film images.(65)
K.R.M. Short argues that American film ignored
Nazism's anti-Semitism until The Great Dictator
(1940) and American entry into the war and even
then hardly imagined the reality of Hitler's "final
solution."(67) Richard Steele discusses the production history of a War Department film intended
to contrast Nazi tyranny and American freedom.(70)
Lawrence Suid maintains that, although presented in
film as evil, Germans fared better than the Japanese because of their European heritage and their
color.(72)

Especially revealing in understanding the
forces behind governmental intervention in filmmaking during World War II are two articles deliv-
ered as part of the Writers' Congress conference
sponsored by the Hollywood Writers' Mobilization in
1943. Harry Kurnitz warned that stereotypes of
stupid Nazis and comical Gestapo lulled Americans
into a false security, that stereotyping the enemy
as a low-grade moron was as dangerous to the American war effort and morale as depicting him as a
superman. Similarly, Virginia Wright and David
Hanna, after reviewing film characterizations of
Nazis from 1939 to 1943, decried the tendency to
separate the German military from the Gestapo, for
they feared such a distinction would encourage
Americans to believe a reasonable peace with Nazi
Germany was possible.(35, 78)

The rehabilitation of the German image after
World War II has impressed, and disturbed, some
authors.(9, 39, 44, 60) So, too, has the persistence of such stereotypes as the monocle and spiked
helmet, which distort the role of class in controlling German society.(30, 31) Several writers
have wondered at television's ability to present
realistic accounts of Nazism, due to the medium's
limited political range which militates against
extremes and seeks to avoid controversy.(7, 46, 74)
The subjects of post-World War II images, visual
symbols, audience responses to media images, and
television's involvement in mirroring and making
images--all remain understudied. The influence of
German cinematic techniques and German emigre
artists needs attention. Less surprising, perhaps,

given the military stamp of the German image in
film and television, has been the absence of work
on the images of German women. Melva Baker made a
few sparing observations on German women in her
study of women in film during World War II, but she
ignored German Americans and did not even try to
locate previous images in the history of popular
culture.(1) Indicative of the military stereotype
attached to Germans is the title of Dwight
Whitney's article about Inga Stevens, who plays the
German housekeeper on the television show Benson.
The "storm trooper" refers to Stevens' seeming
German authoritarian manner. Whitney passes over
the logical and obvious derivation of Stevens'
housekeeper character from the old stereotype of
the German hausfrau.(76) Recurring stereotypes in
film serials have also attracted little scholarly
attention, although Richard Hurst notes the German
case in his study of Republic Studios.(20)
     Although Germans have largely disappeared as an
ethnic group within the United States, and long ago
vanished as German Americans on the screen, the
German marches on in film and television. What is
now needed in scholarship about the German image is
an appreciation of its varied historical roots, its
ties to American popular culture as well as to
political events, and its effects on Germans in
America as well as Americans generally. In that
regard, the most useful directions for research
seem now to be the perspectives of Daniel Leab and
Richard Oehling, who take the long view by observing the evolution of German images over time
and at least in part as outgrowths of popular
beliefs, not just wartime animosities, and the
suggestions of William Everson, John R. Taylor, and
those few others writing about the impact of
foreign film and artists on American filmmakers and
audiences.

     Major discussions of film and/or television
shows include: All Quiet on the Western Front (4,
10, 21, 22, 24, 38, 51, 52, 69), All Through the
Night (17), Barbed Wire (4), Behind the Door (4,
38), Benson (76), Berlin Correspondent (2), Beware
(47), A Bridge Too Far (60), Casablanca (1, 2, 43,
64), Confessions of a Nazi Spy (38, 43, 53, 58, 61,

78), Cross of Iron (60), The Eagle Has Landed (60),
The Enemy Within (68), Escape (43), The Fall of a
Nation (51), Foolish Wives (6, 10, 11, 33, 50),
Foreign Correspondent (17, 53), The Four Horsemen
of the Apocalypse (4, 38, 51, 52), Four Sons (51,
56), The Great Dictator (43, 67), The Guns of
Navarone (19), Hearts of the World (4, 16, 27,
52), High Treason (68), The Hitler Gang (17), Hitler's Children (1, 54, 78), Holocaust (46, 74),
Hotel Berlin (17, 51, 54), The House on 92nd Street
(53), Inside the Third Reich (7), Isn't Life Wonderful? (4, 52), Judgment at Nuremberg (51), Lifeboat (49), The Little American (38, 52), Man Hunt
(17, 43), The Moon Is Down (27, 54, 78), Mortal
Storm (17, 43), My Four Years in Germany (38),
Night Porter (62), Prelude to War (70), Sunrise
(10), Tarzan Triumphs (2), Underground (17), and
the serials during the 1940s (20).

1.   Baker, Melva Joyce. "Images of Women in Film:
     The War Years, 1941-1945" (item II-60).

2.   Black, Gregory D., and Clayton R. Koppes. "OWI
     Goes to the Movies." FOREIGN SERVICE J 51
     (August 1974): 18-23, 29-30.

3.   _____. "OWI Goes to the Movies: The Bureau of
     Intelligence's Criticism of Hollywood,
     1942-1943." PROLOGUE 6 (Spring 1974): 44-
     59.

4.   Brownlow, Kevin. THE WAR, THE WEST, AND THE
     WILDERNESS. New York: Alfred A. Knopf,
     1979.

5.   Butler, Ivan. THE WAR FILM. New York: A.S.
     Barnes, 1974.

6.   Curtiss, Thomas Quinn. VON STROHEIM. New York:
     Farrar, Straus & Giroux, 1971.

7.   Davidson, Bill. "Behind the Scenes Battles at
     'Inside the Third Reich.'" TV GUIDE 30 (May
     8, 1982): 26-28, 30.

8.   de Grazia, Edward, and Roger K. Newman. BANNED
     FILMS (item I-40).

9.   Dworkin, Martin S. "Clean Germans and Dirty
     Politics." FILM COMMENT 3 (Winter 1965):
     36-41.

10. Everson, William K. AMERICAN SILENT FILM
     (item I-45).

11. Finler, Joel W. STROHEIM. Berkeley: University
     of California Press, 1968.

12. Fyne, Robert. "The Unsung Heroes of World War
     II" (item IV-19).

13. Goetz, Alice, ed. HOLLYWOOD UND DIE NAZIS.
     [HOLLYWOOD AND THE NAZIS] Hamburg: 1977.

14. Goldfarb, Alvin. "Adolph Hitler as Portrayed
     in Drama and Film During His Lifetime." J
     OF POPULAR CULTURE 13 (Summer 1979): 55-66.

15. Griffith, Richard, and Arthur Mayer. THE
     MOVIES (item I-62).

16. Henderson, Robert M. D.W. GRIFFITH (item
     II-308).

17. Higham, Charles, and Joel Greenberg. HOLLYWOOD
     IN THE FORTIES (item I-69).

18. Hughes, William. "The Propagandist's Art."
     FILM & HISTORY 4 (September 1974): 11-15.

19. Hunt, Albert. "The Film." DISCRIMINATION AND
     POPULAR CULTURE. Edited by Denys Thompson.
     Baltimore: Penguin Books, 1964, pp. 99-122.

20. Hurst, Richard M. REPUBLIC STUDIOS: BETWEEN
     POVERTY ROW AND THE MAJORS. Metuchen, N.J.:
     Scarecrow Press, 1979.

21. Isenberg, Michael T. "War on Film: The Ameri-
     can Cinema and World War I, 1914-1941."
     Ph.D. diss., University of Colorado, 1973.

22. _____. WAR ON FILM: THE AMERICAN CINEMA AND
     WORLD WAR I, 1914-1941. Rutherford, N.J.:
     Fairleigh Dickinson University Press, 1981.

23. _____. "World War I Film Comedies and Ameri-
     can Society: The Concern with Authoritari-
     anism." FILM & HISTORY 5 (September 1975):
     7-15, 21.

24. Jacobs, Lewis. THE RISE OF THE AMERICAN FILM
     (item I-70).

25. _____. "World War II and the American Film."
     CINEMA J 7 (Winter 1967-68): 1-21.

26. Jeavons, Clyde. A PICTORIAL HISTORY OF WAR
     FILMS. London: Hamlyn, 1974.

27. Joseph, Robert. "From Hun to Nazi by Way of
     the Motion Picture." CALIFORNIA ARTS AND
     ARCHITECTURE 60 (June 1943): 18-19, 54.

28. Jowett, Garth. FILM: THE DEMOCRATIC ART (item
     I-74).

29. Kane, Kathryn Rose. VISIONS OF WAR (item I-
     76).

30. Kayser, Hans Christoph. "The Monocle as Symbol
     of German Arrogance in the American Media."
     ETHNIC IMAGES IN AMERICAN FILM AND TELEVI-
     SION (item I-105), pp. 69-71.

31. _____. "The Sadist and the Clown: The Chang-
     ing Nazi Image in the American Media." J OF
     POPULAR CULTURE 10 (Spring 1977): 848-51.

32. Koppes, Clayton R., and Gregory D. Black,
     "What To Show the World: The Office of War
     Information and Hollywood" (item I-82).

33. Koszarski, Richard. THE MAN YOU LOVED TO HATE:
     ERICH VON STROHEIM AND HOLLYWOOD.   New
     York: Oxford University Press, 1983.

34. Kracauer, Siegfried. "National Types as Holly-
     wood Presents Them" (item I-83).

35. Kurnitz, Harry. "Screen Humor." THE PRO-
     CEEDINGS OF THE CONFERENCE HELD IN OCTOBER
     1943 (item I-173), pp. 230-35.

36. Landry, Robert J. "The Movies: Better Than
     Ever?" PREJUDICE AND THE LIVELY ARTS (item
     I-12), pp. 10-11.

37. Lavine, Harold, and James Wechsler. WAR PROPA-
     GANDA AND THE UNITED STATES. New Haven,
     Conn.: Yale University Press, 1940.

38. Leab, Daniel J. "Deutschland, USA: German
     Images in American Film." KALEIDOSCOPIC
     LENS (item I-106), pp. 156-81.

39. _____. "Goethe or Attila? The Celluloid Ger-
     man." ETHNIC IMAGES IN AMERICAN FILM AND
     TELEVISION (item I-105), pp. 63-68.

40. Lingeman, Richard R. DON'T YOU KNOW THERE'S A
     WAR ON?: THE AMERICAN HOME FRONT, 1941-
     1945. New York: Putnam, 1970.

41. Lyons, Timothy J. "Hollywood and World War I,

1914-1918." J OF POPULAR FILM 1 (no. 1
1972): 15-30.

42. McClure, Arthur F. "Hollywood at War: The
American Motion Picture and World War II"
(item I-91).

43. Manvell, Roger. FILMS AND THE SECOND WORLD
WAR. South Brunswick, N.J.: A.S. Barnes &
Company, 1974.

44. Mariani, John. "Let's Not Be Beastly to the
Nazis." FILM COMMENT 15 (January-February
1979): 49-53.

45. Marion, Denis. "Erich von Stroheim: The Legend
and the Fact." SIGHT AND SOUND 31 (Winter
1961-62): 22-23, 51.

46. Messerschmid, Felix. "Nachuberlegungen zu Hol-
ocaust." [Afterthoughts on Holocaust]
GESCHICHTE IN WISSENSCHAFT UND UNTERRICHT
(West Germany) 30 (1979): 175-78.

47. Mitchell, Charles Reed. "New Message to America: James W. Gerard's Beware and World War
I Propaganda." J OF POPULAR FILM 4 (no. 4
1975): 275-95.

48. Morella, Joe, Edward Epstein, and John Griggs.
THE FILMS OF WORLD WAR II. Secaucus, N.J.:
Citadel Press, 1973.

49. Morseberger, Robert E. "Adrift in Steinbeck's
Lifeboat" (item II-450).

50. Noble, Peter. HOLLYWOOD SCAPEGOAT: THE BIOGRA-
PHY OF ERICH VON STROHEIM. London: Fortune
Press, 1950; New York: Arno Press, 1972.

51. Oehling, Richard A. "The German-Americans,
Germany, and the American Media." ETHNIC
IMAGES IN AMERICAN FILM AND TELEVISION
(item I-105), pp. 51-62.

52. _____. "Germans in Hollywood Films: [part 1]
The Changing Image, 1914-1939." FILM &
HISTORY 3 (May 1973): 1-10, 26.

53.   _____. "Germans in Hollywood Films: [part 2]
        The Changing Image, The Early War Years,
        1939-1942." FILM & HISTORY 4 (May 1974): 8-
        10.

54.   _____. "Germans in Hollywood." [part 3] FILM
        & HISTORY 4(September 1974): 6-10.

55.   Perlmutter, Tom. WAR MOVIES. Secaucus, N.J.:
        Castle Books, 1974.

56.   Peterson, Ruth C., and L.L. Thurstone. MOTION
        PICTURES AND THE SOCIAL ATTITUDES OF CHIL-
        DREN (item I-116).

57.   Ramsaye, Terry. A MILLION AND ONE NIGHTS (item
        I-121).

58.   Roddick, Nick. A NEW DEAL IN ENTERTAINMENT
        (item I-124).

59.   Roffman, Peter, and Jim Purdy. THE HOLLYWOOD
        SOCIAL PROBLEM FILM (item I-125).

60.   Rubenstein, Lenny. "Where Have All the Nazis
        Gone?" CINEASTE 8 (no. 2 [1977]): 32-35.

61.   Sandeen, Eric J. "Anti-Nazi Sentiment in Film:
        Confessions of a Nazi Spy and the German-
        American Bund." AMERICAN STUDIES 20 (Fall
        1979): 69-81.

62.   Sarris, Andrew. POLITICS AND CINEMA. New York:
        Columbia University Press, 1978.

63.   Sauberli, Harry A. "Hollywood and World War
        II: A Survey of Themes of Hollywood Films
        About the War, 1940-1945" (item I-130).

64.   Schickel, Richard. "Some Nights in Casablan-
        ca." FAVORITE MOVIES: CRITICS' CHOICE (item
        I-109), pp. 114-25.

65.   Shain, Russell Earl. "An Analysis of Motion
        Pictures About War Released by the American
        Film Industry, 1930-1970" (item I-134).

66. Shindler, Colin. HOLLYWOOD GOES TO WAR (item
     I-135).

67. Short, K.R.M. "Hollywood Fights Anti-Semitism,
     1940-1945." FILM & RADIO PROPAGANDA IN
     WORLD WAR II. Edited by K.R.M. Short. Knox-
     ville: University of Tennessee Press, 1983,
     pp. 146-72.

68. Skinner, James M. "Cliché and Convention in
     Hollywood Cold War Anti-Communist Films"
     (item V-41).

69. Soderbergh, Peter A. "'Aux Armes': The Rise of
     the Hollywood War Film, 1916-1930." SOUTH
     ATLANTIC Q 65 (Autumn 1966): 509-22.

70. Steele, Richard W. "'The Greatest Gangster
     Movie Ever Filmed': Prelude to War." PRO-
     LOGUE 11 (Winter 1979): 221-35.

71. Stein, Elliott. "Germany in Winter." FILM
     COMMENT 17 (May-June 1981): 20-23.

72. Suid, Lawrence H. GUTS & GLORY: GREAT AMERICAN
     WAR MOVIES (item IV-44).

73. Taylor, John Russell. STRANGERS IN PARADISE:
     THE HOLLYWOOD EMIGRES, 1933-1950. New York:
     Holt, Rinehart & Winston, 1983.

74. Toland, John. "Can TV Dramas Convey the Hor-
     rors of the Holocaust?" TV GUIDE 30 (Feb-
     ruary 13, 1982): 6-8, 10.

75. White, David Manning, and Richard Averson. THE
     CELLULOID WEAPON (item I-166).

76. Whitney, Dwight. "Achtung! It's the Storm
     Trooper." TV GUIDE 29 (May 16, 1981): 19-
     20, 22.

77. Willett, Ralph. "Nativism and Assimilation:
     The Hollywood Aspect" (item I-168).

78. Wright, Virginia, and David Hanna. "Motion
     Picture Survey." THE PROCEEDINGS OF THE

CONFERENCE HELD IN OCTOBER 1943 (item I-173).

VII. HISPANIC AMERICANS

Although Hispanic Americans are the nation's fastest growing minority group according to the 1980 census, they are still proportionately underrepresented in both television shows and feature films. While they comprise approximately ten percent of the population, they are featured in only one percent of the roles on major television shows, and even less so in major films.(27) Hispanic groups also complain that the roles that currently exist perpetuate long-standing stereotypes of Hispanics and Hispanic Americans which date back to the last century.

The earliest representations of Hispanics in American films displayed an extremely violent individual, often known as a "greaser," who soon became a stock villain in silent films.(17, 20) One scholar has even characterized the Hispanic as "the convenient villain" during the first two decades of the twentieth century.(36) The "greaser" robbed, murdered, pillaged, raped, cheated, gambled, lied, and displayed virtually every vice that could be shown on the screen. This image flowered in a series of "greaser" films, such as Tony the Greaser (1911), Broncho Billy and the Greaser, and The Greaser's Revenge (1914). The term "greaser" quickly supplanted "Mexican" or "Latin" as a synonym for the violent Hispanic on the screen.

The coming of the Mexican Revolution in 1910 accentuated the Latin image of violence on the screen as a series of pseudo-documentaries of the conflict were exhibited in American theatres. Real and fictional events soon began to blur, as one of the leading agrarian revolutionaries, Pancho Villa, signed a contract with the Mutual Film Corporation. Villa allowed Mutual cameramen to record his exploits, and, in return, he agreed to fight during daylight hours if possible and delay his attacks

until the cameras were in position. Villa accepted
this unorthodox arrangement since his forces needed
money for munitions. The resultant films tended to
emphasize the gory details of the Mexican
Revolution and ignore the political questions. For
example, The New York Times noted that Barbarous
Mexico (1913) tended to linger on "the burning of
dead bodies on the battlefield."(50, 80)

The Mexican government soon objected to
Hollywood's portrayal of its citizens as "bandits
and sneaks" and threatened to ban all films by
companies which offended its people. This 1922
threat caused screenwriters to treat their
neighbors to the south with more care. The
"greaser" swiftly lost his Mexican nationality in
the attempt to diffuse potential complaints, but
his ghost still haunted new screenplays which
concerned Hispanic characters.(20)

Clever subterfuges often placed an unnamed
"greaser" in a new locale. Rather than use the name
of an actual country and risk offending its
inhabitants, screenwriters began to create mythical
cities and nations. The Dove (1928) provided an
obvious example. The film concerned Don Jose Maria
y Sandoval (Noah Beery), who considered himself
"the bes' damn caballero in . Costa Roja." Costa
Roja, as the title cards explained, was situated in
the Mediterranean!

The flimsy guise hardly fooled anyone. The
Times critic commented: "Taken by and large, Jose
is perhaps a screen character to which the Mexican
government might have objected, for he is greedy,
sensuous, boastful, cold-blooded, irritable, and
quite a wine bibber, but he does dress well. He
hates to have his luncheon spoiled by the noisy
victim of a firing squad."

Nevertheless, the setting of the film in Costa
Roja quieted complaints since Jose was not a
resident of a particular Latin American country.
Unfortunately, when The Dove was remade during the
sound era as Girl of the Rio (1932) with Dolores
Del Rio and Leo Carrillo, the screenwriters
apparently forgot this distinction and situated the
film in a Mexican border town. As a result, Mexico
renewed its threat to ban motion pictures produced
by companies that released films offensive to
Mexicans.

The anger with Girl of the Rio spread beyond

Mexican borders, with Panama and Nicaragua agreeing
to prohibit showings of the film. Spain and other
Latin American countries swiftly followed suit with
a series of reciprocal treaties banning films which
"attacked, slandered, defamed, insulted, or
misrepresented" the various nations of Hispanic
origin. Repeated offenses would warrant an embargo
of all feature films produced by the offending
company. As a result of the growing threat of
economic reprisals, Hollywood tended to downplay
the image of the violent Hispanic in the 1930s.

Despite the Girl of the Rio fiasco, sound at
first offered new opportunities for Hollywood to
redress its ways. In the first flush of enthusiasm
for the new technique, producers attempted to
provide Spanish language films. Some were
originals, while others were shot at the same time
as the English language version. In this fashion,
Latin American audiences saw a Spanish language
Dracula shot on the same sets as the Bela Lugosi
version, but with Hispanic actors!(4, 54) Nevertheless, this approach was soon abandoned in favor
of the cheaper practice of dubbing. Sound's legacy,
therefore, proved to be the introduction of new
stereotypes to films, as the Latin American
inability to speak English properly became the butt
of new jokes. Lupe Velez, as the "Mexican Spit-
fire," later built her career on malapropisms.(76,
80)

Although Hollywood's image of the Latin
softened as the 1930s progressed, certain
stereotyped notions never quite disappeared. Warner
Brothers' Bordertown (1935) best revealed the
ambivalence with which Hollywood viewed its Latin
neighbors. The film featured Paul Muni as Johnny
Ramirez who studies hard at law school and
graduates at the top of his class. Yet, in his
first court appearance he succumbs to anger and
physically attacks the opposing attorney. He is
ejected from the courtroom and quickly disbarred.
Ramirez then drifts outside the law and becomes the
manager of a gambling casino. It is ironic to note
that Ramirez had the perserverance to study in
night school for several years, but is unable to
control his temper for a few brief moments. Once
again, the Latin is depicted as subject to
uncontrollable fits of temper and violent
outbursts. Additionally, when Ramirez is disbarred,

he does not seek a legitimate profession, but
becomes a gambler, a supposed predeliction of the
Latin character.

The final irony of <u>Bordertown</u> concerned its
leading actor. Native Hispanics rarely filled
leading roles. Paul Muni became Warner Brothers'
resident Latin in <u>Bordertown</u> and <u>Juarez</u>, and
Ricardo Cortez (actually Jacob Kranz) also became a
pseudo-Latin. The women fared somewhat better in
this regard in the 1930s, although Lupe Velez once
complained that she portrayed "Chinese, Eskimos,
Japanese, Indian squaws, Hindus, Swedes, Malays,
and Javanese," but rarely an Hispanic. Thus false
Latins often found the road to success easier than
true Latins in the Depression years.

Hollywood finally rediscovered the Latin by
the end of the decade. Suddenly in 1939 films
utilizing Latin stars, locales, and historical
heroes flooded American screens. Such eminent
leaders as Benito Juarez and Simon Bolivar were
immortalized on film. Talent scouts brought
planeloads of Latin American talent to Hollywood,
as viewers discovered and enjoyed Carmen Miranda,
Desi Arnaz, and Cesar Romero. Films also began to
differentiate between varying South American
locales, allowing viewers to spend a <u>Weekend in
Havana</u> and <u>That Night in Rio</u> (1941) or travel <u>Down
Argentine Way</u> (1940).

The reason for this deluge of films with Latin
American themes may be partly due to deliberate
government policy. With the growing threat of war
with Germany, the United States appeared eager to
smooth any remaining tensions with South American
governments in order to maintain hemispheric unity
as a bulwark against foreign threats. President
Franklin Delano Roosevelt thus attempted to
reassert the "Good Neighbor Policy" in order to
promote friendship among the two Americas. Yet,
other motives were also evident. The MGM producer
Arthur Freed attributed the surge in Latin-themed
films to the new interest in South American music
and dances. Others maintained that there were sound
economic reasons for wooing the Latin American
markets since European film markets became severely
restricted after the start of World War II. Only
Latin America remained as a possible area for
profitable expansion.

Hollywood's attitude toward the Latin American

countries soon bordered on reverence. Juarez
(1939), the first film of the South American cycle,
offered a hymn of praise to a nineteenth-century
Mexican president, and portrayed him as an equal to
Abraham Lincoln. This motion picture avoided the
blatant stereotypes of the Mexican and revealed a
newfound sympathy toward Latin characters. Juarez
was the first Mexican hero of the American screen,
and Warners assured that he would be portrayed as
accurately as possible. Juarez so impressed its
intended audience both in the United States and
Mexico that Mexican Président Lazaro Cardenas urged
that the film be shown in the Mexican Palace of
Fine Arts, the first motion picture so honored. The
premiere audience responded warmly to the film, and
interrupted it several times with applause.(68, 75)
     The new filmic Latins of the wartime era were
no longer bandits or ignorant peasants. Many Latins
appeared as well-educated in the films of this
period, and they fulfilled a variety of cinematic
roles. Although Paul Muni portrayed the Mexican
Juarez, real Latins began assuming major film roles
at this time.(18, 19, 62, 70)
     Only one complaint was heard from Latin
American critics. They were disturbed by the
increasing number of South American themed musical
films which showed Hispanics singing and dancing to
the latest samba rhythms. They argued that
Hollywood was replacing one stereotype with
another. True, the Latin might no longer have been
a bandit, but now he was holding a guitar and
crooning the melodies of his native land. Many
Latins worried that Hollywood had gone too far in
its efforts to compensate for earlier
stereotypes.(77, 78)
     When the war ended, Hollywood lost its
extravagant and obsessive interest in Latin America
as a calmer atmosphere pervaded postwar films
concerning "our neighbors to the south." New motion
pictures avoided the musical stereotypes so common
during World War. II and instead considered the
situation of Hispanics in American society. For
example, A Medal for Benny (1945), a John Steinbeck
tale of a deceased Chicano war hero whose memory is
exploited by the citizens of his home town, sharply
reversed previous patterns. Here the Chicanos were
portrayed as sensible and wise, while the Anglo
community leaders were exposed as greedy and

deceitful.
      Several   new factors   seemed to contribute   to
this   new   sensitivity   of   the   postwar   films
concerning Latins.   First,   the   Motion   Picture
Association of America established an advisory
board which could supply information to screenwriters   before   the scripts were   filmed.   In this
fashion, uncomplimentary   stereotypes   could be
eliminated before it was too late.   Co-productions
between the United States and various South American
countries also improved the   Latin image   in   film.
With The Captain From Castile (1947), John Ford's
The   Fugitive (1948), and Way of the Gaucho (1952),
film crews were able to have contact with Latins in
all areas of film production.   John Ford, for
instance, expressed   surprise   when he discovered
that real Latins were far more industrious than the
siesta-prone   caricatures that   Hollywood had been
portraying for years.
      Also remarkable in the postwar period was the
fact that actual Latins were continuing to assume
leading roles in Hollywood films.   For each Marlon
Brando (Viva   Zapata),   there   was   also a   Ricardo
Montalban and a Fernando Lamas.(8, 51, 53, 67) Salt
of the Earth, directed by Herbert Biberman in 1953,
shattered all precedent by casting all major roles
with Mexicans or Mexican Americans.   Although this
film was not widely distributed during the McCarthy
era, it is perhaps the best portrayal of Chicano
life that has yet been filmed.(7, 45, 49)
      Unfortunately, the advances of the postwar
years have not continued to the present day, as
outdated images slowly returned to the   screen   in
the aftermath of the Cuban Revolution. The violent
and bloodthirsty "greaser" reappeared in Bring Me
the Head of Alfredo Garcia (1974), and in Sergio
Leone's "spaghetti westerns"   Duck, You Sucker
(1972) and The Good, the Bad, and the Ugly (1968).
In a similar fashion this rural figure became a
symbol of urban violence in such films as Badge 373
(1973) and Fort Apache--The Bronx (1981), which led
to protests and boycotts after its release.   At the
same time, the bumbling Latin became the object of
ridicule in Viva Max (1970) and Bananas (1971).
Serious attempts   to consider   Latin   American
personalities   went   awry   (Che!   [1969]),   and
pseudo-Latins remained in leading roles in such
films as Alan Arkin's Popi (1975). Even efforts to

woo Hispanic American audiences with such films as
Walk Proud and Boulevard Nights (1979) backfired,
as the undue emphasis on urban gang violence caused
considerable criticism. Yet, more often than not,
Hispanic characters have been excluded or ignored
in recent screenplays.

Television, in general, has followed Hollywood's lead.(59) From Mel Blanc's antics on The
Jack Benny Show to Bill Dana's "Jose Jimenez,"
pseudo-Hispanics have often appeared as comic
figures. Chico and the Man, a NBC television
series, featured Freddie Prinze in the leading role
of Chico. Although a Puerto Rican, Prinze's portrayal of a shiftless Mexican American brought complaints from Chicano groups.(1, 6, 16, 30) Despite
this emphasis on comedy, recent quantitative
studies have found that the predominant image of
the Hispanic American on television is that of
law-breaker. Groups such as "Nosotros" and "LULAC"
(League of United Latin American Citizens) have
attempted to publicize these problems and work for
change.(38)

Despite several of the problems with television's image of Hispanics, there have been some
rays of hope.(23, 25, 26, 46, 60, 63) Children's
television (Carrascolendas and Sesame Street) has
utilized Hispanic characters and has taught elements of the Spanish language.(22, 31) Public
television's American Playhouse has sponsored
several films of either Hispanic content or with
Hispanic actors in leading roles (e. g., El Norte
and The Ballad of Gregorio Cortez).(58, 66, 71) ABC
also provided Norman Lear's comedy, a.k.a. Pablo,
which presented the life of an up-and-coming
chicano comedian and his extended family. Although
short-lived, it attempted to address many of the
complaints concerning the presentation of Hispanic
Americans on network television and in films.
Additionally, more Hispanics have, in recent years,
been involved in writing and directing new films.
While their numbers have been relatively small,
they have managed to provide a new Hispanic-
American viewpoint in such films as El Norte and
Zoot Suit.

Two general surveys of the Hispanic and Hispanic American in film have appeared.(15) Allen

Woll's The Latin Image in American Film analyzes
the Latin image in film from the turn of the
century to the present, as well as the reaction of
Hispanics to these images.(80) Arthur G. Pettit
concentrates on the Mexican-American image in both
film and popular literature in his work.(52) Both
authors argue that filmmakers tended to adopt
existing nineteenth century stereotypes in their
fiction films. (For an analysis of these earlier
stereotypes in both the print media and literature,
see De Leon's study).(17) While these works tend to
concentrate on the filmic image of Hispanics,
others have attempted to utilize studio files in an
attempt to analyze the thinking that gave rise to
these images. Of particular interest in this regard
are the works of Paul Vanderwood concerning Juarez
and Viva Zapata!.(67, 68) Herbert Biberman, the
director of the controversial Salt of the Earth,
also explains conventional Hollywood ideas about
Hispanics in film in his account of the making of
his film.
     The majority of literature on this topic has
focussed on Latin Americans, but there has been a
shift in attention in recent years to Hispanic
Americans. For information on, in particular,
Puerto Ricans, see the articles by Cordasco and
Galanes. (10, 24, 37) Carlos Cortes and Linda
Williams have provided information on Chicano
images in a variety of works.(11, 23, 25, 28, 29,
32, 41, 42, 48, 64, 65, 72, 73)
     Although considerable attention has been given
to the image of Hispanics in motion pictures, there
is no general survey of the Hispanic image in
television. Nevertheless, several provocative
studies provide content analyses of television
images during recent years. Of particular interest
are the works of Bradley Greenberg and the studies
of LULAC.(27, 28, 38) Sociologists and psychologists have also attempted to examine the effects
of television's stereotypes on both Hispanic and
Anglo families, and on adults as well as children.
(3, 6, 12, 22, 23, 25, 26, 31, 34, 55, 61, 65, 66)
Although most scholars recognize television's
problems, a few note certain optimistic trends in
recent years which may promote inter-cultural
communication and improve job prospects both behind
the screen as well as on camera.(33)
     For information about the use of films in edu-

cation, a variety of reference works have appeared. Jane Loy examines films conerning Latin America, while the Chicano Resource Center has published a guide to films concerning Mexican Americans.(43, 44, 9) Cortes and Campbell have considered the uses of film in the examination of broader problems concerning race and ethnicity.(13)

Major discussions of films and/or television shows include: Alambrista (72), Antonio and the Mayor (5), Bananas (80), The Border (58), Boulevard Nights (11, 35), Carrascolendas (71), Che! (39), Chico and the Man (1, 6, 16, 30), El Norte (58), The Gang's All Here (70, 78), The Greaser's Revenge (11), The Gun (40), I am Joaquin (47), Juarez (68, 75), A Medal for Benny (21), Requiem for a Heavyweight (57), Salt of the Earth (7, 45, 49), Scarface (58), Under Fire (56), Viva Villa (50, 80), Viva Zapata! (51, 53, 67), and West Side Story (33).

1. ──────. "Ratings Lightning Strikes one of Season's Bargains." BROADCASTING 87 (October 21, 1974): 40.

2. Abadie Aicardi, Anibal. "El cine como instrumento de la leyenda negra: notas profanas de un espectador." ["Film as an Instrument of the Black Legend: Profane Notes of a Spectator."] HUMANITAS (Mexico) 15 (1974), 621-29.

3. Allen, Richard L. and David E. Clarke. "Ethnicity and Mass Media Behavior: A Study of Blacks and Latinos." (item II-45).

4. Allen, William. "Spanish Language Films in the U. S." FILMS IN REVIEW 1 (July-August 1950): 1-4, 42-45.

5. Armas, Jose. "'Antonio and the Mayor': A Cultural Review of the Film." J OF ETHNIC STUDIES 3 (Fall 1975): 98-101.

6. Berger, Arthur Asa. THE TV-GUIDED AMERICAN (item I-13).

7. Biberman, Herbert. SALT OF THE EARTH. Boston: Beacon Press, 1965.

8. Biskind, Peter. "Ripping off Zapata -- Revolution Hollywood-Style." CINEASTE 7 ([no. 2] 1976): 11-15.

9. Chicano Resource Center. CHICANO RESOURCE CENTER FILM GUIDE. E. Los Angeles: E. Los Angeles Library, 1981.

10. Cordasco, Franceso. "Images of Puerto Ricans in American Film and Television." ETHNIC IMAGES IN AMERICAN FILM AND TELEVISION (item I-105), pp. 131-34.

11. Cortes, Carlos E. "'Greaser's Revenge' to 'Boulevard Nights'" HISTORY, CULTURE AND SOCIETY: CHICANO STUDIES IN THE 1980S. Edited by The National Association for Chicano Studies, ed. Ypsilanti, Michigan: Bilingual Press, 1983, pp. 125-40.

12. ———. "The Role of Media in Multi-Cultural
     Education." VIEWPOINTS IN TEACHING AND
     LEARNING 56 (Winter, 1980): 38-49.

13. ———, and Leon G. Campbell. "Introduction
     to the Study of Race and Ethnicity Through
     Film." RACE AND ETHNICITY IN THE HISTORY OF
     THE AMERICAS (item I-36), pp. 5-21.

14. ———, Leon G. Campbell and Robert Pinger.
     LATIN AMERICA: A FILMIC APPROACH. River-
     side: Latin American Studies Program, Uni-
     versity of California, 1975.

15. Cripps, Thomas. "Mexicans, Indians and Movies:
     The Need for a History." WIDE ANGLE 5 (no.
     1 1982): 68-70.

16. Davidson, Bill. "The Reformation of 'Chico and
     the Man'." TV GUIDE 22 (November 23, 1974):
     25-29.

17. De Leon, Arnoldo. THEY CALLED THEM GREASERS:
     ANGLO ATTITUDES TOWARD MEXICANS IN TEXAS,
     1821-1900. Austin: University of Texas
     Press, 1983.

18. De Usabel, Gaizka S. "American Films in Latin
     America: The Case History of United Artists
     Corporation, 1918-1951." Ph. D. diss., Uni-
     versity of Wisconsin, 1975.

19. ———. THE HIGH NOON OF AMERICAN FILM IN
     LATIN AMERICA. Ann Arbor: UMI Research
     Press, 1982.

20. Delpar, Helen. "Goodbye to the 'Greaser.':
     Mexico, the MPPDA, and Derogatory Films,
     1922-1926." J OF POPULAR FILM AND TELE-
     VISION 12 (Spring 1984): 34-41.

21. Doscher, Luelyne. "The Birth of a Stereo-
     type." HOLLYWOOD Q 3 (Fall, 1947): 90-93.

22. Eastman, Harvey A. and Marsha B. Liss. "Ethni-
     city and Children's TV Preferences." (item
     II-219).

23. Eiselein, E. B. "Television and the Mexican-
     American."   PUBLIC TELECOMMUNICATIONS R 2
     (February 1974): 13-18.

24. Galanes, Adriana Lewis. "The Image of Puerto
     Ricans in American Film and Television."
     ETHNIC IMAGES IN AMERICAN FILM AND
     TELEVISION (item I-105), pp. 135-37.

25. Gamboa, Harry, Jr.   "Silver Screening the
     Barrio." EQUAL OPPORTUNITY FORUM (November
     1978): 6-7.

26. Gerson, Mauricio Eidelman. "Television, Latin
     Portrayal and Spanish Speaking Philadel-
     phians' Acculturation Process." M. A.
     thesis, Annenberg School of Communications,
     University of Pennsylvania, 1978.

27. Greenberg, Bradley S. and Pilar Baptista-
     Fernandez.   "Hispanic Americans -- The New
     Minority on Television."   LIFE ON TELE-
     VISION: CONTENT ANALYSES OF U. S. TV
     DRAMA.   Edited by Bradley Greenberg (in
     collaboration with Charles K. Atkin).
     Norwood: N.J.: Ablex Publishing Corp.,
     1980, pp. 3-12.

28. ————, and Michael Burgoon, Judee K. Bur-
     goon, and Felipe Korzenny.   MEXICAN-
     AMERICANS AND THE MASS MEDIA. Norwood,
     N.J.: Ablex Publishing Corp., 1983.

29. Gutierrez, Felix. "Chicanos and the Media."
     READINGS IN MASS COMMUNICATIONS: CONCEPTS
     AND ISSUES IN THE MASS MEDIA. Edited by
     Michael C. Emery and Ted Curtis. Dubuque,
     Iowa: Wm. C. Brown, 1970, 283-94.

30. ————. "Chico and the Racist." R OF SOUTHERN
     CALIFORNIA JOURNALISM (Fall/Winter 1974):
     1-3.

31. ————. "Moving Beyond Ethnic Stereotypes:
     Latino Americans." TELEVISION AND CHILDREN
     7 (Winter 1984): 16-19.

32. ————, and Jorge Reina Schement. "Chicanos
     and the Media: A Bibliography of Selected
     Materials." JOURNALISM HISTORY 4 (Summer
     1977): 52-55.

33. Hurley, Neil P., S.J. "Using Motion Pictures
     to Aid Inter-Cultural Communication." (item
     II-336).

34. Jeffres, Leo W. and K. Kyoon Hur. "White
     Ethnics and Media Images." (item I-72).

35. Jeffries, Georgia. "The Low Riders of Whittier
     Boulevard." AMERICAN FILM 4 (February
     1979): 59-62.

36. Lamb, Blaine P. "The Convenient Villain: The
     Early Cinema Views the Mexican American."
     J OF THE WEST 14 (October 1975): 75-81.

37. Laufer, Joseph M. "Television in the
     Seventies: Planting the Seeds of Change for
     the Puerto Rican Image." ETHNIC IMAGES IN
     AMERICAN FILM AND TELEVISION (item I-105),
     pp. 139-42.

38. League of United Latin American Citizens, The.
     THE NETWORK BROWN-OUT -- A NATIONAL
     HISPANIC NETWORK AUDIT. San Francisco:
     Public Advocates, Inc., October 6, 1983.

39. Leonard, John. "Will the Real Che Guevara
     Stand Up and Die for Our Popcorn?" THE NEW
     YORK TIMES MAGAZINE, December 8, 1968, pp.
     57ff.

40. Levinson, Richard and William Link. STAY
     TUNED (item I-89).

41. Lewels, Francisco J. THE USES OF THE MEDIA BY
     THE CHICANO MOVEMENT: A STUDY IN MINORITY
     ACCESS. New York: Praeger, 1974.

42. Limon, Jose E. "Stereotyping and Chicano
     Resistance: An Historical Dimension."
     AZTLAN 4 (no. 2.1973): 257-70.

43. Loy, Jane. LATIN AMERICA: SIGHTS AND SOUNDS. A

GUIDE TO MOTION PICTURES AND MUSIC FOR
COLLEGE COURSES. Gainesville, Florida:
Consortium of Latin American Study
Programs, 1973.

44. ———. "Latin America Through Film:
Problems and Possibilities." PROCEEDINGS OF
THE PCCLAS [Pacific Coast Council on Latin
American Studies] 1 (Summer 1973), 30-40.

45. McCormick, Ruth. "Salt of the Earth." CINEASTE
5 (Fall 1972): 53-55.

46. Marshall, Wes, and E. B. Eiselein, John Thomas
Duncan, and Raul Gamez Bogarin. FIESTA:
MINORITY TELEVISION PROGRAMMING. Tucson:
University of Arizona Press, 1974.

47. Martinez, Eliud. "'I Am Joaquin' as Poem and
Film: Two Modes of Chicano Expression." J
OF POPULAR CULTURE. 13 (Spring 1980): 505-
15.

48. Miller, Jim. "Chicano Cinema: An Interview
with Jesus Trevino." CINEASTE 8 ([no. 3]
1978): 38-41.

49. Miller, Tom. "'Salt of the Earth' Revisited."
CINEASTE 13 ([no. 3] 1984): 30-36.

50. Mistron, Deborah E. "The Institutional Revolution: Images of the Mexican Revolution in
the Cinema." Ph. D. diss., Indiana University, 1982.

51. Morsberger, Robert E. "Steinbeck's Zapata:
Rebel Versus Revolutionary." STEINBECK: THE
MAN AND HIS WORK. Edited by Richard Astro
and Tetsumaro Hayashi. Corvallis: Oregon
State University Press, 1971, pp. 43-63.

52. Pettit, Arthur G. IMAGES OF THE MEXICAN AMER-
ICAN IN FICTION AND FILM. College Station:
Texas A&M University Press, 1980.

53. ———. "Viva Zapata! A Tribute to Steinbeck,
Kazan and Brando." FILM & HISTORY 7 (May
1977): 25-33, 45.

54. Pinto, Alfonso. "When Hollywood Spoke Span-
     ish." AMERICAS 32 (no. 10 1980): 3-8.

55. Popp, Lorraine B. "It's All in the Family:
     Structural Determinants of Television's
     Role in Mexican-American and Anglo
     Households." Ph. D. diss., University of
     California, Santa Barbara, 1981.

56. Powers, John. "Saints and Savages." AMERICAN
     FILM 9 (January-February 1984): 38-43.

57. Ramirez, Arthur. "Anglo View of a Mexican-
     American Tragedy: Rod Serling's 'Requiem
     for a Heavyweight.'" J OF POPULAR CULTURE
     13 (Spring 1980): 501-504.

58. Ryan, Desmond. "Films Today Show America's
     Empty Promise." PHILADELPHIA INQUIRER,
     March 11, 1984, p. 2-K.

59. Seggar, John F. and Penny Wheeler. "World of
     Work on TV: Ethnic and Sex Representation
     in TV Drama." (item I-133).

60. Soriano, Michael Esteban. "Minority Access: An
     Analysis of Community Participation in
     Policy, Programing, Production." (item
     II-565).

61. Tan, Alexis S. "Media Use and Political
     Orientations of Ethnic Groups." (item I-
     148).

62. Tavares de Sa, Hernane. "The Film as an
     Instrument of Good Will." THE PROCEEDINGS
     OF THE CONFERENCE HELD IN OCTOBER 1943
     (item I-173), pp. 573-76.

63. Townley, Rod. "Why Many Hispanics Prefer
     Network Stereotyping to SIN." TV GUIDE 31
     (January 22, 1983): 26-28.

64. Trevino, Jesus S. "Chicano Cinema." NEW
     SCHOLAR 8 (no. 1-2 1982): 167-80.

65. Valenzuela, Nicholas. MEDIA HABITS AND

ATTITUDES OF MEXICAN AMERICANS. Austin:
Center for Communication Research,
University of Texas, 1973.

66. ————. PUBLIC TELEVISION AND THE MEXICAN-
AMERICAN AUDIENCE IN THE SOUTHWEST.
Washington, D.C.: Office of Communication
Research, Corporation for Public Broad-
casting, 1974.

67. Vanderwood, Paul J. "An American Cold Warrior:
'Viva Zapata!'" AMERICAN HISTORY/AMERICAN
FILM (item I-113), pp. 183-201.

68. ————, ed. JUAREZ. Madison, Wisconsin: University of Wisconsin Press, 1983, pp. 9-41.

69. ————. "Latin America in Ferment: The Vision
of Saul Landau." FILM & HISTORY 5 (February
1975): 1-7, 23.

70. Walters, Debra. "Hollywood, World War II, and
Latin America: The Hollywood Good Neighbor
Policy as Personified by Carmen Miranda."
M. A. thesis, University of Southern Cali-
fornia, 1978.

71. Williams, Frederick and Geraldine Van Wart.
CARRASCOLENDAS: BILINGUAL EDUCATION THROUGH
TELEVISION. New York: Praeger, 1974.

72. Williams, Linda. "Type and Stereotype: Chicano
Images in Film." FRONTIERS 5 (no. 2 1980):
14-17.

73. Wilson, John M. "Hollywood and the Chicano:
The Slow, Uneasy Beginning." LOS ANGELES
TIMES, September 17, 1978, 1, 5, 7.

74. Woll, Allen L. "Bandits and Lovers: Hispanic
Images in American Film." THE KALEIDOSCOPIC
LENS (item I-106), pp. 54-72.

75. ————. "The Dilemma of 'Juarez'." FILM &
HISTORY 5 (February 1975): 15-18.

76. ————. "From Bandit to President: The Latin
Image in American Films, 1929-1939." J OF

MEXICAN-AMERICAN HISTORY (1974):28-40.

77. ―――――. THE HOLLYWOOD MUSICAL GOES TO WAR. (item I-170).

78. ―――――. "Hollywood's Good Neighbor Policy: The Latin Image in American Film, 1939-1946." J OF POPULAR FILM 3 (Fall 1974): 278-93.

79. ―――――. "How Hollywood Has Portrayed Hispanics." NEW YORK TIMES, March 1, 1981, II, pp. 17, 22.

80. ―――――. THE LATIN IMAGE IN AMERICAN FILM. Los Angeles: UCLA Latin American Center, 1977; revised edition, 1980.

81. ―――――. "'Latin' in Hollywood Films Often Caricature to Latins." VARIETY, April 4, 1979, pp. 43 ff.

VIII. IRISH

The Irish have maintained a continual screen presence since the birth of the movies. The Irish cop, the parish priest, the crooked, but amiable politician, the fiery red-haired "wench," and the street-wise gangster immediately come to mind as enduring stereotypes of the Irish and Irish Americans on screen and on television. Nevertheless, these images draw little of the ire that similar manifestations would elicit from, say, Hispanics, Jews, or blacks. Despite the prevalence of these images, Irish Americans have remained relatively silent on the subject when compared with other American ethnic groups. There is no immediate equivalent of the B'nai B'rith Anti-Defamation League or its Italian-American counterpart. Similarly, any recent film with identifiably Irish portrayals of crooks or gangsters is not greeted with threats of a boycott or cries for censorship. A brief article or two may arise, but generally these portrayals are ignored until their next recurrence.

It is this curious factor which differentiates the portrayals of Irish and Irish Americans on the screen when compared with other racial and ethnic groups. There is no doubt that recurring stereotypes exist, but there seems to be little concern among Irish groups, nor are there calls to eliminate such portrayals. Even the number of scholarly studies of the topic remain remarkably sparse when compared with other ethnic groups. Why have the Irish tended to escape the problems concerning their portrayal in American film and television?

There are three major differences which set the Irish apart from other ethnic groups in questions concerning filmic portrayals. To a certain extent, it may be argued that Irish Americans fought their battles concerning derogatory stereotypes at the turn of the century instead of more recent times. At that time, however, the target of The Ancient Order of Hibernians was the "stage" image of the Irishman as a poor comic buffoon who spent his time drinking, arguing, and fighting. This image was particularly offensive at a time when Irish Americans were enjoying a newfound respect and power in their new home. The former immigrants who had been characterized as apes in nineteenth-century editorial cartoons were beginning to achieve economic as well as political power in turn-of-the-century America. The new "lace curtain" Irish were looking with disdain on the image of the "shanty" Irish which seemed to prevail in newspapers, literature, popular song, and theatre. As a result, the stage Irishman underwent a profound transformation as it was replaced by a more pious and respectable image. When motion pictures adopted earlier stage images of the Irishman, this comic vision found its rough edges softened and its uniqueness diluted. The once dominant image of the stage became one of many Irish images on the screen. Thus the battles that later arriving immigrants would have to fight were already being resolved as the new motion pictures were being born. The "new immigrants" of the late nineteenth century from southern and eastern Europe would soon replace the Irish in the popular iconography of America's new arrivals.

Unlike most ethnic groups, the Irish have maintained a strong participation in all aspects of the business of filmmaking and thus exercised a degree of control over the images which would be presented. Although Jews may be known for their positions as studio heads, the number of Irish men and women who acted, directed, and wrote for Hollywood films is staggering. While John Ford, John Huston, and Raoul Walsh remain the best-known directors, the list of identifiably Irish actors and actresses is impressive. The silent era presented such stars as Nancy Carroll, Alice Joyce, Edgar Kennedy, and Colleen Moore. The age of sound featured a panoply of actors of Irish background: Walter Brennan, James Cagney, Art Carney, Dolores Costello, Bing Crosby, James Dunn, Irene Dunne, Barry Fitzgerald, Errol Flynn, Jackie Gleason, Helen Hayes, Gene Kelly, Grace Kelly, Victor Moore, Margaret O'Brien, Carroll O'Connor, Donald

O'Connor, Maureen O'Hara, Dennis O'Keefe, Peter
O'Toole, Tyrone Power, Ronald Reagan, Mickey
Rooney, Robert Ryan, Maureen O'Sullivan, Spencer
Tracy, and countless other stars of both first and
second rank.(3, 5) As one scans the names, it is
noteworthy that few were "Hollywoodized" as were
those of other ethnic groups. Irish surnames helped
rather than hurt ticket sales throughout the
twentieth century, while Jewish, Polish, or
Hispanic names seemed a box office anathema. As a
result, Irish figures were clearly identified on
the screen as Irish characters portrayed by those
of Irish descent. Similarly, Irish locales (whether
the hills of Erin or the slums of New York) were
strongly defined in both script and title of
countless Hollywood films, as "Irishness" played a
major role in a film's box office draw. In this
fashion, Irish characters maintained a strong sense
of history, culture, and locale, while the film
images of other ethnic groups often did not.(3)

The Irish figures presented on film and
television differ from those of other ethnic and
racial groups in yet another significant fashion.
Filmic images of other groups tended to be plagued
by monolithic stereotypes that change only slightly
from generation to generation. The initial manifes-
tation of this stereotype is usually an "evil"
character. If balance is either demanded or
required, a polar opposite is supplied, either a
noble savage or "greaser" (see chapters VII and
XI). The monolithic stereotype therefore, often
becomes dualistic as time passes, presenting
characters of extreme nobility or evil, with few
intermediate shadings. The Irish, however, have
never been characterized by such continuing
nobility or evil, as a wide variety of identifiably
Irish characters with distinctive personalities
have been presented on the American screen. There
have been Irish cowboys, policemen, gangsters,
whores, loving mothers, laborers, bankers, priests,
"pols," and badmen on the screen throughout the
twentieth century. Therefore, an isolated evil
character fails to excite the same anger that a
similar Hispanic or Asian character might inspire.
The Irish know that this image is merely one of
many that appear on the screen or television, and,
hence, its power to persuade or convince is
naturally diluted.

Within this wide variety of character types
there are certain traits, however, that have become
evident. Unlike other ethnic groups, the balance of
these characteristics are often tilted to the noble
side. Despite problems with excessive anger or
alcoholism, these Irish characters have a remarkable sense of strength that carries them through
all adversity. They are also a people with a strong
religious conviction on film, as strong and noble
priests such as Bing Crosby, Pat O'Brien, and Barry
Fitzgerald, among many others, clearly demonstrate.
They often have large and loving families which
stick together in good times and in bad. This theme
is clearly revealed in the many biographical films
of well-known Irish-American figures such as James
Cagney's George M. Cohan in Yankee Doodle Dandy
(1942). Despite the emphasis on Cohan, the film is
actually the tale of The Four Cohans, who remain
united despite the vagaries of show business life.
Thus, while the Irish characters may remain of a
stock nature, they often contain strong elements of
good to balance any evil habits.

The large numbers of men and women of Irish
descent working in the film industry managed to
fashion a wide variety of identifiably Irish
figures with diverse character traits. These
stereotypes ran the gamut of good to evil, and thus
avoided the monolithic images of other ethnic or
racial groups. The Irish in film and television,
despite clearly identifiable characteristics,
swiftly became just like other Americans. They were
both good and bad, rich, middle-class, or poor, and
they filled a wide variety of occupations. As a
result, the furor surrounding the screen and
television portrayals of other ethnic groups has
remained relatively muted within the Irish-American
community.

This variety of Irish character types dates
back to the earliest days of the cinema, as
companies filmed tales of Irish lads and lassies
both in America and the auld sod as well. The Kalem
Company, displaying the documentary interests of
early filmmaking, dispatched cameramen to Ireland
as early as 1910 to give their early films a
realistic flavor. Sidney Olcott (born Alcott but
renamed after famed stage Irishman Chauncey Olcott)
directed many of these early film efforts. Some
tackled tales of Irish life, such as The Irish

Honeymoon, Rory O'More, The Colleen Bawn, and
Arran-na-Pogue, while others considered the
beginnings of Irish migration to the New World. The
Lad From Old Ireland, for example, told of the
typical Irish boy who wishes to come to America and
make his fortune. The majority of silent films,
however, looked at the Irish on American soil,
particularly in the urban slums of Boston and New
York. Here the Irish experience paralleled that of
other immigrant groups, especially Jews and Italians, with an emphasis on the trials and travails
of life in a new country. There was also a strong
focus on a close family life, wherein an immense
variety of characterizations existed. Indeed, there
might be a drunkard or a fighter, but there were
strong and noble family members as well.(17)
     While the Irish maintained a strong identity
in silent films, they were often paired with their
fellow immigrants (albeit of a later date), the
Jews. These early "ghetto" films investigated the
in immigrant neighborhoods, exploring the interactions of the Irish and their filmic neighbors,
the Jews. They lived together, did business
together, and even, on occasion, fell in love, much
to the consternation of their various families. The
Broadway hit Abie's Irish Rose (1924) triggered a
cascade of interethnic love comedies. Occasionally, Jewish families even adopted Irish orphans,
in such films as Pawn Ticket 210 (1922) and A Harp
in Hock (1927). As a result, multiethnic heroes and
heroines often came to the fore in such films as
Kosher Kitty Kelly (produced by Joseph P. Kennedy)
and Private Izzy Murphy (1926). Despite initial
tensions between the two groups displayed in these
films, endings were often harmonious, as members of
these two immigrant groups learned to live together, and even love each other. Silent comic efforts,
such as a "Cohens and Kellys" series, assumed a
less romantic tone, often utilizing stereotypes of
both the Jews and the Irish in their search for
humor.(See Chapter X.)
     While the 1920s images of Irish men and women
often glorified the notion of the American melting
pot in which all ethnic groups might live together
in harmony, this tone of consensus faded in the
Depression era, as a darker image of urban Irish
life replaced the nostalgic glow of the early
immigrant age. The boom in gangster films in the

late 1920s and early 1930s also claimed its Irish members, particularly one of the most attractive and controversial ruffians, Tommy Powers, played by James Cagney in The Public Enemy (1931). Cagney formed the third member of the triumvirate of 1930s gangster heroes along with Edward G. Robinson and Paul Muni. It would be difficult to claim that the characterization of Powers differed from the screen vision of Italian gangsters in Little Caesar (1930) or Scarface (1932), for all were immigrants pushing their way to the top through illegal means. All were brutal, with Cagney best remembered for carrying both guns and grapefruit. Nevertheless, there are some subtle differences in the way that the Irish mobster is treated from his Italian cohorts. First of all, The Public Enemy does not indicate that all Irish are evil-doers. Tommy Powers has a brother, Mike (Donald Cook), who seeks the way of the righteous. He rejects petty crimes as a youth, and, as an adult, he finances his college education by daytime work on the streetcar. When the United States enters World War I, Mike is among the first to enlist in the Marines because his "country needs him." Similarly, when Tommy tries to offer him some of his ill-gotten gains, Mike refuses the money even though he is struggling to support his family. Tommy Powers' turn to crime is, therefore, not necessarily an Irish characteristic, as even the father of the clan was a policeman. It is mere chance that has made Tommy a gangster, not a depraved family life.

Caesar and Scarface, however, are loners, with no strong counterbalancing family members to give hints of alternative directions for Italian immigrants. This notion of alternative possibilities in Irish life is strengthened in a later Cagney gangster film, Angels with Dirty Faces (1938), which presents an Irish priest (Pat O'Brien) to balance this evil portrayal. Although both Cagney and O'Brien come from the same Irish neighborhood, each chooses a different path in life. Although Cagney's portrayal closely parallels his "Public Enemy" persona, it is interesting to note that he still has a touch of decency within him. The plot reveals that Cagney has a soft spot for the "Dead End" Kids of his slum neighborhood. As Cagney is sentenced to death, O'Brien explains that the true courageous act would be to die like a

coward. In this fashion, the neighborhood kids
would no longer idealize and emulate him. Cagney
refuses at first, expressing the desire to spit in
the eyes of his executors. But, at the last moment,
Cagney changes his mind and "goes to the chair
yellow." The kids realize the shallowness of their
former hero, and begin to consider the paths of
righteousness suggested by the priest. Therefore,
even an Irish gangster has a moral core. As the
gangster films declined in the late 1930s, Cagney
brought his gangster skills to the right side of
the law in such films as G-Men (1935). This sense
of balance tended to allow the Irish to escape any
onus of a gangster past or character, while the
Italians would continue to live with this screen
and television image for decades.

Contributing to this tendency towards Irish
diversity in film was the work of John Ford, which
spanned the silent era to the 1960s. Ford, born
Sean Aloysius O'Feeney, of Irish immigrant parents
in Cape Elizabeth, Maine, in 1895, played a major
role in shaping the screen image of the Irish, in
much the same manner that his films presented a
dominant image of the Native American in American
popular culture. While Ford's image of the Indian
was basically monolithic until the end of his
career, Ford's Irish men and women were of all
kinds.(See Chapter XI.) No single image of the
Irishman dominates Ford's films. His films about
Irish men and women take place in both Ireland and
America during varying historical periods. They
embrace the heroic, the comic, and the evil. Even
Ford's films about non-Irish themes or settings
seem to involve Irish characters, with John Wayne
turning the "cavalry trilogy" into a How the West
Was Won by the Irish. Ford began to utilize Irish
characters early in his silent film career at Fox,
in such films as The Shamrock Handicap (1926),
Mother Machree, Hangman's House (with Victor
McLaglen), and Riley the Cop (all 1928). Perhaps,
as Roger Dooley suggests, Ford's ability to utilize
these characterizations in several films was due to
the presence of studio head Winfield Sheehan, "born
in the same Irish section of Buffalo that had
produced Chauncey Olcott a generation before."(5)

Ford is best remembered for bringing Irish
life to the screen in the RKO classic, The Informer
(1935). Hollywood has rarely presented films which

have glorified informers, but Gypo Nolan (Victor
McLaglen) offers an enigmatic portrayal of a man
who betrays his friend for money. While Ford and
screenwriter Dudley Nichols are able to condemn
Nolan's actions, there is still the sense of heroic
about him as he is able to redeem himself before
the church in a last minute confession. Both Ford
and McLaglen won Oscars for their achievement.
Ironically, despite the ample dramatic possibilities in Irish political history in the twentieth
century, other filmmakers have been hesitant to
follow in Ford's footsteps, leaving the "troubles"
as terra incognita.

Ford's later efforts include adaptations of
Irish plays, such as The Plough and the Stars
(1936) and The Rising of the Moon (1957),
Irish-American playwright Eugene O'Neill's three
one-act plays in The Long Voyage Home (1940), a
comedy of Irish and American cultural conflict in
The Quiet Man (1952), and the classic tale of
Irish-American politics in Boston, The Last Hurrah
(1958).(11) This brief list merely hints at the
extent of the celebration of the Irish heritage in
Ford's works, as Irish and Irish-American actors
and actresses populated all his films. Ford
glorified the Irish contribution to American and
world culture, and helped to prevent the domination
of a single Irish stereotype throughout his films
and throughout this century. Ford's Irish
characters betrayed every vice as well as every
human virtue.(15, 16)

During the 1940s, the Irish joined other
Americans in the prosecution of World War II. Like
other ethnic groups, they entered the foxholes of
the age in order to demonstrate how the American
melting pot had worked in contrast to the ethnically segregated vision of Hitler's Germany.
Kathryn Rose Kane notes that the Irish were among
the most prevalent of ethnic groups featured in
World War II films, appearing almost as frequently
as WASPS. While they maintained certain supposedly
Irish characteristics (such as being home-loving,
sentimental, respectful of authority, and religious), they were among the toughest of America's
fighting men. Interestingly,in former times this
notion was used to the detriment of Irish Americans, as the phrase "fighting Irish" indicated a
profound willingness to brawl at the slightest

notion. This Irish pugnacity was featured in such
silent films as Hogan's Alley (1925), One Punch
O'Day, Blarney (1926), One-Round Hogan, Hard-Boiled
Hagerty, and Knock-Out Reilly (1927), and in the
sound era in Hard Rock Harrigan (1935), Burn 'Em Up
O'Connor (1938), and Killer McCoy (1947). By the
time of such films as The Fighting 69th (1940) and
The Sullivans (1944), this Irish weakness became a
virtual compliment as it demonstrated how the tough
and passionate Irish were willing to fight to pre-
serve America's freedoms. The Irish fighting men
were amply rewarded for their efforts, as Kane also
notes that they represented all ranks in the army
during this period, perhaps a symbol of their
assimilation into American society.(9)

The immediate post-war period brought an
onslaught of amiable Irish images on the screen.
While the Irish priest as hero had been seen
previously in such films as Boys Town and Angels
with Dirty Faces (1938), Bing Crosby's portrayal of
Father O'Malley in Going My Way (1944) brought this
figure a new respectability. Winning several
Academy Awards, the Leo McCarey film also spawned a
sequel with Ingrid Bergman, The Bells of St. Mary's
(1945). With great charm, humor, and emotion, these
films accentuated a sentimental and nostalgic image
of Irish and Irish-American life, which John Ford
would play to the hilt in such later films as The
Quiet Man, with John Wayne and Maureen O'Hara.

A few evil Irishmen remained on the screen,
such as some of the union bosses in On the
Waterfront (1954), but even there the evil was
balanced with considerable good. Karl Malden
portrays a priest who leaves the haven of the
church to bring reform to the waterfront; Eva Marie
Saint, whose brother has been killed by mobsters,
attempts to find the murderer, and Marlon Brando,
as Terry Malloy, virtually singlehandedly over-
throws the corrupt union bosses. Terry Malloy, like
Gypo Nolan, is an informer in this film, but
eventually a remarkably likeable one. These strong
and moral Irish characters manage to stifle the
power of the gun and mob rule.

In recent years, however, this fascination for
Irish themes and characters seems to have disappeared. Since the 1960s few American-produced
films with Irish themes have been released. Among
the few exceptions were Young Cassidy (1965), a

life of the young Sean O'Casey initiated by John
Ford, but completed by Jack Cardiff; Finian's
Rainbow (1968), Francis Ford Coppola's version of
the 1947 Broadway musical hit; and The Molly
Maguires (1970), Martin Ritt's dramatization of
labor troubles in the coal mines of nineteenth-
century western Pennsylvania, with Richard Harris
and Sean Connery. True Confessions (1981), a
reworking of the cop and priest melodramas of the
1930s with Robert DeNiro and Robert Duvall, remains
one of the few Irish-themed films of the 1980s. The
only difference is that the priest is no longer as
incorruptible as O'Brien, Fitzgerald, or Crosby a
few decades earlier.

A similar pattern can be seen in television
shows concerning the Irish. While a great many
policemen of Irish descent seem to be populating
the patrol rooms in such shows as Brenner, The Cop
and the Kid, Car 54, Where Are You?, Naked City,
The Trials of O'Brien, and O'Hara of the U. S.
Treasury, few plots considered the ethnic heritage
of the men in blue. If not enforcing the law on the
beat, the Irish often appeared in the courtroom as
attorneys. Pat O'Brien turned to television as a
lawyer in Harrigan and Son in the 1960s, as did
Peter Falk in The Trials of O'Brien. Anne Meara
followed suit in the 1970s in Kate McShane.
Otherwise attempts to revive popular motion picture
images of Irishmen failed in efforts to resurrect
the popular priests in a remake of Going My Way
with Gene Kelly and Leo G. Carroll in the early
1960s, and In the Beginning, with McLean Stevenson
in the late 1970s. Despite the clear identification
of Irish characters in all of these shows, little
differentiated these individuals from the lawyers,
policemen, and priests of other ethnic groups.

Only a comedy, Bridget Loves Bernie, which
appeared in the 1972-1973 season, managed to hit
the mark in a tale of a love affair between Bernie
Steinberg (David Birney), a struggling Jewish
writer, and Bridget Fitzgerald (Meredith Baxter), a
schoolteacher and the daughter of wealthy Irish
Catholic parents. When the two marry, the parents
of each reveal the prejudices and problems of their
differing ethnic groups and make life difficult for
the newlyweds. This echo of the classic Broadway
hit Abie's Irish Rose achieved good ratings but was
cancelled after one season, after complaints by

both Jewish and Irish groups.
The dimunition of interest in films and
television shows about Irish Americans has occurred
as the Irish, perhaps to a greater extent than any
other immigrant group, have assimilated into the
great American filmic melting pot. While Irish
characters certainly remain on both television and
film, their Irishness is rarely one of the major
points of the story. They just happen to be one of
the many characters populating the American
landscape. To a certain extent this is a reflection
of the passing of the great Irish directors,
screenwriters, and actors, who explored, glorified,
romanticized, and analyzed their Irish heritage. It
is difficult to think of any modern counterpart to
John Ford among current directors or screenwriters.
Although many may be of Irish background, they, and
probably even their parents, have so assimilated
that any questions concerning their Irish heritage
are virtually ignored. While these great directors
and writers have passed from the scene, so have
many of the characters, places, and political
situations that became the basis for many of their
films, as the modern Irish have lost the qualities
that separated them both from America's other
ethnic groups as well as the Protestant majority.

The scholarship concerning Irish images in
film and television reflects the current lack of
concern for such issues. There are fewer articles
on the Irish than virtually any other major
American ethnic group. Although the influence of
the American Irish on the film industry is
acknowledged as considerable, few have studied this
issue.
There are, nevertheless, a few articles of
interest. Roger Dooley provides an excellent survey
of Irish actors, producers, directors, and
screenwriters in Hollywood in two 1957 Films in
Review articles. While the level of analysis is
slight, Dooley effectively documents the importance
of the Irish contribution to the film industry.(5)
Two later articles by Dennis Clark (with the
collaboration of William Lynch on one) review
Dooley's territory, and attempt to offer generalizations on Irish images in film.(2, 3) Some of the

observations are helpful, such as the attempt to
isolate genres of "Irish films," while others offer
difficulties. Clark claims that audiences often saw
"the Irish as seen by Jews" in Hollywood films, a
statement that seemingly negates the Irish
importance in filmmaking.(3)

For information on images of the Irish in
silent film, see works by Anthony Slide on early
films with Irish backgrounds, while Lewis Krohn
considers the "Cohens and the Kellys" series.(10,
17). Patricia Erens' study on the Jewish image in
film also has interesting comments on the tendency
of Jews and Irish to appear together in the ghetto
films of the 1920s.(See X-23.)

The Irish-as-gangster image is considered in a
variety works, with emphasis on Cagney's role in
Public Enemy and Angels with Dirty Faces.(8, 14)
Andrew Bergman also offers interesting suggestions
on the images of gangsters in Depression films in
We're in the Money.(See I-14 and Chapter IX.)

For interesting comments on the images of
Irish men and women, see the works by Brandon
French and Joan Mellen.(6, 11)   Kathryn Rose Kane
considers similar issues, with a focus on World War
II films.(9)

As suggested earlier, John Ford has played a
major role in shaping the film image of the Irish,
a fact considered only in passing in the many
biographies and critiques of the classic filmmaker.
A few observations, however, may be found in works
by Sarris and Sinclair.(15, 16)

Major discussions of films and/or television
shows include: Angels with Dirty Faces (14), The
Cohens and the Kellys (10), The Lad From Old
Ireland (17), The Last Hurrah (15), On the
Waterfront (13), The Public Enemy (4, 8), The Quiet
Man (6, 11, 15), and What Price Glory? (15).

1. Brennan, William J. "The Irish in American
   Film and Television." ETHNIC IMAGES IN
   AMERICAN FILM AND TELEVISION (item I-105),
   pp. 87-89.

2. Clark, Dennis. "The Irish in the Movies: A
   Tradition of Permanent Blur." ETHNIC IMAGES
   IN AMERICAN FILM AND TELEVISION (item I-
   105), pp. 75-82.

3. ———, and William J. Lynch. "Hollywood and
   Hibernia: The Irish in the Movies." THE
   KALEIDOSCOPIC LENS (item I-106) pp. 98-
   113.

4. Cohen, Henry, ed. THE PUBLIC ENEMY. Madison:
   University of Wisconsin Press, 1981.

5. Dooley, Roger. "The Irish on the Screen."
   FILMS IN REVIEW 8 (May 1957): 211-17; 8
   (June-July 1957): 259-70.

6. French, Brandon. ON THE VERGE OF REVOLT: WOMEN
   IN AMERICAN FILMS OF THE FIFTIES. New York:
   Ungar, 1978.

7. Jeffres, Leo W. and K. Kyoon Hur. "White
   Ethnics and Their Media Images." (item I-
   72).

8. Jowett, Garth. "Bullets, Beer and the Hays
   Office: 'Public Enemy.'" AMERICAN HISTORY/
   AMERICAN FILM: INTERPRETING THE HOLLYWOOD
   IMAGE (item I-74), pp. 57-75.

9. Kane, Kathryn Rose. VISIONS OF WAR (item
   I-77).

10. Krohn, Lewis G. "The Cohens and the Kellys."
    CLASSIC IMAGES REVIEW 9 (October 1981):
    6-7.

11. Mellen, Joan. BIG BAD WOLVES: MASCULINITY IN
    THE AMERICAN FILM (item II-435).

12. Moloney, Mick. "Stereotypes in the Media: The
    Irish-American Case." ETHNIC IMAGES IN
    AMERICAN FILM AND TELEVISION (item I-105),

pp. 83-85.

13. Murray, Edward. TEN FILM CLASSICS: A RE-
    VIEWING. New York: Ungar, 1978.

14. Naremore, James. "Actor, Role, Star: James
    Cagney in 'Angels With Dirty Faces.'"
    MOSAIC 16 (Spring 1983): 1-17.

15. Sarris, Andrew. THE JOHN FORD MOVIE MYSTERY.
    Bloomington: Indiana University Press,
    1975.

16. Sinclair, Andrew. JOHN FORD. New York: Dial
    Press, 1979.

17. Slide, Anthony. ASPECTS OF AMERICAN FILM
    HISTORY PRIOR TO 1920. Metuchen, N. J.:
    Scarecrow Press, 1978.

IX. ITALIANS

Italian images in American film and television were products of popular culture, public events, and, since the 1970s, self-conscious promotion by Italian-American actors, directors, and producers. Popular culture and public events, especially the visibility of gangsters during the Prohibition era, cast Italians as criminal types, a screen image that would grow with the popularity of the gangster genre and newspaper stories about organized crime. Despite protests by Italian-American groups from the 1940s on, the Italian images could not shake an association with crime. The highly publicized Italian-American involvement in real crime and, more importantly, their roles in making screen crime commercially and critically successful, especially with The Godfather saga, fixed Italian criminal images in the popular imagination. Even recent introspective films by Italian-American artists about Italian families and their adjustment to America unwittingly have contributed to the stereotype by locating their characters in city milieus, just those places Americans have traditionally identified as the sources of crime and corruption. Alternative images of Italians as buffoons, which Chico Marx, among others, played upon in his comedy, never matched the Italian criminal stereotype in force or appeal, and they lacked the impetus of news accounts to sustain public interest in them. Whatever the image, the Italian has generally appeared as a creature of passion, an emotional being given to excess in love or hatred, whose religion, culture, and condition seemingly explained his exaggerated behavior.

The Italians' Catholicism, culture, and complexion had long made them suspect in English and American Protestant culture. Anti-Catholicism bred fears of popish plots and priestly intrigue. Unable to accept the repressed sexuality of the Catholic clergy as either natural or possible, anti-Catholic

writers, the pornographers of Protestantism, fed
the public imagination with lurid tales of priests
seducing innocent women in the confessionals or
ravishing nuns in convents. In English Protestant
culture Rome stood as the font of corruption and
perversion; its excessive luxuries and abominations
had caused the fall of the Roman Empire and then
entered   the Catholic church. English culture also
marked civilization by color, rendering the savage
side of human nature in dark hues. Gothic fiction
teemed with dark, Mediterranean men and women exuding passion and plotting intrigues, threatening
English virginity and liberty. In English literature dating back to the eighteenth century Italian
men and women appeared as overly sexual, passionate, and mysterious. The men, with their ear-
rings and daggers, bore watching; so, too, did the
women, with their long eye-lashes and full bodies.
American popular literature stole shamelessly from
English traditions and made the passionate Italian
a fixture in scores of melodramas and potboilers.
     Anti-immigrant literature added to the stock of
Italian images by rendering the large number of
southern Italian immigrants coming to America in
the late nineteenth through the early twentieth
centuries as swarthy, prognathic, and hunch-backed,
much like the caricatures of Jews and gypsies. All
the negative images of urban, immigrant life attached to Italians, whose religion, culture, poverty, and color condemned them as dangerous and
dirty in Protestant America. If not sinister, the
Italian was clownish. The musical, buffoonish
street vendor also appeared in the catalogue of
Italian stereotypes--less threatening than the
criminal types, but still excitable and passionate.
The Italian stereotypes passed from print to cartoons and then to the screen, where the Italians'
gesticulations, behavior, and language further
exaggerated their images.
     Still, during the early years of film, Italians
fared no better or no worse than other immigrant
groups who made up the urban movie audiences. Unlike the Irish and the Jews who assumed control
over the industry, however, Italians exercised
little influence in making movies or in shaping
their early screen images. D. W. Griffith and a few
other filmmakers did not always hide their contempt
for the   "black hand dago," or for any of the "new

immigrants," but such prejudices were not film
staples. The immigrant audiences would not likely
have tolerated them. The moviemakers drew on American popular culture and responded to their own
commercial instincts in forming Italian screen
characters. They dressed Italians in the ethnic
costumes and assigned them the ethnic designations
common to vaudeville and popular fiction in order
to establish setting, mood, and situation for comic
or dramatic action. Italian organ-grinders, tough
guys, lovers, and street vendors all appeared in
early films. Wine and passion flowed in such films
as In Little Italy, but so, too, did empathy for
Italian ghetto life.(37, 46, 72)
     Italian figures evinced both good and bad
traits in a host of early film comedies and melodramas. Italian men show courage and honesty in
nabbing Italian criminals in The Detectives of the
Italian Bureau; an Italian butcher helps capture
mafioso kidnappers in The Black Hand; and, in The
Story of a Rose, an immigrant father sacrifices
much to bring his wife to America and, after her
death, to care for his crippled daughter.
     Thomas Ince's extraordinary film, The Italian
(1914), suggested the sympathy some filmmakers felt
toward the new immigrants. Ince used the Italian
experience to compare the myth of the American
Dream with the harsh reality of immigrant ghetto
life. In the film Ince portrays Old World Italy as
a land of beauty, simplicity, and compassion. The
Italian immigrant, played by matinee idol George
Beban, seeks his destiny in America; he works hard,
saves his money, and brings his fiancee to the new
land. But the couple does not prosper. The cruel,
grim city crushes Ince's Italians, as it crushed so
many real immigrants. The couple's child dies from
malnutrition and heat; the father is robbed and
savagely beaten in an alley and later arrested by
police and imprisoned. Ince's gritty realism was
unusual for films of the time, and perhaps commercially fatal among immigrant audiences seeking to
escape reality in the movie houses. The movie,
however, helped to establish the Italian as a metaphor for the new immigrant, with all the promise
and problems of adjustment in the New World. That
Italian image would reappear in the self-con-
sciously ethnic productions of several Italian-
American filmmakers of the 1970s.(18)

During the 1920s Italians lost their appeal as
film subjects. Rudolph Valentino's screen presence
reconfirmed the association of Italians with eroti-
cism and passion, for those observers who chose to
make the connection. Valentino, the romantic idol,
did not, however, play Italian screen characters,
although his pre-stardom roles as a criminal or
gigolo hinted at the darker side of "Italian" passion. When Italian characters cropped up in films,
they most often served as background. Italian
images rarely took center stage. The films treating
immigrant subjects in the 1920s largely pushed the
theme of assimilation. Filmmakers, who were themselves assimilating into American culture, boiled
down ethnic distinctions among their film characters in melting-pot movies about Irish and Jewish
antagonists who find common purpose and love and
end up marrying one another. The screen Italians
remained unassimilated and unwed--when they appeared at all.(18, 37)

Only in the emerging gangster film genre did
Italians assume visible importance. The gangster
film evolved from the early "underworld films"
about petty crime and penny-ante hoodlums. The
gangster films drew on contemporary news and popular prejudices more than historical or literary
sources for their subject matter and characters.
Urban crime had fascinated filmmakers from the
beginnings of the film industry, but the first true
gangster film was probably D.W. Griffith's Musketeers of Pig Alley (1912), which depicted the
city as a seat of crime and corruption. Thomas Ince
advanced the genre with his The Gangsters and the
Girl (1914), which further linked crime to urban
environment. In the early gangster-oriented films
crime remained individual rather than organized,
and Italians had no special claim to criminality.
Hollywood films only occasionally alluded to the
Mafia, for example, and the references were ambiguous and in no way probing. Until the rise of real
gangsterism in the 1920s, filmmakers lacked examples of large-scale crime anyway. Irish, Jews,
blacks, and others all appeared as criminals in
early films. Significantly, however, as William
Everson points out, the early crime films cast
gangsters as aliens, often Mediterranean types such
as Italians, and thereby attached the image of the
"dark" immigrant to criminality in popular imagi-

nation. Many early crime films were shot in immigrant neighborhoods, lending realism to the images
and tightening the association between urban environment, immigrant culture, and crime. Among immigrant groups, however, the Irish and Jews had alternative screen images in the assimilationist
films of the era. The Italians did not.(12, 18, 37,
67, 70, 72)

By the late 1920s the lawlessness of the Prohibition era, combined with the despair and anger of
the early days of the Depression, infused gangster
films with realism and fury. The advent of sound
also gave the gangster film the pace it lacked in
silent form and, as William Everson once observed,
added to its realism, with screaming tires, jazz
music, chattering machine guns, and "staccato delivery of dialogue."(18) A rash of gangster films
in the late 1920s through the early 1930s glam-
orized violence and the underworld. The Hays Office
in 1930 and the Production Code in 1933 condemned
the explicit violence and sympathy toward the criminals in such films and encouraged Hollywood filmmakers to show the efficiency of law enforcement by
bringing the screen criminals to justice in their
movies. Before such strictures took effect, however, the gangster anti-hero was firmly rooted in
popular imagination, and the Italian was identified, in both news accounts and film characterizations, as the embodiment of organized crime.(3,
12, 44, 67, 68, 70, 72)

Little Caesar (1930), more than any other film,
established the gangster film in form and appeal.
The film's commercial success alone invited further
emulation and exploitation of its features. So,
too, did its theme of success, a message of individual possibility amid the Depression, despite
Little Caesar's death in the end. The film drew on
the headlines about organized crime to create a
screen character modeled on a recognizable, contemporary gangster, Al Capone, with all the magnetism
and power that a Capone or any gangster presumably
possessed to seize and hold onto his territory. In
the title role of Little Caesar was Edward G.
Robinson as Caesar Enrico Bandello, a small-town
hoodlum who rose by ruthlessness and savvy to the
top of the rackets before his fall. In the film
Rico lives in an underworld filled with Italians.
Although Rico appears as rootless (without family,

religion, or romantic attachment), his Italian name
and manner, and the obvious parallels to Al Capone,
give his character an ethnic designation no viewer
could miss.(3, 12, 30, 42, 44, 59, 60, 65, 67, 68,
70, 72)

The connection between the Italian film gangster and the real Italian gangster became more
explicit in Howard Hughes's controversial Scarface
(1932), based on the life of Al Capone. Director
Howard Hawks and writer Ben Hecht both claimed a
"working relationship" with the Capone mob in their
efforts to get information about Capone and his
world for the film. The film ran into trouble with
the censors, who in New York required a new ending
showing Capone dying on the gallows rather than
being shot down in a hail of bullets as in the
original version. While censors recoiled from the
violence and the seeming celebration of Capone in
the film, the Italian identity of Scarface (played
by Paul Muni) and his cronies beamed forth. The
quintessential gangster in real life and in film
was Italian.(12, 15, 44, 67, 68, 70)

The film gangsters who followed Little Caesar
and Scarface included several ethnic types, especially the Irish who, like the Italians, were associated in the public mind with urban crime and
corruption. James Cagney as an Irish hoodlum in
Public Enemy exceeded Robinson in screen magnetism.
Still, the Italian image persisted in film depictions of gangsters and criminals. The prominence of
Al Capone in the news, even after his imprisonment,
made the "mob" synonomous with Italian Americans in
popular thought. The Capone story, with all its
ethnic undercurrents, inspired at least eight gangster films about Capone and his gang and continued
to provide material for films into the 1980s. Even
though ethnic criminality was proscribed under
section 10 (on "National Feelings") of the 1933
Production Code, which prohibited any picture that
might "incite bigotry or hatred among people of
differing races, religions or national origins,"
the foreign character of criminality was not completely disguised. In many films of the 1930s and
1940s swarthy gangsters had a "Mediterranean" look
about them. More significantly, when the Production
Code clean-up of crime movies occurred after 1933,
converting the gangsters from heroes into hoodlums,
the Italians did not follow the Irish into roles as

good cops and federal agents. Cagney, for example, switched from gangster to G-man, carrying all his Irish magnetism and energy with him. Irish priests were also available to redeem criminals and sing their way into moviegoers' hearts. Edward G. Robinson played "good guy" characters, but his new roles lacked realistic Italian ascription. And Italian priests did not appear in Hollywood films to convince criminals to do right. If Italian characters showed up on the side of law, they were often indistinguishable in their methods and manner from the criminals they tried to apprehend. Dark and dangerous, the screen Italian lived in, or close to, the underworld.(3, 12, 30, 42, 44, 65, 67, 70)

The deaths of prominent real-life gangsters, the Production Code's strictures, Hollywood's denial of ethnicity altogether in most films of the 1930s through the 1950s, and World War II--all deflected Hollywood away from films assigning ethnic criminality. Even the anti-Nazi espionage films of World War II skirted an explicit ethnic explanation for criminal behavior by blaming the ideology of Nazism rather than the German character for acts of sabotage and treason. Italian criminal types appeared in several films through the 1950s-- powerfully so in Cry of the City (1948) about the divergent paths taken by two slum-bred Italian Americans (one toward crime, the other against it)--but they were eclipsed on the screen by other criminals who had no clear ethnic background.(12, 67, 70)

From the late 1930s until The Godfather in 1972 Italianness did not even count so much in Hollywood's renditions of big-time crime. The Senate Special Committee to Investigate Organized Crime in Interstate Commerce hearings in 1950, chaired by Senator Estes Kefauver, briefly exposed the "Syndicate" to public view, including close-ups of a hand-wringing, sweating Frank Costello on nationwide television. The subsequent interest in organized crime led to several films about professional "hit men," racketeering, and other gangland activities. In The Enforcer (1951) the public learned about the language and style of Murder, Inc., and in On the Waterfront (1954), it discovered a mob composed of Italians, Irish, and even a few East Europeans, whose very ethnicity seemed a

criminal act in the consensus-oriented, assimilationist world of the 1950s. In the 1950s and early
1960s films about organized crime were as likely to
repudiate or neglect ethnic identities as to include them. Filmdom's mobs were run by men in gray
flannel suits, organization men with only ambition
to guide them. In The Big Combo (1955), for example, the aspiring gangster erased his Italian
origins, which reeked of petty crime and a sordid
life, in order to gain acceptance in the crime
syndicate.(12, 42, 67, 70, 72)

Several developments altered the tone and texture of gangster films in the 1960s and restored
ethnic identities to mobsters. The "new ethnicity"
emerging in America during the late 1960s encouraged filmmakers to restore ethnic labels to
their characters. The collapse of effective movie
censorship by the late 1950s allowed filmmakers in
search of young audiences to reclaim the style and
substance of an earlier era; indeed, beginning with
film biographies about Depression-era criminals and
then extending to films about Prohibition-era gangsters, filmmakers copied the violence, language,
locales, and personalities of the pre-Production
Code gangster films in their own works, a practice
that continued into the 1980s. Even some important
anti-establishment films of the day (e.g., Bonnie
and Clyde) attempted to locate the cultural roots
of the criminals they glorified, while seeking a
"ballet of death" through shoot-out scenes shot in
slow-motion and stop-action photography. Gangster
films spoke in their own poetry of violence, from
the rapid fire of machine guns to the gurgling of a
man being strangled, but their emphasis was less on
style than narrative. By 1967, in Roger Corman's
St. Valentine's Day Massacre, real historical
figures with real names had replaced fictional
gangsters in films about the underworld. The film,
which centered on the feud between the predominantly Irish North Side gang of Bugs Moran and the
Italian South Side gang of Al Capone in Chicago,
created an aura of historical authenticity in its
careful chronological reconstruction of the events
leading up to the massacre, an authenticity that
was made believable for ethnically-conscious audiences in 1967 by recognizing ethnic rivalry as the
root cause of the gangsters' feud. The Italian was
not alone in film's line-up of criminal characters

in the 1960s, but filmmakers' interest in ethnicity
and history in making movies about gangsters inevitably pushed the Italian forward.(12, 67)

The Italian gangster was already in the public
eye because of renewed governmental investigations
of organized crime, which probed into the there-
tofore unknown sociology of the Cosa Nostra. The
word Mafia became common parlance for organized
crime by the mid-1960s, if not earlier. The Mafia
served as subject matter for two films based on the
1909 mafioso assassination of a New York City detective in Italy (The Black Hand [1950] and Pay or
Die [1960]) and for The Brotherhood (1968). A smat-
tering of B-pictures, such as The Most Dangerous
Man Alive (1961), further intimated Italian mafioso
activities. Led by the Sons of Italy, Italian-
American organizations, from the late 1940s through
the 1960s, had been largely successful in keeping
even the most oblique allusions to the Mafia from
Hollywood films, but by the late 1960s the Mafia
theme was too attractive for filmmakers to ignore
altogether. It required only a major social or
cinematic event to reconfirm the Italian as the
quintessential gangster.(12)

The Godfather (1972) provided the social and
cinematic event. Amid pressure from the Italian-
American Civil Rights League (headed by Joseph
Colombo and subsequently discredited as a Mafia
front) to remove references to the Mafia, which
were not in the script anyway, Francis Ford Coppola
filmed an epic about an Italian "family." The film
enlisted the talents of numerous Italian-Americans,
including Mario Puzo (who wrote the screenplay
based on his best-selling novel), Al Pacino (who
played Michael Corleone, the youngest son who in-
herits the family empire even as his detached,
business-like manner undermines it), and one Carlo
Russo who got the role of Carlo Rizzo (the son-in-
law who betrays Don Corleone) because of his connections with the Colombo family. The film's production history contributed to the movie's mystique
and prepared audiences to receive The Godfather as
an authentic document on organized crime. Studio
publicity agents, for example, parlayed supposed
threats against the filmmakers into "proof" of the
film's social importance. Coppola's attention to
historical detail in establishing time and setting,
his sympathetic rendering of the Corleone family,

and his own Italian-American background combined
with the participation of other Italian-American
artists in the film's production to give the Italian mafioso images in The Godfather a credibility
no disclaimers could deny. For the millions who saw
the film, its sequel, and the recut, enlarged version made for television, the Italian families of
the Godfather, played by Italian-American actors,
were too real. A flood of articles, books, and
films about the Mafia ensued, suggesting how much
the Italian criminal image recalled primeval fears
and fantasies in the American subconscious.(8, 12,
21, 24, 29, 30, 36, 40, 47, 49, 55, 58, 62, 63, 69,
74, 75)

The Godfather essays the corruption of "the
family," led by Don Vito Corleone (Marlon Brando),
from its traditional ethnic base of respect and
honor to a modern organization, shorn of ethnic
feeling and commitment. Coppola suggests that the
old ways are the best ways, for the Don rejects
attempts to push the family into narcotics--a crime
against children--and seeks to end the war among
the New York families caused by greed and misunder-
standing. In the end, Michael Corleone, who had
seemingly rejected the family traditions and even
once confessed to his American sweetheart that his
Italian family she met at the wedding of the Corleone daughter was not him, succeeds to the Don's
chair. Michael's brother, emotional Sonny (whom
Coppola cuts in the mold of earlier film gangsters), dies in a barrage of bullets, in which
Coppola offered his version of the poetry of death.
His other brother, Fredo, is too weak to assume
control. Michael seemingly demonstrates his legitimate claim to family leadership.by cooly assas-
sinating two enemies, by escaping to Sicily where
he finds a bride (but not his roots) only to see
her murdered, and by orchestrating the final victory over the rival families. But Michael's rise is
the family's fall from the grace its ethnicity had
given it under the old don. Michael converts the
family into a business organization alone. By the
end of film, Michael`plans to uproot the family
from its New York home and relocate its operation
in Las Vegas, a move symbolic of Michael's, and
thereafter the organization's, loss of ethnic
obligation and honor.(8, 9, 11, 12, 14, 19, 20, 29,
30, 42, 55, 67, 70, 71, 72)

The self-conscious ethnic theme in The
Godfather formed a leitmotif in its sequel, The
Godfather, Part II (1974). Coppola contrasted the
lack of ethnic identity and feeling in Michael's
organization with the Italian immigrant roots of
the old don's family. The film included a long
sequence tracing the circumstances and character
of Don Corleone's rise (with Robert De Niro playing
the young Vito Corleone). Don Corleone was an honorable man who had turned to crime because urban
poverty and anti-immigrant hostility left no other
outlet for the young Italian immigrant. He was also
a self-made man who remembered his friends, provided for his family, and respected tradition. In
contrast, Michael represented the epitome of the
modern organization executive who ruled his corporation without feeling or respect for tradition.
Family no longer counted, for it hardly existed.
Michael even arranged the murder of his brother
Fredo. Michael's rise marks his failure, for in the
end he sacrifices family, tradition, and moral
values. He is alone at the top.(12, 23, 30, 36, 40,
42, 55, 67, 70, 72, 75, 76, 78)
     Coppola's theme about the abandonment of ethnic
values in the quest for the American Dream, with
Michael's organization serving as the metaphor for
the modern corporation, became starkly evident in
Mario Puzo's The Godfather: The Complete Novel for
Television (1977), the television compilation of
the two films in which Coppola rearranged the material in chronological order and embellished the
story with scenes cut from the films (approximately
one hour of material). The tale of fathers and
sons, of connections between personal lives and
business, of old ways versus new ones--the television Godfather, like its film forebears, was more
than just a screen account of gangsters, more than
an extension and romanticization of the Mafia mystique; rather, it constituted an extended essay on
American identity. In the age of Roots Italian
Americans sought their own past, and insomuch as
Italians represented the "new immigrants" in popular culture, their history became the collective
trust of many others. The appeal, and the enormous
commercial and critical success, of the entire
Godfather experience bespoke that common bond.(13,
55, 78)

Coppola insisted that the Don Corleone gangster
was a critique of capitalist society. His family
saga extended the traditional gangster film genre
by making explicit the metaphorical connections
between gangsters and capitalist society that went
back to the days of Little Caesar. Coppola's Don
Corleone was a gangster who both embodied capitalist values in his rags-to-riches rise and rejected them in his refusal to countenance drug-
dealing, new investment tainted with immorality.
Coppola sanitized his gangsters by blurring the
criminal dimension to Don Corleone's activities; no
hint of the sources of the family's income appears
in the films. Whatever his crimes, honor redeemed
him. Michael Corleone, by contrast, had succcumbed
to the evils of American capitalism. His ruthlessness gained him the criminal world, but in so
doing he lost his ethnic soul. His great crime was
his Americanization. "Michael is America," concluded Coppola.(12, 30, 55)
    The Godfather saga made gangsters and Mafia hot
commercial properties. A "godfather syndrome" set
in, along with bumper stickers and T-shirts pro-
claiming one's ties to the Mafia. Filmmakers sought
to cash in on the mystique, with numerous films
built on The Godfather model. Some, such as The
Crime Boss (1974), were so transparently rip-offs,
and so badly done, they seemed almost to parody the
Coppola original. Others--especially the Valachi
Papers (1972), which was based on the Peter Maas
best-seller about the testimony of a minor mafi-
oso--benefitted from the interest the The Godfather
had generated and lent added authenticity to the
Italian gangster connection.
    The rash of gangster films, which now included
films about other groups' criminal past (e.g.,
Lepke [1975], an effort to create a Jewish godfather) quickly exhausted the thematic possibilities of the genre. Filmmakers reached back into
history to remake biographies of gangsters (e.g.,
Capone [1975]), but, in the end, they turned to
style rather than metaphor or history to sustain
audience interest. Violence increased as story
lines became less original and compelling. Brian De
Palma, for example, simply transmuted Scarface into
a Cuban gangster (Scarface [1983]).(12, 67, 70)
    The Italian-as-gangster screen image, of
course, became more deeply entrenched in popular

culture with each new release about the Mafia. So, too, the violent excesses of the post-Godfather films further intensified popular association of Italians with passion and lack of control. The effect of gangster films, especially The Godfather, on Italian images, however, was also to redirect attention to themes of family and to relocate the Italian in the mean streets of the city. Along with the screen Jew, the screen Italian became the metaphor for the price of Americanization. The Italian immigrant's struggle to escape urban poverty, as essayed in The Godfather, Part II, even justified petty crime, so long as the Italian did not abandon his ethnic obligations. Italian characters who hustled their way out of poverty, as in Paradise Alley (1978), starring Sylvester Stallone, were romantic, even heroic, figures, providing they did not betray their family and friends for the American Dream. As the second- and third-generation ethnic Americans wrestled with their own cultural identities and with their parents' values, films treating intergenerational struggles and the rootlessness of modern America found receptive audiences.

A host of Italian-American artists began to explore their own cultural roots. Italian-American filmmakers and actors were themselves hot properties following The Godfather successes. Coppola moved away from the Italian-American theme, but Pacino, De Niro, many of the character actors, and a new generation of young actors translated their Italian appeal into successful film careers. Martin Scorsese, especially, peddled his own Italian ethnicity in several films--most explicitly in Mean Streets (1973), his autobiographical evocation of Little Italy and the Italian-American's divided self, and in the documentary Italianamerican (1974), Scorsese's interview with his parents in their Manhattan apartment.(30, 45, 47, 54, 55, 64)

Sylvester Stallone, as writer and actor, openly traded on his Italianness. In Rocky (1976) he combined Italian images with old-time film cliches about little guys making it big in America. His persistent efforts to sell his script, in the face of numerous rebuffs, bespoke Stallone's faith in his story and his sound cultural and commercial instincts. He judged the public mood correctly. The film was a box-office and critical hit in the year

of America's Bicentennial. Set in a south Philadelphia Italian neighborhood, Rocky is the story of
Rocky Balboa, "The Italian Stallion," a hulking
club fighter who gets his chance against the world
champion and who, by dint of hard work and belief
in himself, comes out the real winner, even though
the champion gets the decision in the ring. Rocky
gains its strength from the urban, Italian-American
milieu, which anchors Rocky in a community and
suggests that he will not fall so long as he holds
onto his cultural and familial ties. Reaching for
part of the American Dream did not necessarily mean
losing one's place at the family table. Rocky was
palatable to the middle class, but it found special
favor among white, ethnic working-class Americans.
As Daniel Leab argues, Rocky "endorsed the ethnic's
prejudices, deferred to his fantasies, and highlighted his lifestyle."(50)

Stallone demonstrated the box-office appeal of
an unabashedly ethnic figure. But Stallone tar-
nished the Italian-American image by shamelessly
exploiting the Rocky character in two sequels, and,
in those and other films, he seemed almost to adopt
an Italian stereotype, flexing his overblown pec-
toral muscles and talking "dumb," when, in fact,
Stallone is quite bright. By the same account,
Stallone's and other Italian-American artists'
growing monopoly of roles as street-wise cops
(e.g., Serpico [1973]), boxers (e.g., Raging Bull
[1980]), and young toughs (e.g., Grease [1978])
reinforced popular stereotypes of Italians as emo-
tionally overcharged toughs. Perhaps some Italians
themselves had come to believe the caricatures.

More subtle are the images emerging from such
films as Lovers and Other Strangers (1970) and,
especially, Saturday Night Fever (1977), in which
Italian men come off as ambivalent about their
identities and destinies. The women either know
their place in the wedding march, as in Lovers and
Other Strangers, or upset older rhythms by leaving
the old place, as in Saturday Night Fever where, by
her example, the dancer Stephanie Mangano (Karen
Gorney) invites Tony Manero (John Travolta) to give
up his local status as the disco king of a Brooklyn
Italian neighborhood for "real" life across the
bridge in modern Manhattan. Such films measure the
distance between fathers and sons and render ethnic
neighborhoods and memories in somber tones.(30)

The Italian-American father in Lovers and Other Strangers, for example, is incredulous when he learns that one of his sons is separating from his wife because the son is not happy. Happiness, the father observes, is no prescription for a stable family. According to Daniel Golden, the intro- spective and confused Tony Maneros represent the "attenuated dreams and aspirations of the new gen- eration of Italian-Americans." More than that, such characters move Italian screen images beyond older stereotypes of Italians as unthinking criminal types to sensitive ethnic everymen caught between tradition and the American Dream.(30)

Italian images on television followed the film Italians along the path from criminal types to ethnic everymen. Early television images of Ital- ians, for example, borrowed from film's gangster models. The most explicit case was The Untouch- ables, a series about Treasury Department gang- busters in the Prohibition era, which brought con- troversy and high ratings to ABC between 1959 and 1963. The show's violence disturbed critics (but thrilled audiences), and its weekly presentation of Italian-American criminals outraged Italian-Amer- ican organizations. The producers responded to critics and threats of boycotts by arguing for the show's basic historical accuracy and, finally, by attaching a disclaimer to the end of each show stating that some characterizations and events were fictionalized. The association of Italian-American characters with organized crime gained additional currency from The Godfather saga, which did well on television in its recut form. In The Gangster Chronicles NBC revived the formula, but the series lasted only one season (1980-1981), amid strong protests from Italian-American civil rights groups. With the gangster mystique playing out, and with ethnicity coming into prime-time programming in the 1980s, producers discovered the "new" Italian Amer- ican of popular film. The slicked-back, smart- alecky Italian characters took their place along- side Jews as symbols for urban contemporaneity.(10, 34, 51, 78)

Italian-American characters populated numerous shows in the 1970s and 1980s. Almost invariably, they appeared in urban settings, and in many cases, they came across as street-smart, but excessively emotional individuals. In several long-running,

prime-time series Italian-American characters
played principal roles. In Laverne and Shirley, a
comedy series set in the 1950s, Penny Marshall was
the quick-tempered, man-crazed Laverne DiFazio. The
Laverne character seemed more a female counterpart
of Italian male images than an extension of the
traditional big-breasted, spoon-wielding Italian
mama who dispensed spaghetti sauce (gravy in real
Italian parlance) and advice from her kitchen, as
in television commercials and the recent, short-
lived Mama Malone show. She was as over-sexed,
under-educated, and over-wrought as any of the
Italian-American characters on television. Laverne
and Shirley had spun off from Happy Days, which was
set in the same period and city. In Happy Days
Henry Winkler was Arthur "Fonzie" Fonzarelli, the
"cool" high school dropout, who educated the
straight, WASP Richie Cunningham about cars and
women and made every girl in their Milwaukee soda
shop hangout swoon. Only the motorcycle queen Pinky
Tuscadero was cooler than the Fonz. In Welcome
Back, Kotter John Travolta, as Vinnie Barbarino,
parlayed his Italian good looks and "style" into
stardom. Barbarino was the heart-throb of the girls
in the show's multiethnic Brooklyn high school, but
among the school's toughest, least academic students who made up Kotter's class of "sweathogs,"
Barbarino seemed the only student incapable of
remediation. In Taxi Louie DiPalma (Danny De Vito)
was the unctuous cab dispatcher who squealed orders
and obscenities from his wire cage, and Tony Banta
(Tony Danza) was the sweet, but stupid palooka who
fell victim to the most transparent scams. Whatever
their occupation, sex, or locale, Italian characters seemingly dealt with the world in a primitive way. Still, as Robert Sklar observes, the
Laverne and the Fonz characters especially succeeded with audiences because they were working-
class white knights whose unpretentiousness and
basic decency regularly pricked the self-satis-
faction, arrogance, and dishonesty of better-heeled
antagonists they met..Only the Fonz, after all,
wore a white T-shirt.(7, 10, 17, 26, 49, 51, 57,
73)

    Television's Italian characters retained their
gritty city look and language. They did not live in
suburban split-level homes, wear white collars, or
speak proper English. Many of them continued to

lurk around crime. In television, as in film, Italian-American characters were cops if they were not
robbers. In several popular action shows of the
1970s, Italian-American cops used their urban savvy
and toughness to out-muscle the criminals. First in
Toma (based on a real Newark, New Jersey, policeman's experiences) and then in Baretta television
cultivated the image of the strutting Italian-
American cop who works outside the system and
relies on his street smarts to nab criminals, suggesting that only a proto-criminal type could know
the habits and habitats of the big city criminals
enough to capture them. Italian cops also appeared
in the multiethnic police stations which became
fashionable on television crime series. In Captain
Frank Furillo (Daniel Travanti) of Hill Street
Blues, however, Italian Americans finally got a
character who, in Jean Grillo's description, is
warm without being overly emotional, handsome without being flashy, humane without being simplistic,
and, most of all, who is a thinker rather than a
street-smart cop. Ethnic pride glowed with the
Furillo character, who has received raves from
Italian-American critics. Furillo, they insist,
counterbalances the media-made Italian-American cop
whose propensity for violence and disobeying the
rules of the system makes him almost indistinguishable from criminals and, so, perpetuates notions of
inherent Italian lawlessness and lack of self-
control. The self-controlled Furillo character
promises a new image of an Italian American who can
live in an urban environment without succumbing to
it.(25, 33, 34, 41, 51, 56, 57)

     The scholarship on Italian images in film and
television is surprisingly sparse and thin, considering the size and visibility of the group. Only
Daniel Golden has essayed the evolution of Italian
images in popular culture, tracking "Mediterranean"
characters and symbols from English and American
literature and caricature to the screen and viewing
Italian film images and Italian-American filmmakers' self-perceptions in the historical context
of southern Italians' commitment to family and tradition.(30) In a seminal essay, published in 1978,
Joseph Papaleo suggested that the Italian's image

in film and television has suffered because of its
simplicity. The image, he argued, has consisted of
excessively emotional Italians whose overreactions
indicate their lack of control in a society demanding self-denial and restraint.(56) Papaleo's
insight into the flaw of Italian "excess" has informed other writers, but no one, save Golden, has
attempted to trace either the roots or the foliage
of that image to any extent. In Mirella Affron's
filmography of sixty-eight films featuring Italian-
American subjects or Italian-Americans as principal
characters (from 1918-1971), several images appear,
but Italian-American subjects and characters seem
to have clustered in films about cities and
crime.(1) The principal concern of scholars examining Italian images, however, has been to catalogue the depictions of and, invariably, to condemn
film's (and television's) association of Italians
with criminality. That over one third of all
studies treating Italian media images focus in some
way on The Godfather further bespeaks the powerful
grip that one set of images holds on both popular
imagination and scholarship.

William Everson provides the fullest discussion
of early screen appearances of Italian characters
and subjects, with special attention to Thomas
Ince's important The Italian.(18) Lewis Jacobs,
Jack Temple Kirby, and Ralph Willett note D.W.
Griffith's derogatory images of southern Europeans,
borne of Griffith's ethnocentrism, but Jacobs adds
that in the mood of the Progressive era other
filmmakers presented Italian immigrants in a sympathetic light.(37, 46, 79) Everson and Robert Sklar
also point out that early filmmakers could ill
afford to alienate their immigrant audiences with
negative portrayals of them.(18, 72) In some
cases, then, film softened popular stereotypes.
According to Peter Rollins and Harry Menig, Italians and other minorities benefitted from Will
Rogers' practice of taking negative images from
popular culture and humanizing them in his on-
screen humor.(66)

The Italian-as-gangster screen image had its
cinematic origins in early crime movies set in city
slums. Everson observes that early crime films did
not isolate the Italian as a criminal type, but
they did draw on popular fears about dark cities
and their dark denizens as seedbeds for crime. The

gangster film genre, and the Italian-as-gangster
motif, awaited the rise to public prominence of
organized crime that the newspapers gave it in the
1920s and thereafter.(18)
     Carlos Clarens tracks the evolving character of
movie criminals from the silent era to the late
1970s. He pays particular attention to Italian
images, noting the connection between news accounts
of Italian, and other, gangsters and their corres-
ponding images on screen. More than anyone else
surveying the subject of crime movies, Clarens
places Italian images within the context of the
gangster film genre.(12) Likewise, Eugene Rosow
observes that early gangster movies were shot in
immigrant neighborhoods and that, during the 1920s,
depictions of organized crime in film almost always
had an ethnic signature.(67) Jack Shadoian is less
attentive to ethnic ascriptions in gangster/crime
movies, but he, too, notes the connection between
ethnicity and crime in popular culture.(70) Nick
Roddick states that Warner Brothers especially
liked making gangster movies during the 1930s
because they were cheap to produce (contemporary
dress, minimal sets, and few exterior shots) and
relied on successful formulas.(65) Stephen Karpf
(along with the other authors cited above) ties the
emergence of the gangster film to the Depression
and to newspapers' fascination with organized crime
and attributes the decline of the genre by 1940 to
shifts in public concerns and the exhaustion of the
formula.(44) Stuart Kaminsky concentrates on the
structure of the gangster film genre, arguing that
Little Caesar defined the genre's terms.(42)
     Several authors comment on the importance of
Little Caesar in establishing the style and substance of gangster movies. Clarens,(12) Everson,(18) Golden,(30) Kaminsky,(42) Karpf,(44)
Roddick,(65) Rosow,(67) Shadoian,(70) and Sklar(72)
all do so. Invariably, they compare the personal
magnetism of Edward G. Robinson with James Cagney
in Public Enemy to the advantage of the latter and
suggest that the Italian gangster image had no
monopoly in 1930s movies. Andrew Bergman sees Rico
as an early Depression era anti-hero, a self-made
man who bucks the system.(3) Bergman and the
others concede Rico's ethnic rootlessness while
noting the film's connections to Al Capone's life
story. Gerald Peary develops the point by showing

that Rico, like Capone, has no past, yet lives in an Italian world. The film's success, he adds, derived from its contemporaneity, its obvious parallels to Capone and real-life news accounts of gangsters.(59, 60) Andrew Sarris compared the ethos of Little Caesar and Scarface.(68)

Until the Production Code worked to eliminate the violence, appeal, and ethnicity of the gangster films, the Italian-as-gangster image thrived, fed as it was by newspaper accounts of Al Capone and the popular images of Italian criminality. By the 1940s, however, gangsters had lost their ethnicity and Italians had been incorporated into the melting-pot images of American unity, when they appeared at all. In surveying American war movies, for example, Kathryn Kane found Italian-Americans in the ranks of World War II American soldiers.(43) Peter Biskind argues that ethnicity was absent in the consensus-oriented films of the 1950s. Where it did appear, as in On the Waterfront, which included Italian and other ethnic criminals, it was condemned.(5)

The Godfather established the primacy of the Italian-as-gangster image. Inevitably, the scholarship on gangster/crime films and on Italians grapples with the visual power of Coppola's images. One line of interest follows the film's production history. Seth Cagin and Philp Dray, who describe The Godfather saga as an immigrant epic, detail the production background.(8) Carlos Clarens points to the involvement of the Colombo family in such areas as casting.(12) Fred Ferretti describes producer Al Ruddy's attempts to get the cooperation of Joseph Colombo's Italian-American Civil Rights League by removing references to the Mafia and by promising to hold the film's premiere to support the League's hospital fund.(21) Joseph Gelmis relates the ethnic and political turmoil in making the movie caused by Coppola's controversial subject matter.(24) Though primarily concerned with Coppola's artistry and themes, Robert Johnson briefly recounts Coppola's troubles with the Italian-American Civil Rights League.(40) Nicholas Pileggi shows how producer Al Ruddy finagled his way out of controversy with Colombo interests.(62) Mario Puzo explains his involvement in the movie and analyzes the validity of his Italian images.(63) Vernon Scott and Mary Fiore interview producer Al Ruddy and actors James

Caan and Al Pacino to discover the film's pre-
production problems with the Colombo organization,
which included Colombo enlisting Frank Sinatra to
raise money to halt the movie's production.(69)
     In assessing the meaning and significance of
The Godfather, several authors credit Coppola with
evoking, elaborating, and extending the style and
content of the traditional gangster film.(12, 30,
40, 42, 47, 55, 61, 67, 70, 72)   In early 1972,
Vincent Canby recognized The Godfather as the fully
mature gangster film, free of the false social
pretense of the 1930s variety.(9) Roberta Chappeta
commented on Coppola's recalling the archetypal
1930s style gangster in Sonny Corleone and creating
the new breed gangster-as-businessman image in
Michael Corleone.(11) Philip Strick argues that the
film's Sicilian landscape, Italian-American wedding
sequence, and final holocaust all intersect with
the baptismal scene to establish new cultural and
symbolic boundaries for the gangster genre.(74)
     The cultural boundaries especially included the
Italian ethnicity of the film's story, settings,
and cast. According to Todd Gitlin, the film's
ethnicity accounted for its popularity. Audiences
found Coppola's Italian images credible because
they included such elements as the male competition
for power, the subordination of women, and the
preservation of strong family ties.(29) Giovanni
Sinicropi intimates that the success of Puzo's
novel allowed Coppola to present a romanticized
Mafia myth and an Italian-American ethos that the
public not only accepted but perhaps also expected.(71) So compelling was Coppola's imagery,
observes David Thomson, that Italian-American
viewers could not interpret The Godfather as a slur
about them, even though the film was about Italian-
American gangsters.(76) An Italian scholar, Vito
Zagarrio, found Coppola's work comparable to that
of Bernardo Bertolucci in its themes of Italian
self, family, and roots in America and Italy.(80)
     Several authors essay Coppola's sharpened theme
of ethnic adaptation and the corrupt nature of
modern corporate capitalism in The Godfather, Part
II and in the recut, enlarged television version of
the saga. In 1984 Stephen Farber followed his 1972
assessment of the Don Corleone figure as the symbol
of the self-made man with a fuller exploration of
Coppola's Italian images in the Godfather saga and

their connections to themes of cultural anomie in
modern man.(19, 20) Joel Gelmis argues that Coppola
sought less emphasis on ethnicity in The Godfather,
Part II in order to show that the family had lost
its roots while seeking the American Dream.(23)
Carlos Clarens observes how the chronological arrangement of events in the television version of
the two Godfather films accentuates the immi-
grant/ethnic theme as it also darkens the actions
and character of Michael Corleone by showing how
far he has travelled from the ethnicity that previously had justified the family's "business."(12,
13) David Thomson maintains that the Godfather saga
succeeds because of its "uncomplicated support for
capitalism, conservative attitudes, family solidarity," and the defense of the old order,(75) an
argument echoed by Robert Toll.(78) Likewise,
Golden,(30) Jacobs,(36) Kaminsky,(42) Kolker,(47)
Monaco,(55) Rosow,(67) Shadoian,(70) and Sklar(72)
all view The Godfather, Part II as Coppola's attempt to project Michael Corleone as the embodiment
of modern corporate man.

    Coppola's Godfather saga dominates the liter-
ature on Italian images in film because its images
and themes grip the American imagination and, also,
because its characters have a symbolic importance
unmatched by those from any other film. With the
exception of Martin Scorsese's Mean Streets, other
recent films about Italian subjects or with Italian
characters have commanded little scholarly attention. Scholars, like viewers and critics, have
remained so preoccupied by the gangster/criminal
motifs relating to Italian images and so mesmerized
by Coppola's visual artistry that they have neglected many basic subjects. Only Daniel Golden,
for example, has explored the images of Italian
women in American film (from the 1930s through the
1970s), noting either their passivity and confine-
ment in the family kitchen or, less frequently,
their hot-blooded passion.(30,31) The connection
between the "bankability" of Italian-American directors and stars and the images those bankable
Italian-Americans project remains undeveloped,
despite John Mariani's perceptive comments (in
1978) on the Italians' commercial appeal as symbols
of emotional liberation and sexuality in an age
when Americans are struggling to get in touch with
their true feelings.(54)

The more recent film images of Italian Americans as symbols of the urban working class have
attracted the attention of several scholars. Al
Auster and others compare the Italian working-class
characters in Rocky and Saturday Night Fever with
those of other ethnic groups in such films as Blue
Collar and F.I.S.T.(2) Lynn Garafola observes the
false images conveyed in Hollywood's working-class
subject films.(22) Daniel Leab identifies subthemes
of racism and ethnic identity in Rocky, and he
relates the film's success to its ethnic awareness
and to its message that through self-reliance,
courage, and hard work success was possible for the
working-class man in America.(50) Juan Pedro Mandelbaum argues that during the 1970s Italians and
Jews co-opted the urban and working-class milieu in
Hollywood films because their numerical and political visibility in American society made Italian
and Jewish characters marketable commodities in
movies.(53) James Monaco praises John Cassavetes
for his understanding of the "dehumanizing forces
of working-class life" and his understanding of
"sexist marriage patterns," but notes that Cassavetes does not necessarily depict an Italian ethnic
world, as does Martin Scorsese in his work. But
Monaco also observes how Scorsese moved away from
the themes and subject matter of Mean Streets in
order to establish his screen viability. Scorsese
would return to his roots, but other Italian-American directors (e.g., Brian De Palma) have ignored
ethnic and working-class themes altogether.(55)
Leonard Quart and Paul Rabinow characterize films
about Italian immigrant life and the working class
as melodramatic and comic in their stereotypes,
insisting that in its shallow treatment of the
Italian-American ethos Hollywood has preferred to
stick to formulas rather than risk losing its
middle-class and ethnic audience by "creating a
complex and possibly controversial social universe."(64)
     According to several writers, Martin Scorsese's
Italian images have revealed that social universe.
Quart and Rabinow credit Scorsese's Mean Streets
with subverting Hollywood's Italian-American fantasies by presenting one Italian-American community
(Scorsese's native "Little Italy" in New York City)
in ethnographic detail and by introducing viewers
to the rituals and interactions of Italian-American

men.(64) Pamela Duncan(16) and Diana Johnson(39)
also focus on the social texture of Scorsese's
urban neighborhood, while Daniel Golden observes
Scorsese's reconstruction of family life.(30) Diane
Jacobs characterizes Mean Streets as Scorsese's
"cathartic work," however truly autobiographical,
and concludes that it succeeds as art and sociology
because Scorsese's characters reflect group sensibilities.(36) Mary Pat Kelly finds Scorsese's ethnicity and Catholicism entering in four of Scorsese's films, all set in New York's "Little Italy"--
It's Not Just You, Murray (1964), Who's That
Knocking at My Door? (1969), Mean Streets, and
Italianamerican (1974).(45) Harry Kolker(47) and
James Monaco(55) place Scorsese's work (and that of
Coppola) in the context of the "new American cinema" of social awareness.
     Writings on the Italian image in television
have also noted the connection between Italian
images and characters and urban/working-class settings and themes. The nostalgia for the 1950s provided the impetus for Happy Days and Laverne and
Shirley. Anthony LaRuffa links the posturing and
the low-brow speech and behavior of the Italian
characters in the shows to stereotypes of Italians
as lower-class creatures of emotion.(49) Robert
Sklar, however, found strength in the two shows'
Italian working-class figures, who, in their honesty about themselves, contrasted favorably with
the falsity and corruption of upper-class life.(73)
     In television, as in film, the criminal image
of Italians has remained the focal point of concern
and discussion. In his survey of Italian-American
images in American television from the 1950s into
the 1970s, Anthony Brizzolara points to the recurring stereotypes of Italians as gangsters and
incorrigible teenagers. Only the grandmothers in
kitchens selling pizzas seemed not to threaten the
social order.(7) In their detailed statistical
study of Italian-American characters in television
entertainment, which was commissioned by the Sons
of Italy, S. Robert Lichter and Linda Lichter conclude that television has presented Italian Americans as people who could not speak proper English,
who overwhelmingly held "low-status jobs," who
acted on emotion rather than reason, and who were
disproportionately identified with criminal activities. They added that Italian-American characters

in prime-time television were principally male. The
Italian-American associations with criminality,
however, dominate their findings.(51) That association had earlier led Andrew Greeley to comment
that even as policemen, Italian-American characters
bucked the system and relied on violence more than
reason to combat crime.(33) In essaying the origins
and durability of negative images of Italians in
mass media, Richard Juliani noted the same parallels between television's Italian-American cops
and criminals.(41) Not until the arrival of Captain
Furillo in Hill Street Blues, write Joseph Gior-
dano(25) and Jean Grillo,(34) did an Italian-American policeman character act and think as if he
belonged to the system he was supposed to protect.
     The social or psychological effects of such
images have attracted less attention than has the
catalogueing of the instances of negative portrayals. Part of the problem is the dispute over
how clear ethnic messages are in television. Marc
Eliot maintains that recent prime-time shows are
increasingly sensitive to the ethnic appearance of
their characters, however false in substance they
might be,(17) while Rose Goldson insists that
ratings pressures have blurred cultural pluralism
and left only ambiguous ethnic images, so that
Italians are interchangeable with Hispanics.(32)
Gordon Berry, however, argues that children learn
about social class roles and social issues from
television and, regarding Italians, that the recurring images of Italians as members of gangs or
as criminals helps make such images "reality" to
otherwise uninformed viewers.(4) Joseph Giordano
goes further in his criticism of ethnic stereotyping. He sees the distorted, negative stereotypes
of Italians and other groups on television as evidence of the television industry's inability to
recognize the immigrant/ethnic phenomenon as a
permanent part of American life rather than a transitional phase.(25) He observes that media-made
Italians continue to be relegated to the underside
of American society--low status, criminal, and
unintellectual--and that the stereotypical Italian
individual recently has given way to the stereotypical Italian-American family composed of aggressive
men and passive women. Giordano calls for organized
action to gather data, monitor portrayals, and
protest injustices and inaccuracies.(26) Giordano's

concern arises from his belief that mass-mediated images shape personal and group identities and, if negative, can lead to self-doubt and feelings of worthlessness among members of the group being portrayed.(28) Indeed, ethnic stereotypes such as those of Italian women confined to kitchens and men interacting with others in primitive ways readily insinuate themselves into children's minds and, in the absence of alternative images and information, form children's attitudes toward the group. Giordano suggests that by taking Italian men out of the police station and by focussing more honestly on life at the family table, more sensitive, realistic portrayals of Italian ethnic life will be available to challenge prejudices against Italian Americans. (27) Perhaps, as happened during the 1984 presidential election, television news reporters' focus on the emergence of Italian-American men and women as articulate, intelligent political leaders will provide a new set of public events, personalities, and images to refashion popular attitudes toward the group. That potential remains a subject for investigation, and for hope.

Major discussions of films and/or television shows include: The Gangster Chronicles (34), The Godfather (8, 9, 12, 13, 14, 19, 20, 21, 23, 24, 29, 30, 36, 40, 42, 49, 55, 56, 58, 61, 62, 63, 67, 69, 70, 71, 74, 75, 76, 78, 80), The Godfather, Part II (12, 13, 20, 23, 30, 36, 40, 47, 49, 67, 70), The Godfather Saga [Mario Puzo's The Godfather: The Complete Novel for Television] (13), Happy Days (10, 49, 73), Hill Street Blues (25, 34), The Italian (18), Laverne and Shirley (49, 73), Little Caesar (3, 12, 30, 37, 42, 44, 59, 60, 65, 68, 70, 72), Lovers and Other Strangers (30, 31), Marty (27), Mean Streets (12, 16, 30, 36, 39, 45, 47, 55), Rocky (2, 50), St. Valentine's Day Massacre (12), Saturday Night Fever (2, 30, 49), Scarface (12, 44, 68, 70), The Untouchables (10), and Welcome Back, Kotter (10, 17).

1. Affron, Mirella Jona. "The Italian-American in
    American Films, 1918-1971." ITALIAN AMERI-
    CANA 3 (Spring/Summer 1977): 233-55.

2. Auster, Al, Lynn Garafola, Dan Georgakas,
    Leonard Quart, and Fred Siegel. "Hollywood
    and the Working Class: A Discussion" (item
    I-8).

3. Bergman, Andrew. WE'RE IN THE MONEY (item I-
    14).

4. Berry, Gordon L. "Children, Television, and
    Social Class Roles" (item I-17).

5. Biskind, Peter. SEEING IS BELIEVING (item I-
    19).

6. Brazaitis, Thomas J. "Ethnics Fear Images
    Warped" (item I-23).

7. Brizzolara, Andrew. "The Image of Italian
    Americans on U.S. Television." ITALIAN
    AMERICANA 6 (Spring/Summer 1980): 160-67.

8. Cagin, Seth, and Philip Dray. HOLLYWOOD FILMS
    AND THE SEVENTIES: SEX, DRUGS, VIOLENCE,
    ROCK 'N' ROLL & POLITICS. New York: Harper
    & Row, 1984.

9. Canby, Vincent. "Moving and Brutal Godfather
    Bows." NEW YORK TIMES, March 16, 1972, p.
    56.

10. Castleman, Harry, and Walter J. Podrazik.
    WATCHING TV: FOUR DECADES OF AMERICAN TELE-
    VISION (item I-27).

11. Chappeta, Roberta. "The Godfather." FILM Q 25
    (Summer 1972): 60-61.

12. Clarens, Carlos. CRIME MOVIES: FROM GRIFFITH
    TO THE GODFATHER AND BEYOND. New York: W.W.
    Norton & Company, 1980.

13. _____. "The Godfather Sag-a." FILM COMMENT 14
    (January-February 1978): 21-23.

14.   Dessner, Lawrence J. "The Godfather, the Exe-
      cutive, and Art." J OF POPULAR CULTURE 6
      (Summer 1972): 211-14.

15.   Dooley, Roger. FROM SCARFACE TO SCARLETT (item
      I-41).

16.   Duncan, Pamela. "Mean Streets." RACE AND ETH-
      NICITY IN THE HISTORY OF THE AMERICAS (item
      I-36), pp. 31-32.

17.   Eliot, Marc. AMERICAN TELEVISION (item I-43).

18.   Everson, William. AMERICAN SILENT FILM (item
      I-45).

19.   Farber, Stephen. "Coppola and The Godfather."
      SIGHT AND SOUND 41 (Autumn 1972): 217-23.

20.   _____, and Marc Green. HOLLYWOOD DYNASTIES.
      New York: Delilah Books, 1984.

21.   Ferretti, Fred. "Corporate Rift in Godfather
      Filming." NEW YORK TIMES, March 23, 1971,
      p. 28.

22.   Garafola, Lynn. "Hollywood and the Myth of the
      Working Class." RADICAL AMERICA 14 (No.1
      1980): 7-15.

23.   Gelmis, Joseph. "Fathering a Sequel." LONG
      ISLAND NEWSDAY, December 22, 1974, II, pp.
      3, 11.

24.   _____. "Merciful Heavens, Is This the End of
      Don Corleone?" NEW YORK, August 23, 1971,
      pp. 52-53.

25.   Giordano, Joseph. "Calling Capt. Furillo."
      ADVERTISING AGE, April 16, 1984, p. 18.

26.   _____. "Distorted Images." ATTENZIONE 6
      (March 1984): 47-50.

27.   _____. "Families: What TV Teaches Children."
      (item I-56).

28.   _____. "The Harm of Ethnic Stereotypes."

NEWSDAY [New York edition], February 21, 1984.

29. Gitlin, Todd. "On the Popularity of The God-father." PERFORMANCE no. 4 (September-October 1972): 37-40ff.

30. Golden, Daniel S. "The Fate of La Famiglia: Italian Images in American Film." KALEIDO-SCOPIC LENS (item I-106), pp. 73-97.

31. _____. "Pasta or Paradigm: The Place of Italian-American Women in Popular Film." EXPLORATIONS IN ETHNIC STUDIES 2 (January 1979): 3-10.

32. Goldson, Rose K. THE SHOW AND TELL MACHINE (item I-60).

33. Greeley, Andrew M. "TV's Italian Cops Trapped in Old Stereotypes." NEW YORK TIMES, July 27, 1975, II, pp. 1, 17.

34. Grillo, Jean Bergantini. "Ethnic Slurs Are Back" (item I-63).

35. Helffrich, Stockton. "Editing the Airwaves." PREJUDICE AND THE LIVELY ARTS (item I-12), pp. 14-16.

36. Jacobs, Diane. HOLLYWOOD RENAISSANCE. New York: A.S. Barnes & Company, 1977.

37. Jacobs, Lewis. THE RISE OF AMERICAN FILM (item I-70).

38. Jeffres, Leo W., and K. Kyoon Hur. "White Ethnics and Their Media Images" (item I-72).

39. Johnson, Diana M. "Mean Streets and Manhat-tan." RACE AND ETHNICITY IN THE HISTORY OF THE AMERICAS (item I-36), pp. 33-35.

40. Johnson, Robert K. FRANCIS FORD COPPOLA. Boston: Twayne, 1977.

41. Juliani, Richard N. "The Image of the Italian

in American Film and Television." ETHNIC
IMAGES IN AMERICAN FILM AND TELEVISION
(item I-105), pp. 99-104.

42. Kaminsky, Stuart M. AMERICAN FILM GENRES:
     APPROACHES TO A CRITICAL THEORY OF POPULAR
     FILM. New York: Dell Publishing Company,
     1974.

43. Kane, Kathryn. VISIONS OF WAR (item I-77).

44. Karpf, Stephen L. "The Gangster Film: Emer-
     gence, Variation and Decay of a Genre,
     1930-1940." Ph.D. diss., Northwestern Uni-
     versity, 1969; New York: Arno Press, 1973.

45. Kelly, Mary Pat. MARTIN SCORSESE: THE FIRST
     DECADE. Pleasantville, N.Y.: Redgrave Pub-
     lishing Company, 1980.

46. Kirby, Jack Temple. "D.W. Griffith's Racial
     Portraiture" (item I-80).

47. Kolker, Robert P. A CINEMA OF LONELINESS:
     PENN, KUBRICK, COPPOLA, SCORSESE, ALTMAN.
     New York: Oxford University Press, 1980.

48. Kurnitz, Harry. "Screen Humor." THE PRO-
     CEEDINGS OF THE CONFERENCE HELD IN OCTOBER
     1943 (item I-173), pp. 230-35.

49. LaRuffa, Anthony L. "Media Portrayals of
     Italian-Americans." ETHNIC GROUPS 4 (July
     1982): 191-206.

50. Leab, Daniel J. "The Blue Collar Ethnic in
     Bicentennial America: Rocky." AMERICAN HIS-
     TORY/AMERICAN FILM (item I-113), pp. 257-
     72.

51. Lichter, S. Robert, and Linda Lichter.
     ITALIAN-AMERICAN CHARACTERS IN TELEVISION
     ENTERTAINMENT. West Hempstead, N.Y.: Com-
     mission for Social Justice, 1982.

52. McAlpin, Sally T. "The Deer Hunter and Mean
     Streets." RACE AND ETHNICITY IN THE HISTORY
     OF THE AMERICAS (item I-36), pp. 39-40.

53. Mandelbaum, Juan Pedro. "The Portrayal of Social Class in Hollywood Films" (item I-97).

54. Mariani, John. "Hollywood's Favorite Ethnic Group." NEW YORK TIMES, June 4, 1978, II, pp. 1, 26.

55. Monaco, James. AMERICAN FILM NOW (item I-107).

56. Papaleo, Joseph. "Ethnic Pictures and Ethnic Fate: The Media Image of Italian-Americans." ETHNIC IMAGES IN AMERICAN FILM AND TELEVISION (item I-105), pp. 93-97.

57. Parenti, Michael. "The Italian American and the Mass Media." ETHNIC IMAGES IN AMERICAN FILM AND TELEVISION (item I-105), pp. 105-107.

58. Parker, Jerry. "Mamma Mia! It's The Godfather." CHICAGO SUN TIMES, June 6, 1971.

59. Peary, Gerald, ed. LITTLE CAESAR. Madison: University of Wisconsin Press, 1981.

60. _____. "Rico Rising: Little Caesar Takes Over the Screen." THE CLASSIC AMERICAN NOVEL AND THE MOVIES. Edited by Gerald Peary and Roger Shatzkin. New York: Frederick Ungar Publishing Company, 1977, pp. 286-96.

61. Pechter, William S. "Keeping Up With the Corleones." COMMENTARY 54 (July 1972): 88-90.

62. Pileggi, Nicholas. "The Making of The Godfather--Sort of a Home Movie." NEW YORK TIMES MAGAZINE, August 15, 1971, pp. 7, 36-37ff.

63. Puzo, Mario. THE GODFATHER PAPERS AND OTHER CONFESSIONS. New York: G.P. Putnam's Sons, 1973.

64. Quart, Leonard, and Paul Rabinow. "The Ethos of Mean Streets." FILM & HISTORY 5 (May 1975): 11-15.

65. Roddick, Nick. A NEW DEAL IN ENTERTAINMENT (item I-124).

66. Rollins, Peter C., and Harry W. Menig. "Regional Literature and Will Rogers" (item I-126).

67. Rosow, Eugene. BORN TO LOSE (item I-128).

68. Sarris, Andrew. "Big Funerals: The Hollywood Gangster, 1927-1933." FILM COMMENT 13 (May-June 1977): 6-9.

69. Scott, Vernon, and Mary Fiore. "The Story Behind The Godfather By the Men Who Lived It." LADIES HOME JOURNAL 89 (June 1972): 62, 64ff.

70. Shadoian, Jack. DREAMS AND DEAD ENDS: THE AMERICAN GANGSTER/CRIME FILM. Cambridge, Mass.: MIT Press, 1977.

71. Sinicropi, Giovanni. "The Saga of the Corleones: Puzo, Coppola and The Godfather--An Interpretive Essay." ITALIAN AMERICANA 2 (Autumn 1975): 79-90.

72. Sklar, Robert. MOVIE-MADE AMERICA (item I-138).

73. _____. PRIME-TIME AMERICA (item I-139).

74. Strick, Philip. "The Godfather." MONTHLY FILM BULLETIN 39 (September 1972): 190-91.

75. Thomson, David. AMERICA IN THE DARK (item II-589).

76. _____. "The Discreet Charm of the Godfather." SIGHT AND SOUND 47 (Spring 1978): 76-80.

77. Toeplitz, Jerzy. HOLLYWOOD AND AFTER (item I-149).

78. Toll, Robert C. THE ENTERTAINMENT MACHINE (item I-150).

79. Willett, Ralph. "Nativism and Assimilation:

The Hollywood Aspect" (item I-168).

80. Zagarrio, Vito. "E venne Francis Ford Cop-
     pola." [And then came Francis Ford Coppola.]
     PONTE (Italy) 36 (no. 10 1980): 1078-86.

81. Zuker, Joel S. FRANCIS FORD COPPOLA: A GUIDE
     TO REFERENCES AND RESOURCES. Boston: G.K.
     Hall, 1984.

X. JEWS

Unlike most of the ethnic or racial groups
discussed in this book, Jews have been strongly
represented in the filmmaking process. From the
days of the nickelodeon, Jews have participated in
the production of motion pictures. Jewish writers,
directors, and actors have shaped the American
motion picture industry. Theoretically, Jews have
thus had the power to create their own images in
film, a luxury which blacks and Hispanics, for
example, have been denied. Yet, the results have
been curiously similar. Despite the presence of
Jews in all aspects of the creation of motion
pictures and television films, the same stereotypical visions which plague other groups have
bedevilled Jews as well. Thus, although Indians,
blacks, and hispanics have seen greater
representation in the creative process as a panacea
which would bring an end to the problem of film
stereotyping, the Jewish experience seems to
indicate that this result is not necessarily
automatic. Indeed, one of the major questions
concerning researchers in this field is the attempt
to explain this apparent anomaly.

Eastern European Jews dominated the early
motion picture business. Some have suggested that
the low prestige attributed to this new
entertainment form allowed a greater opportunity
for newly arrived immigrants to obtain a niche in
the profession. Movie moguls such as Adolph Zukor,
William Fox, Carl Laemmle, Sam Goldwyn, and Marcus
Loew entered the business in this fashion.(17, 18,
52)

While critics had previously argued that Jews
were primarily "invisible" in the early silent
films, recent research indicates that the Jew
appeared in a wide variety and great number of
films during the silent era.(78) Lester D. Fried-

309

man, for example, suggests that Jews were identifiable characters in approximately 230 films
between 1900 and 1929.(30)
     It is difficult to identify a specific Jewish
stereotype, due to the wide diversity of roles
during this period, but certain generalizations can
be made. Assimilation and success seem to be among
the most prominent themes in silent films with
Jewish themes. Perhaps as an echo of the immigrant
filmmaker's own swift rise in the movie world, the
films tended to glorify the shedding of Jewish
traits in the Americanization process. While early
films often provided European backgrounds for
Jewish characters, these were soon supplanted with
American settings, with particular emphasis on
activities in the New York ghetto. Assimilation
occurred in a variety of mannners, with marriage to
a Gentile (often of Irish background) as a dominant
theme. (The success of Broadway's long-run hit
Abie's Irish Rose in 1924 no doubt encouraged a
spate of imitators.) Although the various film
versions of, say, The Merchant of Venice or Oliver
Twist, presented long-standing literary or dramatic
stereotypes of the avaricious or evil Jew, many
motion pictures seemed to adopt a sympathetic
attitude towards Jews and their culture, painting
them in a much more favorable light than, for
example, blacks and hispanics during a similar time
period.(11)
     The Jazz Singer (1927) marked both the
culmination of the silent era films with Jewish
themes as well as the beginning of the sound era.
The tale of Jakie Rabinowitz, the cantor's son who
becomes a successful "Jazz Singer" on Broadway,
marks the assimilationist theme prevalent
throughout the silent era. Although Jakie's father
wishes the boy to follow in his (and his father's)
footsteps, Jakie is enraptured by the Broadway
stage and the Gentile chorus girls. His father
disowns him as the young entertainer seeks an
alternate vision of success in America. Yet, Jakie
is never able to reconcile his feelings concerning
his father and his religion. Father and son are
reunited only on his father's deathbed as Jakie
substitutes in the all-important Kol Nidre service.
Despite this hasty reconciliation, there is no
doubt that Jakie will continue his successful
Broadway career. Of all the early films which

concern Jewish life, <u>The Jazz Singer</u> was perhaps
the most widely seen throughout the United States.
Its sympathetic treatment of Jewish life became
many Americans' first introduction to their new
Jewish neighbors.(5, 79, 95, 100)
     <u>The Jazz Singer</u> became a path-breaking film
primarily for the introduction of sound, song, and
dialogue. While its popular reception eventually
heralded the way for "talkies," its depiction of
Jewish life marked the end of an era in the
utilization of Jewish images on film. Rather than
building on the strengths of <u>The Jazz Singer</u>, films
from the sound era tended to ignore Jewish life. It
is here that the charge of "invisibility" maintains
its greatest strength. Although certain film actors
in prominent roles might bear a Jewish name, the
character was essentially de-Semitized. Similarly,
identifiably Jewish actors during this period were
often relegated to minor roles, or (as in the case
of Paul Muni) given a variety of diverse ethnic
roles after adopting Americanized stage names for
their star turns.(90)
     Although Jews consolidated their power as the
heads of major studios during the 1920s and 1930s,
many seemed to lose touch with their roots. A
standard pattern emerged as movie moguls tended to
divorce their first wife (a Jew) and marry a
Gentile. Many of the moguls' children remember the
celebrations of Christmas, and the total lack of
awareness of their Jewish heritage. The ultimate
phase of assimilation in the moguls' lives seemed
to be reflected on the screen, as the Jew became
Americanized into a non-Semite.(7, 94)
     One might expect a change as the situation
worsened for European Jews during the 1930s.(84)
Yet, films dramatizing the plight of Jews facing
the Nazi menace were few and far between. Those
films which considered Hitler's Germany often
managed to omit references to Jewish persecution.
Even as late a film as <u>Confessions of a Nazi Spy</u>
(1939) with Edward G. Robinson remained remarkably
reticent about the situation of Jews.
     This unseemly caution can be partially
explained by two factors. First, it was a continu-
ation of the earlier habit of the non-depiction of
Jews in major roles. Additionally, Hollywood was
continually being called on the carpet by
Washington political critics who argued that the

motion picture industry was engaged in the creation
of "propaganda films" designed to lead Americans to
intervene in a hitherto European war. This concern
blossomed into an investigation in 1941 by a
special Subcommittee of the Interstate Commerce
Commission. Despite patriotic testimony by Harry
Warner, Darryl Zanuck, and others which indicated
that they sympathized with the enemies of Nazism,
they were hardly as forthright in the films coming
from their studios during this period. Perhaps
fearful of government intervention of any sort in
the film industry, their films maintained a
cautious stance, and hinted only obliquely at the
European situation.

Only Charlie Chaplin violated this veil of
silence with The Great Dictator in 1940, which
combined both humor and drama in the depiction of
the madness of Hitler and the plight of Jews in the
European ghettoes. Avoiding the cautious stand of
others, Chaplin argued (in the touching final
scene) that the evils of Hitler and Mussolini would
have to be ended by force. The response to
Chaplin's film revealed the dangers of such a
forthright stand during this period, for critics
called for an investigation of Chaplin's "leftist"
leanings.(15, 46)

The Subcommittee's investigation was abruptly
terminated after the bombing of Pearl Harbor. Jews
reappeared, albeit slowly, as film characters. In
anti-Nazi films, Jews were now clearly identified
and hints of their tragedy were cautiously
revealed. Jews also were featured as members of
every platoon or squadron as one of many obligatory
ethnic groups which were now pitching in to help
America win the war. Although identified by a
Jewish name (or perhaps by reference to his New
York City birthplace), the Jew seemed little
different than the Italian or Irishman. Rather, he
functioned as a symbol of America's new wartime
unity.(51, 85)

Only after the war did Jewish characters
reappear on the screen in an attempt to analyze the
roots of anti-Semitism in America.(86) Interestingly, both Crossfire and Gentleman's Agreement
(1947) were initiated as film projects by non-Jews.
Both films had difficulty being made as a result of
studio pressure but also as a consequence of
pressure from without.(3, 8, 9, 58) Various Jewish

groups argued that bringing the subject of
anti-Semitism into the open would make the
situation worse rather than better. Indeed, they
felt that slow and cautious behind-the-scenes work
would be of greater importance in ending the
scourge of anti-Semitism. Both films were
critically praised for their courage at the time of
release. Although they may seem somewhat dated at
present, both marked a major reversal in
Hollywood's treament of Jewish themes and subjects.
Gregory Peck, a writer, masquerades as a Jew,
Philip Green, in order to prepare a first-hand
expose of the problem of anti-Semitism for an
American Jew. Real Jews were relegated to smaller
(albeit still impressive) roles in the film, and
they revealed to Green how their lives had been
affected by this continuing scourge. Critics and
social scientists debated the effects of these
films on anti-Semitism and concluded that they
would probably ease the problem somewhat.(36, 58,
74, 76, 99)
        Nevertheless, critical acclaim not-
withstanding, these films failed to usher in a new
era of the depiction of Jews on the screen. After
the House Committee on Un-American Activities
hearings, Hollywood remained notoriously hesitant
in tackling controversial topics. As a result, the
fifties continued the wasteland of the 1930s in its
relative absence of Jewish-themed films with the
exception of film biographies or Biblical epics,
such as The Ten Commandments (1956).
        The beginnings of change can be glimpsed with
Marjorie Morningstar in 1958. After that date a
great variety of identifiable Jewish roles are
evident on the screen. Additionally, topics that
had rarely been considered, such as the Holocaust,
the problems of Israel, the immigrant past, and the
difficulties facing Jewish men and women in modern
America, begin to be addressed.(15, 45, 77) Jewish
actors and actresses also come to the fore,
abandoning the WASP patina that had dominated in
earlier years.(21, 38) While the movie moguls had
formerly ignored any performer who "looked" Jewish,
now Barbra Streisand, Dustin Hoffman, George Segal,
and Elliott Gould became potent box office
forces.(34, 37) While drama became the primary
force for the exploration of Jewish themes, comedy
and musical films also joined the resurgence. Woody

Allen brought the plight of the Jewish schlemiel to the screen, while Mel Brooks utilized a treasure trove of Borscht Belt humor in his film parodies.(68, 71, 83) Such musicals as Cabaret and Fiddler on the Roof, both adaptations of Broadway originals, also brought Jewish characters and themes into focus, as did the two remakes of the classic The Jazz Singer.(4, 41, 48)

Television tended to follow Hollywood's lead in this regard as situation comedies (e. g., All in the Family) introduced Jewish characters and flirted with the question of anti-Semitism. In general, however, television has utilized Jewish themes to greatest advantage in a variety of docudramas and mini-series, such as Holocaust, Playing for Time, and Skokie.(33, 39, 66, 70, 93, 98)

Thus, as the 1980s begin, the image of the Jew on television and films is currently in a remarkably healthy state when compared with other ethnic and racial groups. Nevertheless, critics still find that the "sanitized Jews" of 1930s filmdom occasionally reappear, and others warn of the possibility of the evolution of new stereotypes in the 1980s. Of particular concern has been the spate of images of "villainous Jews" in recent years.(1, 67, 75, 88, 89, 92) Despite these fears, the major problems of earlier decades seem to have been overcome.(2, 47)

The Jewish experience in film has been detailed in a variety of sources in recent years. Both Patricia Erens' dissertation and her monograph The Jew in American Cinema attempt to provide a typology of Jewish images on the American screen from the silent era to the present.(22, 23) She purposely avoids another key question: "To what extent do these films represent the reality of Jewish life at the time." Lester D. Friedman, however, provides interesting observations on the historical context of these films in Hollywood's Image of the Jew.(30) This work effectively disputes previous misconceptions concerning the Jewish image on film.

Despite the title, Sarah Blacher Cohen's From Hester Street to Hollywood, spends little time on the Hollywood experience, as most of the book is devoted to essays on the Broadway and vaudeville stage.(10) Nevertheless, the few essays on film history are quite provocative, as they demonstrate connections between the Jewish images and performances on stage and screen. Of particular interest are essays on Woody Allen and Mel Brooks. Cohen's collection also provides Lawrence Langer's observations on the depiction of the Holocaust on the American stage and screen.(55) Annette Insdorf's monograph on the treatment of the Holocaust in American and European film provides interesting observations on both the films as well as the historical context.(46)

All of these works (except the Cohen collection) provide a filmography of motion pictures with Jewish themes. Stuart Fox's work is also important in this regard as it supplies a listing of 700 films with Jewish characters made between the turn of the century and 1970. He includes feature films, Yiddish language films, documentaries and newsreel materials, U. S. Army films, as well as films related to Israel. Fox also provides a fountain of information on television sources, with listings of series and specials, news shows, religious and educational programs, and documentaries about Israel.(27)

The most promising historical work on the Jewish entry into the film industry comes from Lary and Elaine Tyler May who ask the important question: "Why Jewish Movie Moguls?"(59, 59A, 60) Stephen Farber and Marc Green's study of Hollywood dynasties, although a popular work, provides interesting observations on the assimilationist tendencies of movie moguls as they rise to the top.(25) Similarly, James Monaco's study of modern Hollywood, looks at the newer generation of Jews in power.(64)

Major discussions of films and/or television shows include: Air Force (57), Blume in Love (65), Carnal Knowledge (101), Cast a Giant Shadow (82), The Cohens and the Kellys (54), Crossfire (8, 58, 70), Fiddler on the Roof (49), Gentleman's Agreement (9, 62, 76), The Great Dictator (15, 46), The Heartbreak Kid (65), Hester Street (43, 61), The Hitler Gang (57), Holocaust (13), The House of

Rothschild (73), Intolerance (72), The Jazz Singer (100), Lies My Father Taught Me (43), The Little Drummer Girl (74), Love and Death (44), The Merchant of Venice (39), None Shall Escape (57), Objective Burma (57), Portnoy's Complaint (4, 38), Skokie (96), and To Be or Not to Be (46).

1. Alter, R. "Defaming the Jews." COMMENTARY 55
    (January 1973): 77-82.

2. Beloff, M.   "The Anti-Semitic   Persuasion:
    'Roots' and Jewish Identity." ENCOUNTER 53
    (1979): 70-76.

3. Campbell, Russell. "The Ideology of the Social
    Conscious Movie: Three Films of Darryl F.
    Zanuck." Q R OF FILM STUDIES 3 (Winter
    1978): 49-71.

4. Carey, Gary. "The Long, Long Road to Brenda
    Patemkin." THE BLACK MAN ON FILM (item
    II-433), pp. 113-25.

5. Carringer, Robert, ed.   THE   JAZZ SINGER.
    Madison, Wisc.: University of Wisconsin
    Press, 1979.

6. Cawelti, John G. "Reflections on the New
    Western Films: The Jewish Cowboy, The Black
    Avenger, and the Return of the Vanishing
    American." (item II-132).

7. Clarens, Carlos. "Mogul -- That's a Jewish
    Word." FILM COMMENT 17 (July-August 1981):
    34-36.

8. Cohen, Elliot E. "Letter to the Movie-Makers:
    The Film Drama as a Social   Force."
    COMMENTARY 4 (no. 2 1947): 110-18.

9. _____.   "Mr. Zanuck's Gentleman's Agreement:
    Reflections on Hollywood's Second Film
    About Anti-Semitism." COMMENTARY 5 (no. 1
    1948): 51-56.

10. Cohen, Sarah Blacher, ed.   FROM HESTER STREET
    TO HOLLYWOOD. Bloomington: Indiana Univer-
    sity Press, 1983.

11. Cripps, Thomas. "The Movie Jew as an Image of
    Assimilation, 1903-1927." J OF POPULAR
    FILM 4 (no. 3 1975), 190-220.

12. Cutter, William. "Stereotyping--A Dissenting
    View." DAVKA 5 (no. 3 1975): 30-33.

13. Deloria, Vine, Jr. "The Movie Indian and the
     Movie Jew: Stereotyping." THE BLACK MAN ON
     FILM (item II-433), pp. 106-113.

14. Diamond, Sander A. "'Holocaust' Film's Impact
     on Americans." PATTERNS OF PREJUDICE (G.B.)
     12 (no. 4 1978): 1-9, 19.

15. Doneson, Judith E. "The Jew as a Female Figure
     in Holocaust Films." SHOAH 1 (no. 1 1979):
     11-13, 18.

16. Dotort, David. "The Magic Bullet." DAVKA 5
     (no. 3 1975): 26-29.

17. Eckhardt, Joseph P. and Linda Kowall. PEDDLER
     OF DREAMS: SIEGMUND LUBIN AND THE CREATION
     OF THE MOTION PICTURE INDUSTRY, 1896-1916.
     Philadelphia: National Museum of American
     Jewish History, 1984.

18. ————. "The Movies' First Mogul." JEWISH
     LIFE IN PHILADELPHIA, 1830-1940. Edited by
     Murray   Friedman.   Philadelphia: ISHI
     Publications, 1983, pp. 99-124.

19. Epstein, Benjamin R. "The Stereotype Contro-
     versy: 'Art' vs. People." ADL BULLETIN 18
     (April 1961): 1-2.

20. Erens, Patricia. "Between Two Worlds: Jewish
     Images in American Film." THE KALEIDOSCOPIC
     LENS (item I-106), pp. 114-134.

21. ————. "Gangsters, Vampires, and J.A.P.'s:
     The Jew Surfaces in American Movies." J OF
     POPULAR FILM 4 (no. 3 1975): 208-222.

22. ————. "The Image of the Jew in the American
     Cinema: A Study in Stereotyping." Ph. D.
     diss., Northwestern University, 1981.

23. ————. THE JEW IN AMERICAN CINEMA. Blooming-
     ton: Indiana University Press, 1984.

24. ————. "Mentschlekhkayt Conquers All: The
     Yiddish Cinema in America." FILM COMMENT 12

(January-February 1976): 48-53.

25. Farber, Stephen, and Marc Green. HOLLYWOOD DYNASTIES (item IX-20).

26. Fiedler, Leslie. TO THE GENTILES. New York: Stein & Day, 1972.

27. Fox, Stuart, comp. JEWISH FILMS IN THE UNITED STATES: A COMPREHENSIVE SURVEY AND DESCRIPTIVE FILMOGRAPHY. Boston: G. K. Hall, 1976.

28. Friedman, Lester. "The Conversion of the Jews." FILM COMMENT 17 (July-August 1981): 39-48.

29. ———. "The Edge of Knowledge: Jews as Monsters/ Jews as Victims." MELUS 11 (Fall 1984): 49-62.

30. ———. HOLLYWOOD'S IMAGE OF THE JEW. New York: Frederick Ungar Publishing Co., 1982.

31. Friedman, Murray. "The Images of Jews in American Film." ETHNIC IMAGES IN AMERICAN FILM AND TELEVISION (item I-105), pp. 39-42.

32. Friedman, Norman L. "Hollywood, the Jewish Experience, and Popular Culture." JUDAISM 19 ([no. 4] 1970): 482-87.

33. ———. "Responses of Blacks and Other Minorities to Television Shows of the 1970s About Their Groups." (item II-245).

34. Friedman, R. M. "Exorcising the Past: Jewish Figures in Contemporary Film." J OF CONTEMPORARY HISTORY 19 (July 1984): 511-27.

35. Gaber, Samuel Lewis. "Jews in American Film and Television." ETHNIC IMAGES IN AMERICAN FILM AND TELEVISION (item I-105), pp. 43-47.

36. Goldman, Eric A. "The Fight to Bring the Subject of Anti-Semitism to the American

Screen: The Story of the Production of
Crossfire and Gentleman's Agreement." DAVKA
5 (no. 3 1975): 24.

37. Gross, Barry. "No Victim, She: Barbra Streis-
and and the Movie Jew." J OF ETHNIC STUDIES
3 (Spring 1975): 28-40.

38. Hechinger, Fred M. "Portnoy's Complaint: An
Anti-Jewish Joke?" NEW YORK TIMES, July 16,
1972, pp. 1, 7.

39. ———. "Why Shylock Should Not Be Cen-
sored." NEW YORK TIMES, March 24, 1974, II,
pp. 23, 47.

40. Higham, Charles and Joel Greenberg. HOLLYWOOD
IN THE FORTIES (item I-69).

41. Hoberman, J. "Deracinatin' Rhythm: Is The Jazz
Singer Good for the Jews?" VILLAGE VOICE,
January 7, 1981, pp. 1, 31.

42. ———. "Yiddish Transit." FILM COMMENT
17 (July-August 1981): 36-38.

43. Horowitz, Robert F. "Between a Heartache and a
Laugh: Two Recent Films on Immigration."
FILM & HISTORY 6 (no. 4 1976): 73-78.

44. Howe, Irving. "Yiddish Humor--The Adventures
of the Fabulous 'Schlemiel.'" NEW YORK
TIMES, January 4, 1976, II, p. 1.

45. Ilan, Avisar. "The Aesthetics and Politics of
the Holocaust Film." Ph. D. diss., Indiana
University, 1983.

46. Insdorf, Annette. INDELIBLE SHADOWS: FILM AND
THE HOLOCAUST. New York: Random House,
1983.

47. Isaac, Dan. "Some Questions About the
Depiction of Jews in New Films." NEW YORK
TIMES, September 8, 1974, pp. 13-14.

48. Jacobs, Lewis. THE RISE OF THE AMERICAN FILM
(item I-70).

49. Kael, Pauline. "Current Cinema: 'Fiddler on
     the Roof.'" THE NEW YORKER 47 (November 13,
     1971): 133-39.

50. Kakutani, Michiko. "Debate Over Shylock
     Shimmers Once Again." NEW YORK TIMES, Feb-
     ruary 22, 1981, II, pp. 1, 30.

51. Kane, Kathryn Rose. VISIONS OF WAR (item
     I-77).

52. Kanin, Josh. "Jews in Early Motion Pictures."
     DAVKA 5 (no. 3 1975): 9-11.

53. Kliger, Hannah. "Communication and Community:
     Ethnic Media Images and Jewish Group
     Identity." M.A. thesis, Annenberg School of
     Communications, University of Pennsylvania,
     1977.

54. Krohn, Lewis G. "The Cohens and the Kellys."
     (item VIII-10).

55. Langer, Lawrence L. "The Americanization of
     the Holocaust on Stage and Screen." FROM
     HESTER STREET TO HOLLYWOOD (item X-9), pp.
     213-30.

56. Luft, Herbert. "The Screen and the Holocaust."
     DAVKA 5 (no. 3 1975): 17-23.

57. McManus, John T., and Louis Kronenberger.
     "Motion Pictures, the Theater, and Race
     Relations." (item II-418), pp. 152-158.

58. Maltby, Richard. "Film Noir: The Politics of
     the Maladjusted Text." J OF AMERICAN
     STUDIES (G. B.) 18 (April, 1984), 49-71.

59. May, Elaine Tyler. "The Jews in Hollywood."
     M.A. thesis, University of California, Los
     Angeles, 1970.

59A. May, Lary L. SCREENING OUT THE PAST. THE BIRTH
     OF MASS CULTURE AND THE MOTION PICTURE
     INDUSTRY. New York: Oxford University
     Press, 1980.

60.   ————. and Elaine Tyler May. "Why Jewish
       Movie Moguls?: An Exploration in American
       Culture." AMERICAN JEWISH HISTORY 72
       (September 1982): 6-25.

61.   Michel, Sonya. "Yekl and Hester Street: Was
       Assimilation Really Good for Jews?" LITERA-
       TURE/FILM Q 5 (Spring 1977): 142-46.

62.   Middleton, Russell. "Ethnic Prejudice and
       Susceptibility to Persuasion." (item I-
       102).

63.   Miller, Randall M. "Jews in (and on, behind,
       and around) Film." AMERICAN JEWISH HISTORY
       73 (December 1984): 189-93.

64.   Monaco, James. AMERICAN FILM NOW (item
       I-107).

65.   Moss, Robert. "'Blume' and the 'Heartbreak
       Kid' -- What Kind of Jews Are They?" NEW
       YORK TIMES, September 9, 1973, II, pp. 1,3.

66.   O'Connor, John J. "If Shylock Were Not
       Jewish." NEW YORK TIMES, March 19, 1974,
       II, 21.

67.   Pally, Marcia. "Kaddish, For the Fading Image
       of Jews in Film." FILM COMMENT 20 (January-
       February 1984): 49-55.

68.   Perlmutter, Ruth. "The Melting Plot and the
       Humoring of America: Hollywood and the
       Jew." FILM READER (no. 5 1982): 247-56.

69.   ————. "The Sweetening of America:
       The Image of the Jew in Film." ETHNIC
       IMAGES IN AMERICAN FILM AND TELEVISION
       (item I-105), pp. 35-38.

70.   Perret, Marion D. "Shakespeare and Anti-Sem-
       itism: Two Television Versions of 'The Mer-
       chant of Venice.'" MOSAIC 16 (Spring 1983):
       145-63.

71.   Pinsker, Sanford. "Mel Brooks and the Cinema

of Exhaustion." FROM HESTER STREET TO
HOLLYWOOD (item X-9), 245-56.

72. Platt, David. "Griffith's Intolerance." JEWISH
CURRENTS 30 (no. 11 1976): 26-30.

73. Popkin, Henry. "The Vanishing Jew of Our
Popular Culture." COMMENTARY 14 (July
1952): 46-55.

74. Raths, Louis E. and Frank N. Trager. "Public
Opinion and 'Crossfire.'" J OF EDUCATIONAL
SOCIOLOGY 21 (1948): 345-68.

75. Ribalow, M. Z. "Jews as Killers." HADASSAH 66
(February 1985): 41-44.

76. Rosen, Irwin C. "The Effect of the Motion
Picture 'Gentleman's Agreement' on
Attitudes Toward Jews." J OF PSYCHOLOGY 26
(October 1948): 525-36.

77. Rosenfeld, Alvin H. "The Holocaust in American
Popular Culture." MIDSTREAM 29 (no. 6
1983): 53-59.

78. Samuels, Stuart. "The Evolutionary Image of
the Jew in American Films." ETHNIC IMAGES
IN AMERICAN FILM AND TELEVISION (item I-
105), pp. 23-34.

79. Sarris, Andrew. "The Cultural Guilt of Musical
Movies: 'The Jazz Singer,' Fifty Years
After." FILM COMMENT 13 (September-October
1977): 39-41.

80. Schary, Dore. "Censorship and Stereotypes."
SATURDAY R OF LITERATURE 32 (April 30,
1949): 9-10.

81. Schatz, J. "The Image of the Jew." VARIETY 277
(January 8, 1975), 34 ff.

82. Shavelson, Melville. HOW TO MAKE A JEWISH
MOVIE. Englewood Cliffs, N. J.: Prentice-
Hall, 1971.

83. Shechner, Mark. "Woody Allen: The Failure of

the Therapeutic." FROM HESTER STREET TO
HOLLYWOOD (item X-9), pp. 231-44.

84. Short, K. R. M. "The Experience of Eastern
Jewry in America as Portrayed in the
Cinema of the 1920s and 1930s." HISTORY AND
FILM: METHODOLOGY, RESEARCH, AND EDUCATION.
Edited by K. R. M. Short and Karsten
Fledelius. Copenhagen, Denmark: Eventus,
1980: 113-150.

85. ⸻. "Hollywood Fights Anti-Semitism,
1940-1945." FILM AND RADIO PROPAGANDA IN
WORLD WAR II (item VI-67), pp. 146-72.

86. ⸻. "Hollywood Fights Anti-Semitism,
1945-1947." FEATURE FILM AS HISTORY. Edited
by K. R. M. Short. Knoxville: University of
Tennessee Press, 1981: 157-89.

87. Simmons, Ed. "Exit--Keep the Faith." DAVKA 5
(no. 3 1975): 44-45.

88. Singer, David. "The Jewish Gangster: Crime as
Unzar Shtik." JUDAISM 23 ([no. 1] 1974):
70-77.

89. Spiegel, Alan. "The Vanishing Act: A Typology
of the Jew in Contemporary American Film."
FROM HESTER STREET TO HOLLYWOOD (item
X-9), pp. 257-275.

90. Suber, Howard. "Hollywood's Closet Jews."
DAVKA 5 (no. 3 1975): 12-14.

91. ⸻. "Politics and Popular Culture:
Hollywood at Bay, 1933-1953." AMERICAN
JEWISH HISTORY 67 (June 1979): 517-33.

92. ⸻. "Television's Interchangeable Ethnics: Funny, They Don't Look Jewish." TELE-
VISION Q 12 ([no. 4] 1975): 49-56.

93. Toland, John. "Can TV Dramas Convey the
Horrors of the Holocaust?" TV GUIDE 30
(February 13, 1982): 6-8, 10.

94. Tugend, Tom. "The Hollywood Jews." DAVKA 5

(no. 3 1975): 4-8.

95. Tunstall, Jeremy. THE MEDIA ARE AMERICAN (item I-151).

96. Turan, Kenneth. "Making 'Skokie': The Passions Come Flooding Back." TV GUIDE 29 (October 10, 1981): 32-34, 36-37.

97. Weinberg, David. "The Socially Acceptable Immigrant Minority Group: The Image of the Jew in American Popular Films." NORTH DAKOTA Q 40 (Autumn 1972): 60-68.

98. Wertheim, Arthur Frank. "The Rise and Fall of Milton Berle." AMERICAN HISTORY/ AMERICAN TELEVISION (item I-112), pp. 55-78.

99. White, David Manning, and Richard Averson. THE CELLULOID WEAPON (item I-166).

100. Whitfield, Steve. "Jazz Singers: A Hollywood Bomb--But, Inadvertantly, an Accurate Portrayal of the American Jewish Condition." MOMENT 6 (March-April 1981): 19-25.

101. ————. "Jules Feiffer and the Comedy of Disenchantment." FROM HESTER STREET TO HOLLYWOOD (item X-9), pp. 167-82.

XI. NATIVE AMERICANS

American Indians, although inhabitants of this
hemisphere for longer than any other group discussed in this book, have suffered similar problems
with film and television stereotypes. From the
earliest days of the motion picture, Indians have
been characterized either as noble savages or
bloodthirsty beasts. Filmmakers have reduced the
wide variety of Indian cultures in the United
States to a meld of one or two Great Plains tribes
by erasing all geographical and cultural differences among them. Even the term "Indian" is a white
man's invention which plays a further role in
blurring the distinctions among Native American
cultures. ("Indian" will be utilized in this essay
rather than "Native American" since it reflects the
Hollywood vision of America's original inhabitants.)(13)
Additionally, little attempt has been made by
filmmakers to understand Indian motivations for
action, as virtually all activities are characterized from the white man's point of view. Hence,
when Indians attack white settlers, it becomes a
"massacre." When soldiers attack Indian tribes, it
is for the benefit of civilization and the advance
of Western culture.(59)
While Indian roles have been plentiful from
the early days of the motion picture, actual
Indians have rarely earned the acting honors. In
the silent days, whites often portrayed Indians.
Even Japanese star Sessue Hayakawa appeared as a
Sioux warrior in 1914! Nevertheless, this convention (which was commonplace for blacks and Asians
as well) tended to disappear for other racial and
ethnic groups. In general, few Native Amerians have
essayed major roles even to the present day. Only
by the 1970s has there been a slight breakdown in
this pattern in such films as **Little Big Man** (1970)

and One Flew Over the Cuckoo's Nest (1975).
Otherwise, real Indians have tended to remain as
invisible on the screen as behind it, since they
have remained a tiny minority in the technical and
creative realms of filmmaking.

The role of the Indian on the American screen
began with the initial documentary interests of the
first filmmakers. Early films of dances or other
cultural activities were created with a general
veracity. However, as fictional films flourished,
the Indian was quickly given the status of one of
the screen's dominant villains. Film alone cannot
be given credit for creating this image of the
Indian. Early printed sources, such as dime novels,
tent-show posters, and printed etchings painted the
dramatic period of the westward movement of the
mid-nineteenth century in this fashion.(13, 66)
Films tended to adopt images from this earlier
bellicose era, and utilize them in a time of
peaceful settlement in the West. Hence, films
dealing with Indians continued to hearken back to
the frontier days for both themes and plots. This
might not seem surprising in the early silent era,
when the age of western conflict was fairly recent.
Nevertheless, this particular era of American history has continued to dominate thinking (and screen
plots) about the Indian even to the present. As a
result, the Native American is rarely shown on the
screen with regard to his modern problems, but,
rather, remains locked in a limited historical era.
Even into the 1980s, Indians are still involved, on
television and film, in resisting America's
westward movement.

The Indian which evolved in the silent cinema
seemed to have only two functions -- to kill white
men and to rape their women. As a barbaric savage,
the Indian utilized every means possible to exter-
minate the white man. On some occasions a "noble
savage" (often raised by white men) emerged, who
would ally with whites when the situation demanded.
The resultant image proved wholly unsatisfying to
many Indian groups, and one contingent of Shoshoni,
Cheyenne, Arapahoe, and Chippewa even visited
Congress in 1911 to express their concern about
"untrue portrayals of the Indians." (32)

While most silent films of this period
depicted the Indian as the insensitive barbarian
(such as D. W. Griffith's America [1924]), others

managed to depict the Indian in a sympathetic
light. One of the most favorable endeavors was the
1926 film, The Vanishing American, with Richard Dix
(Nophaie) and Lois Wilson. Here the Indian is
capable of loyalty and education, as Nophaie
realizes that the white man is bilking the Indians
on his reservation. Nophaie eventually grows fond
of Marion, a white schoolteacher, but, as was
characteristic of movies of this (and later)
decades, such a relationship could not be
consummated. Like similar counterparts of other
ethnic or racial groups who fell in love with white
women, death was almost always the inevitable
outcome, as the Chinaman also discovered in D. W.
Griffith's Broken Blossoms. Nevertheless, for this
date, The Vanishing American remains a model in its
depiction of Indian characters and their relationship with whites on the reservation. Despite this
optimistic sense, it still remains clear from both
the film's and the original Zane Grey novel's
title, that the Indian way of life is doomed to
extinction.(17, 54)
     The coming of sound changed Indian images very
little, except that it allowed for the curious
supposed grammar of Indian speech to be heard, with
a plethora of "ughs" and "ums." (For an interesting
survey of the difficulties of conveying Indian
dialects in English, see Raymond Stedman's Shadows
of the Indians. Stedman finds that Tonto's dialect,
heard on The Lone Ranger television and radio
shows, has had an enduring effect on film and television Indians [73].)
     John Ford, whose directorial career spanned
the decades from silence to sound, has played a
major role in presenting and perhaps shaping Indian
stereotypes on film. Since the Western was his
favorite genre, this should not come as a surprise.
From the first, Ford utilized the Indian as a violent and anonymous savage, in such films as Stagecoach and Drums Along the Mohawk (both 1939).
However, Ford's "cavalry trilogy," which consisted
of Fort Apache (1948), She Wore a Yellow Ribbon
(1949), and Rio Grande (1950), revealed a slight
change in his viewpoint as he began to examine the
complexities of Indian-white relationships. Perhaps
as atonement, one of Ford's last films (and his
final Western), Cheyenne Autumn (1964), attempted
to provide a sympathetic view of Indian life and

culture, although most of the major Indian roles
were portrayed by whites or Hispanics, such as
Dolores Del Rio, Victor Jory, Ricardo Montalban,
and Sal Mineo. Ford noted in a contemporary
interview that he had "killed more Indians than
Custer, Beecher, and Chivington put together...
Let's face it, we've treated them [Indians] badly--
it's a blot on our shield; we've cheated and
robbed, killed, murdered, massacred and everything
else, but they kill one white man, and, God, out
come the troops."(68) This mature Ford perspective
is evident in Cheyenne Autumn, which follows the
migration of a small group of Indians who leave
their desolate reservation for their own distant
home with tragic results. (For an evaluation of
Ford's use of Indian characters, see the works of
Ellis, Sarris, Sinclair, and Thoene [27, 63, 68,
74].)
      Ford's shift in the portrayal of the Indian
occurs during the liberal reevaluation of America's
ethnic and minority groups in the late 1940s and
early 1950s film. As prejudice against Jews is
decried in such films as Gentleman's Agreement
(1947), and blacks in Pinky (1949), Indians
received a similar reinterpretation in several
films such as Devil's Doorway (1949) and Broken
Arrow (1950). The latter film, which features James
Stewart and Jeff Chandler (as Cochise), paints the
Indian as a proponent of peace in an Apache
society with its own religion, tradition, and
customs. While this examination of Apache life is
not completely historically accurate, the film
reveals a marked sympathy for the Indian for the
first time in many years. Others, however, have
argued that this film merely revives the image of
the "noble savage" from the silent era. Philip
French presents yet another interpretation in his
study Westerns: Aspects of a Movie Genre. He
contends that these "Indian reevaluation" films
are perhaps less about Indians than about blacks.
The Indian therefore becomes a symbol in the
attempt to redirect race relations in the United
States.(30)
      While the Indian as villain has not
disappeared from film or television shows, the
general treatment of Indian roles has softened
somewhat. During the 1960s and 1970s a historical
revisionism directed Hollywood's attention to the

problems that Indians had faced during the settlement of the West. This is particularly noticeable
in such films as Ralph Nelson's Soldier Blue (1970)
and Arthur Penn's Little Big Man. Here the whites
are clearly the violent aggressors, while the
Indians remain the helpless victim until they are
driven to retaliatory violence against Custer and
his troops. Some have argued that both films function as metaphors for the American experience in
Vietnam, but others contend that these films should
be evaluated for their attempt to reverse standard
Indian images in Hollywood films since the turn of
the century. Little Big Man remains one of the few
films to provide a wide variety of Indian character
types. No longer is an Indian either "good" or
"bad." Adding to the critical raves for this film
was the use of an actual Indian, Chief Dan George,
who, in a major role, won the Oscar for Best
Supporting Actor. Nevertheless, despite the
favorable press given to Dan George, this period
still saw Anthony Quinn as a drunken Indian in Flap
(1970), Katherine Ross as an Indian maiden in Tell
Them Willie Boy Is Here (1969), and Dame Judith
Anderson as a village matriarch in A Man Called
Horse (1970).(60)
     When comparing Native Americans to other
groups analyzed in this book, it appears that
change has been glacial. In many cases, the
stereotypes utilized remain characteristic of the
silent era. Few actual Indians appear in acting
roles, and few appear behind the scenes. There have
been some hopeful signs however. In recent years,
there has been a tendency to jettison the Tonto-
esque dialogue of the past, and utilize real Indian
dialects. Windwalker (1980), for example, provided
subtitles to translate the dialogue in the same
manner as any foreign film. Similarly, Public
Television has presented a variety of series
dealing with Indian matters, even one analyzing
Indian images on film and television. Rita Keshena
argues that one further step is needed: "As
American Indians, however, we cannot look to others
to change the distorted image that has been
projected for the past eighty years by a money-
hungry industry. Real change will come only when
Indian people become knowledgeable in the
methodology of film and television. We must step
out of the role that Hollywood has given us and

take up positions in the important areas of
creativity and production. Only then will we be
able to control the way we are presented on
film."(41)

     Five major works have analyzed the images of
Indians in American films and television. Ralph and
Natasha Friar's The Only Good Indian... The Hollywood Gospel provided the first survey of the
subject. The book is arranged in a complex fashion,
as though it were a film script instead of a
literary work. Hence, the work is divided into
scenes, and characters are introduced by script
notations such as "Enter D. W. Griffith." Nevertheless, the Friars clearly identify the dominant
stereotypes in television shows and films concerning Indians. An excellent filmography also
reveals the major themes exhibited in films about
Indians.(32)
     Kevin Brownlow's The War, the West, and the
Wilderness provides only a brief section on the
Indian, but it is useful as an antidote to the work
of the Friars. Brownlow corrects several of their
assumptions concerning early silent films, and
argues that Griffith's films, such as The Battle of
Elderbush Gulch (1913), might not be as unsym-
pathetic as the Friars suggest. Brownlow also
documents the activities of a few Indian actors and
even a director who made a small but important
mark on silent films about the West.(17)
     Raymond William Stedman's Shadows of the
Indian: Stereotypes in American Culture presents a
broader vista than the Friars. In addition to film
and television, Stedman also considers various
aspects of popular culture, such as popular
literature, posters, and dime novels. Yet, he, too,
notes many of the same character types that the
Friars have identified. (73)
     John E. O'Connor's The Hollywood Indian:
Stereotypes of Native Americans in Film was
designed as a guide to a museum exhibit at the New
Jersey State Museum. Nevertheless, it provides a
careful study of ten major films which concern
Indians. O'Connor discusses the making of these
films (based on studies of studio archives) and
analyzes the images they present. He also provides

effective arguments on the historical accuracy (or,
more likely, inaccuracy) of these films. O'Connor's
subjects include: America, The Vanishing American,
Massacre, Drums Along the Mohawk, They Died With
Their Boots On, Devil's Doorway, Broken Arrow,
Cheyenne Autumn, Tell Them Willie Boy Is Here, and
Little Big Man.(54)
     Gretchen M. Bataille and Charles L. P. Silet's
The Pretend Indians, Images of Native Americans in
the Movies offers an excellent collection of
readings on the subject. Their work provides contemporary articles, reviews, and critical commentary. It includes articles (20, 29, 31, 33, 41,
59, 60, 75) listed below. Bataille and Silet are
also the primary bibliographers on the history of
the role of the Indian in film.(6, 7, 10) Their
work, Images of American Indians on Film: An Annotated Bibliography from Garland Publishing, Inc.
should prove the definitive study in the field.
     Information on the role of Indians in film can
also be found in research on the Western, although
in this context the treatment of this subject can
be cursory. Nevertheless, there are some notable
exceptions. These include the works of Brauer (16),
Cawelti (20), Fenin and Everson (28), Lenihan (44,
45), and Sadoux (61). Western "hero" George Armstrong Custer has been a favorite subject for both
motion pictures and television shows. For an
analysis of the changing image of Custer from the
silent days to Little Big Man, see the articles by
Hutton and Langellier.(38, 42) Although the focus
is on Custer, each article offers interesting
observations on the changing depiction of Indians
in these films.

     Major discussions of films and/or television
shows include: America (54), The Ballad of Crowfoot
(19), Broken Arrow (44, 45, 54, 76, 79), Buffalo
Bill and the Indians (14), Cheyenne Autumn (27, 54,
68, 74, 79), Circle of the Sun (77), Custer's Last
Stand (38), Daniel Boone (26), Devil's Doorway
(54), Drums Along the Mohawk (54, 55), Flap (60),
Fort Apache (27, 49), Hanta Yo (80), Ishi in Two
Worlds (77), The Legend of Walks Far Woman (65),
Little Big Man (3, 38, 44, 54, 58, 60), A Man
Called Horse (58), Massacre (54), The Outsider

(60), The Revolutionary (19), Rio Bravo (27), Run of the Arrow (76), The Searchers (49), She Wore a Yellow Ribbon (27), Soldier Blue (60), Stagecoach (74), Tahtonka (77), Tell Them Willie Boy Is Here (54, 60), These Are My People (19), They Died With Their Boots On (44, 54), Ulzana's Raid (52), The Unforgiven (45), The Vanishing American (17, 46, 54, 64, 79), Walk the Proud Land (45), When the Legends Die (35, 56), and You Are On Indian Land (19).

1. ————. "Hollywood, Academia, and Red Pride."
   HUMAN BEHAVIOR 4 (January 1975): 46.

2. ————. THE NATIVE AMERICAN IMAGE ON FILM: A
   PROGRAMMER'S GUIDE FOR ORGANIZATIONS AND
   EDUCATORS. Washington, D. C.: Education
   Services Department of the American Film
   Institute, 1980.

3. Astor, Gerald. "Good Guys Wear War Paint."
   LOOK 34 (December 1, 1970): 56-61.

4. Barber, Rowland. "How Hollywood Made a Treaty
   with the Indians." TV GUIDE 23 (March 8,
   1975): 12-16.

5. Bataille, Gretchen M. "Education and the
   Images of the American Indian." EXPLOR-
   ATIONS IN ETHNIC STUDIES 1 (January 1978):
   37-49.

6. ————, and Charles L. P. Silet. "Bibliography: Additions to 'The Indian in American Film.'" J OF POPULAR FILM AND
   TELEVISION 8 (Spring 1980): 50.

7. ————. "A Checklist of Published Materials
   on Popular Images of the Indian in the
   American Film." J OF POPULAR FILM 5 (1976):
   171-82.

8. ————. "Economic and Psychic Exploitation of
   American Indians." EXPLORATIONS IN ETHNIC
   STUDIES 6 (July 1983): 8-21.

9. ————. "The Entertaining Anachronism:
   Indians in American Film." THE KALEIDO-
   SCOPIC LENS (item I-106), pp. 36-53.

10. ————. "The Indian in Film: A Critical
    Survey." Q R OF FILM STUDIES 2 (February
    1977): 56-74.

11. ————. THE PRETEND INDIANS. IMAGES OF NATIVE
    AMERICANS IN THE MOVIES. Ames, Iowa: Iowa
    State University Press, 1980.

12. Beale, Lewis. "The American Way West." FILMS

AND FILMING 18 (April 1972): 24-30.

13. Berkhofer, Robert F., Jr. THE WHITE MAN'S
    INDIAN: IMAGES OF THE AMERICAN INDIAN FROM
    COLUMBUS TO THE PRESENT. New York: Random
    House, 1977.

14. Bernstein, Gene M. "Robert Altman's Buffalo
    Bill and the Indians or Sitting Bull's
    History Lesson." J OF POPULAR CULTURE 13
    (Summer 1979): 17-25.

15. Blakey, Carla M. "The American Indian in
    Films." FILM NEWS 27 (September 1970):
    6-10; 27 (October 1970): 6-11.

16. Brauer, Ralph, and Donna Brauer. THE HORSE,
    THE GUN, AND THE PIECE OF PROPERTY (item I-
    22).

17. Brownlow, Kevin. THE WAR, THE WEST, AND THE
    WILDERNESS (item VI-4).

18. Calder, Jenni. THERE MUST BE A LONE RANGER:
    THE AMERICAN WEST IN FILM AND REALITY. New
    York: Taplinger, 1975.

19. Callenbach, Ernest. "Short Notices." FILM Q 24
    (Fall 1970): 56-62.

20. Cawelti, John G. "Reflections on the New
    Western Films: The Jewish Cowboy, The Black
    Avenger, and the Return of the Vanishing
    American." (item II-132).

21. ———. THE SIX-GUN MYSTIQUE. Bowling Green,
    Ohio: Bowling Green State University
    Popular Press, 1973.

22. Churchill, Ward, Norbert Hill, and Mary Ann
    Hill. "Media Stereotyping and Native
    Response." THE INDIAN HISTORIAN 11
    (December 1978): 46-47.

23. Cody, Iron Eyes. (As told to Collin Perry). MY
    LIFE AS A HOLLYWOOD INDIAN. New York: Ever-
    est House, 1982.

24. Cripps, Thomas. "Mexicans, Indians and Movies:
     The Need for a History." (item VII-15).

25. Duchineaux, Franklin. "The American Indian
     Today: Beyond the Stereotype." TODAY'S
     EDUCATION 62 (May 1973): 22-23.

26. Efron, Edith. "The Indians vs. Daniel Boone."
     TV GUIDE 20 (January 22, 1972): 42-45.

27. Ellis, Kirk. "On the Warpath: John Ford and
     the Indians." .J OF POPULAR FILM AND
     TELEVISION 8 (Summer 1980): 34-41.

28. Fenin, George N., and William K. Everson. THE
     WESTERN. FROM SILENTS TO THE SEVENTIES. New
     York: Grossman Publishers, rev. ed., 1973.

29. French, Philip. "The Indian in the Western
     Movie." ART IN AMERICA 60 (July-August
     1972): 36-39.

30. ————. WESTERNS: ASPECTS OF A MOVIE GENRE
     (item II-242).

31. Friar, Ralph. "White Man Speaks With a Split
     Tongue, Forked Tongue, Tongue of Snake."
     FILM LIBRARY Q 3 (Winter 1969-1970): 16-23.

32. ————, and Natasha Friar. THE ONLY GOOD
     INDIAN...THE HOLLYWOOD GOSPEL. New York:
     Drama Book Specialists/Publishers, 1972.

33. Georgakas, Dan. "They Have Not Spoken:
     American Indians in Film." FILM Q 25
     (Spring 1972): 26-32.

34. Hanks, Christopher C., Granzberg, Gary, and
     Jack Steinbring. "Social Changes and the
     Mass Media: The Oxford House Cree,
     1909-1983." POLAR RECORD (G. B.) 21 (no.
     134 1983): 459-65.

35. Harrington, John. "Understanding Hollywood's
     Indian Rhetoric." CANADIAN R OF AMERICAN
     STUDIES 8 (no. 1 1977): 77-88.

36. Hartman, Hedy. "A Brief Review of the Native

American in American Cinema." INDIAN
HISTORIAN 9 (Summer 1976): 27-29.

37. Hirschfelder, Arlene Boshes. AMERICAN INDIAN
    STEREOTYPES IN THE WORLD OF CHILDREN: A
    READER AND BIBLIOGRAPHY. Metuchen, N. J.:
    Scarecrow Press, 1982.

38. Hutton, Paul A. "The Celluloid Custer." RED
    RIVER VALLEY HISTORICAL R 4 (no. 4 1979):
    20-43.

39. Kaufmann, Donald L. "The Indian as Media
    Hand-Me-Down." COLORADO Q 23 (Spring 1975):
    489-504.

40. Kendall, Martha. "Forget the Masked Man: Who
    Was His Indian Companion?" SMITHSONIAN 8
    (September 1977): 113-120.

41. Keshena, Rita. "The Role of American Indians
    in Motion Pictures." AMERICAN INDIAN
    CULTURE AND RESEARCH J 1 (1974): 25-28.

42. Langellier, John Philip. "Custer's Last Fight
    and the Silver Screen." GATEWAY HERITAGE 2
    (no. 3 1981-82): 16-21.

43. Larkins, Robert. "Hollywood and the Indian."
    FOCUS ON FILM 2 (March-April 1970): 44-53.

44. Lenihan, John H. "Films and the American
    Frontier." ORGANIZATION OF AMERICAN
    HISTORIANS NEWSLETTER 12 (August 1984):
    17-18.

45. ———. SHOWDOWN: CONFRONTING MODERN AMERICA
    IN THE WESTERN FILM. Urbana: University of
    Illinois Press, 1980.

46. Leutrat, Jean-Louis. "Sur L'image de L'Indian
    dans le Western." [The Image of the Indian
    in the Western.] CAHIERS D'HISTOIRE
    (France) 23 (no. 3 1978): 293-312.

47. Mantell, Harold. "Counteracting the Stereo-
    type." AMERICAN INDIAN 5 (Fall 1950): 16-
    20.

48. Marsden, Michael, and Jack Nachbar. "American
    Indians in the Movies." HANDBOOK OF NORTH
    AMERICAN INDIANS, Vol. 4. Washington, D.C.:
    Smithsonian Institution, 1985.

49. Mellen, Joan. BIG BAD WOLVES: MASCULINITY IN
    THE AMERICAN FILM (item II-435).

50. Murphy, Sharon. "American Indians and the
    Media: Neglect and Stereotype." JOURNALISM
    HISTORY 6 (Summer 1979): 39-43.

51. Nachbar, Jack. "Published Materials on Western
    Movies: An Annotated Guide to Sources in
    English." Ph. D. diss., Bowling Green State
    University, 1974.

52. ————. "Ulzana's Raid." WESTERN MOVIES
    (item XI-58), pp. 139-47.

53. Newton, Ray. "Tribes Rap Mass Media Portrayal
    of Indians." PUBLISHERS' AUXILIARY (Decem-
    ber 12, 1975), p. 12.

54. O'Connor, John E. THE HOLLYWOOD INDIAN:
    STEREOTYPES OF NATIVE AMERICANS IN FILMS.
    Trenton, N. J.: New Jersey State Museum,
    1980.

55. ————. "A Reaffirmation of American Ideals:
    Drums Along the Mohawk." AMERICAN HIS-
    TORY/AMERICAN FILM (item I-113), pp. 97-
    120.

56. O'Donnell, Victoria. "The Great White Father
    and the Native American Son: An Oedipal
    Analysis of When the Legends Die." J OF
    THE UNIVERSITY FILM ASSOCIATION 32 (Winter-
    Spring 1980): 65-69.

57. Oshana, Maryann. "Native American Women in
    Westerns: Reality and Myth." FRONTIERS 6
    (no. 3 1981): 46-50.

58. Pilkington, William T., and Don Graham.
    WESTERN MOVIES. Albuquerque: University of
    New Mexico Press, 1979.

59. Price, John A. "The Stereotyping of North
     American Indians in Motion Pictures."
     ETHNOHISTORY 20 (Spring 1973): 153-71.

60. Rice, Susan. "...And Afterwards, Take Him to a
     Movie." MEDIA AND METHODS 7 (April 1971):
     43-44, 71-72.

61. Sadoux, Jean Jacques. RACISM IN THE WESTERN.
     New York: Revisionist Press, 1980.

62. Sarf, Wayne M. GOD BLESS YOU, BUFFALO BILL.
     East Rutherford, N. J.: Fairleigh Dickinson
     University Press, 1983.

63. Sarris, Andrew. THE JOHN FORD MOVIE MYSTERY.
     Bloomington: Indiana University Press,
     1975.

64. Shales, Tom. "The Vanishing American." THE
     AMERICAN FILM HERITAGE (item II-548), pp.
     52-55.

65. Shaw, David. "Raquel Welch and the Making of
     The Legend of Walks Far Woman." TV GUIDE
     30 (May 29, 1982): 18-19, 21-23.

66. Silet, Charles L. P.   "The Image of the Amer-
     ican Indian in Film."   THE WORLDS BETWEEN
     TWO RIVERS: PERSPECTIVES ON AMERICAN
     INDIANS IN IOWA. Edited by Gretchen M.
     Bataille, David K. Gradwohl, and Charles L.
     P. Silet. Ames: Iowa State University
     Press, 1978, pp. 10-15.

67. Simonoski, T.   "Sioux Versus Hollywood: The
     Image of Sioux Indians in American Films."
     Ph. D. diss., University of Southern Cali-
     fornia, 1979.

68. Sinclair, Andrew. JOHN FORD. New York: Dial
     Press, 1979.

69. Skinner, James M.   "The Silent Enemy: A
     Forgotten Chapter in the Screen History of
     the Canadian Indian." ONTARIO H (Canada) 71
     (no. 3 1979): 159-62.

70. Smith, James R. "Native American Images and
    the Broadcast Media." AMERICAN INDIAN
    CULTURE AND RESEARCH J 5 (1980): 81-92.

71. Smith, Philip, Jr. "There Were So Good
    Indians." TV GUIDE 12 (December 19, 1964):
    10-11.

72. Spears, Jack. "The Indian on Film." FILMS IN
    REVIEW 10 (January 1959): 18-33.

73. Stedman, Raymond William. SHADOWS OF THE
    INDIAN: STEREOTYPES IN AMERICAN CULTURE.
    Norman, Oklahoma: University of Oklahoma
    Press, 1982.

74. Thoene, Bodie and Rona Stuck. "Navajo Nation
    Meets Hollywood." AMERICAN WEST 20 (no. 5
    1983): 38-44.

75. Turner, John W. "Little Big Man, the Novel and
    the Film: A Study of Narrative Structure."
    LITERATURE/FILM Q 5 (Spring 1977): 154-63.

76. Tuska, Jon. THE FILMING OF THE WEST. Garden
    City, N. Y.: Doubleday, 1976.

77. Vickrey, William. "Some Wrongs Righted on
    Film: The Vanishing American: Part II."
    FILM LIBRARY Q 3 (Winter 1969-1970): 46-47.

78. Weatherford, Elizabeth, with Emelia Senbert,
    eds. NATIVE AMERICANS ON FILM AND VIDEO.
    New York: Museum of the American Indian,
    1981.

79. White, David Manning, and Richard Averson. THE
    CELLULOID WEAPON (item I-166).

80. Whitney, Dwight. "Hanta Yo Finally Comes to
    TV." TV GUIDE 32 (May 19, 1984): 37-38, 40,
    42.

81. Yacower, Maurice. "Private and Public Visions:
    Zabriskie Point and Billy Jack." J OF
    POPULAR FILM 1 (Summer 1972): 197-207.

XII. OTHERS

American film and television have never represented the full range and diversity of American
culture, for many ethnic and racial groups have
escaped portrayal altogether and others have appeared infrequently. A group's social, political,
and economic invisibility in the United States
means invisibility in the visual mass media. Groups
unknown or unfamiliar to the general public do not
serve as metaphors or stereotypes for artistic
delineations of class or culture. If such groups
appear at all, they function as backdrops for
others and for other subjects. Thus, Hawaiians sway
hips and strum ukuleles in movies and television
shows set in the islands, but their hula rhythms
are intended only to convey place and pace for,
say, Elvis Presley in Blue Hawaii (1961), Jack Lord
in Hawaii Five-0, or Tom Selleck in Magnum, P.I.
The Hawaiians do not matter much in the story line.
The stories, in fact, could be set anywhere, for
the almost invisible "others" are interchangeable,
blurred together as convenient props for exotic
islands or jungles. They lack the precise ethnic
ascriptions necessary to give them meaning and distinctiveness.

   In a personal statement by a filmmaker or producer, such as Elia Kazan's America, America
(1963), an "invisible" group might step out from
the scenery to establish an identifiable screen
image, but in those few instances where an "invisible" ethnic or racial group has been central to a
film or television show, its ethnicity or race has
been incidental to its presence. Only spear sha-
king, half-clad Africans can claim abundant stereotypical images, borne of racial fantasies and
imperialist apologies from traders, colonizers,
and missionaries essaying the "dark continent."
Those almost invisible "others" with American
screen images (to date, the Africans, Armenians,
Dutch, East Indians, Greeks, Hawaiians, Louisiana

Cajuns, Norwegians, Swedes, and Turks) remain condemned by their small numbers or their regional
isolation in the United States to the periphery of
American mass media. They lack the commercial
strength in America and the historical or cultural
identities in Western society to command attention
in their own right.

The African image constitutes a special case.
It emerged from white visions of a benighted and
savage sub-Saharan Africa, needful of Western commercial and cultural penetration--visions that went
back to the early days of European contact with the
region and visions that sustained three centuries
of anti-black images in American popular culture
and society. But the predominant white version did
not go unchallenged. Black filmmakers in the United
States drew on Afro-American cultural and literary
themes of an idealized, innocent African homeland,
ravished by European/American commercial, cultural,
and political invasion, and created images of African genius and nobility to counter the pervasive
negative stereotypes of black Africa in American
popular culture.(5, 7)

In the former view, Africans were uncivilized
heathens, as primitive in culture as the tangled,
untilled sub-Saharan continent they inhabited.
According to such thinking, white superiority was
incontrovertible and inevitable. The many, and
immensely popular, adaptations and embellishments
of Edgar Rice Burroughs' Tarzan stories on the
screen made the point. They implied that even an
English babe abandoned in the jungle and raised by
apes, but a nobleman by birth of course, readily
achieved mastery over the animals and black Africans who shared his physical world. In that sense,
the Tarzan films suggested that God created only
the white man in His image. The numerous safari
films cast Stewart Granger, Clark Gable, and other
major movie stars as white hunters who knew the
continent's resources better than did the natives.
The Africans carried a double burden in such films,
toting bwana's supplies on expeditions to exploit
their land and, by their color and their condition,
bearing symbols of subservience, supposedly the
proper role for all of black Africa. These African
images were more than scenic backdrops or contrasts
for the white protagonists; however paradoxical,
images of black African savagery and servility were

visual justifications for European colonialism and
white racism.(6-11)
   Such images survived the post-World War II
flush of African nationalism and the collapse of
European colonial rule. Few American films dealt
sympathetically with modern Africa, if they bothered to depict it at all. African nationalism remained locked in the image of spear-wielding savagery, as in Zulu (1964). On television the old
African film images abounded in early morning and
children's hour programming relying on reruns of
the Tarzan and Ramar of the Jungle series, or
Abbott and Costello and The Three Stooges, among
other popular series which occasionally packed the
"heroes" off to Africa, where they met black Africans speaking a mumbo jumbo and seeming as stupid
as the comics. A black African never outwitted a
white in any genre.
   Despite the enormous success of Alex Haley's
Roots, black African history and culture did not
become commercially attractive for American filmmakers or television producers. And nobody grappled
with the complexity and diversity of African cultures in any age. Tribal, ethnic, regional, religious, or whatever differences among black Africans
counted for nothing in screen depictions of them.
Like the film and television images of American
Indians which reduced Indian cultures to a single
stereotype, black Africans were indistinguishable
from one another in costume or culture. Media-made
black Africans were of a piece, invariably dressed
in loin-cloth made of lion or leopard skin, when
dressed at all, and living in crude huts. The same
attitudes that permitted documentaries or even
feature films to show bare-breasted black African
women, despite Production Code and societal strictures against nudity, survived in modern representations of the "dark continent." The black Africans
were objects of ethnographic or anthropological
interest, much like (sometimes less so than) the
great apes, and, so, seemed unlikely candidates for
literary or screen character treatment.(11)
   Afro-American intellectuals and filmmakers decried such depictions of black Africans as racist
and sought to offer a more favorable view in their
own work. As Afro-American scholars celebrated the
history of black Africa before European contact,
so, too, black filmmakers found strength and integ-

rity in the Africans' compatibility with nature and
absolved them of any responsibility for slavery and
the evils of modern capitalism. Still, stereotypes
of Africa persisted. Marketable scripts on African
subjects, for example, borrowed from commerically
or critically successful works by white authors.
Thus, Paul Robeson gained international fame as an
African prince in his strong performances and even
crossed the Atlantic to make a movie free of black
stereotypes (e.g., The Emperor Jones [1933] and the
British-made Sanders of the River [1935]), but his
powerful film presence could not entirely mute the
imperialist undertones of films based on white
works. Black filmmakers turned to black-authored
material for less negative fare, but they had no
national market in which to show their films. They
made black films for black audiences, and the Hollywood African lived on in American popular culture.(3, 7, 11)

No other almost invisible group had so clear an
image, however much distorted, as did the Africans.
In some cases, groups had screen images solely
because they occupied a particular setting. Since
1897 Hawaiians have been present in movies, and
more recently in television shows, using Hawaii as
a locale. In films such as Hawaii (1966) they have
symbolized South Seas primitivism and sensuality in
contrast to the economic progress and rigid moral
order of Western society, but in that guise they
are important because of their location, not because of their own particular attributes. They are,
for example, interchangeable in that role with the
South Seas islanders in the three versions of
Mutiny on the Bounty. Louisiana Cajuns have had a
more varied screen image, but they, too, have generally functioned as metaphors for environment,
walking, talking, and sometimes gawking embodiments
of a backwoods primitivism. Depending on the individual filmmaker's attachment to rural or southern
values, they have appeared as simple, friendly,
childlike people or as brutal, uncivilized, and
menacing like their bayou swamps.(21, 23)

Scandinavian groups, when shown at all, also
remain tied to their physical environment--the land
they till, they symbolize. Concentrated in rural
states, Norwegians and Swedes have never gained
visual media representations proportionate to their
numbers or social/cultural importance in the United

States. Despite a significant ethnic literature
from which to draw, no American filmmaker has had
the intense personal commitment and resources of
the Swede Jan Troell to follow the epic The Emigrants (1971) with other stories about Scandinavian
life and adjustment in America. Rural groups are
underrepresented in film and television generally,
and Scandinavians remain trapped in media obscurity
by their location.(24, 26)
    A single exception proves the rule. The strong
discernible Norwegian image, in the early television show Mama, which aired from 1949 to 1956, was
set in San Francisco, hardly a Norwegian haven.
The forerunner of the American family comedy series
that would later proliferate on television (e.g.,
Ozzie and Harriet), the show's success came from
Mama's commonality with and expression of middle-
class American values. The Norwegian ethnicity of
the family in Mama was apparent in names and a few
seasonal customs, and the Scandinavian background
of two actors on the show provided strong empathy
with their characters and the basis for story ideas
for the writers.(25) But ethnicity was not perti-
nent to the show's themes or popularity. Removed
from a recognizable Norwegian environment, the farm
lands of the Upper Midwest, and placed in the urban
world of Mr. Everyman, the Norwegian identity of
Mama's family lost its resonance and purpose.

    The scholarship on the "other" groups is as
undeveloped as the images. Only one analytical
overview of the connections between American history, culture, and social structure, on the one
hand, and African images, on the other, exists to
provide a context for understanding the evolution
of media images.(11) In a collection of sources and
reprinted short essays, Richard Maynard introduced
the subject of Africa on film to teachers, and
several authors briefly alluded to the relationship
between screen images of black Africans and American and European attitudes toward and interests in
Africa.(5, 6, 10). One writer recorded the negative
reaction of some modern black Africans to American
movie stereotypes, including Paul Robeson's seeming
complicity in purveying colonialist ideas.(3) Several works on Afro-American images discussed in

Chapter II (on Afro-Americans) suggest that images
of Africa grew out of black and white Americans'
different needs to create an Africa to serve their
social and cultural purposes in the United States
(see especially II-181, 387, 423, 473), but such
observations are tangential to the main arguments
in each work. No study has explored deeply the
relationship between American racial and ideological beliefs and the resulting images of black
Africans on screen or shown how and why African and
Afro-American images converged in American popular
culture. Those studies focussing on the Tarzan
phenomenon comment on the subordination of black
Africans to the white king of the apes, and in
Nesteby's studies tie the Tarzan series to colonialism and racism.(2, 4, 7-9). Here, too, however,
the principal concern has been to identify stereotypes rather than to locate the historical under-
pinnings of those screen images. As yet, no study
addresses questions of aesthetics, authorship, or
audience, and no study treats African images in
television.

Discussions of the Armenians, Greeks, and Turks
have turned wholly on Elia Kazan's America, America, and have principally dealt with the film's
autobiographical significance and Kazan's sympathy
for the immigrant's plight.(12, 20). Greeks and
Hawaiians have been mentioned in audience surveys,
and Dutch images have been catalogued for one
film.(13, 17, 22). Setting, as an influence on
ethnic presence, has included both Hawaiians and
Louisiana Cajuns.(21, 23). But, again, the research
to date remains preoccupied with listing instances
of appearance for particular groups, rather than
essaying any group's cultural significance or
linking any group with patterns of mass-mediated
image making. Almost invisible on screen, the other
groups are but dimly and rarely seen in research as
well.

Major discussions of films and/or television
shows include: America, America (12, 20), An Apple,
An Orange (13), The Emigrants (26), The Emperor
Jones (6, 11), Evangeline (23), Louisiana Story
(23), Mama (25), Sanders of the River (3), Southern
Comfort (23), and the Tarzan series (2, 4, 7-9).

AFRICANS

1. Dooley, Roger. FROM SCARFACE TO SCARLETT (item I-41).

2. Essoe, Gabe. TARZAN OF THE MOVIES: A PICTO-RIAL HISTORY OF MORE THAN FIFTY YEARS OF EDGAR RICE BURROUGHS' LEGENDARY HERO. Secaucus, N.J.: Citadel, 1973.

3. Kamphausen, Hannes. "Cinema in Africa: A Survey." CINEASTE 5 (Summer 1972): 29-41.

4. Lee, Ray, and Vernell Coriell. A PICTORIAL HISTORY OF THE TARZAN MOVIES. Los Angeles, Cal.: Golden State News, 1966.

5. McKinley, Edward H. THE LURE OF AFRICA: AMERICAN INTERESTS IN TROPICAL AFRICA, 1919-1939. Indianapolis: Bobbs-Merrill Company, 1974.

6. Maynard, Richard A., ed. AFRICA ON FILM: MYTH AND REALITY. Rochelle Park, N.J.: Hayden Book Company, 1974.

7. Nesteby, James R. BLACK IMAGES IN AMERICAN FILMS, 1896-1954. (item II-466).

8. _____. "The Tarzan Series of Edgar Rice Burroughs." (item II-467).

9. _____. "The Tenuous Vine of Tarzan of the Apes." J OF POPULAR CULTURE 13 (Spring 1980): 483-87.

10. Okoye, Felix N. THE AMERICAN IMAGE OF AFRICA: MYTH AND REALITY. Buffalo, N.Y.: Black Academy Press, 1971.

11. Opubur, Alfred E., and Adeyayo Ogunbi. "Ooga Booga: The African Image in American Films." OTHER VOICES, OTHER VIEWS: AN INTERNATIONAL COLLECTION OF ESSAYS FROM THE BICENTENNIAL. Edited by Robin W. Winks. Westport: Greenwood Press, 1978, pp. 343-75.

ARMENIANS

12. Ciment, Michel. KAZAN ON KAZAN. New York:
    Viking Press, 1974.

DUTCH

13. Berry, Myron. "No Way Out and An Apple, An
    Orange." RACE AND ETHNICITY IN THE HISTORY
    OF THE AMERICAS (item I-36), pp. 49-50.

EAST INDIANS

14. Dooley, Roger. FROM SCARFACE TO SCARLETT
    (item I-41).

GREEKS

15. Ciment, Michel. KAZAN ON KAZAN (item XII-12).

16. Hurley, Neil P., S.J. "Using Motion Pictures
    to Aid Inter-Cultural Communication." (item
    II-336).

17. Jeffres, Leo W., and K. Kyoon Hur. "White
    Ethnics and Their Media Images." (item I-
    72).

18. Kane, Kathryn. VISIONS OF WAR (item I-76).

19. Kelly, Katie. MY PRIME TIME (item I-79).

20. Pauly, Thomas H. AN AMERICAN ODYSSEY: ELIA
    KAZAN AND AMERICAN CULTURE. Philadelphia:
    Temple University Press, 1983.

HAWAIIANS

21. Schmitt, Robert C. "Movies in Hawaii, 1897-
    1932." HAWAIIAN J OF HISTORY 1 (1967): 73-
    82.

22. Seggar, John F., and Penny Wheeler. "The
    World of Work on TV." (item I-133).

LOUISIANA CAJUNS

23. Schuth, H. Wayne. "The Images of Louisiana in

Film and Television." SOUTHERN Q 23 (Fall 1984): 5-17.

NORWEGIANS

24. Roddick, Nick. A NEW DEAL IN ENTERTAINMENT (item I-124).

25. Wilk, Max. THE GOLDEN AGE OF TELEVISION: NOTES FROM THE SURVIVORS. New York: Delacorte Press, 1976.

SWEDES

26. Miller, Randall M. "American History Through Film: The Immigrant Experience." (item I-104).

TURKS

27. Ciment, Michel. KAZAN ON KAZAN (item XII-12).

AUTHOR INDEX

(The numbers following each listing refer to the chapter number and the item number. Thus, 6-2 refers to chapter VI, item 2.)

Abadie Aicardi, Anibal,
    7-2
Abeles, Ronald P.,
    2-636
Adair, Gilbert, 4-3
Adams, Michael, 2-36
Adatto, Kiku, 1-4
Adler, Renata, 2-37, 38
Adler, Richard P., 1-5;
    2-39
Affron, Mirella J., 9-1
Aitken, Roy E., 2-40
Alexander, Francis W.,
    2-41
Allen, Bonnie, 2-42, 3
Allen, Richard L.,
    2-44, 45; 7-3
Allen, William, 7-4
Allsopp, Ralph N., 2-46
Alter, R., 10-1
Alvarez, Michael, 2-47
Anderson, Carolyn,
    2-231
Andrews, Hannah Page
    Wheeler, 2-48
Angelus, Ted, 2-49
Annenberg, Wallis,
    1-87; 2-394
Archer, Leonard, C.,
    2-50
Arenstein, Howard L.,
    2-51
Arlen, Michael J., 1-6;
    2-52, 53, 54
Armas, Jose, 7-5

Armour, Robert A., 2-55
Arvey, Verna, 2-56
Asante, Molefi Kete
    (Arthur L. Smith),
    2-57
Asendio, James, 2-58
Ashton, Charlotte R.,
    2-59
Asian Americans for a
    Fair Media, 4-4
Astor, Gerald, 1-7;
    11-3
Astro, Richard, 7-51
Atkin, Charles K.,
    2-284, 557; 7-27
Auster, Albert, 1-8,
    119; 5-1: 9-2
Averson, Richard,
    1-166; 2-625; 6-75;
    10-99; 11-79
Axthelm, Kenneth W.,
    1-9

Baerg, James R., 3-1
Baker, Melva Joyce,
    2-60; 4-5; 6-1
Baldwin, James, 2-61,
    62, 63
Ball, Sandra J., 2-380
Ball-Rokeach, Sandra
    J., 2-64
Balon, Robert, 2-65
Balsley, Daisy, 2-66

Banks, Cherry A. McGee,
    2-67
Baptista-Fernandez,
    Pilar, 7-27
Barber, Rowland, 11-4
Barcus, F. Earle, 2-68
Barnouw, Erik, 1-10;
    2-69
Barrow, William, 2-70
Barry, Iris, 2-71
Barshay, Robert, 4-6;
    5-2
Bart, Peter, 2-72
Barthel, Joan, 2-73
Bataille, Gretchen M.,
    11-5, 6, 7, 8, 9,
    10, 11, 66
Beale, Lewis, 11-12
Beaupree, Lee, 2-74, 75
Becker, Samuel, 1-11
Belafonte, Harry, 2-76
Beloff, M., 10-2
Belth, Nathan C., 1-12
Benchley, Robert, 2-77
Bennett, Lerone, Jr.,
    2-78
Bennett, Rex, 2-191
Berg, Charles M., 2-79
Berger, Arthur Asa,
    1-13; 4-7; 5-3; 7-6
Bergman, Andrew, 1-14;
    2-80; 5-4; 9-3
Bergsten, Bebe, 1-15
Berk, Lynn M., 1-16;
    2-81
Berkhofer, Robert F.,
    Jr., 1-16; 11-13
Berkman, Dave, 2-82
Bernstein, Gene, 11-14
Berry, Gordon L., 1-17,
    18; 2-83, 84; 9-4
Berry, Myron, 12-13
Biberman, Herbert, 7-7
Birdwell, A. E., 2-567
Birtha, Rachel, 2-85
Biskind, Peter, 1-19;
    2-86; 7-8; 9-5

Black, Doris, 2-87
Black, Gregory D.,
    1-82; 5-24; 6-2, 3,
    32
Blakefield, William J.,
    4-8
Blakey, Carla M., 11-15
Bloom, Samuel W., 2-88
Bloomquist, Linda
    Edwards, 2-480
Bogart, Leo, 2-89
Bogle, Donald, 2-90,
    91, 92, 93
Bond, Jean Carey, 2-94,
    95
Boskin, Joseph, 1-20;
    2-96
Bourne, St. Clair, 2-97
Bower, Robert T., 2-98
Bowmani, Kwame Nyerere,
    2-99
Bowser, Pearl, 1-21;
    2-100, 101
Boyd, Malcolm, 2-102
Brauer, Donna, 1-22;
    11-16
Brauer, Ralph, 1-22;
    11-16
Brazaitis, Thomas J.,
    1-23; 5-5; 9-6
Breitenfield,
    Frederick, Jr., 1-24
Brennan, William J.,
    8-1
Brigham, John C., 2-103
Bright, Hazel V., 2-104
Brizzolara, Andrew, 9-7
Brossard, Chandler,
    2-637
Broun, Heywood Hale,
    2-105
Brown, Cecil, 2-106
Brown, Les, 1-25
Brown, Roscoe C., Jr.,
    2-107, 108
Brown, Sterling A.,
    2-109

Brown, Tony, 2-131
Browne, Louis Alban,
  2-110
Browne, Sherryl, 2-211
Brownfeld, Allan C.,
  2-111
Brownlow, Kevin, 2-112;
  6-4; 11-17
Brunette, Peter, 2-113
Buchanan, Singer A.,
  2-114
Burgoon, Judee K., 7-28
Burgoon, Michael, 7-28
Burke, Frank, 4-9; 5-6
Burke, William Lee,
  2-115
Burrell, Walter, 2-116
Bush, Ronald F., 2-117
Butler, Ivan, 6-5

Cagin, Seth, 9-8
Calder, Jenni, 11-18
Callenbach, Ernest,
  11-19
Cameron, Earl, 2-118
Campbell, Edward D. C.,
  Jr., 2-119, 120, 121
Campbell, Leon G.,
  1-36; 7-13, 14
Campbell, Russell, 10-3
Canby, Vincent, 2-123,
  124; 9-9
Cantor, Muriel G., 1-26
Capra, Frank, 2-125
Carew, Jean V., 2-493
Carey, Gary, 10-4
Carey, James W., 2-126
Carpenter, Sandra,
  2-127
Carringer, Robert, 10-5
Carter, Earl, 2-128
Carter, Elmer, 2-129
Carter, Everett, 2-130
Carter, Virginia, 2-131

Castleman, Harry, 1-27;
  9-10
Cawelti, John G.,
  2-132; 10-6; 11-20,
  21
Ceplair, Larry, 5-7
Chaffee, Steven, 1-31;
  2-146
Champlin, Charles,
  1-28; 2-133, 134
Chan, Kenyon, 4-10
Chappell, Fred, 2-135
Chappeta, Roberta, 9-11
Charren, Peggy, 2-136
Chaudhuri, Arun Kumar,
  2-137
Chicano Resource
  Center, 7-9
Chin, Frank, 4-11
Choy, Christine, 4-12,
  13
Churchill, Ward, 11-22
Ciment, Michel, 12-12,
  15, 27
Clarens, Carlos, 9-12,
  13; 10-7
Clark, Cedric C., 1-29
Clark, Dennis J., 8-2,
  3
Clarke, David E., 2-45;
  7-3
Clift, Virgil A., 2-405
Coakley, Mary Lewis,
  1-30
Cobbey, Robin E., 1-32;
  2-147, 148
Cody, Iron Eyes, 11-23
Cohen, Elliot E., 10-8,
  9
Cohen, Henry, 8-4
Cohen, Sarah Blacher,
  10-10
Cole, Nat King, 2-138
Coleman, Willette,
  2-139
Colle, Royal D., 2-140,
  141

Collier, Eugenia,
    2-142, 143, 144
Comer, James, 2-145
Comstock, George A.,
    1-31, 32, 33; 2-146,
    147, 148, 460
Congressional Black
    Caucus, 2-149
Connor, Edward, 4-14
Conroy, Hilary, 4-14
Cook, Bruce, 2-150
Coppa, Frank J., 2-454
Cordasco, Francesco,
    7-10
Coriell, Vernell, 12-4
Corliss, Richard, 2-151
Corporation for Public
    Broadcasting, 2-152
Cortes, Carlos F.,
    1-34, 35, 36; 7-11,
    12, 13, 14
Couch, William Jr.,
    2-153
Coverdale, Herbert L.,
    2-154
Cowan, Geoffrey, 2-155
Cripps, Thomas R.,
    1-37; 2-156, 157,
    158, 159, 160, 161,
    162, 163, 164, 165,
    166, 167, 168, 169,
    170, 171, 172, 173,
    174, 175, 176, 177,
    178, 179, 180, 181,
    182, 183, 184, 185;
    7-15; 10-11; 11-24
Cross, Donna Woolfolk,
    1-38
Crowdus, Gary, 2-186
Crowther, Bosley,
    2-187, 188, 189
Cruse, Harold, 2-190
Culbert, David, 2-185;
    5-8, 9
Culley, James D., 2-191
Curtis, James C., 2-172
Curtis, Ted, 7-29

Curtiss, Thomas Quinn,
    6-6
Curtwright, Wesley,
    2-192
Cutter, William, 10-12

Damon, Susan, 2-193
Darrach, Brad, 2-194
Dates, Jannette,
    2-195, 196, 197
Davidson, Bill, 6-8;
    7-16
Davidson, Emily S.,
    2-209, 404
Davies, Philip, 1-39
Davis, George, 2-198
Davis, Ossie, 2-199,
    200, 201
de Grazia, Edward,
    2-40; 2-202; 5-10;
    6-8
DelGaudio, Sybil, 2-203
De Leon, Arnoldo, 7-17
De Usabel, Gaizka S.,
    7-18, 19
Deloria, Vine, Jr.
    10-13
Delpar, Helen, 7-20
Dempsey, Michael,
    2-204; 4-15
Dent, Tom, 2-205
Dervin, Brenda, 2-285
Dessner, Lawrence J.,
    9-14
Diakite, Madubuko,
    2-206
Diamond, Sandor A.,
    10-14
Dismond, Geraldyn,
    2-207
Dittus, Erick, 4-17
Dominick, Joseph R.,
    2-208
Donagher, Patricia C.,
    2-209

Donalson, Melvin B.,
  2-210
Doneson, Judith E.,
  10-15
Dooley, Roger, 1-41;
  5-11; 8-5; 9-15;
  12-1, 14
Dorr, Aimee, 1-115;
  2-211
Doscher, Luelyne, 7-21
Dotort, David, 10-16
Douglas, Pamela, 2-212,
  213
Dozier, Carol, 2-587
Drake, Ross, 2-214
Dray, Philip, 9-8
Dreyfuss, Joel, 2-215
DuBois, W. E. B., 2-216
Duchineaux, Franklin,
  11-25
Duncan, John Thomas,
  7-46
Duncan, Pamela, 9-
  16
Durgnat, Raymond, 4-18
Dworkin, Martin S.,
  2-217; 6-9

Easley, Larry J., 2-218
Eastman, Harvey A.,
  2-219; 7-22
Ebert, Alan, 2-220
Eckhardt, Joseph P.,
  10-17, 18
Eckles, Gary, 2-231
Efron, Edith, 1-42;
  2-221, 222; 11-26
Eiselein, E. B., 7-23,
  46
Eliot, Marc, 1-43; 9-17
Ellis, Kirk, 11-27
Ellison, Mary, 2-223
Ellison, Ralph, 2-224
Elliston, Maxine Hall,
  2-225

Emery, Michael C., 7-29
Englund, Steven, 5-7
Epstein, Benjamin R.,
  1-44; 9-18; 10-19
Epstein, Edward, 6-48
Erens, Patricia, 10-20,
  21, 22, 23, 24
Essoe, Gabe, 12-2
Everson, William K.,
  1-45, 46; 2-226;
  5-12; 6-10;
  11-28
Ewen, Elizabeth, 1-47

Fabre, Michel, 2-227
Farber, Stephen, 9-19,
  20; 10-25
Fay, Stephen, 2-228
Fenin, George N., 11-28
Ferguson, Richard D.,
  Jr., 2-229
Ferretti, Fred, 9-21
Fiedler, Leslie A.,
  2-230; 10-26
Fine, Marlene G., 2-231
Finler, Joel W., 6-11
Fiore, Mary, 9-70
Fishbein, Leslie, 2-232
Flamini, Roland, 2-233
Fledelius, Karsten,
  10-84
Fleener, Nickie, 2-234
Fleener-Marzec, Nickie-
  ann, 2-235
Fletcher, Alan D.,
  2-236, 237
Foner, Eric, 1-48
Fontes, Brian F., 2-317
Foster, Joseph, 2-238
Fox, Stuart, 10-27
Fox, Terry Curtis, 5-13
Franchione, Philip,
  1-57
Franklin, Oliver,
  2-239, 240

Freehling, William W.,
    2-241
French, Brandon, 8-6
French, Philip, 2-242;
    11-29, 30
French, Warren, 2-243
Friar, Natasha, 11-32
Friar, Ralph, 11-31, 32
Friedman, Lawrence J.,
    2-244
Friedman, Lester,
    10-28, 29, 30
Friedman, Murray,
    10-18, 31
Friedman, Norman L.,
    2-245; 10-32, 33
Friedman, R. M., 10-34
Frierich, H., 2-389
Fyne, Robert, 4-19;
    6-12

Gaber, Samuel Lewis,
    10-35
Galanes, Adriana Lewis,
    7-24
Gallagher, Brian, 2-246
Gamboa, Harry Jr., 7-25
Gamez Bogarin, Raul,
    7-46
Gans, Herbert J., 1-49;
    2-247
Garafola, Lynn, 1-8,
    50; 9-2, 22
Garfield, John, 2-248
Garland, Phyl, 2-249
Gehman, Richard, 2-250
Gelmis, Joseph, 9-23,24
Gentile, Frank, 1-51
Georgakas, Dan, 1-8;
    2-186; 9-2; 11-33
Gerbner, George, 1-52,
    53, 54; 2-251
Gerima, Haile, 2-252
Gerson, Mauricio, 1-55;
    7-26

Gerson, Walter, 2-253
Ghareeb, Edmund, 3-2
Gibbs, Vernon, 2-254
Giesbrecht, Linda W.,
    2-103
Gill, Glenda E., 2-255
Gillespie, Marcia Ann,
    2-256
Giordano, Joseph, 1-56,
    57; 9-25, 26, 27, 28
Gipson, D. Parke, 2-257
Gish, Lillian, 2-258
Gitlin, Todd, 1-58, 59;
    2-259, 260; 9-29
Gittens, Tony, 2-261
Gitter, George A.,
    2-229
Glaessner, Verina,
    2-262
Glatzer, Richard, 2-267
Glenn, Larry, 2-268
Goetz, Alice, 6-13
Golab, Caroline, 5-14
Goldberg, Albert L.,
    2-269, 270
Goldberg, Melvin A.,
    2-271
Golden, Daniel S.,
    9-30, 31
Goldfarb, Alvin, 6-14
Goldman, Eric A., 10-36
Goldson, Rose K., 1-60;
    9-32
Goldstein, Richard,
    4-20
Goldwyn, Ronald, 2-272
Gomery, Douglas, 2-273
Gordon, Neal J., 1-88
Gordon, Thomas F.,
    2-280
Gould, Louis L., 2-172
Gow, Gordon, 2-274
Gradwohl, David K.,
    11-66
Graf, Herbert, 2-392
Graham, Don, 11-58
Grant, Liz, 2-275
Granzberg, Gary, 11-34

Graves, Sherryl Browne,
    1-88; 2-276
Greeley, Andrew M.,
    9-33
Green, Marc, 9-20;
    10-25
Green, Theophilus,
    2-277
Greenberg, Bradley S.,
    1-61; 2-208, 278,
    279, 280, 281, 282,
    283, 284, 285, 314,
    557; 7-27, 28
Greenberg, Joel, 1-69;
    2-313; 4-23; 5-17;
    6-17; 9-40
Greene, Laura, 2-286
Grenier, Richard, 2-287
Griffith, D. W., 2-288
Griffith, Richard,
    1-62; 3-3; 6-15
Griggs, John, 6-48
Grillo, Jean Bergan-
    tini, 1-63; 9-34
Grisham, William F.,
    2-289
Gromada, Thaddeus V.,
    5-15
Gross, Barry, 10-37
Gross, Larry, 1-54;
    2-251, 290
Grube, Joel W., 2-64
Gulliver, Adelaide
    Cromwell, 2-291
Gunther, Max, 1-64
Gupta, Udayan, 2-204
Gutierrez, Felix, 7-29,
    30, 31, 32

Hafen, Jeffrey, 2-545
Hair, Joseph F., Jr.,
    2-117
Hairston, Loyle, 2-292
Hall, Jane, 1-65

Halliburton, Cecil D.,
    2-293
Halliday, Jon, 2-294
Hammond, Allen Steward,
    2-295
Hammond, John, 2-296
Handelman, Janet, 1-66
Hanks, Christopher C.,
    11-34
Hanna, David, 4-54, 57;
    6-78
Hanneman, Gerhard J.,
    2-281
Hannonen-Gladden, Helena,
    2-545
Hardwick, Leon H.,
    2-297
Harmetz, Aljean, 3-4
Harmon, Sidney, 2-298
Harrington, John, 11-35
Harrison, William,
    2-299
Hart, James, 2-300
Hartman, Hedy, 11-36
Hartung, Philip T.,
    2-301
Harwell, Richard, 2-302
Haskell, Molly, 2-303
Hayakawa, S. I., 2-304
Hayashi, Tetsumaro,
    7-51
Head, Sydney, 1-67;
    2-305
Heald, Gary Robert,
    2-306
Hechinger, Fred M.,
    10-38, 39
Heeter, C., 2-557
Helffrich, Stockton,
    1-68; 9-35
Hellenbrand, Harold,
    2-307
Hellman, John, 4-21;
    5-16
Henderson, Robert M.,
    2-308; 4-22; 6-16
Henry, William A. III,
    2-309

Hernton, Calvin C.,
   2-310
Herring, Robert, 2-311
Higgins, Patricia
   Beaulieu, 2-312
Higham, Charles, 1-69;
   2-313, 314; 4-23;
   5-17; 6-17; 10-40
Hill, Donald K., 2-315
Hill, Mary Ann, 11-22
Hill, Norbert, 11-22
Hill-Scott, Karen,
   2-316
Hinton, James L.,
   2-317, 475
Hirsch, Foster, 2-318
Hirschfelder, Arlene
   Boshes, 11-37
Hoberman, J., 2-319;
   10-39, 40
Hobson, Dick, 2-320
Hobson, Sheila Smith,
   2-321
Hoffman, William, 2-322
Hogan, Linda, 2-284
Holly, Ellen, 2-323,
   324
Horikawa, Herbert, 4-
   24
Horowitz, Robert F.,
   10-43
Hough, Arthur, 2-325
Howard, John, 2-326
Howe, Irving, 10-44
Howes, Paul W., 2-621
Hoyt, Edwin P., 2-327
Hudson, Michael C., 3-5
Huff, Theodore, 2-328
Hughes, Langston,
   2-329, 330
Hughes, William, 6-18
Hunt, Albert, 6-19
Hunter, Robert G.,
   2-331
Hur, K. Kyoon, 1-72;
   2-332, 333, 334;
   5-18, 19; 7-34; 8-7;

   9-38; 12-17
Hurd, Laura E., 2-335
Hurley, Neil P., S. J.,
   2-336; 7-33; 12-16
Hurst, Richard M., 6-20
Hutchins, Charles L.,
   2-337
Hutton, Paul A., 11-38
Hyatt, Marshall, 2-338

Ilan, Avisar, 10-45
Insdorf, Annette, 10-46
Isaac, Dan, 10-47
Isaacs, Harold R., 4-25
Isenberg, Michael T.,
   6-21, 22, 23

Jackson, Anthony W.,
   2-339
Jackson, Harold, 2-340
Jackson, Martin, 1-113
Jacobs, Diane, 9-36
Jacobs, Lewis, 1-70;
   2-616; 6-24, 25;
   9-37; 10-48
Jarvie, I. C., 1-71;
   2-341
Jeavons, Clyde, 6-26
Jeffres, Leo W., 1-72;
   5-18, 19; 7-34; 8-7;
   9-38; 12-17
Jeffries-Fox, Suzanne
   Kuulei, 2-342
Jerome, Victor Jeremy,
   2-343, 344
Jewell, Karen Sue
   Warren, 2-345
Johnson, Albert, 2-346,
   347
Johnson, Diana M.,
   9-39
Johnson, Penny, 3-6
Johnson, Robert K.,
   9-40

Johnson, Sherry, 2-348
Jones, Christopher
   John, 2-349
Jones, Dorothy B.,
   1-73; 4-26; 5-20
Jones, Ken D., 1-92
Jones, Marquita, 2-350
Jones, Robert, 2-351
Jordan, Vernon E., Jr.,
   2-352
Joseph, Gloria, 2-353
Joseph, Robert, 6-27
Jouhaud, C., 2-354
Jowett, Garth S., 1-74,
   90; 2-355; 5-21;
   6-28; 8-8
Juliani, Richard N.,
   9-41
Jurewicz, Edward J.,
   1-75

Kael, Pauline, 2-356;
   10-49
Kagan, Norman, 2-357,
   358, 359, 360
Kaiser, Ernest, 2-361,
   362, 498
Kakutani, Michiko,
   10-50
Kalson, Alfred E.,
   2-363
Kaminsky, Stuart M.,
   9-42
Kamphausen, Hannes,
   12-3
Kane, Kathryn Rose,
   1-76, 77; 4-27;
   5-22; 6-29; 8-9;
   9-43; 10-51; 12-18
Kanin, Josh, 10-52
Karp, David, 1-78
Karpf, Stephen L., 9-44
Kassarjian, Waltraud
   M., 2-364

Katzman, Natan, 1-1;
   2-146
Kauffman, Stanley,
   2-365
Kaufmann, Donald L.,
   11-39
Kayser, Hans Christoph,
   6-30, 31
Kelley, Samuel
   Lawrence, 2-366
Kelly, Katie, 1-79;
   5-23; 12-19
Kelly, Mary Pat, 9-45
Kendall, Martha, 11-40
Keshena, Martha, 11-41
Killens, John Oliver,
   2-367, 368
Kim, Elaine H., 4-28
Kirby, Jack Temple,
   1-80; 2-369, 370;
   9-46
Kisner, Ronald E.,
   2-371
Klapp, Orrin, 1-81
Kliger, Hannah, 10-50,
   53
Kliman, Bernice W.,
   2-372
Klotman, Phyllis Rauch,
   2-373
Knight, Arthur, 2-374,
   375
Koiner, Richard B.,
   2-376
Kolker, Robert P., 9-47
Koppes, Clayton R.,
   1-82; 5-24; 6-2, 3,
   32
Korzenny, Felipe, 7-28
Koszarski, Richard,
   6-33
Kowall, Linda, 10-15,
   16
Kracauer, Siegfried,
   1-83; 5-25, 26; 6-34
Kraus, Sidney, 2-377
Krohn, Lewis G., 8-10;
   10-51, 54

Kronenberger, Louis,
    2-418, 419; 10-53,
    57
Kucharski, Jerzy S.,
    5-27
Kurnitz, Harry, 1-84;
    6-35; 9-48
Kusielewicz, Eugene,
    5-28

Lamb, Blaine P., 7-36
Landay, Eileen, 2-378
Landry, Robert J.,
    1-85, 86; 2-379;
    6-36
Lange, David L., 2-380
Langellier, John
    Philip, 11-42
Langer, Lawrence L.,
    10-52, 55
Lapsansky, Emma Jones,
    2-381
Larkins, Robert, 11-43
LaRuffa,Anthony L.,
    9-49
Laufer, Joseph M., 7-37
Lavine, Harold, 6-37
Lawson, John Howard,
    2-382, 383
Leab, Daniel, 2-384,
    385, 386, 387, 388,
    389, 390, 391, 392,
    393; 5-29; 6-38, 39;
    9-50
League of United Latin
    American Citizens
    (LULAC), 7-38
Leahy, Michael, 1-87;
    2-394
Leckenby, John D.,
    2-395, 396
Lee, Don L., 2-397
Lee, Ray, 12-4
Lehman, Peter, 4-29;
    5-30

Leifer, Aimee Dorr,
    1-88
Leites, Nathan, 2-638
Lemon, Judith, 2-398
Lemon, Richard, 2-399
Lemons, Stanley J.,
    2-400
Lenihan, John, 11-45
Leonard, John, 7-39
Lesage, Julia, 4-30
Leutrat, Jean-Louis,
    11-46
Levinson, Richard,
    1-89; 2-401; 3-7;
    7-40
Lewels, Francisco J.,
    7-41
Lewis, Jill, 2-353
Lewis, Richard Warren,
    2-402, 403
Lichter, Linda, 9-51
Lichter, S. Robert,
    9-51
Liebert, Robert M.,
    2-209, 404
Limon, Jose E., 7-42
Lingeman, Richard R.,
    6-40
Link, William, 1-89;
    2-401; 3-7; 7-40
Linton, James M., 1-90
Liss, Marsha B., 2-219;
    7-22
Loomis, James W., 2-622
Low, W. Augustus, 2-405
Loy, Jane, 7-43, 44
Luft, Herbert G., 10-56
Lynch, William J., 8-3
Lyons, Timothy J., 6-41

McAlpin, Sally T.,
    5-31; 9-52
McBride, Joseph, 2-406
McCabe, Bruce, 2-407
McClure, Arthur F., 1-
    91, 92; 2-409; 6-42

McCombs, Maxwell, 1-31;
2-146
MacConkey, Dorothy
Ingling, 2-408
McCormick, Ruth, 7-45
McCray, Charles, Jr.,
2-410; 5-32
McCreary, Eugene, 1-93
McDermott, Steven
Thomas, 2-411
MacDonald, J. Fred,
2-412, 413
MacDonald, Susan
Schwartz, 2-414
McFarland, Ronald-
Bryant, 2-415
McGilligan, Patrick,
2-416
McKerns, Joseph P.,
2-417
McKinley, Edward H.,
12-5
McManus, John T.,
2-418, 419; 10-53,
57
MacDougall, David, 1-94
Maloney, Martin, 2-420
Maltby, Richard, 1-95;
2-421; 10-54, 58
Manchel, Frank, 1-96
Mandelbaum, Juan Pedro,
1-97; 9-53
Mander, Jerry, 1-98
Mankiewicz, Frank,
2-422
Mantell, Harold, 11-47
Manvell, Roger, 6-43
Mapp, Edward, 2-423,
424, 425, 426, 427
Marc, David, 1-99
Mariani, John, 6-44;
9-54
Marion, Denis, 6-45
Marsden, Michael, 11-48
Marshall, Pluria, 2-428
Marshall, Wes, 7-46
Martin, Bruce A., 2-429

Martinez, Eliud, 7-47
Mason, B. J., 2-430
Mason, Clifford, 2-431
May, Elaine Tyler,
10-55, 56, 59, 60
May, Lary L., 10-56, 60
Mayer, Arthur, 1-62; 3-3;
6-15
Mayer, Martin, 1-100
Maynard, Richard A.,
2-432, 433; 12-6
Mazingo, Sherrie L.,
1-61; 2-282
Meehan, Diana M., 2-434
Melischek, Gabriele,
2-290
Mellen, Joan, 2-435, 436;
4-31; 8-11; 11-49
Meltzer, Milton, 2-330
Mendelsohn, Harold,
1-101
Menig, Harry W., 1-126;
9-65
Merritt, Bishetta D.,
2-437
Merritt, M., 2-438
Merritt, Russell,
2-439, 440
Messerschmid, Felix,
6-46
Metzger, Charles R.,
2-441
Michalak, Laurence, 3-8
Michel, Sonya, 10-57,
61
Michener, Charles,
2-442
Middleton, Russell,
1-102; 10-58, 62
Miller, Jim, 7-48
Miller, Loren, 2-443,
444
Miller, Mark Crispin,
1-103
Miller, Randall M.,
1-104, 105, 106;
10-59, 63; 12-26
Miller, S. M., 1-51

Miller, Tom, 7-49
Mills, Jon, 2-445
Mistron, Deborah, 7-50
Mitchell, Charles, 6-47
Mitchell-Kernan,
  Claudia, 1-18; 2-84
Moloney, Mick, 8-12
Monaco, James, 1-107;
  2-446, 447; 9-55;
  10-60, 64
Moore, Melvin M., Jr.,
  2-448
Morella, Joe, 6-48
Morgan, Michael, 1-54
Morrow, Lance, 2-449
Morsberger Robert, 2-
  450, 451; 6-49;
  7-51
Morsy, Soheir, 3-9
Moskowitz, Suree, 4-32
Moss, Carlton, 2-452,
  453
Moss, Robert, 10-61, 65
Muccigrosso, Robert,
  2-454
Murphy, Sharon, 11-50
Murray, Edward, 8-13
Murray, James P.,
  2-455, 456, 457,
  458, 459
Murray, John P., 2-460

Nachbar, Jack, 11-48,
  51, 52
Nahm, Tom Kagy, 4-33
Naremore, James, 8-14
Nash, Gary B., 2-96
Nasir, Sari J., 3-10,
  11
National Association
  for the Advancement
  of Colored People,
  2-461, 462
Neal, Larry, 2-463
Neale, John M., 2-404

Neale, Steve, 1-108
Nelsen, Anne K., 2-464
Nelsen, Hart M., 2-464
Nelson, Al P., 2-40
Nelson, Richard Alan,
  2-465
Nesteby, James R.,
  2-466, 467; 12-7, 8,
  9
Neve, Brian, 1-39
Newcomb, Horace, 2-468
Newman, Roger K., 1-40;
  2-202; 5-9; 6-7
Newton, Huey P., 2-469
Newton, Ray, 11-53
Nobile, Philip, 1-109
Noble, Gil, 2-470, 471
Noble, Grant, 1-110
Noble, Peter, 2-472,
  473; 6-50
Nobles, Wade, 2-131
Nolan, William E.,
  2-474
Northcott, Herbert C.,
  2-317, 475
Novak, Michael, 1-111
Null, Gary, 2-476

Obatala, J. K., 2-477
O'Brien, Adrienne,
  2-478
O'Connor, John E.,
  1-112, 113; 11-54,
  55
O'Connor, John J.,
  10-62; 66
O'Dell, Paul, 1-114;
  2-479
O'Donnell, Victoria,
  11-56
Oehling, Richard A.,
  4-34, 35; 6-51, 52,
  53, 54
Ogunbi, Adeyayo, 12-11
O'Hallaren, Bill, 4-36

O'Kelly, Charlotte G.,
  2-480
Okoye, Felix N., 12-10
O'Neal, Mary, 2-481
Opubur, Alfred E.,
  12-11
Oshana, Maryann, 11-57

Paik, Irvin, 4-37
Pally, Marcia, 10-63,
  67
Palmer, Edward L.,
  1-115
Pandiani, John A.,
  2-482
Papaleo, Joseph, 9-56
Paperny, David Charles,
  2-483
Parenti, Michael, 9-57
Parker, Jerry, 9-58
Patterson, Lindsay, 2-
  484, 485, 486, 487,
  488
Paul, William, 5-33
Pauly, Thomas H., 12-20
Peary, Gerald, 2-113;
  9-59, 60
Peavy, Charles, 2-489
Pechter, William, 9-61
Peck, Jeff, 5-34
Perlmutter, Ruth,
  10-64, 65, 68, 69
Perlmutter, Tom, 6-55
Perret, Marion D.,
  10-66, 70
Perry, Lincoln, 2-490
Peters, Art, 2-491
Peterson, Bernard L.,
  Jr., 2-492
Peterson, Ruth C.,
  1-116; 5-35; 6-56
Pettit, Arthur G.,
  7-52, 53
Phelps, Erin, 2-211

Pierce, Chester M.,
  2-493
Pierce-Gonzalez, Diane,
  2-493
Pileggi, Nicholas, 9-62
Pilkington, William T.,
  11-58
Pinchot, Ann, 2-258
Pines, Jim, 2-494, 495,
  496
Pinger, Robert, 7-14
Pinsker, Sanford,
  10-67, 71
Pinsky, Mark I., 2-497
Pinto, Alfonso, 7-54
Platt, David, 10-68, 72
Plocha, Edward F., 5-36
Ploski, Harry A., 2-498
Plotkin, Lawrence,
  2-499, 500, 501, 502
Plummer, Joseph T.,
  2-542
Podrazik, Walter J.,
  1-27; 9-10
Poindexter, Paula M.,
  2-503
Poitier, Sidney, 2-504,
  505
Popkin, Henry, 2-506;
  10-69, 73
Popp, Lorraine B., 7-55
Potamkin, Harry A.,
  2-507
Poulos, Rita W., 2-209
Pounds, Michael C.,
  2-508
Poussaint, Alvin F.,
  2-509
Powers, Anne, 2-510
Powers, John, 1-117;
  7-56
Pozner, Vladimir, 1-118
Prelutsky, Burt, 2-511
Price, John A., 11-59
Protinsky, Ruth, 2-512
Pugh, D., 2-501

Puner, Morton, 1-12
Purdy, Jim, 1-125;
    2-528, 529; 5-38,
    39; 6-59
Puzo, Mario, 9-63
Pyron, Darden Asbury,
    2-513

Quart, Barbara, 1-120
Quart, Leonard, 1-8,
    119, 120; 5-1; 9-2,
    64

Rabinow, Paul, 9-64
Rabinowitz, Dorothy,
    2-514
Raddatz, Leslie, 2-515;
    4-38
Raeburn, John, 2-267
Rainer, Peter, 3-12
Ramirez, Arthur, 7-57
Ramsaye, Terry, 1-121;
    2-516; 6-57
Ransom, Jo, 1-122
Raths, Louis, 10-70, 74
Ray, Marla Wilson,
    2-312
Real, Michael, 1-123
Reddick, Lawrence D.,
    2-517
Reeves, Byron, 2-283
Reid, P. M., 2-518
Reimers, K. F., 2-389
Reina Schement, Jorge,
    7-32
Ribalow, M. Z., 10-71,
    75
Rice, Susan, 11-60
Rife, Marilyn Diane,
    2-519
Riley, Clayton, 2-520,
    521, 522

Roberts, Churchill,
    2-523
Roberts, Donald, 1-31;
    2-146
Robertson, Stanley,
    2-131, 524
Robinson, John P.,
    2-333
Robinson, Louie, 2-525
Robinson, Matt, 2-526
Roddick, Nick, 1-124;
    2-527; 5-37; 6-58;
    9-65; 12-24
Roffman, Peter, 1-125;
    2-528, 529; 5-38, 39;
    6-59
Rokeach, Milton, 2-64,
    603; 5-44
Rollins, Peter C.,
    1-126; 2-530; 9-66
Romdhani, Oussama, 3-13
Romero, Patricia W.,
    2-486
Ronan, Margaret, 2-531
Rook, Timothy E., 1-127
Rose, Willie Lee, 2-532
Rosen, Irvin C., 10-72,
    76
Rosen, Marjorie, 2-533
Rosenbaum, Eileen,
    2-378
Rosenberg, Elaine,
    2-534
Rosenfeld, Alvin H.,
    10-73, 77
Rosengren, Karl Erik,
    2-290
Rosow, Eugene, 1-128;
    9-67
Rothbart, George, 2-326
Rubenstein, Eli A.,
    2-460, 566
Rubenstein, Lenny, 6-60
Rubin, Bernard, 1-129
Rubin, Steven Ray, 4-39
Rushdie, Salman, 4-40
Ryan, Desmond, 7-58

Ryan, Michael, 2-535

Sadoux, Jean Jacques,
  11-61
Sampson, Harry T.,
  2-536
Samuels, Stuart, 10-74,
  78
Sandeen, Eric, 6-61
Sandler, Martin W.,
  2-136
Sarf, Wayne M., 11-62
Sarris, Andrew, 2-537,
  538; 6-62; 8-15;
  9-68; 10-75, 79;
  11-63
Sauberli, Harry A.,
  1-130; 6-63
Sayre, Nora, 1-131
Schary, Dore, 10-76, 80
Schatz, J., 10-77, 81
Schechner, Mark, 10-79,
  83
Schickel, Richard,
  2-539, 540; 6-64
Schiller, Herbert I.,
  2-541
Schlesinger, Arthur,
  Jr., 1-132
Schlinger, Mary Jane,
  2-542
Schmitt, Robert, 12-21
Schuth, H. Wayne, 12-23
Scott, Vernon, 9-69
See, Carolyn, 2-543
Seggar, John F., 1-133;
  2-317, 475, 544,
  545, 546; 4-41;
  7-59; 12-22
Senbert, Emelia, 11-78
Shadoian, Jack, 9-70
Shaheen, Jack G., 3-14,
  15, 16, 17, 18, 19,
  20, 21, 22, 23, 24,
  25, 26, 27, 28, 29

Shain, Russell Earl,
  1-134; 5-40; 6-65
Shales, Tom, 2-547,
  548; 11-64
Shatzkin, Roger, 2-113
Shavelson, Melville,
  10-78, 82
Shaw, David, 11-65
Shaw, Ellen Torgeson,
  2-549
Shayon, Robert Lewis,
  2-550
Shepard, Thom, 2-551
Shindler, Colin, 1-135;
  6-66
Shook, Mollie Stella
  Wiggins, 2-552
Short, Bobby, 2-553
Short, K. R. M., 2-161,
  179; 6-67; 10-80,
  81, 82, 84, 85, 86
Shosteck, Herschel,
  2-554
Shulman, Arthur, 1-136
Sidney, P. Jay, 2-555
Siegel, Fred, 1-8; 9-2
Signorielli, Nancy,
  1-53, 137
Silet, Charles L. P.,
  11-6, 7, 8, 9, 10,
  11, 66
Silverman, Joan M.,
  2-556
Simmons, Ed, 10-87
Simmons, Katrina W.,
  2-284, 557
Simonoski, T., 11-67
Sinclair, Andrew, 8-16;
  11-68
Singer, David, 10-83,
  88
Sinicropi, Giovanni,
  9-71
Skinner, James M.,
  5-41; 6-68; 11-69
Sklar, Robert, 1-138,
  139; 2-558, 559,
  560; 9-72, 73

Slide, Anthony, 1-114;
2-604; 4-47; 8-17
Sloan, Lee, 2-326
Sloan, Margaret, 2-561
Sloan, William J.,
2-562
Slout, William, 2-563
Small, Melvin, 1-140;
5-42, 43
Smith, Gaines, 2-564
Smith, James R., 11-70
Smith, Julian, 4-42
Smith, Philip Jr.,
11-71
Soderbergh, Peter A.,
6-69
Soja, Matthew J., 2-622
Solomon, Paul J., 2-117
Soriano, Michael
Esteban, 2-565; 7-60
Spears, Jack, 11-72
Spiegel, Alan, 10-84,
89
Sprafkin, Joyce N.,
2-566
Stafford, J. E., 2-567
Stam, Robert, 2-568
Stappers, James, 2-290
Stavins, Ralph L.,
2-569, 570
Stebbins, Robert, 2-
571
Stedman, Raymond W.,
1-141; 11-73
Steele, Richard W.,
6-70
Stein, Benjamin, 1-142
Stein, Elliott, 6-71
Stein, Howard F.,
1-143, 144
Steinbring, Jack, 11-34
Stephens, Lenora C.,
2-572
Stern, Seymour, 2-573
Sterritt, David, 1-145
Stevens, John D., 2-574
Stewart, Ted, 2-575

Still, William Grant,
2-576, 577
Stoloff, David L.,
1-146
Stone, Arthur, 2-566
Strick, Philip, 9-74
Stroman, Carolyn A.,
2-503, 578
Strong, Lester, 2-579
Stuck, Rona, 11-74
Suber, Howard, 1-147; 10-
85, 86, 90, 91, 92
Sugy, Catherine, 2-580
Suid, Lawrence, 4-43,
44; 6-72
Surlin, Stuart H.,
2-396, 581
Sweeper, George
Wilson, 2-582
Swerdlow, Joel, 2-422
Swertlow, Frank, 2-583

Tajima, Renee, 4-46
Tan, Alexis S., 1-148;
2-584, 585; 4-45;
7-61
Tan, Gerdean, 2-585
Tavares De Sa, Hernane,
7-62
Taylor, Clyde, 2-586
Taylor, Henry, 2-587
Taylor, John Russell,
6-73
Thoene, Bodie, 11-74
Thomer, Penny, 2-588
Thompson, Era Bell,
2-589
Thomson, David, 2-590;
9-75, 76
Thurstone, L. L.,
1-116; 5-35; 6-56
Toeplitz, Jerzy, 1-149;
9-77
Toland, John, 6-74;
10-87, 93
Toll, Robert C., 1-150;
2-591; 9-78

Toplin, Robert Brent,
    2-592
Townley, Rod, 7-63
Trager, Frank N.,
    10-70, 74
Troupe, Quincy, 2-640
Trumbo, Dalton, 2-593,
    594
Tugend, Tom, 10-88, 94
Tunstall, Jeremy,
    1-151, 152; 2-595;
    7-64; 10-89, 95
Turan, Kenneth, 10-90,
    96
Turner, John W., 11-75
Turow, Joseph, 1-153
Tuska, Jon, 11-76
Twomey, Alfred E., 1-92
Tyner, Howard A., 1-154

Unger, Arthur, 1-155
U. S. Commission on
    Civil Rights, 1-156,
    157, 158, 159;
    2-596, 597, 598,
    599; 4-47, 48, 49
U. S. Congress, 1-160,
    161
U. S. House of Repre-
    sentatives, 2-600

Valenzuela, Nicholas,
    7-65, 66
Van Deburg, William L.,
    2-601
Van Tassell, C. E.,
    2-567
Van Wart, Geraldine,
    7-71
Vanderwood, Paul J.,
    7-67, 68, 69
Verschuure, Eric Peter,
    2-602

Vickrey, William, 11-77
Vidmar, Neil, 2-603;
    5-44

Wagenknecht, Edward,
    2-604; 4-50
Walden, Daniel, 1-162
Walker, Alexander,
    1-163; 2-605, 606
Walker, David, 1-152
Walsh, Moira, 2-607
Walters, Debra, 7-70
Walton, Hanes, Jr.,
    2-608
Wander, Brandon, 2-609
Wander, Philip, 2-610
Wanderer, Aviva, 2-611
Ward, Francis, 2-612,
    613
Ward, Renee, 2-614
Ward, Robert, 2-615
Warner, Virginia, 2-616
Washington, Mary Helen,
    2-617
Waters, Harry F., 1-164
Watkins, Mel, 2-618
Weales, Gerald, 2-619
Weatherford, Elizabeth,
    11-78
Weaver, Harold D.,
    2-620
Wechsler, James, 6-37
Weigel, Russel H.,
    2-621, 622
Weinberg, David, 10-91,
    97
Weinberg, Sydney, 2-623
Weiss, Richard, 2-96
Wertheim, Arthur Frank,
    10-92, 98
West, Hollie I., 2-624
Westen, Tracy A., 1-165
Whang, Paul K., 4-51
Wheeler, Penny, 1-133;
    2-546; 4-41; 7-59;
    12-22

White, David Manning,
    1-166; 2-625; 6-75;
    10-93, 99; 11-79
White, Miriam Betty,
    2-626
Whitfield, Steven,
    10-94, 95, 100, 101
Whitney, Dwight, 6-76;
    11-80
Wiggins, H. Curtis,
    2-627
Wildman, Terry M.,
    2-512
Wilford, Red, 2-628
Wilk, Max, 12-25
Wilkerson, Isabel,
    2-629
Willett, Ralph, 1-167,
    168; 2-630; 4-52;
    6-77; 9-79
Williams, Carol
    Traynor, 1-169
Williams, Frederick,
    7-71
Williams, Martin,
    2-631; 4-53
Williams, Robert, 2-632
Williams, Ruthanne,
    2-633
Willis, Ellen, 2-634
Wills, Deborah, 2-493
Wilson, James, 4-54
Wilson, John M., 7-73
Winks, Robin W., 12-
    11
Winston, Brian, 2-635
Withey, Stephen B.,
    2-636
Wolfe, Bernard, 2-637
Wolfe, Ronald G., 3-5
Wolfenstein, Martha,
    2-638
Woll, Allen L., 1-170;
    2-639; 7-74, 75, 76,
    77, 78, 79, 80, 81
Wolper, David L., 2-640
Wong, Eugene, 4-55

Wood, Gerald, 2-641
Wood, Michael, 1-171;
    2-642
Woodward, Patricia Ann,
    2-643
Wright, Charles R.,
    1-172; 2-644; 4-56
Wright, Lois, 2-645
Wright, Virginia, 4-57;
    6-78
Writers' Congress,
    1-173

Yacowar, Maurice,
    1-174; 11-81
Yamada, George, 4-58
Yang, Anand A., 4-59
Yearwood, Gladstone L.,
    2-646, 647, 648, 649
Youman, Roger, 1-136
Young, Vernon, 2-650

Zagarrio, Vito, 9-80
Zieger, Gay P., 2-651;
    5-45
Zieger, Robert H.,
    2-651; 5-45
Zito, Stephen F., 2-652,
    653, 654
Zuker, Joel S., 9-81

FILM AND TELEVISION SHOW INDEX

(This index includes only those films and television shows which receive more than passing attention or mention in the works listed in the bibliography. When more than one version of a film is cited, the release date of each film is set in parenthesis.)

AfterM.A.S.H., 1-87; 4-36
Air Force, 4-27; 10-57
Alambrista, 7-72
Alice, 3-26
All in the Family, 1-5, 10, 27, 59, 150, 157; 2-53, 54, 81, 103, 196, 197, 395, 396, 413, 422, 514, 582, 603; 3-26; 5-3, 15, 44
All Quiet on the Western Front (1930), 1-116; 6-4, 21, 22, 38, 51, 52, 69
All Through the Night, 1-69
America, 11-54
America, America, 12-12, 20
American Romance, An, 1-82
Amos 'n' Andy, 1-10, 29, 43, 78, 150,

151, 157; 2-96, 140, 145, 156, 340, 357, 413, 519, 618
Andy's Lion Tale, 2-652
Angels With Dirty Faces, 1-14; 2-590; 8-14; 9-12, 70
Anna Lucasta, 5-14, 15
Annie Hall, 1-107, 150
Antonio and the Mayor, 7-5
Apache, 1-19
Apocalypse Now, 5-16; 9-20, 80, 81
Apple, An Orange, An, 12-13
Ashanti, 3-21
Autobiography of Miss Jane Pittman, 2-95, 122, 142, 601, 623

Ballad of Crowfoot, The, 11-19

Banacek, 1-111
Bananas, 7-80
Band of Angels, 2-506,
    601
Barbed Wire, 6-4
Baretta, 9-33
Barney Miller, 5-15
Bataan, 1-73, 76;
    2-238, 387, 418, 466
Battle Cry of Peace,
    The, 6-4
Beast of Berlin, 1-124
Beau Geste (1926), 3-8,
    11
Bedford Incident, The,
    1-107
Behind the Door, 6-4,
    38
Behind the Rising Sun,
    4-5, 54
Benson, 1-103; 2-413;
    6-76
Berlin Correspondent,
    6-2, 38
Best Defense, 1-19;
    3-19
Beulah Land, 1-59;
    2-106, 413, 462,
    583, 601
Beware, 6-47
Big Parade, The, 6-4,
    21, 22, 69
Bill Cosby Show, The,
    2-402, 413
Bingo Long Travelling
    All-Stars and Motor
    Kings, The, 2-150
Bionic Woman, The,
    3-17, 26, 29
Birth of a Nation, The,
    1-45, 50, 74, 80,85,
    108, 121, 138, 150,
    151, 166, 174; 2-40,
    55, 61, 71, 91, 105,
    112, 120, 121, 122,
    130, 140, 141, 151,
    157, 160, 162, 168,
    169, 180, 181, 187,
    207, 210, 223, 230,
    234, 235, 244, 246,
    258, 288, 296, 308,
    328, 368, 370, 374,
    387, 400, 435, 439,
    440, 452, 461, 464,
    466, 479, 494, 495,
    496, 516, 537, 540,
    556, 573, 601, 604,
    626, 627, 631, 632,
    641
Birth of a Race, The,
    2-90, 91, 157, 158,
    160, 168a, 181, 206,
    358, 384, 387
Biscuit Eater, The,
    2-372
Bitter Tea of General
    Yen, The, 1-138
Black and White, 2-181
Black Fury, 1-14, 124;
    5-14, 15, 39
Black Girl, 2-85, 335,
    561, 607
Black Hand, The, 9-12
Black Legion, 1-14,
    124; 5-39
Black Stallion, The,
    1-22; 3-8, 22
Black Sunday, 3-8; 9-12
Blackboard Jungle,
    1-19, 163, 366
Blood of Jesus, The,
    2-159
Blue Collar, 1-8, 107,
    119; 2-12, 186, 410,
    529, 651; 5-14, 32
Blues Brothers, The,
    2-106
Blume in Love, 10-65
Body and Soul (1924),
    2-177, 181, 384,
    387
Bolero, 3-19
Border, The, 7-58
Borderline, 2-177, 181

FILM AND TELEVISION SHOW INDEX   373

Bordertown, 1-124,
  7-76, 80
Boulevard Nights, 7-11,
  35
Brewster's Millions,
  2-301
Brian's Song, 2-273
Bridge on the River
  Kwai, The, 4-39
Bridge Too Far, A, 6-60
Bridget Loves Bernie,
  1-64
Broken Arrow, 1-19; 11-
  44, 45, 54, 76, 79
Broken Blossoms, 1-45;
  2-308, 604, 631;
  4-22, 30, 47, 50
Bronze Buckaroo, The,
  3-359
Brother from Another
  Planet, The, 2-151
Buck and the Preacher,
  2-366, 370, 471
Bucket of Cream Ale, A,
  2-181; 6-38, 39
Buffalo Bill and the
  Indians or Sitting
  Bull's History Les-
  son, 1-107; 11-14
Busted Dreams, 2-550
Bustin' Loose, 2-529

Cabin in the Cotton,
  2-91, 120, 121, 181,
  370
Cabin in the Sky,
  1-170; 2-314, 387,
  466, 572
Cagney and Lacey, 3-20,
  25, 26
Callahan, 3-25
Cannon, 3-17, 26
Caine Mutiny, The, 5-14
Call Northside 777,
  1-69; 5-14

Cannonball Run II, 3-19
Carmen Jones, 2-62, 90,
  91, 387
Carnal Knowledge,
  10-101
Carrascolendas, 7-71
Carwash, 1-107; 2-535
Casablanca, 2-60, 161,
  181, 238; 3-8; 6-2,
  43, 64
Cast a Giant Shadow,
  10-82
Chan is Missing, 4-17
Charlie Chan films, 1-
  46; 4-2, 11, 14, 20
Charlie's Angels, 3-8,
  17
Che!, 7-39
Check and Double Check,
  2-181
Cheyenne Autumn, 1-174;
  11-27, 54, 68, 74,
  79
Chico and the Man,
  1-24, 27, 43, 60,
  156, 157; 7-1, 6,
  16, 30
CHiPs, 3-26
Circle of the Sun,
  11-77
Claudine, 2-127, 324,
  387, 435
Cleopatra Jones, 2-561,
  572
Coffy, 2-561, 572
Cohens and the Kellys,
  The, 1-104; 8-10;
  10-54
Columbo, 9-33
Comrade X, 5-42, 43
Confessions of a Nazi
  Spy, 1-124, 170; 6-
  21, 22, 38, 43, 51,
  52, 61, 78; 9-12
Conrack, 2-36, 370
Cool World, 2-163, 347

Cotton Comes to Harlem,
    1-107, 149; 2-292,
    387
Counter-Attack, 5-34
Crime and Punishment,
    1-46
Crimson Kimono, The,
    1-168
Crossfire, 1-74, 125,
    168, 171; 10-8, 58,
    70
Cross of Iron, 6-60
Curse of the Cat
    People, The, 2-418
Custer's Last Stand,
    11-38

Dallas, 2-600
Daring, The, 6-2
Death of a Princess,
    3-7, 26
Deer Hunter, The,
    1-119; 4-9, 16, 21,
    29; 5-1, 6, 13, 14,
    16, 31
Defiant Ones, The, 1-
    166; 2-47, 274, 366,
    387, 423, 459, 504
Desert Fox, The, 6-38,
    51
Desert Song, The, 3-8
Diff'rent Strokes,
    1-103; 2-413, 635
Dirty Dozen, The, 2-38
Disraeli, 1-124
Dixiana, 2-120, 121
Doctor Bull, 1-126
Down Argentine Way,
    1-170
Drum, 2-119, 120, 121
Drums Along the Mohawk,
    11-54, 55

Eagle Has Landed, The,
    6-60
Eagle's Eye, The, 6-4
East Side/West Side,
    2-413
Edge of the City,
    1-171; 2-274, 310,
    346, 347, 366
El Norte, 7-58
Emperor Jones, The,
    2-90, 91, 169, 181,
    327, 360, 387, 507,
    547, 571
Enemy Below, The, 6-38
Enemy Within, The, 6-68
Escape, 6-38, 43
Evangeline, 12-23
Evening in Byzantium,
    3-23, 26, 27, 28
Evils of Chinatown,
    The, 4-18
Exodus, 3-8

Fall of a Nation, The,
    6-51
Farewell to Manzanar,
    1-48
Fatal Hour, The, 1-45
Fiddler on the Roof,
    10-49
Fighting Coward, The,
    2-120, 121
Final War of Olly
    Winter, The, 2-52
F.I.S.T, 1-8, 119;
    2-651; 5-14
Flame of New Orleans,
    The, 2-120, 121
Flap, 11-60
Flash Gordon (serials),
    4-6; 5-2
Flip Wilson Show, The,
    1-100; 2-94, 268,
    413
Flower Drum Song, The,
    4-46

For Love of Ivy, 2-225,
    323
Foreign Correspondent,
    1-69; 6-52
Fort Apache, 11-27, 49
Fort Apache, The Bronx,
    1-154; 7-79
Four Horsemen of the
    Apocalypse, The
    (1921), 6-4, 21,
    22, 38, 51, 52
Foxes of Harrow, The,
    2-120, 121
Free, White, and 21,
    2-163
Fu Manchu films, 4-6,
    18

Gang's All Here, The,
    7-70, 78
Gangster Chronicles,
    The, 1-63; 9-34
Ganja & Hess, 1-107
Gentleman's Agreement,
    1-74, 102, 125;
    10-9, 62, 76
Get Christy Love,
    1-157; 2-95, 413
Ghetto, 2-489
Giant, 1-19
Go For Broke, 4-55
Godfather, The, 1-107,
    150, 168; 9-8, 9,
    10, 12, 13, 14, 19,
    20, 21, 23, 24, 29,
    30, 31, 33, 36, 40,
    41, 42, 49, 56, 58,
    61, 62, 63, 67, 69,
    70, 71, 72, 74, 75,
    76, 80, 81
Godfather, Part II,
    The, 1-107, 138,
    150; 2-590; 9-12,
    13, 20, 23, 30, 31,
    36, 40, 46, 47, 49,
    67, 70, 80, 81

Godfather Saga, The,
    1-35, 119; 9-13
Goldbergs, The, 1-78
Gone Are the Days,
    2-188, 347
Gone With the Wind,
    1-85, 138; 2-90,
    91, 120, 121, 140,
    141, 169, 181, 183,
    203, 210, 223, 233,
    302, 345, 370, 387,
    466, 472, 473, 494,
    495, 496, 513, 532,
    574, 601, 634, 641
Good Earth, The, 4-26,
    46
Good Times, 1-10, 139,
    156, 157; 2-95,
    131, 142, 145, 155,
    195, 196, 231, 245,
    413, 414, 422, 434,
    449, 514, 579, 582
Greaser's Revenge, The,
    7-11
Great Dictator, The,
    6-21, 22, 43, 67;
    10-15, 46
Great O'Malley, The,
    1-14
Great White Hope, The,
    2-363, 538
Greed, 1-168
Green Berets, The,
    1-149; 4-3
Green Pastures, The,
    2-181, 184, 387,
    572
Guadalcanal Diary, 1-76,
    167; 4-27
Guess Who's Coming to
    Dinner?, 2-38, 90,
    91, 140, 225, 366,
    379, 387, 421, 423,
    427, 459, 504, 552
Gun, The, 7-40
Guns of Navarone, The,
    6-19

Halka, 5-27
Hallelujah!, 1-163; 2-
    90, 91, 181, 216,
    311, 314, 370, 387,
    466, 472, 473, 571,
    572
Hanta Yo, 11-80
Happy Days, 1-27, 139;
    9-25, 49
Harlem Rides the Range,
    2-391
Harris and Company,
    1-139
Hart to Hart, 3-25, 26
Hawaii Five O, 3-17
Heartbreak Kid, The,
    10-65
Hearts in Dixie, 2-77,
    90, 91, 120, 121,
    140, 162, 181, 207,
    210, 216, 370, 387,
    466, 472, 473
Hearts of the World,
    1-45; 2-308; 6-4,
    22, 27, 38, 52
Heroes for Sale, 1-14
Hester Street, 1-104;
    10-43, 61
High Treason, 6-68
Hill Street Blues,
    1-59, 63, 87, 99;
    2-316, 413; 9-25, 34
His Darker Self, 2-652
His Trust Fulfilled,
    2-120, 121
Hitler Gang, The, 1-69;
    10-57
Hitler's Children,
    1-134, 170; 2-60;
    6-38, 54, 78
Hogan's Heroes, 1-10;
    6-30, 31, 38, 51
Holocaust, 1-35, 59;
    6-46, 74; 10-13
Home of the Brave, 1-
    169; 2-153, 163,
    368, 370, 375, 387,

    466, 619
Hotel Berlin, 1-69;
    6-51, 54
House Divided: Denmark
    Vesey's Rebellion,
    A, 2-241, 592
House of Rothschild,
    The, 10-73
House on 92nd Street,
    The, 6-38, 39, 52;
    9-12
Huckleberry Finn,
    2-120, 121
Hun Within, The, 6-38
Hurry Sundown, 2-464,
    627

I Am a Fugitive From a
    Chain Gang, 1-14,
    124; 9-12
I Am Joaquin, 7-47
I Married a Communist,
    5-29
I Spy, 1-10; 2-340,
    376, 413, 519, 618
I Will Fight No More
    Forever, 2-54
Idol Dancer, The, 2-604
Imitation of Life
    (1934), 2-90, 91,
    109, 140, 181, 203,
    210, 387, 466, 553,
    571
Imitation of Life
    (1959), 2-90, 91,
    115, 140, 203, 217,
    294, 346, 387, 466
Immigrant, The, 1-47,
    104, 138; 2-590
In Old Kentucky (1909),
    2-120, 121, 126,
    181
In Old Kentucky (1924),
    2-162
In Our Time, 5-15

In the Heat of the
   Night, 1-149; 2-38,
   90, 91, 102, 366,
   370, 387, 650
Indiana Jones and the
   Temple of Doom, 4-1
Inside the Third Reich,
   1-59; 6-7
Intolerance, 1-80;
   10-72
Intruder in the Dust,
   1-69, 131; 2-163,
   224, 370, 375, 387,
   392, 466, 619
Ironside, 1-150; 2-468
Ishi in Two Worlds,
   11-77
Island in the Sun,
   2-346, 387, 506,
   572
Isn't Life Wonderful?,
   6-52
Italian, The, 1-45, 47,
   104

Jazz Singer, The, 1-
   104, 116, 163, 170;
   2-181; 10-5, 100
Jeffersons, The, 1-6,
   10, 43, 59, 139,
   156, 157; 2-53, 54,
   131, 145, 195, 196,
   211, 231, 245, 309,
   325, 413, 414, 422,
   434, 449, 514, 549,
   579, 582, 617, 618
Jezebel, 2-120, 121
Juarez, 1-124, 170;
   7-68, 75
Judgment at Nuremberg,
   6-51
Julia, 1-10, 157; 2-26,
   315, 376, 403, 413,
   420, 434, 519, 543,
   582, 618

Jungle, The, 2-489

Kaiser -- The Beast of
   Berlin, The, 6-4
Khartoum, 3-8
Kid Galahad, 9-30
King, 2-413, 417
King Kong, 2-307, 647
Kojack, 1-79, 111
Know Your Enemy --
   Japan, 4-8
Knute Rockne -- All
   American Boy, 1-124
Kung Fu, 4-7, 38

Lad From Old Ireland,
   The, 8-15
Lady Sings The Blues,
   2-61, 438
Last Hurrah, The, 8-15
Laverne and Shirley,
   1-139; 9-49
Lawless, The, 1-125
Lawrence of Arabia, 3-8
Leadbelly, 1-107; 2-551
Legend of Walks Far
   Woman, The, 11-65
Learning Tree, The,
   1-149; 2-6, 366, 504
Leathernecks, The, 5-34
Lies My Father Taught
   Me, 10-43
Lifeboat, 1-167; 2-181,
   255, 387, 450, 466
Liberation of L.B.
   Jones, The, 1-149;
   2-262
Life With Luigi, 9-57
Lilies of the Field,
   2-188, 310, 336,
   347, 366, 504, 552
Little American, The,
   6-4, 21, 22, 38, 52

Little Big Man, 1-149,
    174; 11-3, 38, 44,
    54, 58, 60
Little Caesar, 1-14,
    70, 124, 150; 9-12,
    30, 31, 42, 44, 59,
    60, 68, 70
Little Colonel, The,
    2-120, 121
Little Drummer Girl,
    The, 10-74
Littlest Rebel, The,
    2-601
Little Tokyo, U.S.A.,
    1-82
Lost Boundaries, 1-69,
    125; 2-88, 466
Lost Man, The, 2-463
Louisiana Purchase,
    12-23
Love and Death, 10-44
Love at First Bite,
    2-193, 633
Lovers and Others
    Strangers, 9-30, 31
Lucky Luciano, 9-12
Lying Lips, 2-181

McCloud, 3-26, 29
Mack, The, 2-365
Man Called Horse, A,
    1-174; 11-58
Made for Each Other,
    9-31
Making the Grade, 5-34
Mama, 12-25
Mama Malone, 9-25
Mandingo, 2-119, 120,
    121, 122
Manhattan, 5-20; 9-39
Man Hunt, 1-69; 6-43
Manila Calling, 6-2
Man With the Golden
    Arm, The, 5-14
Mannix, 2-434

Marty (1955), 9-30
Marty (TV), 1-10, 56
Massacre, 1-14, 124;
    11-54
Matt Houston, 3-26
Mean Streets, 1-107,
    119; 5-31; 9-12, 16,
    30, 33, 36, 39, 41,
    45, 47, 64
Medal for Benny, A,
    7-21
Medical Center, 3-26,
    29
Merchant of Venice,
    The, 10-39
Michael Strogoff, 1-116
Miracle in Harlem,
    2-652
Mission Impossible,
    1-10; 2-27, 94
Mission to Moscow, 1-
    134; 5-7, 8, 9, 42
Mississippi, 2-120, 121
Mississippi Gambler,
    The, 2-120, 121
Mr. Moto (series), 1-46
Mr. Wang Detective,
    1-46
Mod Squad, The, 1-99,
    157; 2-94, 468
Moon Is Down, The,
    6-27, 38, 54, 78
Moon Over Harlem,
    2-181, 652
Mork and Mindy, 3-25
Mortal Storm, 1-69,
    170; 6-21, 22, 38,
    43
Mrs. Miniver, 6-43
Mummy, The, 3-8
Murder on Lenox Street,
    2-453
Musketeers of Pig
    Alley, The, 9-12
My Baby Is Back, 2-163
My Four Years in
    Germany, 6-4, 38
My Sweet Charlie, 1-89

Mystery in Swing, 2-652

Naked City, The (1948),
    9-12
Nat King Cole Show,
    The, 1-27, 99, 157;
    2-138, 340, 412,
    413, 519
Native Son, 2-113, 173,
    307
Negro Soldier, The,
    2-125, 159, 160,
    161, 162, 165, 181,
    185, 267, 387, 418,
    508, 616
Network, 3-8
New Era, The, 2-234
Night Porter, The, 6-62
Ninotchka, 1-83; 5-33,
    34, 42, 43
Norma Rae, 2-36, 651
North Star, 5-34, 42,
    43
Nothing But a Man,
    2-159, 205, 347,
    370, 387
Notorious Elinor Lee,
    2-181
No Way Out, 2-47, 387,
    389, 466, 638;
    12-13
None Shall Escape,
    10-57

Objective Burma, 1-125;
    4-27; 10-57
Officer and a
    Gentleman, An,
    2-529
Oil for the Lamps of
    China, 1-124
Old Heidelberg, 6-38,
    51
Oliver Twist, 1-85

On the Waterfront,
    1-19; 8-13; 9-12,
    70
One Day at a Time,
    3-17, 23, 26
100 Rifles, 2-389
One Potato, Two Potato,
    2-205, 347, 387
Ordeal, The, 6-4
Outcasts, The, 2-376,
    413
Outsider, The, 1-22;
    11-60

Paradise, 3-8
Paris, 2-600
Pass, The, 2-387, 489
Passion Plantation,
    2-119, 120, 121
Patria, 1-168
Pawn Shop, The, 1-85
Pinky, 1-69, 125, 167,
    169; 2-90, 91, 115,
    163, 217, 224, 349,
    370, 375, 387, 392,
    466, 619
Police Woman, 3-26
Porgy and Bess, 2-589
Portnoy's Complaint,
    10-4, 38
Prelude to War, 6-70
Pressure Point, 2-421
Pride of the Marines,
    1-125
Producers, The, 6-38
Prussian Cur, The, 6-4
Public Enemy, The,
    1-14, 124, 150;
    2-590; 8-4; 9-12,
    44, 70
Putney Swope, 1-149;
    2-262

Quiet Man, The, 8-6,
    11, 15

Ragtime, 1-120; 2-529
Raiders of the Lost
    Ark, 3-8
Rains Came, The, 4-26
Raisin in the Sun, A,
    2-387
Ramona, 1-80
Realization of a
    Negro's Ambition,
    2-181, 387
Red Menace, The, 5-43
Red Dust, 1-93
Reds, 1-119
Requiem for a
    Heavyweight, 7-57
Revolutionary, The,
    11-19
Richard Pryor Show,
    The, 2-413
Richard Pryor Live on
    the Sunset Strip,
    2-287
Riffraff, 5-39
Rio Bravo, 11-27
River of Romance,
    2-120, 121
Rockford Files, 3-17,
    23, 26
Rocky, 1-8, 107; 2-386;
    9-30, 49, 50
Roll Out, 2-144
Rollover, 3-6, 8, 12,
    25
Rookies, The, 2-468
Roots, 1-48, 59, 139;
    2-16, 65, 106, 120,
    121, 227, 232, 241,
    326, 332, 333, 334,
    413, 415, 417, 422,
    447, 512, 532, 558,
    579, 581, 601, 610,
    630, 640, 653

Roots: The Next Gener-
    ation, 1-48; 2-64,
    120, 162, 232, 271,
    413, 630, 640
Rose Tattoo, The, 9-30,
    31
Run of the Arrow, 11-76
Russians Are Coming,
    The, 5-43

Sahara, 2-238
St. Louis Blues, 2-159,
    169, 466
Saint Valentine's Day
    Massacre, The, 9-12
Salt of the Earth,
    1-125; 7-7, 45, 49
Sanders of the River,
    2-177, 181, 387;
    12-3
Sanford and Son, 1-24,
    27, 156, 157; 2-53,
    54, 131, 142, 196,
    215, 231, 245, 325,
    396, 413, 414, 514,
    579, 582, 618
Santa Fe Trail, The,
    1-124; 2-218, 451
Saturday Night Fever,
    1-8, 107, 119;
    9-30, 49
Saturday's Hero, 5-14,
    15
Scarecrow and Mrs.
    King, 3-36
Scarface, 7-58; 9-12,
    44, 68, 70
Scar of Shame, 2-159,
    162, 165, 178, 181,
    272, 384, 652, 654
Searchers, 1-19; 11-49
Seventh Cross, The,
    6-39

Shaft, 1-107, 149, 157;
    2-11, 90, 91, 105,
    142, 144, 162, 215,
    356, 387, 413, 435,
    442, 455, 456, 459,
    529
She Wore a Yellow
    Ribbon, 11-27
Sheik, The, 1-138;
    3-38, 11
Shop Around the Corner,
    The, 5-33
Showboat, 2-162, 181,
    207, 327, 387
Since You Went Away,
    2-60
Sinking of the Lusi-
    tania, The, 6-4
Six Million Dollar Man,
    The, 3-26
Sixteen Candles, 4-1
Skag, 1-79
Slaves, 2-119, 120,
    121, 122, 463, 601
Soldier Blue, 11-60
Soldier's Story, A,
    2-151
Somewhere in the
    Sahara, 6-27
Song of Russia, 5-34
Song of the South,
    2-30, 120, 121,
    181, 210, 387, 441
Son of the Sheik, 3-8,
    11
So Red the Rose, 2-120,
    121, 181, 601
Sonny and Cher Comedy
    Hour, 3-26
Sons of the Gods, 1-124
Sounder, 2-36, 370,
    387, 389, 551, 572,
    607, 624
Southern Comfort, 12-23
Stagecoach, 11-74
Stalag 17, 6-51

Steamboat 'Round the
    Bend, 2-530
Stormy Weather, 1-170;
    2-466
Story of the Three Day
    Pass. See Pass, The
Story of G.I. Joe, The,
    4-27
Streetcar Named Desire,
    A, 5-14, 15
Super Fly, 1-74; 2-14,
    356, 442, 459, 613;
    9-12
Sweet Sweetback's
    Baadasssss Song,
    1-107, 149, 166;
    2-78, 90, 91, 124,
    159, 206, 292, 387,
    397, 435, 436, 442,
    458, 459, 469, 489,
    522, 561, 601a, 612,
    646, 647, 648

Tales of Manhattan,
    2-177, 181
Tall, Tan, and
    Terrific, 2-387
Tahtonka, 11-77
Tarzan of the Apes,
    2-466, 467
Tarzan (series), 2-181,
    466, 467; 12-2, 4, 5,
    7, 8, 9, 10, 11
Tarzan Triumphs, 6-2
Taxi Driver, 9-8, 12,
    36, 46
Teahouse of the August
    Moon, The, 4-46
Tell Them Willie Boy Is
    Here, 11-54, 60
Tenafly, 1-157; 2-144,
    215
Tender Comrade, 1-169
Tennessee Johnson,
    2-161, 171
That's My Mama, 2-516

These Are My People,
    11-19
They Call Me Mister
    Tibbs, 2-262
They Came to Blow Up
    America, 9-12
They Died With Their
    Boots On, 1-124;
    11-44, 54
They Met In Argentina,
    1-170
They Were Expendable,
    4-27
They Won't Forget, 1-14
Thief of Baghdad, The,
    3-8
Things Are Tough All
    Over, 3-25
Thunder Boy, 12-23
Tick...Tick...Tick...,
    2-370
To Be or Not to Be,
    5-33; 10-46
Toma, 9-33
Tomorrow The World,
    1-74
Topsy and Eva, 2-652
To Sir, With Love, 2-
    257, 366, 485, 552
Toy, The, 1-145; 2-529
Trading Places, 2-529
Traitors, The, 2-410;
    5-32
Trapper John, M.D.,
    3-17, 26
Treasure of the Sierra
    Madre, The, 1-25
Trooper of Troop K,
    2-654

Ulzana's Raid, 11-52
Uncle Tom's Cabin
    (1903), 1-85; 2-48,
    96, 106, 119, 120,
    121, 140, 181, 563

Uncle Tom's Cabin
    (1914), 2-120, 121,
    122, 140, 181, 563
Uncle Tom's Cabin
    (1926/27), 2-48,
    96, 106, 119, 120,
    121, 162, 169, 181,
    563
Uncle Tom's Cabin
    (1965/68), 2-119,
    120, 121, 563
Under Fire, 7-56
Underground, 1-69
Unforgiven, The, 11-45
Untouchables, The,
    1-27, 63, 150; 9-57
Up Tight, 2-36
Uptown Saturday Night,
    2-93, 366, 504

Vanishing American,
    The, 11-17, 46, 54,
    64, 79
Vega$, 3-17, 26
View From the Bridge,
    A, 9-30
Viva Villa!, 7-50, 80
Viva Zapata!, 7-51, 53,
    67
Voice of the Violin,
    The, 6-38
Volga Boatman, The,
    5-34

Wake Island, 6-2
Walk the Proud Land,
    11-45
Warm December, A, 2-33
Warriors, The, 2-223
Watermelon Man, 2-262,
    387
Wattstax, 2-455
Way Down South, 2-120,
    121

We Got It Made, 2-316
Welcome Back, Kotter,
    1-27, 43, 103, 157
West Side Story, 7-33
What's Happening?,
    1-139; 2-195, 196,
    197, 413
What Price Glory?, 8-15
When the Legend Dies,
    11-35, 36
White Rose, The, 2-604
Wind and the Lion, The,
    3-8
Within Our Gates, 2-181
World, the Flesh, and
    the Devil, The,
    2-310, 346, 387
Wrong is Right, 3-8

You Are On Indian Land,
    11-19
You Dig It?, 2-489
You Only Live Twice,
    4-31
Young Lions, The, 6-38
Young Men, 6-2
Young Savages, The,
    9-30

Zandy's Bride, 1-107
Zorba the Greek, 12-16

SUBJECT INDEX

Africa: depictions of,
in film, 2-181, 227,
354, 466, 467, 485;
3-8, 11, 21; 12-2,
3, 4, 5, 6, 7, 8, 9,
10, 11
Africans: stereotypes
of, in film, 2-181,
354, 466, 467, 485;
3-21; 12-1, 2, 3, 4,
5, 6, 7, 8, 9, 10,
11. See also
specific film and TV
show titles
Afro-Americans: as
actors, 2-2, 6, 15,
17, 18, 20, 22, 32,
33, 35, 38, 43, 59,
63, 70, 73, 74, 76,
87, 90, 91, 95, 123,
151, 159, 161, 162,
167, 168, 169, 170,
175, 177, 181, 183,
185, 189, 190, 200,
207, 210, 214, 225,
233, 239, 240, 255,
274, 277, 287, 292,
298, 310, 315, 320,
327, 340, 366, 378,
387, 389, 392, 393,
399, 402, 403, 412,
413, 427, 431, 443,
465, 466, 471, 476,
486, 498, 504, 505,
511, 515, 519, 530,

536, 543, 547, 549,
553, 573, 592, 601,
605, 606, 612, 613,
615, 617, 618, 620,
647; and advertising
(TV), 2-110, 117,
191, 212, 229, 257,
364, 413, 480, 493,
499, 500, 542, 567,
611; as audience,
1-9, 47, 74, 105,
106; 2-8, 12, 17,
23, 32, 33, 44, 45,
46, 148; 2-57, 64,
65, 68, 75, 84, 98,
103, 126, 152, 195,
196, 219, 236, 237,
278, 279, 280, 281,
282, 283, 285, 306,
332, 333, 339, 384,
396, 404, 408, 411,
483, 512, 552, 574,
575, 579, 584, 585,
601, 614, 636; bib-
liography and/or
filmography about,
2-338, 361, 373,
385, 423, 495, 510;
comedic tradition
of, 2-97, 108, 181,
287, 652; dialect
of, on TV, 2-231;
effects of World War
II (films) on, 1-73,
91, 125, 130, 134,

Afro-Americans (con't)
135, 170; 2-91, 125,
159, 160, 161, 162,
164, 171, 179, 181,
185, 238, 267, 297,
301, 355, 387, 418,
466, 508, 616, 639;
and film market,
2-3, 45, 384, 416,
568; as filmmakers,
1-66, 105, 106, 107;
2-2, 6, 9, 15, 18,
32, 85, 90, 91, 107,
127, 150, 157, 158,
159, 160, 162, 164,
166, 167, 169, 170,
175, 178, 181, 194,
198, 206, 234, 239,
240, 252, 261, 289,
292, 319, 358, 384,
387, 389, 391, 393,
443, 446, 457, 458,
459, 465, 466, 471,
489, 492, 498, 536,
539, 551, 575, 601,
609, 624, 643, 648,
649, 654; and inter-
racial setting on
TV, 2-401, 566, 587,
621, 622; music of,
in film, 1-122, 163,
170; 2-56, 79, 181,
443, 455, 577, 637,
639; positive images
of, in film, 2-36,
85, 97, 159, 160,
162, 177, 186, 239,
240, 418, 419, 601,
616; 5-14; and
programming (TV),
1-27, 55, 59, 139,
156, 157, 158, 160;
2-10, 46, 176, 201,
212, 249, 412, 413,
422, 592, 596, 597,
600; and protests
against stereotypes,

1-25, 42, 59, 64,
65, 74, 89, 139,
156, 157, 158, 160;
2-1, 13, 14, 30, 31,
50, 72, 78, 114,
156, 163, 180, 181,
187, 212, 215, 221,
222, 226, 234, 235,
245, 249, 261, 272,
329, 355, 357, 437,
441, 461, 462, 583,
589, 596, 597, 600,
601; representation
of, in film, 1-28,
76, 77, 97, 124,
125, 145, 149, 170;
2-3, 7, 62, 74, 86,
150, 159, 160, 161,
162, 163, 164, 170,
171, 175, 178, 179,
181, 184, 185, 188,
204, 205, 207, 217,
223, 224, 242, 243,
254, 268, 274, 277,
292, 298, 299, 301,
302, 313, 318, 327,
330, 331, 338, 346,
347, 375, 377, 383,
392, 416, 423, 555,
628, 629; repre-
sentation of, on TV,
1-13, 17, 18, 29,
43, 53, 55, 60, 61,
67, 78, 87, 88, 90,
103, 150, 156, 157,
158, 160, 161; 2-
8, 10, 52, 66, 67,
72, 82, 89, 104,
136, 149, 155, 176,
195, 196, 201, 208,
209, 212, 214, 215,
220, 221, 222, 250,
251, 259, 276, 278,
279, 280, 281, 282,
283, 284, 285, 306,
309, 312, 316, 317,
321, 330, 340, 348,

395, 396, 398, 399,
412, 413, 414, 420,
422, 428, 447, 454,
468, 475, 480, 482,
491, 499, 500, 501,
502, 503, 523, 524,
525, 526, 534, 544,
545, 546, 557, 565,
566, 569, 570, 578,
579, 582, 587, 588,
591, 592, 596, 597,
600, 617, 618, 621,
622, 640, 644;
socialization of, by
film, 2-62, 107,
552; socialization
of, by TV, 2-84,
128, 142, 145, 146,
147, 148, 176, 195,
196, 236, 237, 247,
251, 253, 276, 278,
279, 280, 281, 282,
283, 284, 285, 304,
306, 315, 333, 342,
404, 411, 483, 493,
514, 554, 578, 584,
585, 587, 618;
stereotypes of, in
film, 1-20, 21, 25,
45, 62, 70, 73, 74,
80, 85, 86, 107,
114, 120, 121, 126,
151, 157, 160, 161,
168; 2-1, 13, 14,
24, 29, 35, 38, 42,
43, 59, 61, 62, 63,
71, 77, 80, 86, 90,
91, 96, 100, 101,
102, 105, 106, 107,
109, 111, 112, 113,
115, 118, 119, 120,
121, 122, 129, 130,
132, 133, 135, 137,
140, 153, 154, 160,
162, 163, 168, 169,
173, 174, 177, 181,
182, 183, 192, 199,

202, 203, 210, 223,
226, 228, 246, 262,
293, 308, 311, 324,
328, 329, 343, 344,
355, 368, 369, 370,
372, 374, 379, 381,
384, 386, 387, 388,
389, 390, 392, 400,
407, 418, 426, 427,
432, 433, 435, 436,
444, 448, 450, 452,
453, 459, 465, 466,
467, 472, 473, 476,
485, 488, 494, 495,
496, 497, 498, 507,
511, 528, 529, 531,
532, 537, 538, 540,
559, 561, 562, 571,
573, 576, 577, 580,
589, 590, 593, 594,
596, 597, 601, 608,
612, 613, 614, 620,
625, 627, 632, 634,
637, 638, 639, 643,
646, 647, 648, 652,
654;   stereotypes
of, on TV, 1-6, 20,
22, 27, 37, 59, 65,
100, 139, 150, 156,
157, 158, 160, 161;
2-46, 53, 54, 68,
69, 83, 95, 106,
108, 131, 142, 143,
144, 145, 149, 156,
197, 209, 212, 213,
215, 221, 222, 290,
295, 315, 317, 321,
323, 340, 367, 376,
413, 445, 448, 449,
477, 518, 519, 582,
596, 597, 600, 601;
and women, in film,
1-21, 169; 2-22, 25,
29, 60, 109, 116,
168, 181, 183, 203,
210, 216, 275, 286,
291, 294, 302, 303,

Afro-Americans (con't)
345, 371, 387, 424,
425, 438, 481, 533,
561, 572, 586, 641,
646; women, on TV,
1-156, 157; 2-26,
95, 295, 323, 345,
353, 403, 434, 543,
544, 545, 546, 549,
582, 596, 597, 615,
617, 618. See also
blaxploitation
films; specific film
and TV show titles
Allen, Woody, 1-107;
10-44, 83
Altman, Robert, 1-107;
9-36, 47; 11-14
Anderson, Eddie, 2-181
Anti-Semitism: in film,
1-102, 125, 167,
169; 6-67; 10-1, 2,
3, 8, 9, 36, 62, 80,
85, 86. See also
Jews; specific film
and TV show titles
Arabs: as filmmakers,
3-8; and protests
against stereotypes,
1-89; 3-2, 7, 8, 13,
15, 16, 23, 26;
representation of,
on TV, 1-78; 3-2, 8;
stereotypes of, in
film, 1-62, 121;
3-3, 4, 6, 8, 10,
11, 12, 15, 16, 19,
21, 25; stereotypes
of, on TV, 3-2, 9,
13, 14, 15, 16, 17
18, 20, 22, 23, 25,
26, 27, 28, 29;
as villains, 3-6, 8,
11, 12; women, in
film, 3-8, 10, 11.
See also specific
film and TV show

titles
Armenians, 12-12. See
also specific film
and TV show titles
Asians: as actors,
1-46, 158; children
and stereotypes,
4-10, 25; college
courses on film
images, 4-59; as
detectives, in film,
1-46, 74; 4-2; and
James Bond films,
4-31; and Korean
War, 4-36, 39, 42;
literature, 4-6, 18;
masculinity, 4-31;
Pacific Americans,
4-9; and protests
against stereotypes
in film, 4-51;
psychological
effects of films on,
4-24; racism and,
4-1; representation
of, in film, 1-145,
149, 161; repre-
sentation of, on TV,
1-13, 29, 53, 55,
61, 79, 87, 156,
157; 4-41, 47, 48;
socialization of, by
film, 4-12; stereo-
types of, in film,
1-21, 25, 45, 70,
73, 80, 117, 125,
161; 2-181; 4-1, 49;
stereotypes of, on
TV, 4-45; survey of
images of, 4-13, 25,
32, 33, 34, 35, 37,
45, 47, 54, 55; TV
programming for,
1-146; and Vietnam
War, 4-3, 9, 16, 21,
29, 39, 42, 44, 54;
as villains, 4-6,

18; women, 1-21;
4-5, 47, 48, 49;
World War II images
of, in film, 1-74,
76, 77; 4-8, 19,
23, 27, 44, 52, 57.
See also Chinese;
East Indians; Fili-
pinos; Japanese;
Korean War; Vietnam
War; specific film
and TV show titles
Assimilation, 1-77, 83;
4-12; 5-14, 25;
10-43, 61
Audience (film): char-
acter of, 1-107,
151; 2-85, 181, 384;
10-59a; socializa-
tion of, 1-20, 74,
102, 105, 106, 116,
138, 140; 2-88, 140,
269, 270, 377, 552,
619; studies of, 1-
74, 102, 116; 2-12,
23, 88, 140; women
as, 1-47, 74. See
also film; televisi-
on; specific groups
Audience (TV): in
foreign countries,
2-227, 595; 6-46;
and protest, 1-23,
25, 59, 64, 65, 105;
and public TV, 1-2;
2-152; 7-66; social-
ization of, 1-17,
18, 20, 26, 29, 31,
32, 38, 52, 53, 54,
56, 105, 110, 144;
2-45, 46, 57, 64,
65, 68, 98, 136,
142, 145, 146, 147,
148, 195, 196, 211,
236, 237, 247, 251,
253, 271, 276, 278,
279, 280, 281, 282,

283, 285, 304, 306,
333, 342, 408, 460,
483, 512, 578, 581,
584, 585, 602, 636;
3-22; 5-44; survey
of, 1-2, 11, 17, 18,
31, 33, 52, 53, 54,
72, 127, 137; 2-23,
44, 45, 46, 64, 65,
98, 103, 126, 128,
152, 219, 326, 332,
334, 396, 397, 414,
460; 5-18, 19. See
also children;
minority program-
ming; public TV;
television; and
specific groups

Barthelmess, Richard,
1-45, 70, 121
Beavers, Louise, 2-181
Beban, George, 1-45
Belafonte, Harry, 2-2,
76, 413
Berle, Milton, 10-98
Biberman, Herbert, 7-7,
45, 49
Biograph Company,
1-15, 45, 121, 138.
See also Griffith,
David W.
Black Efforts for Soul
in TV (BEST), 2-437
Blaxploitation films:
character of, 2-59,
85, 87, 90, 91, 100,
105, 169, 194, 254,
356, 365, 427, 435,
436, 442, 456, 458,
459, 481, 489, 531,
551, 575, 609, 643;
decline of, 2-43,
416, 624; market
for, 2-3, 4, 5, 19,

Blaxploitation films
(con't)
42, 49, 75, 416,
575; opposition to,
by Afro-Americans,
2-9, 11, 13, 14, 18,
21, 31, 78, 111,
139, 154, 199, 256,
324, 352, 397, 430,
469, 509, 612, 613,
614; realism of,
2-28, 647; social
effects of, 2-18,
21, 24, 107, 111,
124, 277, 292, 509.
See also Afro-
Americans
Bourne, St. Clair,
2-459
British: stereotypes
of, in film, 1-83;
5-26. See also
specific film and TV
show titles
Brooks, Mel, 1-107;
10-71
Burton, LeVar, 1-87

Caan, James, 9-69
Cagney, James, 8-4, 8,
14
Capra, Frank, 1-138;
2-267
Carroll, Diahann, 2-26,
315, 403, 413, 519,
543, 618
Cassavetes, John,
1-107; 9-36
Chaplin, Charlie, 1-45,
70, 74, 138
Chicago, Illinois:
early filmmaking in,
2-289
Chicanos: accultur-
ation of, 7-26; as

actors, 7-7; as
audience, 7-66;
bibliography and/or
filmography about,
7-9, 32; cinema,
7-48; and mass
media, 7-23, 28, 29,
41, 46, 55, 60, 61,
65; in Philadelphia,
7-26; and protests
against stereotypes,
7-42; stereotypes
of, in film, 7-7,
11, 25, 35, 36, 45,
49; stereotypes of,
on TV, 7-16, 27, 30,
40, 57; survey of
images of, 7-17, 42,
51, 7-52, 72, 73.
See also specific
film and TV show
titles
Children and Tele-
vision, 1-3, 17, 18,
31, 32; 7-22; favor-
ite characters of,
2-219, 278, 280;
lack of study about,
1-32, 33; and lack
of study of ethnic
minority, 1-32, 33;
programming for,
1-88; 2-8, 68;
socialization of, by
TV, 1-32, 33, 34,
35, 88, 110; 2-45,
46, 51, 68, 145,
146, 147, 148, 211,
236, 237, 251, 276,
278, 279, 280, 283,
306, 342, 404, 411,
460, 483, 512, 578,
636; 3-22; 7-12, 22,
31; and TV stereo-
types, 1-3, 17, 18,
31, 56, 88; 2-46,
51, 68, 145, 211;

4-10; 7-31
Chinese: audience
  reaction to, in
  film, 1-116; as
  detective, 1-46;
  4-2, 11, 14, 17, 20;
  representation of,
  in film, 1-124, 125;
  stereotypes of, in
  film, 1-45, 73, 114;
  4-22, 30, 34, 35,
  50, 53; survey of
  images of, 4-25, 26,
  34, 35, 55; women,
  4-5; World War II
  images of, in film,
  1-74; 4-19, 23, 27,
  52. See also Asians;
  specific film and TV
  show titles
Cimino, Michael, 4-9,
  16, 29; 5-13, 14, 30
Cold War: on film,
  1-19, 74, 105, 106,
  125, 131, 134; 5-7,
  29, 41, 43, 6-9, 38,
  68; 7-67; 10-58
Cole, Nat King, 2-138,
  412, 413, 519
Colombo, Joseph, Sr.,
  9-62
Communists: and film,
  1-134; 5-7, 8, 9,
  10, 29, 34, 40, 41,
  43; 6-68
Coppola, Francis Ford,
  1-107; 9-9, 11, 12,
  19, 20, 23, 24, 36,
  40, 47, 71, 80, 81
Cosby, Bill, 2-402,
  413, 519, 618
Cowboys, Jewish, 10-6
Custer, General George
  Armstrong, 11-38, 42

Davis, Ossie, 2-4, 334,
  340, 459, 615;
  racial themes in
  films by, 2-85, 292,
  446
Davis, Sammy, Jr.,
  2-220, 413
Dee, Ruby, 2-615
De Niro, Robert, 1-107
Directors: Afro-Amer-
  icans as, 2-15, 85,
  90, 91, 159, 162,
  166, 170, 178, 181,
  206, 234, 239, 240,
  252, 261, 289, 358,
  384, 387, 391, 393,
  446, 457, 459, 466,
  471, 492, 536, 551,
  575, 609, 648;
  Germans as, 1-45;
  5-33; 6-6, 11, 33;
  Italians as, 1-105,
  106, 107; Jews as,
  1-45, 105, 106, 107;
  10-64; Poles as,
  5-27; Russians as,
  5-33. See also
  specific groups;
  specific film and TV
  show titles; names
  of specific di-
  rectors
Detectives: Asians as,
  4-2, 11, 14, 20;
  films about, 1-45,
  46, 74, 107; images
  of, on TV, 2-414,
  591; 4-2; 9-41. See
  also police;
  specific ethnic
  groups
Dutch, 12-13. See also
  specific film and TV
  show titles

East Europeans: as
   audience, 1-23;
   representation of,
   in film, 1-124, 125;
   5-1, 6; represen-
   tation of, on TV,
   1-79; 5-18, 19, 23;
   stereotypes of, in
   film, 5-2, 5, 10,
   14, 37, 38, 45; as
   villains, 5-2;
   women, in film,
   5-14; as working-
   class metaphor,
   5-45; World War II
   images of, in film,
   1-74, 82; 5-22. See
   also Poles, Rus-
   sians, Ukrainians
East Indians, 12-14
Ebony Film Corporation,
   2-289
Edison, Thomas
   (studios), 1-45
Education, bilingual,
   7-71
Education, college
   courses on: Asian
   images in film,
   4-59; Hispanic
   images in film,
   7-12, 7-14, 7-44;
   race and ethnicity
   in film, 7-13

Fairbanks, Douglas,
   1-45, 121; 3-8
Feiffer, Jules, 10-101
Filipinos, 6-2. See
   also specific film
   and TV show titles
Film: audience of, 1-9,
   20, 47, 74, 102,
   105, 106, 116, 138,
   140, 151; 2-8, 12,
   17, 23, 88, 140,
   172, 174, 175, 269,
   270, 272, 336, 351,
   377, 384, 419, 459,
   471, 474, 506, 552,
   574, 601, 605, 606,
   614, 619; 9-29;
   10-57; censorship
   of, 1-40, 70, 74,
   124, 125, 138;
   2-163, 181, 235,
   301, 601, 10-80; and
   civil rights move-
   ment, 2-37, 59, 74,
   85, 160, 162, 163,
   187, 217, 268, 331,
   392, 459, 466, 474,
   489, 528, 590, 591,
   593, 594, 601, 619,
   625; crime depicted
   in, 1-107, 124, 125,
   128, 138; 8-4; 9-8,
   11, 12, 41, 44, 59,
   60, 65, 67, 68, 70,
   71, 78; 10-29, 88;
   directors, 1-45,
   105, 106, 107; 2-15,
   85, 90, 91, 159,
   162, 166, 170, 178,
   181, 206, 234, 239,
   240, 252, 261, 289,
   358, 387, 391, 393,
   446, 457, 459, 466,
   471, 492, 536, 551,
   575, 609, 648; 5-27,
   33; 6-6, 11, 33;
   10-64; educational
   role of, 1-34, 36,
   37, 62, 74; 2-88,
   252, 269, 270, 336,
   377, 517, 552, 590;
   4-59; 7-12, 13, 14,
   43, 44; 11-5, 78;
   9-28; ethnographic
   aspects in, 1-94;
   2-466, 601; 9-64;
   foreign settings in,

1-118; 2-181, 354,
466, 467, 485, 568,
642; 5-7, 8, 24, 25,
26, 34, 40, 42; 6-2;
7-14, 18, 19; 12-2,
3, 4, 5, 6, 7, 8, 9,
10, 11, 21; heroes
in, 1-81, 124, 125;
2-20, 277, 327, 389,
601, 647; 5-14, 34,
42; immigration
depicted in, 1-47,
104, 106, 138, 151;
2-181; 5-14; 7-58;
10-11, 43, 97; mas-
culinity in, 2-435,
580, 612, 613, 643,
647; 4-31; 5-14; 8-
11; 11-49; minor-
ity employment in
production of,
1-157, 158, 159,
160; 2-150, 159,
177, 181, 204, 207,
216, 239, 240, 268,
298, 299, 331, 355,
383, 387, 392, 394,
407, 416, 427, 443,
459, 465, 466, 476,
521, 564, 573, 591,
601, 605, 606, 654;
4-47, 48, 49; 7-38;
politics and, 1-70,
106, 107, 124, 125,
151, 152, 166; 2-41,
162, 181, 343, 344,
355, 556, 590, 591,
601; 3-6, 8, 12;
4-42; 5-7, 8, 9, 14,
15, 26, 29, 37, 38,
40, 41, 42, 43; 6-2,
3, 4, 5, 8, 9, 10,
12, 13, 14, 15, 16,
17, 18, 19, 20, 21,
22, 23, 24, 25, 27,
28, 29, 32, 34, 37,
38, 39, 40, 41, 42,

43, 44, 51, 52, 54,
61, 63, 65, 75; 7-7,
50; 8-8, 91; 9-57;
protests against
stereotypes in,
1-45, 74, 104, 105,
106, 154, 157, 160;
2-1, 11, 13, 14, 30,
31, 40, 41, 50, 114,
141, 157, 180, 181,
187, 234, 235, 288,
329, 355, 441, 461,
589, 601; 3-8; 4-51;
7-42; 9-21; 11-22,
53; racism and,
1-93, 107, 122, 124,
157, 160, 161, 166,
167, 169; 2-41, 129,
157, 163, 169, 172,
179, 180, 181, 182,
183, 210, 244, 246,
248, 261, 296, 308,
310, 328, 351, 368,
369, 370, 383, 387,
388, 389, 390, 392,
439, 440, 452, 464,
465, 466, 474, 484,
485, 506, 517, 521,
532, 537, 538, 540,
559, 573, 590, 591,
593, 594, 601, 604,
612, 620, 627, 651;
4-1, 4, 55; 5-14;
6-70; 11-61; rural
images in, 12-23;
slavery depicted in,
1-45; 2-48, 55, 77,
96, 119, 120, 121,
122, 140, 181, 183,
203, 216, 218, 230,
233, 243, 302, 308,
370, 387, 451, 463,
466, 512, 540, 562,
601; 3-21; social
consciousness of,
1-19, 71, 73, 74,
75, 76, 77, 82, 95,

Film (con't)
  105, 106, 107, 119,
  120, 124, 125, 138,
  151, 154, 166, 169,
  170, 171; 2-160,
  161, 162, 163, 164,
  167, 168, 170, 171,
  175, 177, 178, 179,
  181, 184, 185, 188,
  199, 206, 216, 217,
  223, 224, 225, 239,
  240, 252, 261, 262,
  313, 327, 341, 346,
  347, 349, 355, 360,
  366, 370, 375, 382,
  383, 387, 392, 418,
  419, 421, 436, 453,
  466, 484, 489, 506,
  522, 527, 528, 551,
  559, 590, 591, 601,
  607, 609, 619, 624,
  625, 628, 629, 638,
  643, 646, 651; 3-8;
  5-6, 7, 8, 9, 10,
  14, 26, 29, 30, 34,
  37, 38, 39, 40;
  6-36, 51, 52; 9-8,
  9, 15, 20, 22, 42,
  45, 47, 49, 50, 53,
  64, 65, 77; 10-3, 8,
  36, 57, 62, 74, 85,
  86; 12-12, 13, 20;
  social mythology
  and, 1-4, 45, 62,
  95, 107, 125, 138,
  171; 2-160, 181,
  224, 370, 381, 435;
  4-21; 11-55; Spanish
  language, 7-4, 54;
  star system and,
  1-45, 62, 74, 105,
  106, 107, 138, 181;
  2-210, 378, 601;
  studio system and,
  1-45, 62, 74, 105,
  106, 107, 138;
  2-168, 181, 188,
    210, 355, 466, 471,
    513, 559, 590, 601;
    7-18; urban images
    in, 1-106, 107, 124,
    125, 138; 2-164,
    181, 559; 5-20; 9-5,
    12, 15, 16, 20, 22,
    39, 42, 44, 45, 47,
    64, 65, 74; 12-13;
    uses of history in,
    1-28; 2-55, 164,
    175, 181, 234, 370,
    387, 439, 440, 497,
    559, 601, 626;
    3-8, 11; 6-38;
    women, 1-21, 74;
    2-25, 29 34, 60, 91,
    101, 109, 116, 210,
    216, 275, 286, 291,
    294, 302, 303, 345,
    371, 424, 425, 438,
    481, 533, 561, 572,
    586, 641, 646; 3-8,
    10, 11; 4-5, 46, 49;
    5-14, 30; 6-1; 7-7,
    45, 49; 8-6; 10-5,
    10, 15, 21, 23, 37;
    working-class themes
    in, 5-1, 4, 13, 14,
    15, 30, 32, 37, 38,
    39, 45; 9-22, 49,
    50, 52, 53; 11-17,
    18. See also
    specific groups;
    specific film titles
Film noir, 1-107, 138;
  10-58
Filmethics Inter-
  national, 2-9
Florida: early film-
  making in, 2-
  465
Ford, John, 1-45;
  2-181; 8-11, 15, 16;
  11-27, 63, 68
Fox, William, 1-70,
  74, 138

Foxx, Redd, 2-21

Gangsters: films about,
    1-70, 105, 106, 107,
    128, 138, 149; 9-3,
    8, 9, 11, 12, 14,
    15, 19, 20, 21, 30,
    42, 44, 58, 59, 60,
    61, 65, 69, 70, 71,
    74, 75, 76, 78; Nazi
    as, 6-70; TV shows
    about, 1-63; 9-13,
    41, 51, 78
Garbo, Greta, 1-45
German-American Bund,
    6-61
Germans: as actors in
    Hollywood, 1-45; 5-
    33; 6-6, 11, 33, 45,
    50, 57, 73, 76, 77;
    audience reaction
    to, in film, 1-116;
    6-6, 11, 20, 33, 46,
    50, 56; and Cold
    War, 6-38, 44, 51,
    68; and ethnic hu-
    mor, on TV, 1-78; as
    filmmakers in Holly-
    wood, 5-33; 6-6, 11,
    33, 50, 57, 73; in-
    fluences of, on
    film, 1-45, 70,
    138; 5-33; 6-57, 73;
    as Nazis, 6-5, 9,
    13, 14, 17, 25, 26,
    27, 30, 31, 38, 39,
    42, 43, 44, 48, 51,
    53, 54, 55, 60, 61,
    62, 63, 64, 65, 66,
    67, 68, 70, 72, 74,
    78; representation
    of, in film, 1-124;
    6-13, 20, 21, 22,
    34, 36, 38, 51, 56,
    58, 59, 71; repre-
    sentation of, on TV,
    1-78; 6-7, 12, 76;
    stereotypes of, in
    film, 1-83; 6-1, 2,
    3, 4, 5, 8, 9, 10,
    11, 12, 13, 15, 16,
    17, 18, 19, 20, 21,
    22, 23, 24, 25, 26,
    27, 28, 29, 30, 34,
    35, 37, 38, 39, 40,
    41, 42, 43, 44, 45,
    47, 48, 49, 50, 51,
    52, 53, 54, 55, 57,
    60, 61, 62, 63, 64,
    65, 66, 67, 68, 69,
    70, 72, 75, 77, 78;
    stereotypes of, on
    TV, 6-30, 39, 52; as
    villains, 6-4, 5,
    10, 11, 13, 14, 16,
    17, 19, 21, 22, 23,
    24, 25, 26, 27, 30,
    31, 33, 37, 38, 39,
    41, 42, 43, 45, 46,
    48, 49, 50, 51, 52,
    53, 54, 55, 61, 63,
    65, 66, 69, 70, 72,
    75, 78; women, 6-1,
    76; World War I
    images of, in film,
    1-45; 62, 70, 74,
    121, 168; 6-4, 5, 6,
    10, 15, 16, 21, 22,
    23, 24, 26, 27, 28,
    33, 37, 38, 39, 41,
    47, 50, 51, 52, 55,
    57, 69, 75, 77;
    World War II images
    of, in film, 1-69,
    74, 76, 77, 82, 84,
    86, 91, 125, 130,
    134, 135; 6-1, 2, 3,
    5, 8, 9,, 12, 13,
    14, 17, 18, 19, 20,
    25, 26, 27, 28, 29,
    30, 31, 32, 34, 35,
    36, 38, 39, 40, 42,

Germans (con't)
43, 44, 48, 49, 51,
53, 54, 55, 60, 61,
62, 63, 64, 65, 66,
67, 70, 72, 75, 78;
World War II images
of, on TV, 6-7, 30,
31, 39. See also
specific film and TV
show titles
Gish, Lillian, 1-45,
121; 2-258
Good Neighbor Policy,
7-62, 70, 77, 78
Greasers, 7-17, 20
Greaves, William, 2-459
Greeks: as audience,
1-72; as filmmaker,
12-15, 20;
representation of,
in film, 1-77;
12-17; representa-
tion of, on TV,
12-19; stereotypes
of, on TV, 1-72;
sympathetic portrait
of, in film, 12-15,
20; World War II
images of, in film,
12-18. See also
specific film and TV
show titles
Griffith, David W.:
defense of images
by, 2-40, 258, 288,
300, 573; ethnic/
racial imagery of,
1-45, 70, 74, 80,
114, 121, 138, 168;
2-61, 71, 90, 91,
112, 120, 121, 122,
130, 140, 181, 192,
226, 230, 244, 246,
308, 369, 370, 374,
387, 388, 389, 439,
440, 516, 537, 540,
573, 604, 631; 4-22,

30, 50, 53, 72; 6-
16; 10-59a; oppo-
sition to films of,
2-40, 71, 157, 187,
234, 235, 461, 540
Guevara, Che, 7-39
Gunn, Bill, 2-446

Haley, Alex, 2-232, 413
Hawaii: early film-
making in, 12-21
Hawaiians, 12-21, 22.
See also specific
film and TV show
titles
Hays Office, 1-40, 74,
106, 138; 8-8
Hispanics: as audience,
for film, 2-336;
7-18, 19; as
audience for TV,
1-32, 33; 2-45, 219;
audience reaction
to, on film, 7-3,
33; audience
reaction to, on TV,
7-6; bibliography
and/or filmography
about, 7-9, 43;
children and TV,
7-22, 31; and Cold
War, 7-67; and
education, 7-12, 13,
14, 26, 43, 44; and
ethnicity, 7-3, 13,
22, 34; Good
Neighbor Policy and
7-62, 70, 77, 78;
as greasers, 7-17,
20; and immigration
problems, 7-58; and
Mexican Revolution,
7-8, 50; MPPDA and,
7-20; newspapers,
7-61; Nosotros,

7-35; protests
against stereotypes
of, 1-25, 64, 89,
156, 157, 158, 159,
160; and public TV,
7-66, 71; and
racism, 7-17; repre-
sentation of, in
film, 1-76, 77, 97,
145, 158, 159;
representation of,
on TV, 1-6, 7, 17,
18, 29, 43, 51, 53,
55, 60, 87, 156,
157, 158, 159, 160,
161; 7-28, 59;
socialization of, by
TV, 1-18, 148; 7-26,
55, 71; and Spanish
language films, 7-4,
54; stereotypes of,
in film, 1-25, 62,
70, 80, 124, 125;
stereotypes of, on
TV, 1-22, 27, 65,
88, 156, 157, 158,
159, 160, 161; 7-27,
40, 41, 58; survey
of images of, 7-1,
2, 13, 52, 72, 73,
76, 79, 80, 81; TV
programming for,
1-146, 156, 157,
158; 7-38, 46, 60;
as villains, 7-36,
74. See also
specific film and TV
show titles
Hitler, Adolph, 6-13,
14. See also Germans
Hoffman, Dustin, 1-107;
10-20, 21
Holly, Ellen, 2-214
Holocaust, the:
audience reaction to
films about, 10-14;
in European film,

10-34; in film;
10-34, 45, 55,
56; in popular
culture, 10-77; on
TV, 10-93; women's
images in films
about, 10-15
Humor: ethnic, in film,
8-10; 10-44, 68,
71; ethnic slur,
1-34; 5-3; on TV,
1-5, 63, 78, 105,
139, 147; 2-103,
325; 5-3

Immigrants: depiction
of, in film, 1-47,
104, 138, 151; 9-64,
77; 12-12, 15, 20,
27; and film, 1-45,
70, 107, 151; 10-43,
97
Immigrant Problems: in
film, 1-45, 47, 74,
82; 2-181; 5-14;
7-58
Ince, Thomas H., 1-45,
121, 138
India: in film, 4-26,
40
Indians. See Native
Americans
Irish: as gangster,
1-128; humor, 8-7,
10; Hays Office and,
8-8; and Kalem
Company, 8-17; and
Jews, 10-54; mascu-
linity of, 8-11;
representation of,
in film, 1-76, 77,
104, 120, 124;
representation of,
on TV, 1-51, 64, 79;
silent film images

Irish (con't)
    of, 8-17; stereo-
    types of, in film,
    1-70; survey of
    images of, 8-5, 12,
    17; women, 8-6;
    World War II images
    of, in film, 8-9.
    See also specific
    film and TV show
    titles
Italian-American Civil
    Rights League, 9-21,
    40
Italians: as actors,
    1-8; 9-54, 56, 58,
    69; audience reac-
    tion to, in film,
    9-29, 54; as
    author, 9-63, 71;
    bibliography and/or
    filmography about,
    9-1; as filmmaker,
    1-104, 106, 107;
    9-16, 19, 20, 36,
    40, 45, 47, 54, 56,
    71, 80, 81; as folk
    hero, 9-54; as
    gangster, 1-63, 70,
    105, 106, 107, 124,
    128, 149, 168; 9-3,
    8, 9, 11, 12, 13,
    14, 15, 18, 21, 23,
    24, 29, 30, 41, 42,
    44, 49, 51, 55, 56,
    58, 59, 60, 61, 62,
    65, 67, 68, 69, 70,
    71, 72, 74, 75, 76,
    78, 79; as police,
    9-33, 41; positive
    images of, in film,
    9-37, 45, 77;
    protests against
    stereotypes of, 9-6,
    21, 34, 40, 78;
    representation of,
    in film, 1-76, 77,
    97, 124; 9-43, 53;
    representation of,
    on TV, 1-17, 43, 44;
    9-17, 32, 38, 51,
    73; as self-made
    man, 9-19, 59;
    stereotypes of, in
    film, 1-8, 47, 50,
    70, 80, 84, 105,
    106, 107, 126, 150,
    168; 9-2, 3, 5, 8,
    9, 11, 12, 15, 18,
    20, 21, 23, 24, 26,
    28, 30, 31, 41, 42,
    44, 46, 49, 53, 56,
    57, 59, 60, 64, 65,
    66, 67, 68, 70, 71,
    72, 75, 76, 78, 79;
    stereotypes of, on
    TV, 1-23, 27, 56,
    57, 60, 63, 68, 105,
    139; 9-4, 7, 10, 13,
    25, 26, 27, 28, 33,
    34, 41, 49, 51, 56,
    78; urban environ-
    ment of, in film,
    9-2, 5, 8, 16, 20,
    39, 42, 44, 45, 47,
    55, 64, 65, 71, 74;
    women, 1-56; 9-31;
    as working-class
    metaphor, 9-2, 3, 5,
    10, 22, 47, 49, 50,
    52, 53, 55; World
    War II images of, in
    film, 9-43, 48. See
    also specific film
    and TV show titles

Japanese: as detective,
    1-46; representation
    of, on TV, 1-79;
    4-48, 49; stereo-
    types of, in film,
    1-168; 4-31; survey

of images of, 4-25,
26, 34, 35, 55;
women, 4-5; World
War II images of, in
film, 1-74, 76, 77,
82, 84, 86, 91, 125,
130, 134, 135; 4-8,
19, 23, 27, 52. See
also Asians; World
War II; specific
film and TV show
titles
Jews: as actor, 1-45,
105, 106, 107, 138,
150; and anti-
Semitism, 10-2, 3,
8, 9, 36, 62, 80,
85, 86; audience
reaction to, in
film, 1-116; 10-74,
76; audience
reaction to, on TV,
10-33, 53; bibli-
ography and/or
filmography about,
10-27; and Cold War,
10-58; as cowboys,
10-6; as directors,
10-64; and East
Europeans, 10-84; as
filmmakers, 1-45,
74, 105, 106, 107,
138, 150, 151; as
gangster, 1-128;
humor of, 1-107,
138; 10-44, 68, 71;
and film noir,
10-58; and the Holo-
caust, 10-14, 15,
34, 45, 46, 55, 56,
77, 93; and Indians,
10-6, 13; and Irish,
10-54; as moguls,
1-45, 74, 105, 106,
138; 10-7, 17, 18,
25, 49, 59, 60;
protests against

stereotypes of, 1-59,
64, 89; repre-
sentation of, in
film, 1-76, 77, 97,
105, 106, 107, 120,
124, 125; represen-
tation of, on TV,
1-43, 51, 60, 78;
2-259, 260; and
Shakespeare, 10-39,
50, 66, 70; in
silent films, 10-11,
52, 54; sociali-
zation of, by film,
10-43, 61; stereo-
types of, in film,
1-80, 85, 104,
105, 106, 107, 145,
151; 2-181; 10-43,
61; stereotypes of,
on TV, 1-68; 10-19,
92; survey of images
of, 10-20, 22, 23,
28, 30, 31, 35, 47,
67, 69, 78, 81, 89;
as villains, 10-75,
88; women, 10-15;
and World War II,
1-125; 10-40, 51,
85; Yiddish cinema,
10-24. See also
anti-Semitism; the
Holocaust; specific
film and TV shows
Johnson, George
P. (George Perry),
2-181
Johnson, Noble, 2-181
Jones, James Earl,
2-413

Kalem Company, 8-17
Kazan, Elia, 7-67;
8-13; 12-12, 20
Kelly, Jim, 2-43

Korean War, 1-134;
  4-36, 39, 42
KTAL-TV: licensing
  dispute and, 1-7

Landau, Saul, 7-69
Lear, Norman, 1-6; and
  All in the Family,
  1-5, 27, 143; 2-53;
  and black images by,
  2-53, 142, 413, 514,
  635
Lebanese: stereotypes
  of, on TV, 1-72. See
  also Arabs
Lee, Canada, 2-255
Lincoln Motion Picture
  Company, 2-181, 654
Literature: Asian,
  4-28, 59; Asian-
  American, 4-28
Lockhart, Calvin, 2-43
Lone Ranger, The, 11-40
Louisiana: depictions
  of, in film, 12-23
Louisiana Cajuns, 12-23
Lubin, Siegmund, 10-17
Lubitsch, Ernst, 1-45,
  121; 5-33

McDaniel, Hattie, 2-90,
  91, 92, 181, 183
Mammy: film images of,
  2-25, 29, 34, 60,
  91, 101, 109, 183,
  203, 210, 275, 294,
  302, 345, 572, 641;
  TV images of, 2-295,
  345
Martin, D'Urville, 2-18
Marx Brothers, 1-138;
  10-68
Masculinity: in film,

2-435, 580, 612,
  643, 647; 4-31;
  5-14; 8-11; 11-49
Mayer, Louis B., 1-45,
  138; 10-25
Mazursky, Paul, 1-107;
  9-36
Merritt, Theresa, 2-515
Mexicans: Black Legend
  and, 7-2; history
  of, 7-68, 75; and
  Native Americans,
  7-15; and Mexican
  Revolution, 7-8, 50,
  51, 67; stereotypes
  of, 7-17; stereo-
  types of, in film,
  7-19, 20. See also
  specific film and TV
  show titles
Micheaux, Oscar, 2-58,
  170, 175, 181, 206,
  319, 466, 492
Minnelli, Vincente,
  2-314
Miranda, Carmen, 7-70
Miscegenation:
  censorship of, in
  film, 1-41; in film,
  1-45, 121, 125, 138;
  2-91, 109, 181, 346,
  347, 466, 506; 3-8,
  11. See also
  specific groups;
  specific film and
  TV show titles
Moguls, Jewish, 1-45,
  70, 74, 138; 10-7,
  17, 18, 25, 48, 59a,
  60
Morris, Greg, 2-27, 94
Moseley, Lillian, 2-34
Moss, Carlton, 2-159,
  161, 185
Motion Picture
  Producers and
  Distributors of

America (MPPDA),
7-20
Murnau, Friedrich
Wilhelm, 1-45
Murphy, Eddie, 2-151
Muse, Clarence, 2-181
Musical comedy, film:
and Afro-Americans,
2-639; and Hispan-
ics, 7-77

NAACP, 2-40, 71, 157,
181, 187, 357, 461,
462
Native Americans:
audience reaction
to, 11-22; Canadian,
11-69; children and
stereotypes, 11-37;
and education, 11-5;
bibliography and/or
filmography about,
11-2, 6, 7, 11, 51,
78; elimination of
stereotypes of, on
TV, 1-44; and Jews,
10-6, 13; and
Mexicans, 11-24;
masculinity of,
11-49; as Navajo,
11-79; as outsider,
1-22; protests
against stereotypes
of, 1-25, 65, 159;
and racism, 11-61;
representation of,
in film, 1-97, 124,
149; representation
of, on TV, 1-13, 53,
55, 61, 159; Sioux,
11-67; stereotypes
of, 11-22, 25;
stereotypes of, in
film, 1-21, 25, 45,
70, 80, 86, 125;

2-182; stereotypes
of, on TV, 1-6, 22,
65, 98, 159; survey
of images of, 11-9,
10, 11, 13, 15, 16,
32, 33, 36, 39, 41,
43, 44, 46, 48, 50,
53, 54, 59, 66, 70,
72, 73; in westerns,
11-16, 17, 18, 20,
21, 28, 30, 45, 58,
62, 76; and women,
1-21; 11-57, 58;
women on TV, 11-80.
See also specific
film and TV show
titles
Nazis. See Germans
Negri, Pola, 1-45
Norman Film Manu-
facturing Company,
2-465
Norwegians: family on
TV, 12-25; rep-
resentation of, in
film, 12-24. See
also specific film
and TV show titles
Nosotros, 7-35

O'Neal, Ron, 2-43
Oxford House Cree,
11-34

Pacino, Al, 9-69
Pacific Americans, 4-10
Paramount, 2-181
Parks, Gordon, 2-6,
446, 551
Penn, Arthur, 9-47
Perry, Lincoln, 2-35;
defamation suit by,
2-1; defense of

Perry, Lincoln (con't)
  character role by,
  2-406, 490. See also
  Stepin Fetchit
Peters, Brock, 2-74
Pickford, Mary, 1-45
Poitier, Sidney, 1-107;
  2-47, 134, 298, 336,
  466, 486; characters
  of, 2-73, 93, 123,
  189, 225, 274, 292,
  318, 347, 366, 387,
  389, 431, 435, 463,
  504, 505, 511, 650;
  racial themes in
  films of, 2-15, 33,
  38, 61, 63, 90, 91,
  102, 310, 379, 421,
  471, 504, 505, 625
Poles: as ethnic joke,
  on TV, 5-3, 15, 36,
  44; as filmmakers,
  5-27; representation
  of, on TV, 1-13;
  stereotypes of, in
  film, 5-4, 14, 15,
  28, 36, 38, 39;
  stereotypes of, on
  TV, 5-15, 28, 36,
  44; as victim, in
  film, 5-17; as
  working-class met-
  aphor, 5-14, 15, 32,
  37, 38, 39. See also
  East Europeans;
  specific film and TV
  show titles
Police: images of, on
  TV, 1-31, 105, 414,
  460, 591; 9-33, 41,
  51. See also
  detectives
Production Code
  Administration,
  1-70, 74, 106, 138
Pryor, Richard, 1-107;
  2-106, 151, 287, 629

Puerto Ricans, 7-10,
  24, 37
Puzo, Mario, 9-63, 71

Revolution: Latin
  American, 7-56;
  Mexican, 7-8, 50
Ritt, Martin, 2-36
Robeson, Paul, 2-32,
  90, 91, 92, 177,
  181, 190, 327, 360,
  387, 389, 466, 547,
  620, 647; proscrip-
  tion of, on TV,
  2-412, 413
Robinson, Bill, 2-90,
  91, 92, 181, 466
Robinson, Eddie, 2-301
Roker, Roxie, 2-549
Rollins, Howard E.,
  Jr., 2-151
Roundtree, Richard,
  2-42
Ruddy, Al, 9-62, 69
Russians: as
  anti-communists, in
  film, 5-34; audience
  reaction to, in
  film, 1-116; 5-35;
  as communists, in
  film, 1-134; 5-7, 8,
  9, 10, 29, 40, 41,
  43; as detectives,
  in film, 5-12;
  disappearance of, in
  film, 5-25; as film-
  maker in Hollywood,
  5-33; as heroes,
  5-8, 34, 42; stereo-
  types of, in film,
  1-73, 83; 5-7, 26,
  29, 40, 42, 43; World
  War II images of,
  in film, 1-134; 5-7,
  8, 9, 11, 20, 22, 24,

25, 26, 40, 42. See
also East Europeans;
specific film and TV
show titles

St. Jacques, Raymond,
2-486
Sambo, 2-96
Schultz, Michael, 2-446
Schrader, Paul, 1-107;
2-186
Scorsese, Martin,
1-104, 107; 9-16,
36, 39, 45, 47
Scott, Emmett, 2-157,
181
Selznick, David, 2-183,
513
Serling, Rod, 7-57
Shakespeare, William,
10-39, 50, 66, 70
Silver, Joan Micklin,
1-104
SIN, 7-63
Sioux Indians, 11-67
Slavery: in film, 1-45;
2-48, 55, 77, 96,
119, 120, 121, 122,
140, 181, 183, 203,
216, 218, 230, 233,
243, 302, 308, 370,
387, 451, 463, 466,
540, 562, 601; on
TV, 2-241, 415, 512,
601, 630, 640. See
also specific film
and TV show titles
Stallone, Sylvester,
1-8; 9-50
Steinbeck, John, 7-51,
53
Stepin Fetchit:
stereotypical role
of, 2-35, 90, 91,
92, 181, 200, 387,

389, 406, 466, 490,
530. See also Perry,
Lincoln
·Stereotypes: definition
of, 1-12, 68, 96,
154, 174; 5-14;
10-19. See also
specific groups
Streisand, Barbra,
1-107; 10-37
Swedes: immigration
experience of, in
film, 12-26. See
also specific film
and TV show titles

Television: advertising
on, 1-10, 59, 60,
64, 78, 139, 150;
2-69, 89, 110, 117,
191, 212, 229, 257,
259, 364, 413, 478,
480, 493, 499, 500,
542, 567, 611;
audience of, 1-10,
11, 13, 17, 18, 26,
31, 52, 59, 88, 100,
127, 137; 2-44, 45,
64, 65, 69, 98, 99,
136, 142, 146, 147,
148, 152, 195, 196,
212, 219, 227, 251,
253, 259, 271, 278,
279, 280, 281, 282,
283, 284, 285, 326,
332, 333, 334, 339,
396, 397, 408, 411,
413, 414, 437, 460,
482, 483, 578, 579,
581, 584, 585, 587,
595, 596, 597, 600,
602, 636; 3-22, 23,
26; 5-44; 6-46; 7-
65, 66; 10-14, 33;
and children, 1-3,

Television (con't)
    17, 18, 31, 32, 33,
    35, 88, 99, 108,
    110, 123; 2-45, 46,
    51, 68, 145, 146,
    147, 148, 211, 219,
    236, 237, 276, 278,
    279, 280, 282, 283,
    285, 306, 342, 404,
    411, 460, 483, 512,
    578; 3-22; 7-22; and
    civil rights aware-
    ness, 1-11, 52, 59;
    2-64, 99, 104; 176,
    259, 279, 285, 413,
    470, 526, 554, 581,
    596, 597, 598, 600,
    618; class bias of,
    1-16, 17, 23, 31,
    43, 49, 51, 60, 99,
    103, 111; 2-81, 259,
    279, 280, 285, 422,
    482, 541, 569, 570,
    579, 591, 596, 597,
    600, 630; 9-33, 51;
    content analysis and
    methodology for,
    1-31, 32, 33,
    67, 137; 2-334; 4-
    41; 7-27; crime de-
    picted on, 1-63,
    142, 150; 2-69, 251,
    279, 280, 312, 398,
    414, 422, 460, 482,
    560, 566, 591, 636;
    3-18, 26; 9-7, 13,
    33, 41, 51, 78; cul-
    tural influences on,
    1-13, 59, 99, 150;
    2-280, 285, 290,
    560, 591, 596, 597;
    3-2, 5, 15, 16, 17,
    22, 25, 26; deviance
    on, 1-22, 460; dis-
    trust of images on,
    1-58, 79, 99, 104;
    2-215, 227, 283,

    414, 482, 560; 6-74;
    docudramas on,
    1-48; 2-16, 232,
    592, 610, 623, 630,
    640, 653; 3-7, 26;
    6-7, 46, 74; educa-
    tional role of,
    1-17, 18, 29, 31,
    32, 33, 34, 37, 38,
    52, 53, 54, 56, 59,
    99, 123, 144; 2-23,
    57, 64, 65, 69, 98,
    128, 136, 196, 237,
    247, 253, 278, 279,
    280, 281, 282, 283,
    285, 304, 342, 396,
    460, 483, 512, 578,
    584, 585, 596, 597,
    600; 3-22; 7-22, 26,
    71; 9-27, 28; ethnic
    dialect on, 2-231;
    ethnic humor on,
    1-5,63, 78, 139,
    147; 2-103, 325;
    5-3; masculinity in,
    2-429; minority
    programming on, 1-7,
    24, 42, 49, 87, 100,
    146; 2-8, 10, 212,
    259, 260, 321, 412,
    413, 422, 524, 534,
    554, 565, 569, 570,
    578, 596, 597, 599,
    600; 5-18, 19; 7-23,
    41, 46, 60; minority
    representation in,
    1-7, 10, 31, 42, 53,
    55, 60, 61, 67, 78,
    79, 87, 88, 103,
    111, 147, 153, 155,
    156, 157, 158, 159,
    160; 2-8, 10, 16,
    26, 53, 66, 67, 68,
    69, 99, 136, 146,
    149, 196, 201, 208,
    209, 212, 214, 220,
    221, 222, 250, 259,

260, 276, 278, 279,
280, 282, 284, 305,
309, 316, 317, 321,
330, 340, 376, 395,
396, 398, 412, 413,
414, 420, 422, 428,
454, 475, 480, 482,
491, 498, 499, 500,
501, 502, 503, 523,
524, 525, 534, 544,
545, 546, 550, 557,
566, 569, 570, 578,
579, 588, 591, 596,
597, 598, 599, 600,
615, 617, 618, 621,
622, 640, 644; 3-2,
5; 4-48; 5-18, 19,
23; 7-28, 29, 37,
38; 10-92; political
functions of, 1-54,
59, 99, 111, 123,
142; 2-99, 259, 290,
321, 413, 422, 491,
569, 570, 587, 591,
596, 597, 600; 3-1,
5, 9, 14, 18, 20,
23, 26, 27, 29;
and producers'
sensitivity to
ethnic concerns,
1-10, 13, 30, 32,
43, 44, 49, 59, 63,
78, 87, 89, 100,
147, 156, 157, 160,
164; 2-104, 165,
212, 215, 259, 260,
273, 290, 315, 325,
348, 376, 413, 414,
422, 468, 524, 560,
565, 578, 579, 582,
587, 591, 596, 597,
598, 599, 600, 617,
635, 640; 3-1, 5,
14, 20, 26, 27;
5-15; 9-34, 51;
protests against
stereotypes on, 1-6,

10, 25, 42, 64, 65,
87, 89, 156, 157,
158, 159, 160, 161,
164; 2-8, 156, 212,
215, 245, 249, 357,
413, 437, 462, 477,
583, 596, 597, 600;
3-2, 5, 7, 15, 16,
23; 7-16, 40; 9-34,
78; 11-26, 53;
racism in, 2-138,
350, 412, 413, 587,
591, 596, 597, 600;
revisionist history
on, 1-48; 2-16, 601,
652; slavery
depicted on, 2-241,
592, 601, 630, 640;
social consciousness
of, 1-75, 78, 105,
142, 143, 147;
2-104, 142, 152,
176, 259, 273, 413,
422, 447, 460, 468,
491, 565, 569, 570,
578, 579, 587, 591,
596, 597, 600, 621,
622, 652; 3-1, 5,
26, 27; 5-15; 9-34,
51; 10-93, 96;
station licensing,
1-7, 105; 2-249,
596, 597, 598, 599,
600, 645; urban
images on, 1-20,
259; 2-560; uses of
history in, 2-232,
271, 326, 417, 512,
591, 592, 601, 610,
630; 3-7, 26; 6-7,
74; violence on,
1-1, 30, 31, 90;
2-142, 155, 251,
259, 279, 280, 285,
312, 380, 460, 560,
587, 591, 636; and
westerns, 1-22, 44;

Television (con't)
    2-132, 591; and
    women, 1-21, 31;
    2-26, 95, 295, 323,
    345, 353, 403, 434,
    475, 515, 519, 543,
    544, 545, 546, 549,
    582, 596, 597; 4-36,
    47, 48; 6-76; 7-38;
    11-65; working-class
    themes on, 1-133;
    2-546, 591; 5-15;
    9-7, 10, 49. See
    also specific
    groups; and specific
    TV show titles
Third World Cinema Film
    Company, 2-4, 127
Travolta, John, 1-8
Trevino, Jesus, 7-48
Troell, Jan, 1-104
Turks, 12-27. See also
    specific film and TV
    show titles

Ukrainians: and loss of
    ethnicity in film,
    5-6; representation
    of, in film, 5-1; as
    working-class meta-
    phor, 5-13, 14, 16,
    30, 31. See also
    East Europeans;
    specific film and TV
    show titles
United Artists
    Corporation, 7-18
United States govern-
    ment. See specific
    agencies
United States Depart-
    ment of War, 6-70
United States House
    Un-American Activi-
    ties Committee,

1-19, 74, 125, 138
United States Office of
    War Information, 1-74,
    82; 2-59, 125, 161,
    171, 185, 508; 6-2, 3,
    25, 27
Universal Studio, 2-181

Valentino, Rudolph,
    1-45, 70, 121, 138;
    3-8, 11
Van Peebles, Melvin,
    1-159; 2-446; Afro-
    Americans' protests
    against films of,
    2-78; social
    consciousness of,
    2-124, 206, 292,
    458, 459, 648
Vidor, King, 2-181, 314
Vietnam War: in film,
    1-107, 134, 149;
    5-1, 6, 13, 14, 16,
    30, 31; 4-3, 9, 16,
    21, 29, 39, 42, 44,
    54; on TV, 2-52
Villains. See specific
    groups
Violence: and ethnic
    minorities on TV, 1-
    90; 2-83, 84, 560,
    587, 636; and film,
    1-107; 2-111; 9-8; and
    TV, 1-1, 30, 31, 90;
    2-142, 155, 251, 259,
    279, 280, 285, 312,
    380, 460, 587, 636
Von Stroheim, Erich, 1-
    45, 121, 168; 6-6, 11,
    24, 33, 45, 50, 73

Walsh, Raoul, 1-45
Walton, Lester, 2-181

Wang, Wayne, 4-17
Warner Brothers, 1-138;
    1930's films of,
    1-124, 184
Welch, Raquel, 11-65
Westerns: Afro-
    Americans and,
    2-132, 181, 242,
    359, 391; Native
    Americans and,
    11-16, 17, 18, 20,
    21, 28, 29, 45, 62,
    76; on TV, 1-22, 44
Williams, Spencer,
    2-166, 181
Williamson, Fred, 2-20,
    43, 87
Wilson, Flip, 2-94, 413
Wisconsin: Polish
    filmmaking in, 5-27
WLBT-TV: licensing
    dispute and, 1-7
Women: as actors,
    1-107; 2-22, 25, 26,
    29, 34, 95, 168,
    181, 183, 210, 291,
    302, 403, 475, 515,
    519, 543, 549, 615,
    618; 6-76; as
    audience (film),
    1-47, 74; as
    audience (TV), 1-53;
    as liberating ele-
    ments in film,
    1-169; 2-216, 646;
    stereotypes of,
    1-21, 53, 56, 107,
    156, 157, 160, 161;
    2-22, 25, 29, 34,
    68, 95, 101, 116,
    203, 210, 275, 286,
    291, 294, 302, 303,
    323, 335, 345, 353,
    371, 387, 424, 434,
    438, 481, 518, 533,
    544, 545, 546, 561,

    572, 582, 586, 596,
    597, 617, 641; 3-8;
    4-46, 47; 5-14, 30;
    6-1; 8-6; 9-31;
    10-15; and TV
    advertising, 2-191;
    World War II images
    of, in film, 4-5;
    6-1. See also
    specific groups
World War I: in film,
    1-45, 62, 70, 74,
    105, 106, 138; 168,
    181; 6-1, 4, 5, 6,
    10, 11, 15, 16, 20,
    21, 22, 23, 24, 26,
    27, 28, 33, 37, 38,
    39, 41, 47, 50, 51,
    52, 55, 57, 69, 75,
    77
World War II: in film,
    1-69, 73, 74, 76,
    77, 82, 84, 86, 91,
    105, 106, 125, 130,
    134, 135, 138, 167,
    170; 2-267, 639; 4-
    19, 23, 27, 44, 52,
    57; 5-7, 8, 9, 20,
    22, 26, 40, 42; 6-1,
    2, 3, 5, 8, 9, 12,
    13, 14, 17, 18, 19,
    20, 25, 26, 27, 28,
    29, 30, 31, 32, 34,
    35, 36, 38, 39, 40,
    42, 43, 44, 48, 49,
    51, 53, 54, 55, 60,
    61, 62, 63, 64, 65,
    66, 67, 70, 72, 75,
    78; 7-51, 85; 8-9;
    9-43, 48; 10-40; and
    Latin America, 7-70;
    racial themes in,
    2-60, 159, 160, 161,
    162, 164, 171, 179,
    181, 185, 238, 297,
    418, 508, 593, 594,

World War II (con't)
    616; on TV, 6-7, 30,
    46; and women, in
    film, 2-60; 6-1
Wright, Richard, 2-173,
    307

Yiddish Cinema, 10-24
Young, Otis, 2-320

Zanuck, Darryl F.,
    1-138; 10-3, 9
Zukor, Adolph, 1-138